Twentieth Century DRESS in the United States

TWEN

Dr

TIETH CENTURY

ess

IN THE UNITED STATES

Jane Farrell-Beck and Jean Parsons

IOWA STATE UNIVERSITY

FAIRCHILD PUBLICATIONS, INC.

NEW YORK   2007

Director of Sales and Acquisitions: Dana Meltzer-Berkowitz
Executive Editor: Olga T. Kontzias
Senior Development Editor: Jennifer Crane
Development Editor: Sylvia L. Weber
Senior Production Editor: Elizabeth Marotta
Art Director: Adam B. Bohannon
Assistant Development Editor: Justine Brennan
Manuscript Editor: Roberta Mantus
Photo Researcher: Photosearch, Inc.
Copyeditor: Chernow Editorial Services, Inc.
Cover Design: Adam B. Bohannon
Cover Art: Corbis and Condé Nast Publications
Text Design: Susan C. Day
Page Makeup: Ron Reeves
Second Printing 2008

Library of Congress Control Number: 2006928241

ISBN: 978-1-56367-415-0

GST R 133004424

Printed in the United States of America

CH01, TP15

To Marvin

Martin

Alex

and Louise

CONTENTS

PREFACE

Americans today live in a world of celebrity designers, cult labels, sprawling shopping malls, giant luxury conglomerates, and Internet shopping. The clothes on our backs are made in every part of the world, for consumer groups with numerous ethnic, regional, and religious affiliations and based on size range, age group, and overall lifestyle. Fashion trends spread at digital speed and rule breaking has become the rule, as we look to stars of film, television, and music for clues to the newest looks in clothes, hairstyling, grooming, and cosmetics. Our closets and dresser drawers bulge with a volume of clothing that would have flabbergasted our great-grandparents.

How did Americans arrive at this abundance, these mega industries, and this variety of choices? To help answer those questions, we will examine the history of dress in the United States from 1898 to 2004. Along the way we give due recognition to influences from Europe, Asia, Africa, and the rest of the Americas. However, focusing on the United States allows us to cover some of the complexity of dress, and the events and trends that shaped that complexity. Contrary to popular misconceptions, men and children have pursued changing fashions just as women have; fashion-conscious Americans have lived in small towns as well as megalopolises; and every period of fashion has embraced variety. In other words, the clothes of any given decade show much greater diversification than embodied in stereotypes of such periods as the "Twenties" and the "Sixties."

Because styles do not change abruptly at the start of each new decade, the chapters in this book sometimes cover fewer or more than 10 years, and they begin on years other than 1920, 1950, and so forth. Each chapter explores the social, economic, cultural, artistic, and technological themes that helped to shape the fashions of the era, both high fashion and mass fashion. Innovations in retailing and manufacturing contribute to changes in design, and new sources and methods of design help retailing to flourish, so we consider both of these functions in each period. We profile important designers in the period of their greatest influence and illustrate the text with high fashion images and photos of Americans in both festive and everyday clothing. Whenever possible, we mention the major fashion photographers and illustrators and show examples of their work.

History is exciting . . . yes, *exciting*! We hope that as you study twentieth-century dress, you will come to agree with that statement and will gain a fuller appreciation of the dress history of your own family and friends. We are all part of this story.

JANE FARRELL-BECK AND JEAN PARSONS
AMES, IOWA

ACKNOWLEDGMENTS

Many helpful colleagues, students, and friends helped to make this book possible, directing us to resources, answering our questions, and assisting with research. We want to recognize especially: Sara Kadolph, Grace Kunz, Rita Marinko, Diana Shonrock, Susan Torntore, Geitel Winakor, Tanya Zanish-Belcher and the whole staff of Special Collections, Iowa State University Library, plus graduate assistants Jessica Havlicek and Brenda Ackerman. We appreciate Sarah Marchetti's preparation of the Instructor's Guide that accompanies this book. Thanks also to Victoria Van Voorhis and LouAnn Doyle for secretarial support.

We received knowledgeable guidance and encouragement at various stages of the project from Barbara Chernow of Chernow Editorial Services, Deborah Bull and Susan Weschler of Photosearch, Inc.; Roberta Mantus; and the following members of the staff of Fairchild Books: Olga Kontzias, executive editor; Carolyn Purcell, former associate acquisitions editor; Joseph Miranda, acquisitions editor; Jennifer Crane, senior development editor; Elizabeth Marotta, production editor; Adam Bohannon, art director; Ginger Hillman, production manager; and our faithful developmental editor, Sylvia Weber. Thank you, also, to the following reviewers, selected by the publisher: Diana Cone, Georgia Southern University; Sally Helvenston-Gray, Michigan State University; Lisa L. Lopez, Katherine Gibbs College; Lisa Hopkins Newell, IADT; Lynne Richards, Oklahoma State University; Teresa B. Robinson, Middle Tennessee University; Susan Stark, San Francisco State University; and Phyllis Tortora, professor emerita, Queens College, City University of New York.

Twentieth Century DRESS in the United States

CHAPTER 1

1898

U.S. Events and Trends

Spanish-American War

Average work week: 57.3 hours

Immigration averages 1 million per year

Theodore Roosevelt becomes president after McKinley assassination

Illiteracy drops to 10.7 percent

Twenty percent of women earn wages

 **1898**

 **1899**

 **1900**

 **1901**

1902

U.S. Fashions

Bloused bodice, trumpet skirt for women

Cuffed, creased trousers for men

Blocky silhouette for men

Spaulding makes Olympic uniforms

Men's shirtwaist controversy

Shirtwaist style continues for women

New Century,

1907

Wright
brothers fly at Kitty
Hawk, N.C.

1903

American
Federation of Labor:
1,676,000 members

1904

Name brassiere
applied to bust
supporter

First tooth
cream/paste

Spiegel catalog
started

1905

Women's
silhouette
begins to
become slim

1906

Financial panic

44,000 cars
manufactured

Sears, Roebuck and
Co. issues 3.6 million
catalogs

1907

Princess
silhouette
accepted

New Fashions

As noted in the Introduction, periods of history and fashion rarely coincide with the beginnings of centuries and decades. So it was with the twentieth century. In many ways, 1898 marked important changes for the United States. Victory in the Spanish-American War revealed the United States as a world power, someone to reckon with. Domestically, 1898 brought an end to a severe economic depression that had beset the country in 1893, causing some businesses to fail and others to merge. A watershed year in fashion, 1898 introduced styles such as the bloused dress front and trumpet-shaped skirt that remained popular well into the 1900s.

Prelude to the Twentieth Century

Conditions in the United States in 1898 grew out of the events and trends of the last half of the nineteenth century. In the 1850s and early 1860s, there was no assurance an entity called "the United States" would survive. The country endured a bloody and wrenching Civil War (1861–1865) to reestablish union between North and South and to end slavery. In the aftermath of that war, many Americans moved westward to the Great Plains and the Pacific Coast, aided in part by the reach of the railroads across the continent. Large-scale industries and big business enjoyed growing power in the economy, although agriculture still employed almost half of American workers.

The Growth of Cities

National population tallied at 62,979,766 in 1890, with New York accounting for 2.5 million people and Chicago for 1 million. Philadelphia and St. Louis ranked as third and fourth in size, respectively. Even smaller cities such as Denver and Minneapolis were growing rapidly. Within those cities and in small towns and rural areas, the U.S. population was becoming more diverse. To the earlier nineteenth-century immigrants from Ireland, Scotland, Germany, and Scandinavia were added Greeks and Italians, Russians and Czechs, Chinese and Japanese.

Cities began to assume a modern aspect. San Francisco's quintessential cable cars began to run in 1873, an innovation that Chicago adopted in 1882. Electric trolleys, first installed in 1887 in Richmond, Virginia, served more than 200 U.S. cities by 1889. Trolleys and other modes of transportation acted as centrifugal forces drawing population away from city centers, while the city boundaries reached ever outward. Subdivision of cities accelerated, creating racial and ethnic neighborhoods, occupational enclaves, and socio-economic groupings. Both illumination and transportation began to modernize the country. San Francisco and Cleveland boasted carbon arc lamps in 1879, and electric lights reached New York City in 1882. The telegraph and the telephone, nineteenth-century breakthroughs in long-distance communication, were every bit as remarkable as the Internet in the late twentieth century.

The Spread of Education

Not only were Americans becoming more urban but also better educated. Public kindergartens, devised in Germany, reached the United States in 1873. Primary and secondary education grew steadily, although in 1890 only about 4 percent of Americans aged 14 to 17 years stayed in school. Not until 1918 did all states have compulsory schooling laws. Land Grant colleges and the historically black 1890 colleges educated middle- and lower-middle-class boys and girls for careers in agriculture or engineering and domestic science, respectively. Ivy League universities and the elite women's colleges, called the "Seven Sisters," offered a classical education for the professions to those who could afford it. Professional opportunities for women remained limited. A growing number of young girls, although by no means the majority, finished high school, and by 1900, a full one fourth of college students were women.

Part of the drive for education came from the increasing variety and complexity of jobs. Whereas farming, factory labor, retailing, and the learned professions had constituted the majority of jobs in the 1860s, by the 1890s significant employment could be found in business offices. Men and women worked as secretaries, clerks, typists, telephone operators, and bookkeepers—jobs for which they needed more years of schooling, a mastery of English, *and* appropriate clothing. The idea of the white-collar worker, which began with the use of detachable collars by men, spread to women's fashions in the period.

The Sale and Manufacture of Ready-made Apparel

By the 1890s, Americans could buy ready-made clothing in department stores, specialty shops, and from the mail-order catalogs of Montgomery Ward; Sears, Roebuck & Co.; and a handful of department stores (Figure 1.1). People in the United States still looked to Europe—particularly France and England—for fashion leadership, but Americans were already putting a national stamp on ideas generated abroad. Large-scale production of uniforms and laborers' clothing, which began in England in the late seventeenth century, flourished in U.S. factories. Other more fashion-driven products were also made in volume. Custom tailoring and dressmaking, not to mention home sewing, still provided a significant portion of American

Figure 1.1 Men's and boys' sweaters. *Sears, Roebuck & Co. Catalog,* Number III, 990.

wardrobes, but economic and stylistic pressures favored the growth of ready-mades.

Embarking on a New Century

Vast changes in many aspects of life awaited Americans as the twentieth century approached. The economy gyrated between prosperity and recession, political trends crystallized around progressivism, and fashion embraced features that would continue to predominate in the twentieth century.

Economic and Social Conditions in the United States, 1898–1907

After the woeful mid-1890s, the turn of the twentieth century brought healthier economic conditions. Unemployment fluctuated between 5.4 percent and 2.8 percent during those years, and gross national product rose every year except 1904, when it held steady. Inflation was mostly mild, except for a 4.5 percent spike in 1906. Cumulatively, of course, inflation ate into people's earnings, especially those of people on fixed salaries. A financial panic struck in 1907. Although intervention by a combination of government and bankers resolved the crisis, a rise in unemployment followed in 1907–1908.

Large corporations exerted enormous power in turn-of-the-century America. United States Steel, which swallowed up 158 smaller companies, controlled $1.4 billion—three times the federal budget. Three hundred huge firms owned more than 40 percent of America's industrial wealth. By 1909, a scant 1 percent of American companies manufactured 44 percent of the nation's goods. On the one hand, strong companies delivered efficiently made goods and contributed to America's annual per capita income of $569, the highest in the world. On the other hand, large industrial trusts and holding companies (which controlled several firms) led to price fixing, political shenanigans, and disregard for decent wages and working conditions. Reformists, collectively called Progressives, launched attacks on the trusts and secured stronger enforcement of the formerly feeble Sherman Antitrust Act to break up the most damaging monopolies.

No discussion of progressivism should omit mention of Theodore (Teddy) Roosevelt, who became president in September 1901 when William McKinley was assassinated. Teddy Roosevelt espoused reform in business and industry and supported the establishment of the Department of Commerce and Labor. He used the power of the federal government to break up the monopolies established by the most egregious trusts. Under Roosevelt's administration, the Meat Inspection Act and the Pure Food and Drug Act were put into effect to halt the scandalously unsanitary practices in food industries and to ensure that medicines were not contaminated or falsely labeled. Roosevelt instigated conservation of natural resources, a movement that added national parks and other protected areas to the nation's heritage.

As early as the 1880s, employment in business and industry surpassed farm employment in the nation as a whole. In 1890, millions of men, women, and children worked in manufacturing and mining, often putting in 10- to 12-hour days, 6 days a week. The average work week in 1900 totaled 57.3 hours. Five million women and 1.7 million children under the age of 16 years worked full time. Efficiency drives in industry delivered lower cost products but subjected workers to monotonous tasks performed at a grueling pace. Wages often fell below the poverty line of $500 annual income. Steelworkers made $450 per year; textile workers—many of them women and children—averaged $350 a year. In New York City, from 1903 to 1909, the average working-class family of four to six members had an income of $800, although their expenses were higher than elsewhere in the country. Unemployment was relatively low, but people who were out of work had no source of short-term relief from government or private sources.

Progressives began to chip away at workers' problems. Real wages rose one third between 1890 and 1910, and ultraprogressive Wisconsin enacted state laws to limit working hours for women and children and to provide compensation for injured workers. The American Federation of Labor—mostly directed to white males in skilled trades—united a variety of small unions and totaled 1,676,000 members by 1904. Apparel unions increased in numbers and activity, including the National Women's Trade Union League, formed in 1903. Middle-class women, members of the National Consumers' League founded in 1898, criticized factory working conditions and supported union activity.

Services for the Poorer Classes

By 1900, 90 percent of all U.S. manufacturing took place in cities, whereas small industries in towns and rural areas had predominated a century earlier. New York grew by 1 million inhabitants between 1890 and 1900, and the U.S. population reached 75.9 million, including a large contingent of recent immigrants. Knowing no English, and often entirely illiterate, immigrants were confined to unskilled labor and housed in squalid tenements, with poor lighting and ventilation. Only one tenth of all tenements had indoor toilets or running water. Social services were offered by religious groups such as the Salvation Army, clergy of all major faiths, and settlement houses in the slums of cities such as New York and Chicago. Staffed mostly by female social workers, these community centers offered recent arrivals education, moral guidance, physical care, and orientation to American life. Numbering 100 nationwide in 1900, settlement houses increased fourfold by 1911. Social workers, scandalized by the misery around them, campaigned for laws to regulate tenements, secure consumer protection, and improve working conditions and access to schooling. They also frequently provided women with job skills, most often in sewing, either for their own clothing or for the many jobs in factory work, especially in New York.

Less altruistic helpers, the politicians in big-city party machines, assisted immigrants in finding jobs and offered a few social services in exchange for votes. Corruption flourished in all too many city governments. Progressives set out to tackle this problem, starting at the city level and working up through the states to the federal government. As a conglomeration of different reform movements, progressivism encompassed Republicans and Democrats, women and men, and citizens from all regions, who were inspired by American ideals and the Social Gospel (Christianity directed to societal betterment) to solve the problems precipitated by urban congestion, burgeoning industrialism, and massive immigration, averaging 1 million per year in the early 1900s.[1] Progressives secured passage of the federal Civil Service Act, which removed almost 100,000 jobs from political patronage and improved opportunities for qualified applicants.

Largely untouched by reform, African Americans lost their modest nineteenth-century gains in suffrage by the early twentieth century and, along with Native Americans and Mexican immigrants, suffered job discrimination and were subjected to inferior schooling. Literacy rates among blacks did rise slightly in the early 1900s.

Medicine

At the turn of the century, forward-looking medical professionals and many lay people fostered health reform, a complement to political, social, and industrial reform. Medical science had begun to earn that name in the later 1800s, as the most forward-thinking physicians accepted the germ theory of disease. The American Medical Society reorganized to encourage sounder practices; medical education also advanced at Johns Hopkins University, in Baltimore, and elsewhere.

Through the efforts of physicians, nurses, and social workers, Americans came to realize that disease could be transmitted through contact with public toilets, trolley cars, and even clothing manufactured in disease-ridden slums. No longer could the well-off assume that their status shielded them from the tuberculosis, diphtheria, and typhoid and scarlet fevers that ravaged the poor. Strenuous efforts were made to teach middle-class standards of home hygiene and personal care to working-class people, within the limits of their circumstances. At middle- and upper-class levels, households redoubled their vigilance against sewer gasses, dust, and microscopic organisms in every object of daily use.

Public health proponents tackled purification of municipal water supplies, launched antispitting campaigns, and taught people the necessity of covering their mouths when coughing or sneezing. Paper tissues replaced cloth handkerchiefs, and paper drinking cups supplanted communal water ladles. Electric trolleys replaced horse-drawn conveyances and the manure that formerly polluted city streets.

Standards of household and personal cleanliness rose gradually, although habits of bathing and hair washing fell far short of today's standards. Working-class city dwellers could frequent the public baths that offered cleanliness and recreation, because tenements often lacked access to the clean water essential to personal hygiene. Dress came under scrutiny, too. Women were urged to shorten their skirts enough to clear the dirty streets. Physicians, especially surgeons, abandoned the frock coat for a washable surgical gown and covered their beards during surgery. In due course, a fashion for being clean-shaven banished the beard among most young men, not just men who practiced medicine (Figure 1.2).

Technology

Americans lived up to their reputations as a nation of inventors and tinkerers at the turn of the twentieth century. The Bessemer steel process, the foundation of the fortune amassed by Andrew Carnegie, made possible steel railroad tracks, plows, bridges, and high-rise buildings. The latter became practicable with iron framing and elevators; in 1889 the first electric elevator was installed in a New York high-rise office. At the individual level, Americans enjoyed steel sewing machines, parallel to the diversified factory machines that handled knitted fabrics and performed specialized manufacturing operations, such as forming buttonholes. Apparel itself became the subject of hundreds of inventions,

Figure 1.2 Middle-class couple from Macon, Missouri, circa 1898–1899. Note the man's clean-shaven face. Author's collection.

including improvements to corsets and brassieres and devices to secure the fashionable silhouette of shirtwaist and flaring skirts for women and crisp shirts and suits for men.[2]

Transportation and communications modernized in the early twentieth century. Automobiles insinuated their way into American life. Only 2,500 were manufactured in 1899, but by 1907 output rose to 44,000, easily surpassing the numbers in both Britain and continental Europe. Accustomed to the personal transportation made possible by bicycles, upper-middle-class Americans were eager to procure automobiles. Even more limited, although dramatic, was America's entrance into the Air Age on December 17, 1903, when Wilbur and Orville Wright flew their airplane over Kitty Hawk, North Carolina. Commercial and military development of airplanes lagged until the 1910s.

Rotary press and linotype inventions lowered the cost and raised the quality of periodicals at the start of the twentieth century. An impressive 2,226 daily newspapers and 14,000 weeklies reached a circulation of 42,500,000 in 1900. Illiteracy declined to 10.7 percent in 1900. Clearly, a substantial percentage of Americans had access to news, opinion, and consumer advertising—just the thing to stimulate the spread of fashionable clothing. Newspapers also began to publish more fashion engravings in apparel advertisements, and stores could purchase fashion-display images from manufacturers and trade publications. Middle-class amateur photographers, using inexpensive cameras, charted the spread of apparel styles. Telephones were becoming more common; by 1900 one U.S. home in 13 had a telephone.

America in the World, 1898–1907

Foreign policy under President Theodore Roosevelt was built on the assertiveness demonstrated in the Spanish-American War, which brought the United States control of Cuba and the Philippine Islands, as well as annexation of Guam and Hawaii. Believing that America and advanced European nations had a duty to police the world, Roosevelt oversaw the modernization of the American navy and the establishment of a War College, in Carlisle Barracks, Pennsylvania. He sent the U.S. Great White Fleet around the globe to demonstrate American prowess and to counter the rising naval might of Japan and Germany. American officials warned European powers against meddling in Central and South America, deemed to be a U.S. sphere of influence. By various means, direct or indirect, the United States acquired the land where the Panama Canal was built between 1904 and 1914. This critical waterway vastly expedited shipping between the East and West Coasts of North America. Not all of Roosevelt's foreign ventures involved saber rattling. He received the Nobel Peace Prize in 1905 for helping to negotiate the end of a war between Russia and Japan. In short, American policy abroad involved maintaining stability at home and a balance among powers and securing recognition of U.S. interests in its own geographic neighborhood.

Turn-of-the-century Work and Roles of Men and Women

A common misperception assigns a passive role to women until almost the 1920s. However, teenage girls and adult women, both working and middle class, earned wages in record numbers at the turn of the century. In 1900, 4,834,000 women worked for wages, representing 21 percent of all women. That number rose to 7,011,000 by 1910, and the proportion grew to 24 percent. In 1900, the principal job category among all working women included domestic (Figure 1.3), hotel, and laundry-related jobs (44 percent); followed by factory work and other manual labor (34 percent). For women, skilled labor often meant dressmaking or millinery and sometimes factory sewing—skills considered essential to their eventual role as homemakers.

The third largest classification encompassed professional work (12 percent), primarily teaching and social work. Women seeking to enter college teaching, medicine, or law needed a high degree of intellectual ability and determination, because these male bastions vigorously resisted women's encroachments. Clerical and sales jobs employed only 5 percent of women workers but were growing in appeal and availability, especially because women often remained in high school longer than men did, which better prepared themselves for office jobs. Whereas factory work paid women $1.50 to $8.00 per week in 1900, office jobs commanded between $6.00 and $15.00. In addition, factory work, especially in the apparel industry, was often seasonal, which meant women were frequently unemployed for at least a portion of the year. Clerical and sales work offered a cleaner environment and an opportunity to wear more fashionable attire, such as suits or separate skirts and jackets, worn with **shirtwaists** (shirt-style blouse). This corresponded to the white-collar man's ensemble of three-piece suits, shirts, and ties. Some women factory workers wore fashionable clothes, but probably saved their best finery for leisure hours.

Education, including vocational courses for women, was increasingly tied to the types of jobs men and women obtained. Large percentages of men labored in factories and mines or on farms at tasks that were arduous and often dangerous. Working-class youngsters were often relegated to low-paid manual labor. Vocational education, offered in special schools or through courses in conventional schools, pre-

CARRIAGE GOWNS

FOR DESCRIPTIONS SEE "DESCRIPTIONS OF FASHIONS—SOCIETY—MUSIC—ART" SECTION

Figure 1.3 Fashionable carriage gowns. Note the maid's trim dress, apron, and frilly cap and the little girl's loosely cut jacket. *Vogue*, May 11, 1905, 707.

pared both boys and girls for their expected careers. Typical laboring men's clothing centered on denim dungarees or wool work pants and shirts; cold-weather labor required woolen sweaters or shirts similar to today's lumberjack shirts. Farm laborers sometimes wore bib overalls.

Office work continued to attract somewhat better educated men into corporations and service organizations. Technical skills and education prepared some men for the rising occupations in various branches of engineering, both applied and theoretical. A few large companies supported their own engineering laboratories, and therefore competed with those in universities. Most prestigious and often lucra-

tive were the learned professions, although earnings could not compare with the riches acquired by successful industrialists. Men's wages or salaries were typically double those of women who had the same types of jobs. Despite inferior pay, women who worked for wages enjoyed more power in their families because they contributed to family coffers.

Suffrage remained a preserve of (mostly white) men in the early 1900s. However, Colorado, Idaho, Utah, and Wyoming had enfranchised women. By 1900, suffragists struggled to reinvigorate a formal campaign to win the vote, spearheaded by the National American Woman Suffrage Association. Aggressively masculine politics in both major parties in the 1890s meant mainstream politicians were unsympathetic toward women's suffrage.

Nonvoting women indirectly exercised political influence in the early twentieth century by lobbying legislators for laws protecting women, children, and consumers; helping the poor; and cleaning up government. Women's clubs counted 150,000 members in 1900 and were growing rapidly. At the turn of the century, some activist women supported prohibition of alcohol because of the abuse and neglect alcoholic men inflicted on their families. Five states had enacted prohibition by 1900, and the movement progressed quickly, especially in the South and in rural areas. Upper- and middle-class women supported their working-class counterparts by fighting for better working conditions, including recognition of their unions.

Most middle-class women regarded marriage and children as an ultimate goal. Systemization of household tasks, via application of scientific principles, was preached by home economists, who believed in the possibility of improved status for home management and child-rearing. Between 1897 and 1908, home economists professionalized, building on the origins of their field in sanitary science. Although housework gradually became less physically arduous for middle-class women because of improvements in household technology (washing machines, vacuum cleaners), standards of housekeeping rose concurrently, so the time spent on household chores decreased little, if at all.

American Retailing and Manufacturing

France inaugurated the Age of the Department Store in 1850, with the opening of Le Bon Marché in Paris. England and countries of the Continent followed suit, and, after the Civil War, retailers in American cities began to experiment with departmentalization. Notable early examples were A. T. Stewart in New York City and John Wanamaker in Philadelphia. Dry goods stores, which sold fabric and some ready-to-wear items, often metamorphosed into department stores. Wanamaker sold military goods during the Civil War, shifted to civilian men's and boys' wear in the postwar years, and added other lines in the later nineteenth century. In some of the southern and western states, peddlers, who had carried goods on their backs for door-to-door sale, saved their profits, opened "general" stores, and ultimately departmentalized. By the turn of the century, few cities with any claim to importance lacked a major store—one cornerstone of civic pride.

What set department stores apart from earlier specialty stores were the fixed prices, clearly marked on merchandise. Formerly, shoppers had to haggle with clerks over any purchase. Lookers were perfectly welcome in department stores, whereas earlier retailers high-pressured customers to make a purchase. People flocked to the department stores to browse the vast array of merchandise and to gawk at the marvelous windows, mirrors, colorful displays, and special lighting. Shopping in such stores constituted recreation, quite different from the old drudgery of going to the market for necessary goods. Stores provided lounges and restrooms, tea rooms for midday refreshment, delivery services, and even nurseries.

After the downturn of the mid-1890s, department stores spruced up even more. They remodeled to give staff more efficient access to merchandise and to show products attractively. Stores such as Macy's in New York and Marshall Fields in Chicago sought to disarm customers with a club-like or homey atmosphere, making the ladies—the main shoppers—more willing to part with their money. Charge accounts, installment buying, and flexible return policies further enticed customers. Exteriors as well as interiors blossomed with lovely merchandise. Window decoration became a significant art, its practitioners all men, and its audience the throngs on the city sidewalks.[3] Performance art also flourished in stores, which held cultural events, including classical music concerts. The first fashion shows in the United States were staged at Erich Brothers in New York in 1903, bringing to a wide audience what had formerly been the preserve of elite women in Paris.[4]

The growth of in-city transportation helped department stores to thrive, and the reach of the railroad proved a similar boon to mail-order houses, another feature of turn-of-the-century retailing. Aaron Montgomery Ward launched mail order in the United States in 1872, offering a small array of goods to Americans who lived far from cities and were weary of the high markups charged by general stores. Seventeen years later, Richard Sears purveyed pocket watches and other small items to mail-order customers. Both the Ward and Sears, Roebuck, & Co. firms rapidly expanded their lines and their customer bases. No local store, not even Woolworth's 5-and-10-cent stores, could beat the mail-order outfits' prices on a limited number of loss leaders. Prices on a wide array of merchandise were attractive, and customers could place orders without sending money. This reassured purchasers who would otherwise have been reluctant to part with money for something they had not seen from someone they did not know. The emergence of Rural Free Delivery in 1896 brought catalogs to the farm family's mailbox, and mail order proliferated. Sears boasted a circulation of 300,000 by 1897, swelling to 3.6 million by 1907. Spiegel inaugurated its catalog in 1905. Mail order offered a full range of fashion goods for women, men, and children, and places such as Sears, Roebuck, & Co. and Ward offered housewares and farm implements. People of various economic levels, and in most geographic areas, could now aspire to some degree of fashionability (see Figure 1.1).

Changes in Apparel Manufacturing

Apparel manufacturing and the growth of ready-to-wear clothing began in the mid-nineteenth century, with shirts for men and outerwear and some undergarments for women. Both corset and shirt manufacturers outpaced other apparel firms in developing large-scale industrial organizations, because they were able to standardize their product and create vertically integrated firms.[5] Standardized products in high volume proved vital to mail order and to department stores, which did some of their own manufacturing. By 1900, virtually all types of apparel could be purchased ready-made. Particularly significant for women was the rise of the shirtwaist, which began to be produced in huge quantities by the mid-1890s. Department stores sometimes advertised availability in the thousands in what seemed an infinite variety of styles and fabrics.

The popularity of the shirtwaist also led to new organizational structures in the apparel industry. New York City was becoming the center for wholesales and showrooms. While there were apparel factories all over the United States, a significant amount of manufacturing also occurred in New York. As numerous manufacturers entered into production of women's apparel, they were forced to find ways to compete and to differentiate their products for buyers, often with rapid style changes and pricing. Production began to shift to contractors and jobbers, with a resulting increase in the number of sweatshops. Labor in these factories was supplied by the strong contingent of Eastern and Central European immigrants who entered New York via Ellis Island. While many companies focused only on price, a few made the ethical treatment of their workers a selling point. The C. Kenyon Company of Brooklyn, New York, made a point of stating, "It is reassuring to know that Kenyon products are made in bright, sanitary factories without sweatshop work,"[6] thereby proclaiming its products free of contamination and its conscience free of worker exploitation. Starting in 1898, the National Consumers' League offered labels to manufacturers who met League labor standards.

Fashion Influences

Paris, considered the center of style and fashion for centuries, continued to provide a major source of inspiration for both dressmakers and the rising U.S. ready-to-wear industry. Fashion publications such as *Vogue* and *Harper's*

Bazar reported on the styles from Paris and London, and women considered the possession of a Paris-designed gown the pinnacle of dressing. However, by this period an increasing number of new sources began to exert an influence, and, while fashion continued to trickle down from European designers, it also came from the theater, ready-to-wear manufacturers, and art styles and artists. U.S. manufacturers sent their stylists to European events that attracted the wealthy clientele of French and English designers to observe and borrow design ideas. Despite the prominence of France, people began calling for an American style of dress, particularly as U.S. designers adapted French styles to American tastes.

Celebrities

Stars of theater, opera, and vaudeville—an amalgam of music, comedy, and dance—cut elegant, fashionable figures in early 1900s America. Lillian Russell helped to enshrine the fashion of a small waist bracketed by ample bosom and hips. Nellie Melba, an opera diva, and Lillie Langtry, an actress, also represented mature beauty (Figure 1.4). More

Figure 1.4 Actress Lillie Langtry. *Vogue*, September 24, 1903, 307.

modern and youthful in image were Maude Adams, who created the role of Peter Pan; vaudevillian Eva Tanguay, known for her blonde hair and spirited temper; and Mary Pickford, an ingénue who specialized in youthful roles. A contemporary observer reported: "An Annie Russell, Ethel Barrymore, Mary Mannering, or Maxine Elliott 'first night' is as good as an 'opening' to theatre-going women, and not only a dressmaker's opening, but a milliner's as well."[7] Isadora Duncan, exponent of modern dance and uncorseted, barefoot freedom, debuted in the United States in 1904, after gaining celebrity in Europe. Among the men, star quality was represented by Lionel and John Barrymore and Douglas Fairbanks (who married Mary Pickford), and bodybuilders could look to "The Strongman" Eugene Sandow for a model.

Starting in 1894, primitive motion picture parlors opened in some cities; by 1907, the United States boasted 5,000 movie houses. Even middle-class patrons, including families, were gradually attracted to public places of recreation, many of which cleaned up their acts to broaden their audience. Vaudeville offered family-type polite shows and bawdier versions for all-male audiences.

For All Out-of-Door Sports. For Men, Women and Children
In weights and styles for all. At the leading shops throughout the country

DOES NOT SHRINK

Figure 1.5 Gibson Girl attire and athletic competence. Note how the man has shed his jacket for active sport. *Vogue*, April 13, 1905, 567.

The latter type skirted close to erotic burlesque shows. Musical innovation included emergent jazz and its most notable early offshoot, ragtime, blending African and European musical traditions into a syncopated beat that shocked older Americans but delighted young dancers. In due course, faster dancing encouraged lighter and shorter dresses for women.

Socialites

At the top of the social pinnacle stood King Edward VII of England and Queen Alexandra, his shy consort. Even as prince and heir apparent, Edward cut a fashionable, although portly, figure. He helped to confirm the fashions for sack coats, tweed, and trousers with creases. Alexandra, handicapped socially by deafness and a limp, nonetheless wore clothes beautifully. Socialites and actresses often frequented the European couturiers or expensive U.S. dressmakers.

Grande Dames of American plutocracy, such as Mrs. O. H. P. Belmont, symbolized extravagant style in quality and quantity of clothing. A first daughter, the irrepressible Alice Roosevelt gave her name to a popular shade of blue for young women, enshrined in the 1910s song "In My Sweet Little Alice Blue Gown." Society women shoppers, including members of department-store–owning families, gave working-class saleswomen a glimpse of high fashion and a yearning to imitate the latest styles.

Other Trend Setters

One powerful fashion symbol at the turn of the century was Charles Dana Gibson's beautifully illustrated creature, the Gibson Girl. Despite her aristocratic demeanor and milieu, she cut across class lines to appeal to rich and poor women. Her skirts and shirtwaists, worn with élan, presented an image to which many might aspire (Figure 1.5). Men also felt comfortable with the Gibson Girl, who engaged in New Woman pursuits of sports and outdoorsy living but avoided radicalism. Men's equivalent of the Gibson Girl, arriving at the end of this period, was the Arrow Collar Man, a clean-cut, square-jawed paragon of vigorous but fashionable masculinity.

Not all trendsetters were upperclass. Social life for urban working-class young people revolved around commercial recreations, notably dance halls and amusement parks, where boys and girls could mingle without parental supervision. In these locales and on city streets, where prostitutes paraded, stylish dress was on view for working-class girls to admire and imitate. Young factory women might skimp on meals or stay up half the night refurbishing their apparel—anything to own some swell outfit that helped them break out of the monotony of daily work and look fashionable in the social scene of city street life.[8]

One huge boon of expanding ready-to-wear offerings at varied prices was that it allowed working-class women to secure fashionable styles. Immigrants, too, used up-to-date apparel to help them make the transition from greenhorns to assimilated Americans. Shawls were exchanged for fashionable hats; Hasidic Jewish women's wigs and shaven heads gave way to hairdos augmented by rats and puffs of false hair; and serviceable shoes were replaced by tight but elegant high-heeled boots.[9] Factory girls and saleswomen also looked to their coworkers for advice on clothing and personal appearance. Immigrant men and children, too, adopted the attire of their new country as speedily as they could.

The Arts

Art nouveau style developed at the end of the nineteenth century as an attempt to create an international style of decorative art and architecture that was at least in part a response to the industrial age. Art nouveau designers aimed to create a cohesive look that included buildings, furniture and interiors, textiles, apparel, and jewelry. Inspiration for their stylized and organic forms included the curvilinear rococo style of the eighteenth century; the arts of Japan, China, and the Islamic world; the Pre-Raphaelite artists; and the arts and crafts movement. Although the most direct influence on fashion is sometimes assumed to be the curvilinear shape of the popular woman's fashion silhouette, art nouveau was most visible in surface embellishments and the ornamentations used in textile and lace patterns (Figure 1.6). Although the art nouveau style did not have a significant influence on the fashion illustration style of the period, it can be seen in advertising posters.

Chinese art became increasingly familiar to Americans, partly as a result of U.S. involvement in suppressing the Boxer Rebellion and enforcing an Open Door policy that allowed various countries to compete in China. The 260-year-old Qing Dynasty was nearing its end, and a two-way trade in Western–Eastern goods flourished. Short or long outer robes called *pao* found their way into wealthy Americans' loungewear. Brilliant silks and intricate embroideries enhanced these robes' appeal. In a few years, a more pervasive Chinese and Japanese influence would alter the shapes of American women's dress.

Fashion Illustration and Art

Upper- and middle-class Americans read a number of influential fashion publications of this period. *Vogue* and *Harper's Bazar* appealed to moneyed readers, with fash-

GREEN CREPE with Black Velvet Ribbon edged with Ruchings of White Mousseline de Soie.

Figure 1.6 Gown trimmed in art nouveau style. *Harper's Bazar*, June 9, 1900, 361.

ion and society news, features on gracious living, and—especially in the case of *Bazar*—fiction. *Delineator*, *McCall's*, and *Ladies' Home Journal* directed their articles to middle-class women, with ready-made fashion images, dressmaking patterns and instructions, and household hints. Those who could not afford subscriptions to the fashion press acquired their information from newspapers, catalogs, and—in the case of city dwellers—store windows.

By the late nineteenth century there were many opportunities for women to learn about the latest fashions. Most styles that women saw in the fashion and other publications of the period were drawings, with the exception of society columns, which included photographs of wealthy or titled women at social events. Although photography was beginning to be adapted to fashion, it was most frequently used to show actresses and society women in the latest styles. Some couture designers took fashion photographs as a means of record keeping. Not intended for publication, these were used in-house and may also have served as a source for illustrators of the period to depict the precise details of a design. The quality of fashion illustration, reproduced through engraved plates, had begun to decline in the last quarter of the nineteenth century; but several illustrators revived the fashion plate and produced high-quality work, most often of couture designs. One of the more skilled illustrators was Adolphe Charles Sandoz, whose work was published in high fashion magazines such as *The Queen*.

The Authority of the Designer

The influence of French designers and dressmakers was given a helping hand by English-born Charles Frederick Worth in the last half of the nineteenth century. Although not the first couturier, he is often considered the father of haute couture and the first designer to achieve celebrity. Worth died in 1895, but the House of Worth continued under the direction of his sons. Other well-known design houses included those of Doucet, Redfern, the Callot Sisters, and Paquin. There were, however, dozens of designer dressmakers in London and Paris who exerted an influence on fashion, some with prominent design houses, and others in smaller dressmaking shops. These artisans did the custom work required of couture, but they did not have to present the twice-yearly fashion collections that were mandatory for couturiers.

During the last half of the nineteenth century, and indeed well into the twentieth, the **House of Worth** was considered the definitive couture *maison*. It was established in 1857 and was frequented not only by royalty and the wealthy but also by actresses and the socially ambitious. Newly wealthy Americans, including Mrs. Potter Palmer from Chicago and the Hewitt sisters from New York, formed a significant portion of its clientele. As an astute businessman, Worth developed techniques for producing and distributing his designs, which remain the most influential part of his legacy. Son Jean-Philippe Worth took over as designer after his father's death, while his brother Gaston handled the financial end of the business. Gaston also served as the first president of the Chambre Syndicale de la Haute Couture Française, a governing body that oversaw the couture houses. The design approach under Jean-Philippe remained the same as his father's. He continued to dress royalty, American heiresses, and opera stars in opulent styles, often inspired by visits to art galleries. Dressing royalty also meant frequent masquerade balls, for which a study of historic costume was essential. Although Jean-

Philippe preferred many of the classic silhouettes created by his father, tastes and styles were changing, and by 1910 he decided to design only major commissions. He turned the majority of the designing over to his nephew, Jean-Charles.

Jeanne Paquin was one of Worth's principal competitors, and at the time she was considered an equally prominent fashion authority and artist. She and her businessman husband, Isadore, opened her *maison de couture* next door to Worth's on the rue de la Paix in 1891. Her fashion business was one of the most prominent, at one time employing as many as 2,000 workers, and she herself was described as the dictator of the fashion couture aristocracy. Paquin was the first couturière to open foreign establishments, first in London, and later in Buenos Aires and Madrid. She was also president of the Chambre Syndicale de la Haute Couture from 1917 to 1919. Her customers included both royalty and actresses, and, while she was known for her innovative designs, she also modified the more extreme styles to provide her customers with some comfort and practicality. She died in 1936.

The **House of Doucet** was one of the oldest in Paris, with an emphasis on lingerie, and, in the mid-1800s, on men's haberdashery. The creation of women's outerwear became the focus after Jacques entered the family business in the 1870s. Jacques Doucet's creations were considered equal to Worth's in influence and were, like Worth's, often exported for copying by U.S. dressmakers and department stores. Doucet preferred more fluid fabrics and incorporated ribbons and chiffons into his designs. His use of intertwining vines and other organic motifs as surface design is very much in keeping with the art nouveau aesthetic of the period. An avid art collector, Doucet often took his design inspiration from art and historic costume styles. The increasingly clean-lined fashion styles of the 1910s and post–World War I period were less in tune with his tastes, and he began to participate less and less in the actual designing. The house was merged with a smaller house, Doueillet, in 1924, and ultimately closed in 1932. Although Doucet dressed some of the same clients as Worth, his soft and feminine designs also appealed to actresses and other stage personalities, such as Réjane and Sara Bernhardt.

The house of **Callot Soeurs** was operated by four sisters, daughters of a Paris antique dealer who specialized in laces and old fabrics. Their designs of the period reflect this taste for lace, often used on extravagantly decorated, ornate dresses. Their most prominent customer was New York–born socialite Rita de Acosta Lydig, but the Callots' simpler designs were copied or adapted by the U.S. fashion trade. The sisters built a design house that was known for its high standards of workmanship and continued to produce fashionable clothing through the 1920s. It closed in 1937.

The **House of Redfern** was opened in the mid-nineteenth century on the English Isle of Wight and catered to the dressing needs of the women who went to the island's elite resort, Cowes, for racing and yachting. The company became Redfern and Sons and expanded to include a ladies' tailoring business and couture houses in London and Paris in 1881. Best known for his elegantly tailored outfits, Redfern had a substantial U.S. clientele and ultimately opened branches in New York and Chicago. The house expanded to Paris and, by the turn of the century, gained recognition as a member of the Chambre Syndicale de la Haute Couture. Redfern was adept at keeping up with changing fashions, and was a leader in the development of the high-waisted styles that began the emerge shown in 1908.

Fashion Trends

Men's and women's silhouettes had begun to diverge in the 1860s, with the square-cut sack suit, a trend that went even further in early twentieth-century America. Blocky suit styles gave men an oblong shape, whereas women's dresses and suits accentuated a slim waist with billowing curves above the waist and rounded hips below. An S-bend posture (see Figure 1.6), also called the **pouter pigeon silhouette**, emphasized these contours. Only in certain styles of coat did women's outlines approach those of men. Softer, more flowing fabrics emphasized the more fluid lines. Young boys wore suits, and girls wore short jackets, with a relatively boxy effect. Despite the clearly different silhouette, however, the contemporary impression of some women's dress was often one of borrowing from brothers or husbands. Shirtwaists and tailor-made suits, with a visual link to men's and boys' dress, often led contemporaries to see it as masculine. Publications and cartoons often commented on the mannish woman. Women's eveningwear shunned tailoring and stressed décolleté necklines, soft pale colors, and frills. The high-waisted, Empire line that would become popular in the 1910s made an early appearance in a few evening gowns and in **tea gowns** for entertaining at home.

Occasion-specific dress ruled among the uppercrust and upper-middle-class social climbers. The motto might have been "Change early and often." Etiquette dictated loose gowns at breakfast, dresses with trains and tea gowns for receiving at home, suits for promenading, and finely discriminated dressy clothes for family dinners and grand balls. Well-to-do men also had to observe the niceties of suits proper to business office, sports, formal daytime occasions, and evening events (Figure 1.7). In addition to all of these rules were conventions of mourning for the death of a close relative, which required several months of black garb.

Another trend was the growing impression that fashions changed with increasing rapidity in the last quarter of the nineteenth century. Comments to that effect permeated women's fashion publications. Articles related to the problems of keeping up with fashion were directed at shoppers, home sewers, and dressmakers. One woman supposedly exclaimed, "Sleeves have changed again this month!"[10]

The increased number of women in clerical and sales work helped to increase the demand for ready-to-wear apparel. They required clothing that gave a polished appearance but were encouraged not to look too extravagant or flashy. For office workers, fashion advice literature recommended tailor-made suits with dress shirts and ties or plain skirts, shirtwaists, and jackets. What the clerical staff needed were sturdy, inconspicuous clothes, able to hold up to long wear. Such clean-lined garments were now available at reasonable prices. Working-class men's wardrobes might be limited to a suit of Sunday-best clothes and work clothes—either a uniform (see Figure 1.7) or trousers and shirts.

Textiles

For all practical purposes, four fibers dominated the clothing scene in the early twentieth century. Coats and suits were usually of wool, either firm, shiny worsteds or softer woolens. Flax, woven into linen cloth, appeared in some suits for summer and in **dusters**—coats worn for riding in an automobile or a carriage. Men's shirts and women's and children's blouses or **waists** might be of plain-weave cotton or linen, as might the washable white dresses that dominated summerwear during this period. Linen was the more prestigious fabric for men's shirts. To achieve the look of a crisp linen shirt, they could purchase a cheaper shirt in cotton and a linen collar and cuffs. Most luxurious were the silk dresses, blouses, and shirts of the well-to-do American woman. During this period, thin woven silks such as chiffon and crepe enjoyed great popularity, although heavier satin, brocade, and velvet appeared in costly evening dresses. Lace trims, both hand and machine made, appeared on quality clothing for women and girls. Although a form of rayon was developed in France in 1892, and viscose rayon was brought out in 1903, these were not yet sufficiently reliable for commercial use. Celluloid, a plastic made from cellulose nitrate and camphor, patented in 1870, was used for buttons and washable collars and cuffs during the early twentieth century. Wearers had to be careful with smoking materials, because celluloid was highly flammable.

Major Garments

Women's streetwear underwent subtle but important changes in shape during this period. Shifts in menswear styling were even less obtrusive.

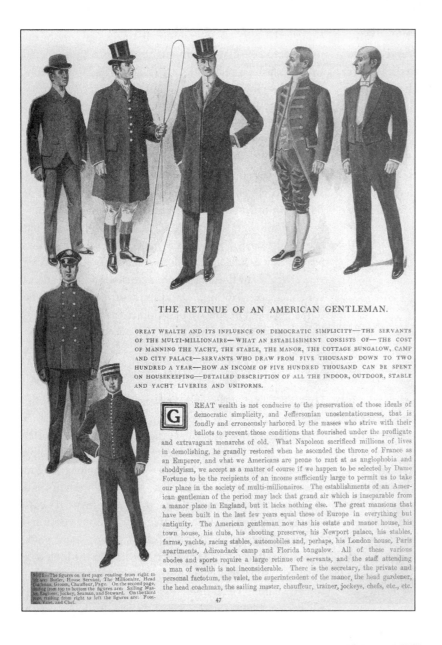

THE RETINUE OF AN AMERICAN GENTLEMAN.

GREAT WEALTH AND ITS INFLUENCE ON DEMOCRATIC SIMPLICITY—THE SERVANTS OF THE MULTI-MILLIONAIRE—WHAT AN ESTABLISHMENT CONSISTS OF—THE COST OF MANNING THE YACHT, THE STABLE, THE MANOR, THE COTTAGE BUNGALOW, CAMP AND CITY PALACE—SERVANTS WHO DRAW FROM FIVE THOUSAND DOWN TO TWO HUNDRED A YEAR—HOW AN INCOME OF FIVE HUNDRED THOUSAND CAN BE SPENT ON HOUSEKEEPING—DETAILED DESCRIPTION OF ALL THE INDOOR, OUTDOOR, STABLE AND YACHT LIVERIES AND UNIFORMS.

G REAT wealth is not conducive to the preservation of those ideals of democratic simplicity, and Jeffersonian unostentatiousness, that is fondly and erroneously harbored by the masses who strive with their ballots to prevent those conditions that flourished under the profligate and extravagant monarchs of old. What Napoleon sacrificed millions of lives in demolishing, he grandly restored when he ascended the throne of France as an Emperor, and what we Americans are prone to rant at as anglophobia and shoddyism, we accept as a matter of course if we happen to be selected by Dame Fortune to be the recipients of an income sufficiently large to permit us to take our place in the society of multi-millionaires. The establishments of an American gentleman of the period may lack that grand air which is inseparable from a manor place in England, but it lacks nothing else. The great mansions that have been built in the last few years equal those of Europe in everything but antiquity. The American gentleman now has his estate and manor house, his town house, his clubs, his shooting preserves, his Newport palace, his stables, farms, yachts, racing stables, automobiles and, perhaps, his London house, Paris apartments, Adirondack camp and Florida bungalow. All of these various abodes and sports require a large retinue of servants, and the staff attending a man of wealth is not inconsiderable. There is the secretary, the private and personal factotum, the valet, the superintendent of the manor, the head gardener, the head coachman, the sailing master, chauffeur, trainer, jockeys, chefs, etc., etc.

NOTE—The figures on first page reading from right to left are: Butler, House Servant, The Millionaire, Head Coachman, Groom, Chauffeur, Page. On the second page, reading from top to bottom the figures are: Sailing Master, Engineer, Jockey, Seaman, and Steward. On the third page, reading from right to left the figures are: Footman, Valet, and Chef.

47

Figure 1.7 (LEFT) Attire of a gentleman and some of his servants. *Haberdasher*, March 1903, 47.

Figure 1.8 (OPPOSITE, LEFT) Princess dress in black and white. *Delineator*, September 1906, 319 (from Textile and Clothing Collection, Department of Apparel, Education Studies, and Hospitality Management [AESHM], Iowa State University).

Figure 1.9 (OPPOSITE, RIGHT) Shirtwaist novelties. *Delineator*, May 1902, 747 (from Textile and Clothing Collection, Department of Apparel, Education Studies, and Hospitality Management [AESHM], Iowa State University).

Women's Dresses, Suits, and Coats

From 1898 to 1906, women's major garments featured a bloused bodice with long sleeves and a skirt that hugged the hips, fanning out into a trumpet-shaped hemline (Figure 1.8 and Plate 1.1). Except for shirtwaist styles, bodices (and even some waists) were constructed with a boned lining. Sleeves became elbow length and fuller cut about 1904–1905, and the blousiness began to shrink. A much greater change came in 1905–1907, with the arrival of the smooth-fitting **princess** silhouette, shaped by long seams from shoulder to hem rather than by gathers or pleats. From this point forward, women's posture lost its forward tilt, and a slim ideal prevailed (see Figure 1.8).

In addition to dresses, women's wardrobes included tailor-made suits, often with more or less fitted short jackets, and flared or pleated skirts that touched the toe of the shoe. Such skirts were worn with **shirtwaists**, modeled on men's shirts, and usually with a jacket (see Figure 1.5). Although shirtwaists began life as clones of men's shirts, frilly edgings and insertions of lace crept into their styling (Figure 1.9). All sorts of coat lengths could be seen in the early 1900s: long, three-quarter length, or hip length. Their common feature was a squared-off cut that hung from the shoulders with no waistline indentation; some suit jackets assumed a similar shape in about 1906 (Figure 1.10). When there was a waistline indentation, it came at the back, leaving the front flat, echoing the line of the dress at center front. By 1906–1907, designers offered wraps made from soft materials, without stiff tailoring.

THE DELINEATOR.   *Novelties in Shirt-Waists.*   MAY. 1902.
DESCRIBED ON PAGES 758 AND 760

Men's Suits, Coats, and Shirts

Most men wore three-piece suits, including **sack coats** with no waistline seams (see Figure 1.2). Jackets were longish three- or four-button styles; vests were waist length. Trousers had acquired creases and cuffs by the end of the 1890s, whereas earlier trousers were smooth-fronted and uncuffed. Creases, acquired in folded storage, were found to give the leg a slim look, and cuffs (also known as turn-ups), originated from the efforts of laborers to protect the hems of their pants from wear and soiling. Cuffs remained avant-garde, worn by younger men.

Dress shirts were tailored and usually white, with collars that were almost as stiff and uncomfortable as women's corsets. Evening shirts featured heavily starched fronts—called **bosoms**—and back neck closures. In the very hot summers of 1901 and 1902, men ventured to adopt a version of the women's shirtwaist, defying rigid definitions of masculinity. These scandalous shirts were intended to be worn with *no jacket*, outraging the more traditional-minded members of the public, who regarded a shirt as underwear.[11] Indeed, not only did men in offices with no air-conditioning wear jackets, but laboring men on worksites sometimes kept their vests on as well, even if they shed their jackets. At least one dermatologist reported cases of skin rashes resulting from this dysfunctional convention of dressing. Other, more relaxed shirt styles began to appear. Most notable was the **négligé**, a front-button shirt with attached collar that was sold in various colors and patterns and was intended for sport or casual occasions (Figure 1.11; see also Figure 1.5).

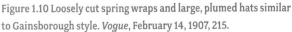

Figure 1.10 Loosely cut spring wraps and large, plumed hats similar to Gainsborough style. *Vogue*, February 14, 1907, 215.

Figure 1.11 Négligé shirt. *Haberdasher*, March 1903, 11.

Sports-Related Styles

Americans embraced various sports in the last half of the nineteenth century. People with money sailed yachts, followed horseracing, and pursued tennis. Middle-class citizens played baseball, swam, practiced calisthenics, followed football, and engaged in croquet, golf, and fencing. The middle class turned bicycling from a diversion for a few rich wheelmen in the 1880s into a national craze for men, women, and children by the 1890s.

Sports uniforms and equipment evolved, developing into an apparel category in its own right and ultimately influencing everyday streetwear (see Figure 1.5). Spaulding became a major producer of both equipment and team uniforms, including for the 1900 and 1904 Olympic Games. Sports items of the late nineteenth century, including sweaters and canvas shoes, became part of informal wardrobes (see Figure 1.1). As early as the beginning of the twentieth century, the United States began to adopt more informality in daily dress, particularly compared with the greater decorum in Europe.

Women's participation in cycling made them more independent and demonstrated the confinement of conventional fashion, leading some wheelwomen to adopt **bloomers**—full knee-length pants—and shorter, more flexible corsets. Women who didn't feel comfortable wearing bloomers opted to wear shorter skirts. Men's cycling togs included canvas shoes and **knickers**—snug, knee-length pants—which had formerly been worn only by young boys. By 1895, four million Americans owned bicycles, and at least as many rented them.

Bicycle manufacturers, along with carriage makers and marine-motor companies, branched into production of automobiles for the ultrarich by the mid-1890s.[12] In their early campaign for better roads, cyclists also paved the way for the success of the auto. Motoring gear included a long duster coat, a cap for men or a brimmed hat with a veil for women, gloves, goggles, and leather boots (Figure 1.12). Because cars lacked windshields and most roads were unpaved, protection of the face, hair, and clothing was essential. Even at a then breathless 15

THE FIRST LESSON
See text

Figure 1.12 Duster coats and headgear for motoring. *Vogue*, October 15, 1903, 409.

Figure 1.13 Men's swimsuit. *Haberdasher*, June 1903, 123.

miles per hour, a horseless carriage could kick up considerable dust.

Turn-of-the-century swimwear covered an astounding portion of the body, despite shrinkage in women's swimwear from the all-enveloping styles of the 1860s. Men wore either one- or two-piece suits with sleeveless or short-sleeved tops and above-knee-length trunks (Figure 1.13). Rubber shoes often cushioned swimmers' feet, because beaches were sometimes littered with stones. Away from the public eye, in private swimming areas or in gender-segregated public pools, women might wear suits like the men's styles, but on public beaches a short skirt, hose, rubber shoes, and sometimes headgear were added for modesty's sake (Figure 1.14). Professional performers sometimes wore tights or other streamlined outfits.[13] Being obsessive about catching a chill, Americans often opted for lightweight woven wool or knits, although some cotton was used. Wool also kept its shape better than cotton or linen textiles. Suntans had not yet won acceptance, so coverage of the skin was de rigueur. Untroubled by consider-

ations of health or modesty, young boys sometimes skinny-dipped in secluded lakes or rivers.

Underwear and Sleepwear

Women squeezed themselves into straight-front **corsets**—very uncomfortable, but requisite to the S-bend shape so much in vogue. Corsets stopped below the bust, so the gap was bridged by a fitted corset cover of cotton or linen (Figure 1.15). Hip pads augmented that part of the anatomy to help skirts hang better. When the princess dress came into fashion, something more was needed. Enter the **brassiere,** as it was called in 1904 (Figure 1.16). From the 1860s through the 1890s, bust supporters had been fashionable among a health-conscious and corset-averse minority. With the arrival of the princess line, brassieres moved into the mainstream. They were waist-length, boned lightly, fastened in the front, and had no cup contour. "One, not two" represented the fashion ideal; even a décolleté gown did not normally reveal actual cleavage.

Figure 1.14 Women's bathing suits. *Vogue*, May 11, 1905, 704.

Figure 1.15 Straight-front corset, WB brand. *Delineator*, October 1902, unpaginated front matter (from Textile and Clothing Collection, Department of Apparel, Education Studies, and Hospitality Management [AESHM], Iowa State University).

Drawers (loose, knee-length underpants) came with closed or open crotches and tended to have full-cut legs and, at the higher price levels, lots of frills (Figure 1.17). Drawers with an open crotch made toileting and changing sanitary pads (or cloths) much easier. Only in the twentieth century did the closed crotch prevail. Fullness in drawers helped to support the skirt silhouette, as did the frilly petticoats of cotton, linen, or thin china silk or crisp taffeta. In cold climates a crocheted woolen petticoat might be added. Winter brought in **union suits** (shirts attached to drawers) of wool, cotton, or some mixture of materials. George Munsing, a Midwestern underwear magnate, owned patents on a technique for covering wool with silk in the yarn to mitigate the itchiness of wool. Girls wore unshaped underwaists, drawers, and petticoats.

Men, boys, and girls wore union suits much like those worn by women (Figure 1.18). Sleepwear consisted of pajamas and a few nightshirts for men and mostly nightgowns and a few frilled pajamas for women. Women wore lounging robes, frilly morning gowns, and plainer cotton dusters for strictly private domestic routines, including breakfasting and doing housework. Men had hip-length **smoking jackets** and longer robes for leisure hours.

Infants' and Children's Styles

Convention dictated that infants be dressed in white, in as many layers as the budget could afford. Babies wore diapers, **barrow coats**—long skirtlike garments with extrawide waistbands—petticoats, and dresses, not to mention coats for outings in the pram (Figure 1.19). If fear of chilling was presumed to affect adults, it applied doubly to infants. After a year or two, babies were put into ankle-length dresses more conducive to toddling. Gender made no difference as long as they were in diapers. Kilts were worn by small boys, such as the three-year-old in Figure 1.20, who wears his kilt with a fancy shirt. After toilet training, girls wore short dresses with full skirts and decorative sashes. Such relative freedom lasted until adolescence, when skirts began to creep down the leg (Figure 1.21), until full length was achieved at age seventeen.

Figure 1.16 DeBevoise brassiere. *Vogue*, May 25, 1905, 741.

Figure 1.17 Corsets and corset covers. *Vogue*, September 17, 1903, 277.

Toilet-trained boys wore short trousers that were well above the knee. These, too, gradually lengthened until full-length was reached, at about the same time as girls graduated to adult styles. Boys might also wear shirts that buttoned to the short pants, as well as vests and jackets. Military, naval, and similar themes dominated small-boy wear (see Figure 1.21). Boys and girls usually wore cottons during warm weather and wools during winter. Dressy dresses might have silk sashes; except in the case of budding socialites, who would wear all silk. Most startling to present-day viewers is the choice of heavy black or dark-colored stockings and shoes, worn by boys and girls, with no regard to the color of the rest of the outfit (see Figure 1.21). Low- or high-buttoned or laced leather shoes predominated for all children. Sometimes girls wore **Mary Janes** with straps over the instep.

Accessories

In this period of relative formality, accessories were mandatory to complete the costume for both genders and all ages.

Hats

Headwear constituted a vital accessory for women, men, and children. Flights of fancy and, sometimes, defiance of gravity characterized women's and girls' hats: some were brimless **turbans**; others modified the **Gainsborough style** with wide brims and plumes; still some had deep-crowned **toques** with upturned brims. By the end of this period, three-cornered hats and other curved shapes laden with **flowers, fruit, leaves, feathers**, and whole birds were perched on up-swept hairstyles (Figure 1.22; see also Figures 1.3, 1.6, 1.8, 1.9, 1.10). The Audubon Society began to protest angrily because of the devastation of the bird population.

Men's **derbies** continued their 1890s popularity, but the creased-crown **fedora** enjoyed a following among businessmen. Laborers and sportsmen favored the soft cloth cap with a small brim. Flat-brimmed and low-crowned **straw boaters** or **skimmers** signified the coming of the summer season. Young boys wore caps, and young girls wore deep-crowned versions of their mama's hats.

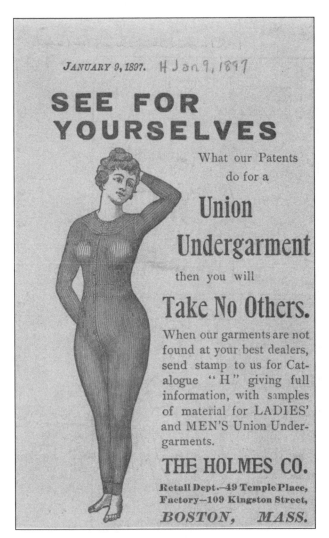

INFANTS' FLANNEL SKIRT OR PETTICOAT 8745.

Footwear and Hosiery

Stylishness trumped comfort in footwear for both men and women. Narrow shapes and tapered toes showed up on men's Oxfords and women's buttoned-up boots. Although high tops from the 1890s remained popular, many styles for women were low topped, with blocky heels (Figure 1.23). Canvas shoes with rubber soles, which had made an appearance in the late 1800s, provided comfort for sporting activities and were even adopted by a few nurses.

Men's socks reached mid-calf and were supported by garters. Women wore thigh-length cotton lisle,[14] worsted, or silk stockings, the most luxe of them boasting embroidered ankle decorations called **clocks** (see Figure 1.23).

Other Accessories and Jewelry

Gloves constituted a social necessity for well-dressed women and men. Gloves protected hands against the weather and also completed the look of an outfit. Heavy gloves were for driving, and thin white or light-colored kid gloves were for evening and daytime streetwear for both women and men.

Women carried small leather, velvet, or silver mesh purses with dainty handles. **Parasol** means "against the sun" and their function was to shield a woman's complexion from tanning or from the almost equally deplorable freckling. Not until the 1920s did a tan signify leisure at the beach rather than working-class labor in a field or on a hot construction site. Parasols of silk or linen were carried; longer handles typified the twentieth century versions compared with those of the 1860s and 1870s (see Figures 1.6, 1.8, 1.9).

During the period, men often wore **bow ties** or long, **four-in-hand ties** with suits, both formal and business-appropriate (see Figure 1.2). Sporting occasions called for neckerchiefs (see Figure 1.11), which were also worn by laborers. Women favored small bows and narrow ties (see Figure 1.9), but usually high, ornate collars and lacy frills provided neck trim.

Jewelry is represented only occasionally in fashion im-

Figure 1.18 (OPPOSITE, LEFT) Union suit for women. *Harper's Bazar*, January 9, 1897. *Picture collection*, The Branch Libraries, The New York Public Library, Astor, Lenox and Tilden Foundations.

Figure 1.19a and b (OPPOSITE, RIGHT) Infants' gowns and petticoats. *Delineator*, October 1905, 567 (from Textile and Clothing Collection, Department of Apparel, Education Studies, and Hospitality Management [AESHM], Iowa State University).

Figure 1.20 (LEFT) Walter Weissenbaum, age three, sports a kilt and fancy shirt. February 1898. Author's collection.

Figure 1.21 (RIGHT) Girls' and boys' everyday attire. *Vogue*, March 9, 1905, 340.

ages, usually in the form of beads and other necklaces (see Figures 1.10 and 1.22). With clothes being so ornate, jewelry would be lost in the total effect. Evening dress, with its décolleté neckline, was perfectly designed so women could wear impressive necklaces and ropes of pearls.

Grooming Aids

Cosmetics and cleansers have a history nearly as long as that of clothing, and for much of that history, beautifiers were the preserve of the wealthy. Democratization of these products came in the nineteenth and early twentieth centuries, and this change brought a gradual acceptance of the social propriety of enhancing personal appearance.

Commercial soaps replaced homemade versions in the late 1800s, with professional beauties such as the English Lillie Langtry endorsing Pears' Soap. American popular brands included Lifebuoy and Palmolive. Household water was still an urban and middle- to upper-class amenity, so

the application of soap varied from daily ritual to sporadic effort, depending on class. Commercial shampoos arrived by the turn of the twentieth century, and their use was at best a semimonthly event; brushing substituted for washing in the removal of dust and dirt, even among the wealthy. Odo-ro-no, a commercial deodorant, appeared in the 1890s. Dental powders promised whiter teeth, and Colgate ribbon dental cream came to market in 1904.

Actual cosmetics suffered from a dubious image in mid-nineteenth-century America. Women who wore it were considered prostitutes at worst and fast women at best. Women concocted most beauty aids at home from recipes in household books and periodicals, and from ingredients obtained at the general store or drugstore. A few house-brand preparations were dispensed by the town druggist. By the end of the 1800s, even respectable women would apply powder to their shiny faces or use whiteners and liquid powders of doubtful efficacy and even more doubtful safety. Tragic stories appeared in the press, tracing the demise of some damsel who used arsenic or lead-based skin improvers. Papier poudre, a thin, powdered piece of paper was smoothed over the face to remove shine. *Vogue* reported in 1903 on the use of imported French pencils, red for lips and black for eyebrows. At $2.00 to $2.50, these were for wealthy women only. African Americans applied skin lighteners, too, and used hot combs or other techniques to smooth out their hair.[15] By 1900, wholesale drug catalogs offered local pharmacies a range of about 50 types of face cream, a similar number of powders and skin treatments, and almost a dozen brands of cosmetic. Jergens hand lotion debuted in 1901. Use of these enhancements cut across social classes, but only a fraction of American women bought them, despite the urgings of celebrities such as Lillie Langtry and Adelina Patti, the famed opera diva.

During the nineteenth century, American women got a clearer idea of their appearance from photography and from wider availability of good-quality mirrors. Compared with the images of celebrated beauties, what the average American saw of herself displeased her. She wanted to ape the new ideal image, and cosmetics promised to help her. Drugstores no longer had this market to themselves. Department stores began to carry cosmetics, at first discreetly and then forthrightly, placing these desirable products in prime locations to attract customers.

Solvent-based cleaning began in France in the 1830s and spread to Austria, Germany, and England in the 1840s and 1850s. By the 1870s, a few major U.S. cities offered so-called French cleaning to those who could afford it. Of course the very wealthy had cleaning services at home, courtesy of valets and ladies' maids. With slow diffusion of dry (waterless) solvent cleaning services, came pressing and delivery of the finished garments on clothes hangers. Department stores and specialty shops displayed their ready-made merchandise on hangers, too, introducing Americans to a tool that would help their clothing keep a smooth, shapely look. Use of hangers also betokened larger wardrobes, as clothing prices dipped relative to incomes, except for the poorest Americans. One hook in a closet or a small drawer could no longer accommodate middle-class wardrobes. Rods and hangers became an important amenity in bedrooms.[16]

Clothing and Comfort

Comfort is subjective—shaped by psychological perceptions and habit as much as by physical conditions. Consider, then, that fully clothed adult Americans from 1898 to 1907 routinely carried around 20 or more pounds of apparel. From his stiff derby hat through his cumbersome wool overcoat to the tops of his leather shoes, a man was well-armored. Suit, shirt, wooly union suit—all added weight. Women fared no

MIDWINTER MILLINERY. DESCRIBED ON PAGE 298

better. Hats were heavy, coats weighty, suits all wool, and layers of underwear numerous, including long, beruffled petticoats and metal- or bone-stiffened corsets. During the 1910s, this would change, as slimmer and lighter fashions came into favor for both men and women.

Few concessions were made, even in hot weather. Linen might replace wool in suits and underwear (Figure 1.24), but Americans hesitated to shed layers. Weather could be changeable, and a fine day might turn raw and windy. Remember, weather forecasting remained at the level of folk-wisdom, and no radio or television broadcasts prepared one for the day's weather. Caution seemed vital, because a chill could lead to a cold, which could lead to pneumonia and an early grave.

Besides being heavy, clothing was tight: tight collars on men and women, tight corsets, and tight shoes. Perhaps this restrictive apparel contributed to reserved behavior, what one present-day wardrobe consultant calls boundaries—keeping people from being too familiar.[17] Children wore looser and lighter clothing, in deference to their youth and to the need to exercise muscles in play so they would grow strong (see Figures 1.3 and 1.21).

A word about corsets: tight lacing to reduce the waistline several inches was relatively rare, confined to the

Figure 1.22 (OPPOSITE) Fashionable hats for women. *Designer*, January 1905, 300.

Figure 1.23 (RIGHT) Ladies' shoes and hosiery. *Delineator*, October 1902, 549 (from Textile and Clothing Collection, Department of Apparel, Education Studies, and Hospitality Management [AESHM], Iowa State University).

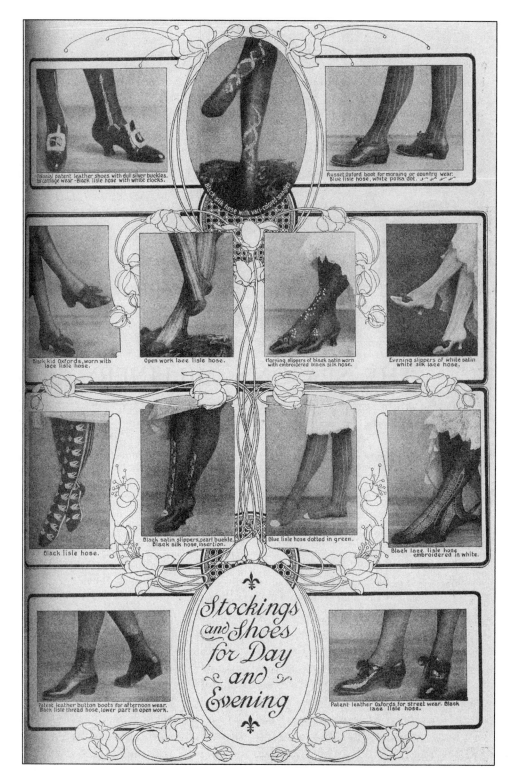

ultra-fashionable and for formal occasions. Many women loosened the laces to leave a gap of 2 or 3 inches in the back, for practical necessity in doing household or farm chores. Why then did they wear the corset at all? It was a matter of respectability—a loose woman was morally suspect—and of achieving a fashionable figure. The so-called health corset of the early 1900s, straight in front and curved behind, created the desired shape, but at the cost of comfort when walking and standing, insofar as can be judged from twentieth-century experiments (see Figure 1.15).[18]

For pregnant women, modifications of the corset allowed loosening at the sides; at a minimum a sling-like supporter held the abdomen, guarding the child within and, coincidentally, offering support to the mother's lower back. Maternity outerwear was just beginning to make an appearance, with Lane Bryant's work for her New York custom clients who desired dresses that suited their delicate condition.[19] Women of lesser means wore **wrappers** and loose robes (Figure 1.25), frilly **tea gowns,** and oversized dresses. Often, in the last stages of pregnancy, women limited their appearances in public out of modesty or embarrassment at a protuberant belly.

Summary

By 1907, American style was moving toward a trim silhouette for women, with the exception of bulky hats. Men and, to some degree, children retained a fuller or blockier shape. Although many women's styles flaunted ruffles and lace, crisp tailoring gained social cachet and suited office environments, where an increasing number of American women and men were employed. Men, of course, dressed in tailored garb for all occasions except for active sports.

Despite the continued prominence of the haute couture in creating new styles, clothing manufacturers in the United States drew on other sources of ideas, including entertainers, artists, and various celebrities. Newer modes of transportation—bicycles and automobiles—stimulated changes in styling, from bloomers and sport corsets for women to duster coats for men and women. Along with breadth of

CARE and precision are the characteristics of Ivory Soap manufacture. Each cake is just as good as any other and all are from soap that is as pure as it can be made. For these reasons the continued use of Ivory Soap gives confidence and pleasure; confidence by its harmlessness, and pleasure in the delightful sense of cleanness it brings.

fashions went varied sources of clothing and grooming products, including mail-order companies, department stores, and specialty shops.

Much clothing of this era hints at an urban appeal—polished and formal. Cities became ever more dominant in manufacturing, in the general economy, and in Americans' consciousness. Fashion news was disseminated and fashion products shipped from cities to small towns and rural areas. In every part of America, there were fashion followers and those who remained loyal to outmoded styles. Younger or more affluent Americans were more inclined to embrace changing fashions. As the next period unfolded, the inclination of fashion to emphasize and celebrate youthfulness grew stronger.

Suggested Readings

Cashman, Sean Dennis. *America in the Age of the Titans*. New York: New York University Press, 1988.

Friedel, Frank. *America in the Twentieth Century*, 4th ed. New York: Alfred A. Knopf, 1976.

Leach, William. *Land of Desire: Merchants, Power, and the Rise of a New American Culture*. New York: Pantheon Books, 1993.

Mahoney, Tom, and Leonard Sloane. *The Great Merchants: America's Foremost Retailers and the People Who Made Them Great*. New York: Harper & Row, Publishers, 1966.

Milbank, Caroline Rennolds. *New York Fashion: The Evolution of American Style*. New York: Harry N. Abrams, 1996 (paperback edition).

Peiss, Kathy. *Cheap Amusements: Working Women and Leisure in Turn-of-the-Century New York*. Philadelphia: Temple University Press, 1986.

Reeves, Thomas C. *Twentieth-Century America: A Brief History*. New York: Oxford University Press, 2000.

CHAPTER 2

1908-

U.S. Events and Trends	Ford introduces Model T	Shirtwaist sewers strike, New York City		Triangle Waist Company fire; many deaths and pressure for labor reforms	Fan magazines for movie devotees

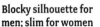    

1908 **1909** **1910** **1911** **1912**

U.S. Fashions	Blocky silhouette for men; slim for women	Condé Nast buys *Vogue*; fashion content expands substantially		Men's silhouette slims; empire styling for women	Drapy shapes for women; hobble skirt debuts

The Twentieth

1918

Ford's moving assembly line at Highland Park, Michigan

Income tax starts in the United States

Armory Show in New York: modernism

1913

Paul Poiret tours the United States

World War I begins

1914

Full, shorter skirts for women reveal ankles

War-induced dyestuff shortages become evident

1915

First shopping center, Lake Forest, Ill

1916

Erté begins to create fashions for *Harper's Bazar*

America enters Great War; women and minorities find work in factories

Russian Revolution climaxes; Communists take over

1917

Reduced variety of products, apparel included; shorter hair for women; "womanalls" and trench coats

Armistice signed November 11, ending Great War

Influenza pandemic kills millions worldwide

1918

Reduced use of metal in corsets

More evident use of eye makeup, lipstick, and rouge

Century Takes Hold

To understand why the period from 1908 to 1918 may be regarded as the *real* beginning of the twentieth century, consider that the decade brought a world war and the drawing of battle lines between communism in Russia and democracy and capitalism in the West. The emergence of fully fledged mass production, the success of a major drive to secure woman suffrage in the United States, and wide swings in the American economy add to the sense of familiarity for present-day readers. The first feature-length movies drew millions of fans, and movie stars came to be known by name, with rising salaries to match their fame. Modernity appeared in the clothing and how it was depicted through illustration and photography. Relatively lean shapes, soft textures for women, and general lightness predominated compared with the apparel of about 1900. Childrenswear presented a straight or loose outline compatible with easy movement for young bodies.

Figure 2.1 Men's lounge suit. *Haberdasher*, February 1918, 45.

Social and Cultural Context

The American economy swung wildly during this period, as a tense peace gave way to the Great War. Some progressive causes such as woman suffrage came close to fruition, but progressivism itself was blunted by the diversion of effort to win the war.

Economic Trends in the United States

In 1908, American unemployment stood at a shocking 8 percent, but by 1913 it had declined to 4.3 percent. The following 2 years brought another spike, topping at 8.5 percent, followed by steady decline to an amazing 1.3 percent in 1918. Industry was hurt in the early 1910s by the deepening crisis and eventual war, which curtailed available credit from overseas. Demand for American agricultural products and manufactured goods was stimulated by World War I (known to contemporaries as the Great War) and escalated to a climax when the United States entered the fray in April 1917.

Whereas rebounding employment signaled good times, inflation pinched many purses, especially those of salaried office workers and others on fixed incomes. Prices rose slowly or declined slightly during the years 1908 to 1915, but inflation soared as the Great War intensified and U.S. sabers began to rattle. Contemporaries referred to inflation as advanced prices for many goods, with annual inflation running from 11 to 23 percent between 1916 and 1918. Labor did command higher wages, which partly eased the burden of steep price rises. Apparel makers responded to the rising cost of fabric by favoring lightweight wool and silk fabrics or substituting inexpensive cottons. Existing trends toward skinny suits for men (Figure 2.1) and narrower, slightly shorter skirts for women received an extra impetus from price inflation because the fabric yardage in a garment had a significant impact on its retail cost. Throughout the 1910s *Vogue* featured columns entitled "Dressing on a Limited Income" and "Dressing on a War Income" to help fashionable women cope with changed economic circumstances. In other magazines, writers encouraged women not to pursue style changes too avidly.

Not everything rose in price. Henry Ford conceived of a simple, low-cost, reliable automobile as early as 1907–1908 and began to realize his dream after 1910.[1] In 1911, 39,640 Fords were made; by 1917, that figure rose to 740,770. Systematization of manufacturing made this possible by breaking down each task and assigning a worker one task that he could do very rapidly and cost-effectively. By the end of 1913, with the help of ingenious engineers, Ford inaugurated a moving assembly line at his vast plant in Highland

Park, Michigan. This meant greater acceleration of production, which was fatiguing to the workers but resulted in great price reductions. In 1909, a Ford Model T cost $950; by 1916, the price had plunged to $360, putting a tin lizzie or flivver within the reach of middle-class families.[2] To mollify the overworked production men and keep them from leaving the company, Ford dramatically announced a doubling of typical wages, to a startling (for the era) $5 per day for an 8-hour day.[3] This gave workers greater income and slightly more leisure time that might persuade them to buy a Model T. In one stroke, Ford reduced worker turnover and absenteeism while building a wider market for his brainchild.

As the automobile industry flourished, allied industries prospered, too. Producers of metal, glass, rubber, and gasoline, not to mention leather and textiles, found Ford and his competitors to be excellent customers. Even the federal government got into the act, passing a bill in 1916 to pump $75 million into highway construction over 5 years. The great American love affair with the automobile had begun in earnest. Its ramifications were felt in Americans' willingness to commute to work from greater distances, to shop in major population centers, and to take day trips and family vacations farther from home. Although specialized clothing for driving continued to include caps, gloves, and duster coats, better-off Americans who could afford the newer, enclosed cars drove in regular daytime or evening clothes (Figure 2.2).

The Great War

European politics had simmered throughout the opening decade of the twentieth century, as various countries formed alliances and nurtured rivalries. Germany's rising industrial and naval power put it on a collision course with England and its allies, notably France and Russia. Smaller countries lined up behind mightier ones or struggled to remain neutral. A Serbian nationalist assassinated the German ally Archduke Ferdinand of Austria and his wife, bringing the pot to a boil. Successive countries declared war on one another, and in August 1914 the guns began to boom. They would do so for more than 4 years, causing about 10 million deaths and the demolition of significant parts of the Continental landscape. Ultimately, 27 countries were involved, and almost an entire generation of young French, British, and German men was wiped out by battle wounds or disease. What prolonged the war and made it so deadly was resort to trench warfare. Unable to score a quick victory, both sides dug in and bombarded each other with very little change in positions for nearly four years.

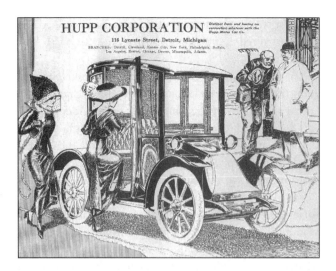

Figure 2.2 Attire for riding in a closed automobile. Hupp Corporation advertisement, reprinted with permission of *Vogue*, November 15, 1911, 67.

At first, the United States refrained from joining the fight, although American citizens held strong views favoring either the Allies (principally Britain, France, Italy, and Russia) or the Central Powers (principally Germany, Austria-Hungary, and Turkey). In some cases, these views were shaped by Americans' feelings for their ancestral countries; in others, by antipathy to one side or the other for past aggressions on their former homelands. Hence a large contingent of Americans of Irish descent opposed England and half-hoped for a Central Powers victory. Various connecting links drew the United States inexorably toward war. One was America's sheer prowess in industry and agriculture. Both sides wanted to buy armaments and food from America. In an effort to starve England into submission, Germans used submarine warfare, destroying American ships. The English also interfered with American shipping. As American lives were lost, the clamor for intervention rose. The Zimmerman telegram in which the Germans seemed to offer Mexico the return of several southwestern American states if Mexico would join the Central Powers proved too great a threat for all but the most dedicated pacifists. America declared war on Germany and its allies on April 6, 1917.

President Woodrow Wilson, a Progressive Democrat and international idealist, couched the American war effort as a crusade to preserve democracy and strike down autocratic governments, such as Kaiser Wilhelm's rule in Germany. America shifted from simply manufacturing armaments and supplying food to desperate Europeans to drafting and training millions of soldiers for active duty in Europe. Ultimately, about 6.4 million men were drafted, and of these more than 2 million served in the military in Europe. Although discrimination against African Americans was still rampant, the United States finally trained and commissioned 1,200 African American officers to lead black troops.

On the home front, the war wrought enormous changes. Industries that had made consumer goods were retooled to supply munitions, trucks, ships, and aircraft. Added to this was the demand for rations, tents, and uniforms for the soldiers. Europe needed food desperately—all the United States could supply. Faced with these exigencies, President Wilson called for the establishment of a War Industries Board (WIB) to coordinate the work of thousands of factories and control which products were made and for whom. Daylight Savings Time was introduced to concentrate factory and farm labor during periods of natural daylight, thus conserving electricity. Under the leadership of Bernard Baruch, the WIB oversaw drastic rationalization (streamlining) of manufacturing. Gone were the hundreds of variations of products. Leather was produced in just three colors—black, white, and tan—instead of the dozens formerly available. Corsets were redesigned to maximize the use of rubber and woven cloth and to minimize the use of metal in stays and fastenings, thereby saving 8,000 *tons* of steel annually (Figure 2.3). Food, too, needed to be conserved, so the Food Administration (FA), another wartime bureau, campaigned for abstinence from wheat on Mondays and Wednesdays, from meat on Tuesdays, and from pork on Thursdays and Saturdays. Americans honored Herbert Hoover, head of the FA, by coining the term Hoover-

ize to describe measures to economize and simplify products for the duration of the war.

With millions of men training for military service at the very time when industry was running full throttle and immigration from Europe plunged, opportunities opened for those not often employed in heavy industry: black Americans and women. The Great Migration drew African Americans from the South to northern cities, where they earned far better wages and suffered fewer curtailments of their civil rights.[4] There were spurts of racial violence, but not enough to deter long-term settlement of transplanted southern families. Women, too, found employment in jobs previously barred to them, as factory workers (Figure 2.4), telegraph operators, barbers, streetcar conductors, railroad workers, and police officers. Women also farmed, on either a full-time or casual basis.[5] These jobs, sadly, were returned to men once the war was over. Not all was lost, however, because wartime service gave women an added argument in their final, successful push to secure national suffrage (voting rights) with the passage of the nineteenth amendment in 1920.

Paying for the war entailed heavy use of the recently enacted income tax. Approved in 1913, with very low rates on only the highest incomes and on corporations, the tax rose dramatically as the United States engaged in war. Even larger contributions to the war chest came from sale of war bonds and stamps. The bonds constituted loans to the federal government, with a promise of repayment with interest

Figure 2.3 (BELOW) Corset with little metal. *Harper's Bazar,* March 1917, 127.

Figure 2.4 (RIGHT) Coveralls for women war workers. *American Machinist,* July 4, 1918, 8.

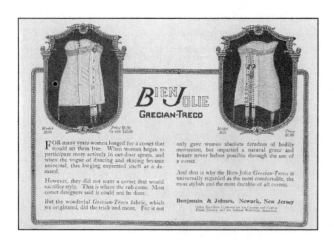

when the bond reached maturity. Posters, four-minute speeches (organized public oratory), and other promotional efforts coaxed Americans to invest in war bonds. Government borrowing drove the demand for money, putting more cash in circulation and contributing to price inflation.

From spring 1917 through late autumn 1918, Americans fought in Europe or served on convoy ships that protected merchant and troop shipping from U-boat (submarine) attack. Serving with French, British, and Italian troops, Americans engaged in several major battles. By late October 1918, the Central Powers were being repulsed and, with the abdication of Kaiser Wilhelm, peace negotiations began. As a major, although late-arriving, combatant, the United States had a substantial role in the conferences to end the war. Woodrow Wilson earnestly sought to have the peace accords pave the way for reconciliation among the warring nations through his Fourteen Points,[6] but he was defeated in this goal by Allied countries' desire to punish Germany and by his own reluctance to compromise. Heavy war reparations crushed the German economy and paved the way for the hyperinflation and misery that helped bring Adolph Hitler to power in 1930–1933. A League of Nations—forerunner to the United Nations—was part of Wilson's ideal for shaping lasting peace. It came to pass, but America did not join, again because of political missteps and rigidity by Wilson, Senator Henry Cabot Lodge, and other government leaders. Indeed, the 1920s and early 1930s marked a time of decreased American involvement in European affairs.

The Russian Revolution, brought to a culmination in 1917 by wartime hardship in Russia, put the Communists in control. In the wake of the Red Communist persecution of middle- and upper-class Russians, many emigrated to Western Europe and to the United States. Russia lapsed into a dictatorship—a one-party rule as harsh as the former lordship of the czars.

War exerted long-term effects on the United States, too, including increased government regulation of business, mass shaping of public opinion via the press and other media, and demographic shifts that made northern cities more racially diverse. In the economic realm, the war fostered a streamlined assortment of goods. The somewhat chaotic variety of prewar years did not return.

Progressive Reforms

In a certain sense, the war effort diverted energy from Progressive social causes and is believed to have spelled the decline of progressivism as a major force in American life. Nonetheless, a few cherished social reforms came to fruition, notably woman suffrage, which was finally passed by Congress as the nineteenth amendment to the Constitution in 1919 and ratified in 1920. Even before they secured national suffrage, women worked through clubs and professional associations to secure kindergartens, playgrounds, public bathhouses (important to those in tenements with no residential bathrooms), parks, and libraries for their communities. Women pressed for cleaner streets and sanitary milk and processed foods. As they had since 1898, the National Consumers' League criticized miserable working conditions in factories. Women reformers, who might have been expected to lead the campaign for comfortable, healthful dress held back, fearing that radical clothing would prejudice their case for the vote. One magazine columnist suggested that a woman could get away with expressing revolutionary sentiments, as long as she conformed in her style of dress.

Education expanded and changed during the years of 1908 to 1918. In 1914, the Smith-Lever Act set aside money for the states to establish extension services, bringing the new knowledge generated in public universities to farmers and their families. Kindergartens and public high schools proliferated, and their enrollments grew, yet the numbers were small: only one third of children finished elementary school, and only one tenth graduated from high school. The Smith-Hughes Act subsidized vocational education, including home economics, in public secondary schools, helping many students prepare for trades. By 1915, enrollment in high school commercial courses exceeded that in private commercial schools. Colleges and universities enrolled 350,000 students by 1910. College curricula expanded, with broader course offerings, including applied science and engineering, and the opportunity to take a few electives. Professional and graduate schools reformed. For example, the scathing Flexner Report, a published evaluation of U.S. medical schools and educational practices, forced poorer schools to close and those that survived to reach for the standards set by Johns Hopkins University.

National death rates declined by almost 25 percent because of progress in treating syphilis and other venereal diseases, and typhus, typhoid, diphtheria, and tuberculosis. Chlorination of water helped, as did improvements in food and milk sanitation. Some setbacks occurred, including the devastating influenza pandemic of 1918, which killed millions worldwide and at least 588,000 in the United States; one fourth of the U.S. population had the infection. Because the flu was caused by a virus, medical researchers of the time could not even see the microbe that caused influenza let alone treat its effects. In many cities people wore masks to help protect them from the disease. Red Cross volunteers made thousands of masks, because police and soldiers were required to wear them. Fashion also responded to the crisis. *Women's Wear Daily* advertised a safety first chiffon hat veil intended to protect the wearer against the virus (Figure 2.5).

Arts and Entertainment

Popular as well as classical music enjoyed a heyday during the 1910s. Consider that popular songs of those years are still sung today on special occasions. On St. Patrick's Day people sing "Danny Boy," "When Irish Eyes Are Smiling," and "Too-Ra-Loo-Ra-Loo-Ra;" and "Take Me Out to the Ball Game" is a baseball tradition. "St. Louis Blues" remains a jazz standard, and the marches of John Philip Sousa are staples of the many marching bands' repertories. Jazz (originally spelled *jass*) spread to northern cities with the Great Migration of black Americans, from New Orleans to Chicago, and then to New York. Phonograph records, available to the affluent, captured the artistry of the most prominent orchestras and opera singers.

Movies grew up, too. Seeking to escape a monopoly combination in New York, filmmakers migrated to a balmy California suburb with the bucolic name of Hollywood. Important studios came into being, notably Metro-Goldwyn-Mayer, Paramount, and United Artists. Famous directors such as Cecil B. DeMille and D. W. Griffith helped push the medium further, with spectacles that ran for several reels instead of the usual one. Griffith pioneered shooting multiple perspectives and focal distances, and he coached actors to subdue their gestures to accommodate the intimate closeups that set film apart from the stage. Along with stirring stories and new effects, the movies needed the personal draw of popular actors, and so the star system was born, bringing to fame Mary Pickford (Figure 2.6), Charlie Chaplin, Theda Bara, and Rudolf Valentino. Mack Sennett's Keystone Studios cranked out hugely popular comedies whose cops became a staple of the frenetic action film and a byword for fruitless chases. Where there are stars, there are fans, so, beginning in 1912, fan magazines capitalized on the public's thirst for information about their favorite actors and actresses.

Radio, still in its infancy, produced very limited broadcasts, such as the offering of two New York Metropolitan Opera features with Enrico Caruso. San Jose broadcaster Charles D. Herrold began transmitting regular news bulletins and music in 1904, and his station broadcast from the 1915 World Exposition in San Francisco. Ship-to-shore communication by radio continued to be important, as did the constant experiments of amateurs, who numbered about 8,000 by 1917. After the armistice ending World War I, competing radio manufacturers agreed to pool their patents, leading to the manufacture of radios on a large scale.

Figure 2.5 (BELOW) Safety veil against influenza. *Women's Wear Daily*, October 23, 1918, 1.

Figure 2.6 (OPPOSITE) Mary Pickford and her fashions. *Theater*, June 1916, 376 (from Textile and Clothing Collection, Department of Apparel, Education Studies, and Hospitality Management [AESHM], Iowa State University).

Dramatic changes in the visual arts began in, or just before, this period and had an impact not only on painting but also on all the decorative arts. This included fashion presentation through illustration and photography and surface decoration of textiles. A group of painters, dubbed the fauves or wild beasts because of their use of bold, unnaturalistic colors and other distortions, began to present their work in 1905. Although short-lived, this movement had a lasting influence on twentieth-century art. The 1913 Armory Show in New York introduced the U.S. public to the shock

Miss Pickford in one of her "raggedy" gowns.

Mary Pickford in her newest evening frock. A wild-rose Pompadour effect that Watteau might have designed.

Miss Pickford's "picture dress." Forget-me-not blue taffeta with touches of coral and silver.

IF you were an actress with a salary of four thousand real dollars every week, wouldn't you wear gowns like those of the Queen of Sheba, or her latest prototype, Florence Walton?

Of course you would, and so would Mary Pickford, who really gets that unbelievable salary, only—but let the little Queen of the Movies tell her own story: "Sometimes," said our Mary, with a smile that disclosed a very big dimple, "Sometimes when I read my contract, and think about my pleasant home and my capital chum I think I am the luckiest girl on earth, and life looks like one long Thanksgiving day, with plump young turkeys browning pleasantly in the oven and mince pies cooling on the pantry shelf. Then along comes Mr. Frohman and hands me a part, and the sky grows gray and a chill wind springs up in my soul. Because, of course, I have to play another of those ragged little girls, or tattered boys, instead of doing a Pauline Frederick part in gorgeous gowns all plastered over with jewels."

It is too bad that Miss Pickford's voice is lost to the speaking stage; it is one of the most wonderful voices I have ever heard. It registers comedy in rippling syllables fuller of mirth and youth than any voice I can recall; it trembles with sympathy when Miss Pickford is sorry for herself and you feel that you could squeeze tears out of it when she deplores her tragic and ragged fate. It quivered with regret as she went on: 'It is too disgusting to have to be a waif of a newsboy when Thurn has just sent home a new frock that would delight every one of the millions of women who see a Famous Player film every day. Why is heaven so kind to Valeska Surratt and Mary Nash and Jane Cowl, who always have parts that wear stunning clothes, while Fate casts me for rags and rags and rags? It doesn't seem fair!"

"But the public likes you best in pathetic little raggedy rôles," interposed Miss Pickford's chum, soothingly.

"Of course, that helps some," admitted the actress, rather ruefully.

"But you can afford to wear lovely frocks off the screen," I said with dazzling recollections of certain splendors in which

I had seen Miss Pickford arrayed at theatre and opera. Unbounded mirth greeted my remark. Miss Pickford smoothed out her ragged sleeve and laughed until tears ran down her cheeks.

"I *had* some pretty frocks, a whole lot of them," she said, "but then came the big call for clothing for the Belgian sufferers—and pouf!—they all went. No, I didn't send my evening gowns to Belgium, really, I am afraid there aren't any parties or theatres there, where they would be the correct thing to wear, but I sold and raffled and chanced them all off and sent the money to the Belgian relief."

This was quite disappointing because I wanted to sketch Miss Pickford in her prettiest frocks and here she was without a single Bendel creation left! It was too discouraging.

"But then I ran straight to Julie and Tappé and Thurn and bought some sweet new things for the summer, and please let me show them to you," she said.

Miss Pickford was right. They were "sweet new things for the summer," and I am glad to sketch them for you in all their radiant June freshness.

First is a lovely wild rose frock that might have been designed by Watteau which Miss Pickford will wear to the

---

of modernism, including postimpressionism (Van Gogh and Cézanne) and abstraction (Picasso and Duchamp). Duchamp began to paint in the style of fauvism but then experimented with the cubist style. Perhaps his most famous work, "Nude Descending a Staircase, No. 2" caused a furor at the Armory Show. The cubist movement in twentieth-century art focused on breaking forms down into basic geometric shapes. The cubists' abstractions in particular lent themselves to fashion, both through surface design and through the use of intricate, geometric seaming. This be-

came more obvious in the 1920s. American modernists who later became famous also exhibited at the Armory Show, including John Marin, Max Weber, Marsden Hartley, and Georgia O'Keefe. Ironically, lay audiences proved more receptive to new art than did the critics. Even department stores occasionally placed fine art in their show windows, including works by old masters and newer talents.[7]

Architecture featured luminaries such as the firm of McKim, Mead and White, and Louis Sullivan, who pushed skyscrapers higher and made them more ornate; and Frank

Lloyd Wright, who continued to develop his prairie style of house begun in the early 1900s. Its design expressed a clean-lined, horizontal, and physically dark aesthetic. These private spaces, of course, were experienced only by those Americans wealthy enough to pay for highly original architecture. The multitudes could enjoy the skyscraper, with amenities that included a forerunner of air-conditioning, notably in the 1904 Larkin Building in Buffalo, New York.

Retailing and Manufacturing

Retailers modernized as much as the arts, using rational techniques such as model stocks, which entailed careful or-

Figure 2.7 DeBevoise brassiere. *Vogue*, April 15, 1918, 94.

dering of sizes, colors, and styles based on what the local population bought. Price-lining created a sharp differentiation among a smaller number of price levels for each category of goods instead of the dozens of prices that prevailed at the turn of the century. Brand names began to make inroads via national and regional advertising (Figure 2.7). No longer was private-label merchandise, specific to each store, the only form of goods. Ad campaigns primed consumers to ask for their favorites, and woe to the retailer who could not satisfy them. Promotion embraced colorful billboards and posters and continued to refine window displays and in-store fashion shows, including children's shows and even fashion movies.[8] As chains such as JC Penney spread around America, independent retailers battled these newer outlets for customer loyalty. Filene's Automatic Bargain Basement opened in Boston in 1909, inaugurating discount retailing and applying the theories of Edward Filene, including the use of model stocks. In 1916, the first shopping center in American opened in Lake Forest, Illinois. Significant to the growth in the ready-made industry for women's clothing, *Women's Wear Daily* began publication in 1910. Retailing remained one field in which women could establish careers. Some joined store medical departments, served as saleswomen and assistant merchandise managers, and—most promisingly—worked their way up to buyer positions. By 1915, one third of the 10,849 buyers in the United States were women.

Almost any category of clothing could be purchased ready-made in the 1910s. The number of dressmakers declined dramatically, as most women purchased at least a portion of their wardrobe off the rack. Manufacturers competed with one another by offering a multitude of styles and changing their styles frequently. Retailers created images and used advertising language that associated style with a mass-produced product. The rapid growth of the ready-to-wear industry put stress on manufacturers and led to increasing abuses of factory labor, mostly women. Many joined the new industry unions, including the International Ladies' Garment Workers' Union, and, in 1909, 30,000 female shirtwaist makers went on strike in New York City. This brought attempts to improve conditions, but one of the worst factory accidents since the beginning of the industrial revolution occurred in 1911. A fire at the Triangle Waist Company killed 146 immigrant women who had been locked into the ninth-floor sewing rooms of the factory and were unable to escape when a fire broke out. Many plunged to their deaths trying to escape the flames.

World War I brought other changes to the industry. National branding and wartime simplification created both winners and losers among apparel firms. Those whose price ranges fell outside the price lines approved by major stores

SERVICE AND PLEASURE FROCKS

FROCKS NOWADAYS ARE STRICTLY FOR SERVICE OR PURELY FOR PLEASURE

Shirt 7915
Skirt 7907

Waist 7899
Skirt 7791

7899—7791   7915—7907   7803   7931   Dress 7803
Transfer Design No. 822

Dress 7931

For descriptions of models illustrated, see page 46

Figure 2.8 Sport frock and separates. *McCall's Magazine*, September 1917, 33.

could fail; makers who did not fix their names in the minds of consumers could dwindle away, as clever rivals took up their business.

One area of manufacturing in which the United States was caught short was dyestuff production. Americans had relied on the German organic chemicals industry for medicines and dyestuffs. Between the English naval blockade of Germany and German redirection of chemical production toward explosives, dyestuffs ceased to be exported. The United States had to gear up to produce its own synthetic dyes. Meanwhile, American companies substituted less durable, vivid, and diverse natural dyestuffs. Between 1915 and 1917, dyes were limited in variety, often dull in tone, and stretched as far as possible by the combination of small amounts of color with major areas of white in plaids, stripes, and other prints (Figure 2.8).[9] Fads for white or white-and-black ensembles helped Americans cope with this unanticipated wartime exigency. By the time the war ended, U.S. chemical companies had begun to supply the needed dyestuffs and to accelerate production of modified cellulose fibers, including rayon and experimental acetate.

Fashion Influences

Movies became so prevalent by the 1910s that movie stars served as important models of the latest fashion. Maude Adams earned $225,000 in 1912, when a few thousand dollars per year constituted a comfortable income. She and Mary Pickford, who achieved star status in 1914 and earned $104,000 that year, could well afford to wear fashionable clothing. Annette Kellerman, notorious for being arrested in 1907 for wearing a one-piece knitted swimsuit on a Boston-area beach, starred in an aquatic movie and doubtless helped accustom Americans to more comfortable and functional swimwear. Max Factor, a creator of theatrical makeup, developed flexible greasepaint suited to movie close-ups. By 1920, Factor had expanded his line to society make-up for everyday use. Made-up looks, familiar to moviegoers, gradually gained acceptance from American girls and women.[10]

Figure 2.9 Irene Castle, new star of motion pictures. *Harper's Bazar*, July 1916, 35.

Between 1908 and 1918, before Vernon Castle died in a military plane crash, he and his wife Irene were household names, as they popularized such energetic dances as the turkey trot, fox trot, and tango. For these types of dances, lighter, less encumbering clothing was needed. Irene sported ankle-length skirts and bobbed hair in 1912, at a time when most women still wore their tresses and skirts long. Widowed, she continued to dance professionally, act in movies, and be a fashion setter (Figure 2.9).

Bohemians, although not strictly celebrities, enjoyed a certain notoriety for their radical political and social views, expressed in literature and the visual arts. Clustered in the Greenwich Village neighborhood of New York City, bohemians wore informal clothing. Women donned loose dresses that hung free of the waist, and they even espoused sandals at a time when pointy-toe pumps and cloth-topped boots represented conventional fashion. In due course, these styles spread to relatively conservative American women via images in New York City guidebooks and adaptations presented in the fashion press.[11]

Paris and the French couture designers continued to exert a significant influence on fashion, although Americans began to demand a design approach that was less extreme. Many of the most theatrical French fashions of the period were created by **Paul Poiret**. The influence of designers can sometimes become distorted because of the publicity that surrounds them; Poiret was dramatic, in both style and personality, and adept at promoting his designs. His influence was coupled with changes in illustration and the popularity of exotic Asian (especially Persian) motifs and colors. His early designs under his own name[12] revived the empire or directoire style along with the narrow column of a skirt. This required a change in understructure from the S-shape to a more linear silhouette. Poiret commissioned Paul Iribe to illustrate his 1908 creations in an exclusive and unique album called *Les Robes de Paul Poiret*. This album initiated a transformation in fashion illustration. Iribe's drawings showed the bold colors and lines of Poiret's styles and ignored traditional design details in favor of broad, flat planes of color.

A vogue for Asian motifs and colors had recurred periodically since the opening up of Japan to the West in 1854 and was expanded with exposure to Japanese art at the 1900 World's Fair in Paris. Poiret and others were influenced by Sergei Diaghilev's Ballets Russes, which created a sensation when the company first performed in Paris in 1909. Their exotic ballets *Cleopatre*, *Les Orientales*, and, a year later, *Scheherazade* had brightly colored costumes by Leon Bakst that enthralled audiences and fascinated Poiret. He introduced such dramatic, avant-garde styles such as the **lampshade dress, harem-style** trousers, **turbans,** and the narrow **hobble skirt**, all at least partially inspired by the ballet (Figure 2.10). Although these styles were controversial and not universally adopted, the narrower line and bright colors were.

There were links between Poiret and many of the designers and illustrators of the period. Although **Leon Bakst** was primarily a costume and stage designer, his exotic costumes for the ballet inspired both designers and dressmakers. Many of the artists and illustrators of the day were also considered creators of fashion.[13] Illustrators Paul Iribe, Georges Lepape (Plate 2.1), and Drian sometimes created their own designs, in addition to illustrating the work of others. One of the most prolific of these illustrator–designers was Romain de Tirtoff, who went by the name **Erté**. He moved in 1912 from Russia to Paris, where he worked as an illustrator for Poiret until 1914 (Figure 2.11). When he left the House of Poiret, he designed sets and costumes for numerous music hall productions, including the Ziegfeld Follies. Erté began creating original fashion illustrations for *Harper's Bazar* in 1916 and continued through 1936, illustrating hundreds of covers as well as designs in the magazine. Erté's stylized designs epitomized the art deco style that began to evolve in this period, although it would not be so named until the 1925 Paris Exposition Internationale des Arts Décoratifs et Industriel Modernes. He continued to illustrate and design until his death in 1990.

Lady Duff Gordon, known professionally as **Lucile**, was a pioneer in both business and design. At first she experimented with the high-waisted line, but she usually took a romantic and sensual approach to fashion, creating designs in laces or soft and drapable fabrics. She often gave her designs suggestive names such as "Kiss Me Again" or "Do You Love Me?" Lucile creations could also be quite theatrical, and she was very attuned to the theater potential of fashion. Lucile and Poiret were among the first designers to develop theater stages and lighting for live-mannequin shows. They also recognized the importance of the U.S. ready-to-wear market, despite problems of design piracy. Poiret toured and lectured about fashion in numerous American and Canadian cities in 1913, but Lucile preceded him in opening a branch of her design house in New York City.

Other French fashion designers, important at the time, have fallen into obscurity today. Jeanne Sacerdote, known as **Madame Jenny,** opened her dressmaking business in 1908. Her designs were frequently reported in the fashion magazines and in *Women's Wear Daily*. Her style tended to be simpler than Poiret's, making it easy to copy by ready-to-wear manufacturers in the United States. Unlike most designers, Madame Jenny made a profit during World War I,

Feder

An unusual combination of white and navy blue has been exploited in a Martine silk known as Rameau. And Poiret has adapted it in quite as novel a fashion to the black charmeuse afternoon frock designed expressly for John Wanamaker by using it for the bell-shaped sleeves and side insets of the tunic. The flaring tunic and wide sash are typical Poiret features which he has continued in his spring costumes.

Figure 2.10 Poiret gown designed for John Wanamaker. *Harper's Bazar*, April 1914, 25.

and her popularity continued through the 1920s. Her house closed in 1940.

A group of Viennese artists and designers influenced fashion and the decorative arts throughout the first part of the twentieth century. Formed in 1897 as the Vienna Secession, it became the **Wiener Werkstätte** (Vienna Workshop) in 1903. The aim was to bring good design and art into every part of people's lives. As a result, these applied-arts workshops created glass, metalwork, jewelry and even some textile and clothing designs (Figure 2.12). Poiret, in particular, drew upon their example and opened his Martine art school and studios. There he encouraged girls to draw and paint in a primitive style to create designs to be used on textiles, carpets, and other decorative objects. The studio attracted the interest of painter Raoul Dufy, who contributed textile designs.

The avant-garde movement in art also influenced fashion, beginning before World War I and extending through the 1920s. Futurists experimented with geometric lines and unisex garments, while the Russian constructivists and supremacists created both practical apparel and abstracted textile designs.

The designs of **Mariano Fortuny** influenced clothing

PARIS—
The Dictator

By NITA NORRIS

The impression prevails in America that the dressmaking establishments in Paris have entirely suspended work. This is not the case. Although many of the famous couturiers have gone to the front, some creators of fashions for women still remain in the workrooms, behind closed doors. The selling force in many places has been lessened, as there is practically no effort being made to sell gowns to Parisiennes, but the creations continue to find their way to North and South America. The designs on these pages, for example, were produced in the establishment of Paul Poiret, and other couturiers have sent designs so that there will be no interruption in the supply of fashions direct from Paris and shown exclusively in Harper's Bazar. Nita Norris explains why Paris was, is, and always will be the Fashion Dictator.

HOW can I make you in America understand the fashion situation as it is in Paris to-day? For you cannot appreciate it, else you would not persist in sending to us rumours to the effect that there will be no spring fashions in Paris this year.

War—women in mourning—upset financial conditions—no trade, all these misfortunes, argued, I have no doubt, for a cessation of fashions. But did you think of the hundreds of sewing women, *midinettes*, and others in the big dressmaking establishments who would be left without means of support should these ateliers close? If you did

A.—Described by the French as a *petit vêtement*, it is developed in ermine, two lengths being joined to a sleeve embroidered in a polychrome design and outlined in skunk.

B.—A Poiret colourful wrap in coral velvet, lined with cloth of silver and collared in chinchilla enhanced by festoons of silver embroidery. The scarves falling from the neck terminate in silver tassels.

C.—Not satisfied with a full skirt of rose taffeta, the designer added pantaloons of silk embroidered in antique silver and old rose and outlined in skunk.

D.—Typical winter costume—full skirt of black satin topped by a short jacket of white cloth with sleeves of satin.

stored is just another proof of the splendid ability of the French women in times of emergency.

And oh, how they have worked, these noble French women, who have had to show the business alertness of a man and the courage and sympathy of a woman! And the *vendeuse* who formerly greeted you with a smile? She is there, but the smile is a very pathetic attempt which is belied by the swollen lids and trembling hands. Yet when it comes to a matter of business she is the same alert, clever saleswoman, a little more gracious

Figure 2.13 Erté ensemble, showing full skirt. *Vogue*, January 15, 1914, 14.

styles in this period, although he avoided a traditional fashion approach. His styles did not change seasonally like other designers' offerings, but kept a unique aesthetic. Inspired by both the velvets and brocades of fifteenth- and sixteenth-century Italy and by the ancient pleated styles of Greece, Fortuny created a series of pleated gowns and robes. Also trained in chemistry and dyes, he patented numerous processes to create special effects, including a unique pleating process.

Numerous other designers opened their businesses during this fertile period before the Great War, but they achieved greater creative impact in the decades after the war. These included Coco Chanel, Jeanne Lanvin, Jean Patou, and Madeleine Vionnet. All except Lanvin closed their houses at least briefly during the war. Lanvin continued to design throughout the war and was one of the designers who introduced the fuller skirt as early as 1914. It was knocked-off by American fashion houses, as shown in Figure 2.13. Lanvin continued to champion this silhouette, eventually called the *robe de style*, through the 1920s.

Photographers **Edward Steichen** and **Baron Adolphe de Meyer** slowly began to transform fashion photography into a glamorous occupation and an art form for showing both

the clothing and the backgrounds in an elegant and striking manner. De Meyer, already well known, came to New York in 1913 to work for Condé Nast. Nast bought *Vogue* in 1909 and immediately set out to make it a significant fashion publication. Although the idea of a professional fashion model did not really exist at this time, these photographers captured contemporary style modeled by actresses and society beauties. De Meyer even designed clothing for his models (Figure 2.14).

Fashion Trends

The period brought decided change to fashion silhouettes for women and men. The slim ideal, so long-lasting in American aesthetics, took hold during the years 1908–1918. A softer look prevailed at the end of the era than had typified its first years.

Textiles and Colors

Textures of popular textiles evolved through this decade.

Relatively firm and heavy between 1908 and 1912, they became softer and thinner thereafter. It was partly a response to changing tastes, away from the stiffness of turn of the century toward the relaxed shapes of the second decade. Wools included firm twills and tweeds but fashion also embraced crepes and voiles. As the pressure on wool supplies intensified in the mid-1910s, partly resulting from the need for wool for military uniforms, silk and cotton filled the void. Dressy attire made use of satin, China crepe, chiffon, and taffeta, which was used for hats as well as for dresses and petticoats. Silky, printed twill foulard remained popular for day dresses. Rough-textured shantung and sport silk became durable wartime expedients.

Cottons ranged from washable poplin for boyswear to corduroy for some men's suits to fine batistes for women's blouses and lingerie. Linen remained popular for children's clothes as well as for adult garments, including dusters for motoring. Rayon had just begun to be produced in quantity at the end of this period; its first era of serious use was from 1918 to 1928.

Colors might have remained vivid during the period

CORRECT AUTUMN DRESS

except for the outbreak of war. Orientalism promoted by French designer Paul Poiret, exhibited in the *Ballets Russes* costumes, and applied by artists Leon Bakst and Georges Lepape, introduced strong blues, greens, and reds into fashion from 1908 until the beginning of the war. However, the somber mood of wartime and the curtailed output of synthetic dyes from 1914 through 1918 meant that black, white, navy, and tan became fallbacks. Subdued pastels met the need for summery looks.

Silhouettes for Women and Men

Men's and women's suits and women's dresses shrunk in length and width to a startling degree between 1907 and 1918. Indeed, one of the best refutations of the statement "men's clothing does not change much" is to show the barrel-chested suits of the early 1900s and the cigarette-skinny outfits of the 1910s. The pants, vests, and jackets are still there, but their proportions contracted drastically (Figure 2.15). Women's voluptuous curves of 1905 collapsed into a wafer-thin silhouette by 1918. Styles that had common knowledge

attributes to the 1920s really began in the 1910s. In part, these changes sprang from very different lifestyles between the first and second decades of the twentieth century. Relative speed of travel, even in cars that rarely exceeded 25 miles per hour, rapid dances, and the increased number of women workers in heavy industries encouraged stripping fashion of its excess fabric and fripperies. Efficiency became a social virtue, and clothing that expedited work and leisure gained cachet.

Women's Styles

Women's fashion showed perceptible yearly changes, even in the pages of middle-class periodicals such as *Delineator* and *Ladies' Home Journal*. Accelerated factory production put fashionable attire in stores more quickly and at different price levels. With more women working, notably in the later 1910s, a larger pool of customers had discretionary money to buy fashion. One clothing textbook defined a business or professional woman's clothing budget as $150 per year. No wonder slow-changing, hard-wearing clothes were supplanted by less-durable, but appealing, fashions that came and went in quick succession. Intense competition in the U.S. ready-to-wear industry and a society in flux also contributed to constant change in fashions.[14] From narrow shapes in 1908–1911, dresses shifted to drapy silhouettes in 1912–1913, then to full, shortened skirts in 1914–1916, and back to slim, slightly longer styles in 1917–1918.

Dresses and Suits

In 1908, mainstream styles for women featured gored or pleated skirts that fanned out from smooth hiplines. Bodices hugged the body, with minimal blousing, and waistlines remained tiny (Figure 2.16). Princess-seamed shapes continued to be popular. High-fashion periodicals such as *Harper's Bazar* presented a sheath-like shape in dresses in 1909, a trend that spread to mainstream consumers. From shoulder to hemline the look was lean, with the sole exception of huge hats (Figure 2.17). Women truly resembled mushrooms: a lean stalk topped by a large cap. Moderate-priced catalogs in 1910 offered princess-style sweaters that came to midthigh, with double or single-breasted buttoning, to be worn with trim skirts.

Two years of an unbroken line ended in 1911, when **empire styling** appeared in dresses. Raised waistlines joined smooth skirts to slightly bloused bodices. A number of designers began to experiment with higher waistlines, and the empire waist was popular in many of the tea dress styles of the previous period. Skirts tapered inward slightly at the hem, in anticipation of the 1911–1912 **hobble** silhouette, with a narrow circumference at the bottom of the skirt. Floating panels, tunic layers, and sashes relieved the plain-

Figure 2.16 (LEFT) Shirtwaist dress. *Good Housekeeping*, December 1908, 702.

Figure 2.17 (BELOW) Women's suits. *McCall's Magazine*, October 1909.

Figure 2.18 (BOTTOM, RIGHT) Bridge (card game) gown. *Harper's Bazar*, January 1911, 32.

Figure 2.19 (OPPOSITE, LEFT) Drécoll gown. *Harper's Bazar*, January 1914, 77.

Figure 2.20 (OPPOSITE, RIGHT) Full-skirted ensemble. *Harper's Bazar*, August 1916, 61.

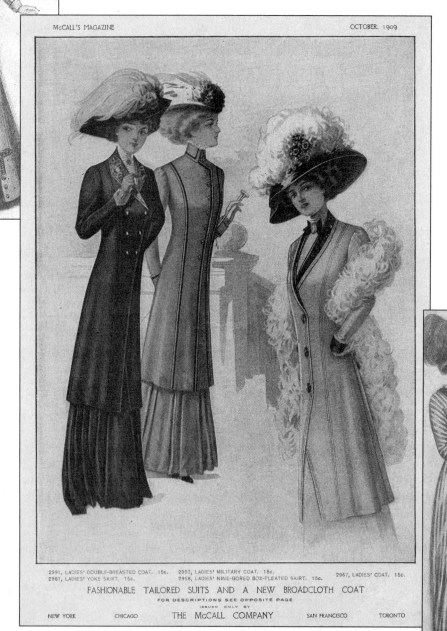

McCALL'S MAGAZINE   OCTOBER, 1909

2991, LADIES' DOUBLE-BREASTED COAT. 15c.   2952, LADIES' MILITARY COAT. 15c.
2981, LADIES' YOKE SKIRT. 15c.   2958, LADIES' NINE-GORED BOX-PLEATED SKIRT. 15c.   2967, LADIES' COAT. 15c.

FASHIONABLE TAILORED SUITS AND A NEW BROADCLOTH COAT
FOR DESCRIPTIONS SEE OPPOSITE PAGE
ISSUED ONLY BY
NEW YORK   CHICAGO   THE McCALL COMPANY   SAN FRANCISCO   TORONTO

ness (Figure 2.18). By 1912, a drapy quality softened both skirts and bodices. Collars came in several flat styles, from the small, round **Peter Pan** to the drooping **bertha**. No longer was the high collar de rigueur. Sleeves varied— elbow- or wrist-length—and were usually set in at the shoulder. Hip-level drapery made of bias cowls was featured in many dresses in 1913—which was a difficult style to wear well for any but the slimmest women. Photographs of the era show how much the fashions enlarged women's apparent size, despite the extremely slender silhouette of fashion illustrations of the period. Blousing continued to develop in the bodice, and batwing **dolman sleeves** showed up in coats and dresses, partly influenced by Chinese and Japanese gar-

ments (Figure 2.19). Some jackets even had a hip-band with blousing, complementing the banded bottom on some of the most constricting hobble skirts. Later scholars often ridiculed this inconvenient style, which constricted women's stride just as they were marching to demand the vote and moving in ever greater numbers into business. Whether or not the new style had a psychological dimension, its narrow lower margin was the physically necessary outcome of draping the hips in cowls or shaping the waistline with pleats or gathers in a technique called **pegging**. The effect was that of a flared skirt turned upside-down, with the narrow part at the hem and the wide part at the waist. Paul Poiret claimed credit for introducing the hobble skirt.

18410

18410   18411   18412

READ "HOW TO ORDER CORRECT SIZES" ON PAGE 218.

18410—Youth's Combination Overcoat of All Wool Herringbone Cheviot, in medium grey or medium brown effects. This handsome coat is made of warm, durable material, is cut on the newest lines, and represents one of the leading styles for young men. The stylish collar may be worn turned down when a dressy effect is desired, or in cold and stormy weather may be adjusted as shown in the smaller picture, to afford more complete protection. The back is slightly shaped at the side seams and has a center vent, and the entire garment is lined throughout with a durable quality of serge. The coat is supplied with outside and inside breast pockets, the side pockets having a soft, warm lining, and the shapely sleeves are finished with strap cuffs. This smart model will be found very stylish, warm, and thoroughly serviceable. It is a "NATIONAL" offering of exceptional merit. SIZES: 30 to 38 chest. $9.98

18411—Youth's Double-Breasted Auto or Tourist Coat of selected All Wool Tweed, in smart grey or brown colorings. The stylish lines that distinguish this model will appeal to the young man who wishes a coat embodying both appearance and serviceability in the highest degree. It is made of handsome, firmly woven material noted for its warmth-giving qualities and for its ability to withstand hard wear. Details which insure perfect comfort in coldest weather are the high collar, and the strap cuffs which finish the sleeves. The model is slightly form-fitting in the back, is made with a deep center vent, and the full number of pockets is provided, the outside pockets having soft, warm linings. Marked excellence is the keynote of this becoming overcoat, which exemplifies the most expert skill of "NATIONAL" designing and workmanship. The model is correct in cut and fit, for it is made by tailors whose ability is unsurpassed, and it will always retain its attractive lines because of its good material and the care exercised in its making. This stylish coat will prove a most desirable and serviceable selection. SIZES: 30 to 38 chest. $12.98

18412—Youth's Suit of full Winter weight pure worsted navy blue Serge; or of fine All Wool Tweed, in medium grey or medium brown effects. This desirable model is sufficiently dressy for all occasions, and will be found both warm and serviceable. The stylish, perfectly tailored coat is made with a close-fitting notched collar, and slightly shaped back with center vent, and is lined with a fine quality serge. The vest has one inside and four outside pockets. The trousers will be found perfect-fitting and of lasting good shape. They are supplied with two side pockets and two strap-buttoned hip pockets, also a change or watch pocket, side buckles, and loops for a belt. Unusual value is offered in this stylish suit, for the material is of a handsome, durable texture, and possesses excellent wear-resisting qualities. The model is carefully made throughout, no pains having been spared to make it perfect in every detail. SIZES: 30 to 38 chest. $12.98

Mrs. George J. Butler, Bowling Green, Florida, writes:

"I am delighted with my son's 'NATIONAL' suit, and so is he. We are glad to know where to get such nicely finished suits. Thank you for your prompt attention and for the suit, which is more than satisfactory."

We never publish a letter without the writer's permission.

Figure 2.21 (LEFT) Men's coats and suits. *National Style Book*, 1910, 221.

Figure 2.22 (OPPOSITE, LEFT) Trench coat. *Haberdasher*, November 1918, 29.

Figure 2.23 (OPPOSITE, RIGHT) Evening suits for formal (left) and semiformal (right) occasions. *Haberdasher*, October 1915.

Young women's fashions continued to exhibit hip emphasis with cowls or flounces, but adult women embraced a more flattering line in 1914, with overskirts and jumper-like components adding layers with less bulk and offering slightly greater hemline circumference. Concurrent with these developments, the waistline expanded, something not seen since the early 1800s. By 1915, widening hemlines also rose. Adult women of fashion showed most of their insteps and even an inch or two of ankle, camouflaged by dainty cloth-topped boots.

Skirt width and leg exposure seem to peak in 1916, when fullness recalled the skirts of the 1850s, but with a drastic change in length (Figure 2.20). Several inches of lower calf were exposed, which would have caused even the doughty Amelia Bloomer, advocate of shorter skirts, to reach for her smelling salts. More staid women kept to an ankle-length style. Typical dresses had peplumed jackets that skimmed the waist. Ornate shoes and hose peeked demurely out of the hems. With the drama focused on the legs, the breasts went into hiding under soft draperies. By the end of 1917, breasts were practically flat, waistlines wide, and hems slightly longer and a bit narrower. Clingy effects marked 1918 fashions for women: shoulders sloped, chests were almost concave, and skirts tapered in at the hem. As they had in about 1911, evening dresses of the late 1910s featured long, slender trailing panels at back. The shapes of 1918 blended by slow degrees into the styles of the 1920s.

Work Attire

Quite distinct from fashionable attire and the social statements made by bohemian modes, pragmatism shifted the way women dressed, especially from 1917 to 1918. Factory

ADLER-ROCHESTER
Overseas SERVICE COAT

L. Adler, Bros. & Co.
ROCHESTER NEW YORK

Correct Dress for Formal and Informal Evening Wear

workers in conventional dresses or skirts could not work safely with machinery, so **womanalls**, a modified bib overall or coverall with gathered pant legs, were accepted (see Figure 2.4). Women serving in the army motor corps wore uniforms with above-ankle-length skirts, topped by no-nonsense jackets. These styles, like those of the bohemians, illustrated a departure from the ideas of French, English, or New York authorities in some realms of dress.

Men's Styles

During these years menswear underwent changes parallel to those in womenswear. What had been wide and long became progressively narrower and shorter. Styles destined for enduring popularity came into use.

Topcoats remained boxy and long, with single- or double-breasted closings in 1910 (Figure 2.21). By the end of the war, outercoats achieved a more fitted line, and **trench coats**, based on army officers' practical coats, began to pass into civilian use (Figure 2.22). Suits exhibited a trend toward snug fit, with a preference for single-breasted more than double-breasted styles. Jackets remained long throughout the period, but indentation at the waist increased and waist position rose slightly. One-button models were seen in the earlier 1910s, but two- and three-button styles gained popularity later. Some jackets were too tight to button in front, but a snug vest filled the gap. Trouser legs shortened steadily, eventually skimming the ankle. To create a smooth visual transition, men of fashion wore felt or twill **spats,**[15] fitted ankle-covers, over the tops of their shoes, paralleling women's use of cloth-topped boots. By the end of the Great War, civilian suits were downright skimpy, possibly reflect-

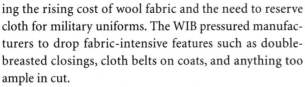

Figure 2.24 Swimwear for men and women, circa 1918. Author's collection.

Figure 2.25 Envelope chemise and nightgown. *Harper's Bazar,* January 1918, 4.

ing the rising cost of wool fabric and the need to reserve cloth for military uniforms. The WIB pressured manufacturers to drop fabric-intensive features such as double-breasted closings, cloth belts on coats, and anything too ample in cut.

Men's dress clothes had two levels of formality. **Tails** for the most formal events included a **cutaway jacket** that revealed a white vest (**waistcoat**), a white tie, and **top hat**. Semiformal wear, the **tuxedo** (Figure 2.23), barely showed the waistcoat and included a black tie. Even the shirts differed in that the formal shirt had a stiff bib front, and the tuxedo shirt had a tucked front that buttoned with studs.

High, stiff, round collars continued to afflict men in business dress, but relief was in the offing with softer collars in sport shirts and in some front-buttoning business shirts.

Many shirts were white, but some informal shirts came in colors, stripes, and small patterns.

Sport Styles

Bathing suits lightened up compared with early 1900s styles. Men's swimsuits still had tops; women's became slimmer and in some cases sleeveless, to the shock of the older generation, which still deplored any trace of a suntan. Most women wore hosiery and rubber slippers or flat, cloth boots at the beach; men went barelegged as a rule (Figure 2.24).

Riding outfits for women departed from the long-standing tradition of trailing, cumbersome skirts. As riding astride became a respectable alternative to the side-saddle position, some women chose **jodhpurs** or **divided skirts**. Less-daring equestriennes retained tailored jackets

Figure 2.26 Brassiere and low corset. John Wanamaker advertisement. *Harper's Bazar*, February 1918, 4.

joined with petticoats to form **slips** in a loose style unlike nineteenth-century versions. The **envelope chemise**, combining drawers and camisole, heralded the light, easy-fitting lingerie of the 1920s (Figure 2.25).

Not new but increasingly popular were brassieres (see Figure 2.7) and even *bandeaus*, the former with full shoulder coverage, the latter with slender straps. These controlled the breasts but did not yet emphasize cleavage. Mostly their function was to provide a bridge between the new low corset and the upper chest. Otherwise, an ugly break in the silhouette might be marked by a roll of flesh. Older women favored the longer, stiffer brassieres; younger ones, the brief bandeaus or delicate lace brassieres (Figure 2.26).

For centuries, the function of the corset had been to constrict the waistline and smooth the upper torso. Suddenly, the focus shifted downward to taming the hips. Therefore, the portion of the corset above the waist shrunk, while the part below became longer and more confining. Most adult women still wore some form of corset, its style depending on their fashion preferences and their approximation to a willowy, youthful body type. One columnist said, "A woman is as old as her corsets,"[16] explaining that a woman needed to switch from the old waist-cinching style to a hip confiner to successfully wear contemporary dress styles. As the war in Europe dragged on and U.S. involvement increased, corsets were redesigned with fewer metal stays, to the undoubted relief of many wearers. Fully elastic corsets, such as those knitted by Treo, gained a following. Of course, the bohemians shunned all these bourgeois underpinnings and didn't wear any corset. Madeleine Vionnet, Paul Poiret, and other designers claimed that they rid women of corsets, but changing foundation materials and social expectations as much as newer outerwear styles brought about the demise of old ironsides as they were called.

Nightgowns or sleep garments (pajamas) held to the flat-chested, slim line (Figure 2.27), in contrast to the full-bodied, flouncy sleepwear of the early 1900s. By 1916, a French style of sleeveless slumber robe appeared in fashion features.

Girls wore knitted vests, drawers, and petticoats, full or slim depending on the dress style of the year. Men's and boys' underwear was usually a sleeved or sleeveless suit that united drawers with a shirt. Knits were popular, but woven cottons such as striped dimity might be used in summer.

and midcalf skirts. Jodhpurs, with a puffy hipline above a snug calf, gained cachet for men and women from their use by officers in World War I. Checked or plaid sport suits, with knickers and matching or contrasting jackets, served for various sports, including golf. **Gaiters** over heavy knee-socks completed the outfit. Gaiters were cylinders of leather or heavy cloth that covered the legs from knee to ankle.

Underwear and Sleepwear

In keeping with the general slimming of outerwear, underwear shifted from flouncy petticoats to trim ones. Then came short, full petticoats or shallow **hoops** to hold out the flouncy skirts of 1914–1916. Numerous undergarments combined into a few compact pieces: corset covers or camisoles merged with drawers, and corset covers were

Children's Styles

Children dressed relatively comfortably in the second decade of the century. Skirts on little girls showed their knees and had loose bodices and low waistlines (Figure 2.28). Older girls wore skirts a few inches below the knee, shorter than those for adult women. Jumpers with **guimpes**

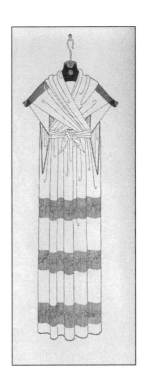

Figure 2.27 (RIGHT) Night robe drawn by Erté. *Harper's Bazar*, April 1918, 50.

Figure 2.28 (LEFT) Flapper dresses for young adolescents. *Harper's Bazar*, April 1917, 4.

Figure 2.29 (BELOW) Girls' dresses. *Harper's Bazar*, May 1911, 230.

(short underblouses) became an option in the mid-1910s. Tunic and overskirt styles for young adolescents, called flappers, imitated some of the features of women's clothing, but with less fussy detail (Figure 2.29). The flapper debuted as a 12- to 16-year-old in the mid-1910s, and—seemingly—the term grew up with the generation to whom it was applied. By the 1920s, any modern, unmarried twenty-something could be a flapper. By 1918, little girls' dresses resembled smocks, with no waistline indentation. A 1913 *Delineator* image implied the propriety of short rompers for the youngest girls (Figure 2.30).

Little boys who were out of diapers wore short pants or rompers that combined shirts with bloomer bottoms. As boys grew, the trousers lengthened to below the knee, and

the style assumed a crisply tailored look. Soft-collared shirts, including sailor-style middies, were suited to boys (Figure 2.31). Some jackets tended to follow the **Norfolk** line, with self-belt and vertical pleats to give room for movement and growth (Figure 2.32). For small boys, so-called **Russian styles,** featuring asymmetrically closed tunics, remained popular. During the war years, especially after 1916, boys' and young girls' outfits exhibited military and naval motifs (Figure 2.33).

Accessories

All types of accessories changed in tandem with the lightening and softening of the 1910s fashions.

Figure 2.30 (LEFT) Rompers for little girls. *Vogue*, October 1, 1911, 39.

Figure 2.31 (RIGHT) Boy's Norfolk suit. *Harper's Bazar*, August 1917, 5.

Figure 2.32 (BELOW) Boy's outfit. *Harper's Bazar*, May 1911, 231.

Headwear and Hairstyles

One of the most striking changes in the woman's silhouette between 1908 and 1918 is a lightening up of hair and headwear. From 1908 to 1912, wide-brimmed, deep-crowned hats drooped under the burden of plumes, flowers, and anything that imagination could devise and factory or nature could supply. One hat style was aptly dubbed the **mushroom.** Women's hats retained their depth or bulk until about 1913, and even thereafter a few weighty styles continued to be shown, (see Figures 2.17 and 2.18) including the **peach basket**, which consisted of a deep, broad crown with little or no brim. Orientalism contributed **aigrettes** (upright tufts of feathers) to the array of hat decorations (Figure 2.19).

Under the hats, however, hairstyles were shrinking. First the pillowy upsweeps of circa 1907 deflated into waves. Then a snug-to-the head coiffure rather like a **French twist** came to the fore. Finally, **bobbed** (cut) **hair** openly declared itself. As hats became smaller, they no longer needed support from mounds of hair and false padding.

Wide-brimmed hats continued to be offered, but deep-crowned shapes with minimal brims were the latest rage. By 1915, headwear acquired dramatic focus, with stiff brims tilted at rakish angles or angular brimless styles pointing skyward. Hairstyles reached new levels of coquettish compactness in 1916, and hats appeared almost dainty, whether they were brimmed or brimless (Figure 2.20). At the end of this period, small hats that pulled down to the eyebrows

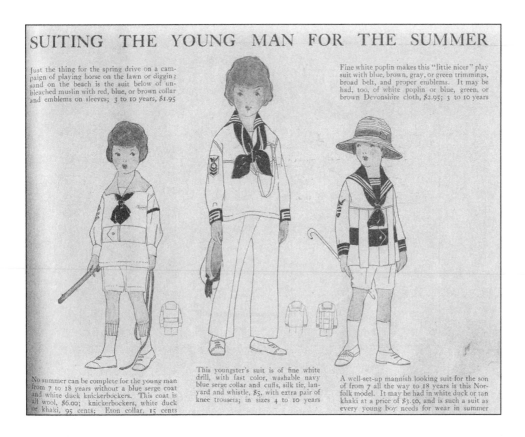

Figure 2.33 (LEFT) Boys' summer suits, with sailor motifs. *Good Housekeeping*, May 1917, 65.

Figure 2.34 (OPPOSITE) Ladies' Keds brand slippers. *Good Housekeeping*, July 1917, 107.

foreshadowed the 1920s cloche (Figures 2.8 and 2.13). Girls' hats remained simpler and less dramatic in shape than adult versions, with broad, flat brims or deep crowns and no brim.

Caps represented the ultimate in informality or youthfulness for men and boys; they were the usual option for young boys and were worn by adults with sport outfits. Tubular, knitted **stocking caps** served for sports or work in the coldest weather. At the other end of the continuum fell top hats, mandatory with full evening dress, although not with the semiformal tuxedo. Derbies held their own for businesswear, but increasingly competed with softer, creased-crowned **fedoras**. Summertime at East Coast resorts brought out straw boaters, often accompanying light-colored trousers and **buck shoes**. Light-colored straw **Panama hats** were worn in the South. Men's hairstyles were generally short and minus sideburns; both center and side parts are seen in photos. A few men cultivated mustaches or small beards, but most went clean-shaven.

Footwear and Hosiery

At the lower end of the woman's silhouette, a revolution was brewing—the appearance of fancy hosiery. As skirts crept up from the toe to above the ankle, more stocking was revealed, and clumsy, dark woolen stockings looked frumpy. Fine cotton lisle and even silk hose decked well-off ladies' legs. Embroidered clocking became very popular. For those unwilling to expose a stockinged ankle, cloth-topped boots provided discreet coverage. Often in pale gray or other pastels, the boot tops functioned as a surrogate for hosiery. Except for the rebellious sandals of the bohemian set, shoes sported pointed toes, heedless of the consequences for foot comfort and health. Incurving **King Louis heels**[17] and decorative vamps made slippers a charming accessory to the willowy shapes of women's apparel.

For active wear, canvas slippers were available in semi-dressy styles (Figure 2.34). Low shoes and slippers were deemed appropriate for children, and small heels for the flappers (see Figure 2.29).

Boys' shoes might be high or low topped, and stockings long and dark or shorter and lighter in color. Men suffered from shoes as constricting as women's styles, although without the raised heels. Oxford ties predominated. Boots were for sport, as were buck and even canvas shoes with rubber heels.

Miscellaneous Accessories and Jewelry

Blouses, so-named in the late 1910s, featured soft shapes, variable sleeves, and lowered necklines compared with the waists with high collars that dominated the early 1910s. Although both terms coexisted, by the late 1910s, waist was becoming obsolete.

Keds

Make Their First Bow to You

Women continued to carry small, ornamental rather than functional purses that were flat and soft. Daytime materials included leather; for evening, velvet, embroidery, mesh, and knitted-beaded bags were popular. All had small handles. From time to time during this decade, long feather boas decorated daywear. Fur muffs and narrow scarves came out in winter. Long ropes of pearls reached below the breast, a popular dressy style in the 1910s. Dangling earrings were worn in the evenings.

Grooming and Cosmetics

Tonics and creams for everything from the hair to the feet dominated the cosmetic advertisements in 1910. A dry shampoo was marketed as Swedish hair powder. Deodorant creams, such as Mum brand, were advertised and alluded to in beauty columns in *Vogue*. Advertising with before and after images touted a skin rejuvenation system that used no surgery or injections—80 years before Botox.

By 1918, heavy eye makeup, sharply delineated lips, and rouge were evident on socialites. Permanent waves promised relief from straight tresses. Liquid makeup and Max Factor's "pan-cake" began to replace heavier washes. Cutex advertised a line of nail products that included cuticle cream and polishing pastes. The latter gave a shine and a tinge of color to the nails.

Elite beauty salons reached New York by 1918: both Elizabeth Arden and Helena Rubinstein, rival queens of cosmetics, opened their doors in the 1910s. African American entrepreneurs Annie Turnbo Malone and Madam C. J. Walker purveyed hair care products in the South and West to women who wanted to smooth out and lengthen their hair and improve the texture of their complexions.

Summary

Without a doubt, apparel looked more modern in 1918 than it did in 1908. Slimness replaced burliness in men and luxuriant curves in women. Materials became thinner and often softer, colors—except for wartime exigencies—more vivid. Americans cast off stiff, stately clothing in favor of designs that allowed for greater mobility. America's evolving economy and participation in the Great War helped to establish streamlined clothing. Old taboos fell, even the proscription of divided garments for women. Fashions were quickly adopted and discarded as designers who offered avant-garde styles to their customers were rapidly copied by ready-to-wear manufacturers. Besides prolific designers, stars of the world of entertainment helped to popularize various fashions, in makeup and hair styling as well as apparel. The future promised yet more rapid and dramatic change.

Suggested Readings

Cashman, Sean Dennis. *America in the Age of the Titans.* New York: New York University Press, 1988.

Friedel, Frank. *America in the Twentieth Century,* 4th ed. New York: Alfred A. Knopf, 1976.

Milbank, Caroline Rennolds. *New York Fashion: The Evolution of American Style.* New York: Harry N. Abrams, 1996 (paperback edition).

Peiss, Kathy. *Hope in a Jar: The Making of America's Beauty Culture.* New York: Henry Holt, Metropolitan Books, 1998.

Reeves, Thomas C. *Twentieth-Century America: A Brief History.* New York: Oxford University Press, 2000.

Tapert, Annette, and Diana Edkins. *The Power of Style.* New York: Crown Publishers, 1994.

CHAPTER 3

1919

U.S. Events and Trends	Prohibition approved in Congress	Nationwide woman suffrage First commercial radio station, KDKA	First Miss America contest Price deflation begins	Country Club Plaza shopping center	Economic rebound begins Exhibit of Tutankhamen's treasures

	1919	**1920**	**1921**	**1922**	**1923**
U.S. Fashions	Curves flattened in women's wear	Kotex marketed		Men's silhouette slims	Hips emphasized in women's dresses Uplift bra first patented Shingle bob hairstyle becomes popular

1928

First talkies and
Academy Awards

Charles Lindbergh's
transatlantic flight

Exposition des Arts
Decoratifs (France)

1924

1925

1926

1927

1928

Uplift bras marketed

**Dresses feature
elongated panels**

**Oxford bag trousers
introduced**

**Celanese acetate in-
troduced**

**Chanel's simple
Ford dress**

**Daytime hemlines
skim knee**

**Finger waves for
women**

**Evening hemlines dip
to floor in back**

**Jeans presented as
fashion apparel**

Thoroughly Modern Americans

Mention the 1920s and almost everyone, whatever the age, has some mental image—of speakeasies and bathtub gin, flappers and gilded youth, exuberant prosperity and gravity-defying stock markets, Al Capone and his gangland rivals, or the first real heydays of jazz and Harlem. None of these impressions is false, but even taken together they paint an incomplete picture of a highly complex era. Americans old enough to remember the 1920s often regard with nostalgia a decade bracketed by the Great War of the 1910s and the Great Depression of the 1930s. Others, looking at those postwar years with detachment, recognize that they set a seal on many modern trends: urbanism, hedonism, gender-bending, sophisticated modernism, and the abandonment of older mores and manners. American literature and arts flourished, achieving recognition even from the worldly Europeans. Clothing reached new levels of comfort. In fact, at least one veteran dress reformer expressed delight that mainstream fashion had adopted healthful dress.[1]

Despite the image of an era of revolution, the twenties did not break totally with the past. Americans' attitudes had, after all, been shaped by their experience—however abbreviated—of a world war and its dispiriting aftermath. Nor did the decade bring prosperity to everyone. Farmers struggled with declining prices after the wartime boom. Despite a generally probusiness mood, some companies collapsed under stiff competition or from the deadweight of outmoded products. Finally, 1919–1928 was not wholly dominated by the younger generation. Politicians were not young, nor were many captains of industry. Nonetheless, youth had a definite cachet, and the fashions of the era looked best on young, slim bodies (Figure 3.1) . Many adult Americans *wanted* to look young and peppy. They counted calories, exercised, and bought all sorts of products that promised to remove extra poundage or to tone sagging skin. In short, this period has more in common with the early twenty-first century than with the early 1900s.

Domestic and International Politics

After the zeal of Progressives' reformism and the crusade of the Great War, many Americans took a breather, turning away from utopian ideals toward the cultivation of business and the embrace of pleasure. They elected pro-business presidents, Warren Harding, Calvin Coolidge, and Herbert Hoover. Harding appealed to Americans' desire to return to normalcy after the stresses of the war years. Although Harding chose several capable cabinet members, some of his close friends engaged in large-scale graft and larceny. The impending revelation of the scandal precipitated Harding's fatal stroke in 1923. Calvin Coolidge, his vice president, took the reins and then successfully campaigned for a full term. Coolidge cleaned up the mess left by the Harding administration and oversaw the paying down of the national debt. He favored business and encouraged its growth. Hoover, who had shown organizational talent and humanitarian instincts during the Great War, won the presidency in November 1928, unhappily less than a year before America's business boom went bust.

One notable aspect of the domestic political scene during this era was Prohibition. Passed in October 1919, the Eighteenth Amendment outlawed the production and sale of alcoholic beverages. Adoption of the amendment represented a triumph of rural, native-born, Protestant sentiments over urban, immigrant, Catholic views. Liquor consumption did plummet, and death from cirrhosis of the liver dropped by two-thirds, but smuggling burgeoned, reaching $40 million just in 1924. Illegal stills produced dangerous brews; hidden bars called speakeasies numbered 10,000 in Chicago alone; and organized crime flourished. Al Capone was the most notorious of the many criminal figures who prospered on the liquor trade, protection rackets, gambling, and prostitution. Most destructive of societal cohesion were the corruption of law enforcement officials by bribes and the ordinary American's contempt for the law. A doggerel poem of the era jeered "Prohibition is an awful flop," but it was not repealed until 1933.

Labor unions and management engaged in outright battles in the early 1920s, with victory going to managers. Popular opinion supported moves against the radical communist and socialist unionists, with the more moderate organizations suffering setbacks as a result. In part, unionization efforts were blunted by businesses' embrace of welfare capitalism, by which some firms offered workers improved conditions and pay, plus social benefits, in exchange for remaining nonunionized. The entry of more women into the workforce may also have hampered unionization, because most unions, except for those in the apparel industry, refused to accept women as members.

On the other end of the political spectrum, the Ku Klux Klan, a Nativist secret society, persecuted not only labor organizers but also immigrants, blacks, Catholics, and Jews. Lynchings (mob murders) of African Americans occurred frequently. Even in places such as Chicago, where the Klan had less influence than it did in the South, race riots blighted the decade. African Americans were seen as competitors for jobs in a market made tight by business recession and thousands of returning war veterans. *Crisis*, the name of the National Association for the Advancement of Colored People's (NAACP) publication of the era, suggests the trauma that black Americans were experiencing. In 1925, the Ku Klux Klan's supreme leader was convicted of murder, a scandal that weakened the Klan's hold on some southwestern and midwestern state governments.

After the Great War, the United States reduced its involvement in international affairs. Wilson's refusal to compromise on the Paris treaties, including the League of Nations covenant, hardened Congressional opposition. Instead of signing the treaties, the United States negotiated separate peace accords with Germany and the other Central Powers. America stayed out of the Geneva-based League of Nations, which remained ineffectual as a deterrent to war. Equally seriously, American withdrawal from postwar negotiations exposed Germany to the full wrath of the European allies. Crushing reparation payments created drastic inflation, ruining Germany's economy and enabling Adolph Hitler and his thugs to rise to power in 1930–1933. Washington did host an arms conference in November 1921, capping naval buildup among Britain, Japan, France, Italy, and the United States. Various other pacts were negotiated to cool international tensions, but these did not achieve long-term success.

Economic Ups and Downs

In 1919–1920, as the war ended and price controls were dropped, consumer prices continued an upward surge and then plunged in 1921. Farmers, in particular, suffered from lower demand, as Europe recovered from war and began to grow its own foodstuffs. Domestic consumption of starches, such as grains and potatoes, declined as well, because fewer Americans were working at jobs that required heavy labor, as mechanization gradually replaced muscle in factories. Large-scale farms coped with changing demand through expanded use of machinery. Specialty cultivators, including dairy farmers, fruit growers, and truck farmers,[2] fared better than did small-scale commodity growers. California's nascent wine industry declined sharply with the coming of Prohibition. Farm tenancy and mortgages grew, as independent farming became untenable for many.

American businesses also had to retrench in 1921–1922, having lost the power to raise prices to keep pace with manufacturing costs. By 1923, a rebound came, lasting into 1929. From 1923 through 1928, America's gross national product grew by 40 percent, with low inflation. Business combinations continued to absorb smaller companies. For example, 8,000 mining and manufacturing companies were merged into a few hundred huge corporations during this decade. Secretary of the Treasury Andrew Mellon favored big business, just as Herbert Hoover, Secretary of Commerce, helped small businesses. Mellon encouraged the formation of trade associations to develop codes of ethics, standardize production, and save costs through efficiency.

THE FASHION ART LEAGUE OF AMERICA BULLETIN

From the Bailey Studios

Sports costume, three-piece, of Reseda Green and White Flannel. The coat of White Flannel is trimmed with a design of the green material.

Figure 3.1 Sports costume of white and reseda green flannel. *Fashion Art League of America Bulletin*, Chicago, March-April 1923, 8.

Two thousand trade associations existed by 1920. In that milieu, many trade journals prospered, including *Women's Wear Daily*,[3] *Corset and Underwear Review*, and the *Dry Goods Merchants Trade Journal*, rich sources of information for historians of dress. Business theory promoted scientific management, continuing a trend that had begun in the 1910s. Schools of management were founded, and businesses embraced professionalism, teamwork, and careful budgeting. Productivity grew, boosted by these practices and by improved levels of education in America, notably in an increased percentage of high school graduates.

One unfortunate trend of the decade was rising tariffs on foreign-made goods. Steep duties were alleged to protect American businesses, but declining trade deprived European nations of the income they needed to repay wartime debts to the United States. Some historians believe this situation contributed to the depth and length of the Great Depression in the 1930s. Another shortsighted policy was curtailment of immigration, especially from Asian and southern European countries. This led to injured feelings in countries that were discriminated against—such as Japan—and heightened the tensions that would ultimately produce another major war.

Despite these problems, optimism prevailed in the United States in the 1920s. America's wealth was almost equal to that of all of Europe. Some Americans enjoyed huge fortunes. The number of millionaires increased from 4,500 in 1914 to 11,000 in 1926. Much wealth was based on business and industry, but some came from speculation in the stock market or on land schemes, notably in Florida. Although few Americans enjoyed large incomes, the living standards of many were rising, with food and clothing constituting only 40 percent of family expenditures in 1928 versus 58 percent in 1899. Between 1914 and 1928 real wages increased by about one third, and the average work week declined from 60 hours to 47.3 hours in 1923 and to 45.7 hours in 1929. A half day of work on Saturday remained typical well into the 1940s. The most enlightened companies began to offer employees medical plans and paid vacations. Perceived increases in economic well-being eroded traditional values of thrift and saving for what one wanted, stimulated by the availability of buying on credit through store charge accounts and layaway plans. These applied not only to large purchases of cars and appliances but also to apparel and accessories.

Sociocultural Trends

The social scene of the period was decidedly international. Paris had been considered a cultural center for centuries, but a very favorable exchange rate and freedom from Prohibition induced American and British tourists and expatriate authors, journalists, and artists to spend both time and money there. As a result, not only did French art and style provide a source of inspiration, but Paris couture designers were also influenced by their American customers.

Literature

In an era when business was idolized by the many, serious writers predictably turned their pens against it. Novelist Sinclair Lewis satirized the money-grubbing businessman, small-town life, and even the medical profession. H. L. Mencken, from his post as editor of the magazine *American Mercury*, ridiculed the middle-class *booboisie* (a pun on the French *bourgeoisie*). Some writers who were unhappy with postwar America gathered regularly at the Algonquin Hotel in New York City to trade witticisms and barbs. While living in the South, William Faulkner exposed the seamy side of life in Dixie. One satirist chose humor rather than angry commentary. She was Anita Loos, who wrote *Gentlemen Prefer Blondes* and its sequels, satirizing women out to snag rich husbands or sugar daddies.

In Harlem, a strongly black neighborhood in New York City, the relative prosperity of the 1920s nurtured an outpouring of literature about the African American experience. Most famous among the writers were James Weldon Johnson, Countee Cullen, and Langston Hughes, who used literature to argue for racial justice. Another component of this Harlem Renaissance was jazz, discussed later. Harlem became a destination for white as well as black enthusiasts of African American arts. Louis Armstrong, famed jazz trumpeter and singer, moved to New York from Chicago in 1924 (Figure 3.2).

Women's Advancement

Women's emancipation from traditional restrictions progressed further between 1918 and 1928. For one thing, the number of women employed outside the home increased fivefold, although women represented only 22 percent of the total workforce by 1930. Almost 79 percent of working women in 1920 were single. Young women's work often represented less an economic necessity for their families than a transition to adulthood for themselves. Most college graduates worked for at least a period before marriage or the arrival of the first child. Working couples ceased to be a rarity. Although industrial and service jobs excluded women once the war ended, the bureaucratization of business created more office positions, many of them readily available to suitably educated (white, usually native-born) women. Banking, insurance, real estate, publishing, trade, and transport all needed hordes of office workers. Collegiate women entered social work and libraries in substantial numbers, feminizing those professions just as school teaching and nursing had been in the previous period. However, engineering, law, medicine, dentistry, and the ministry counted only tiny percentages of women among their practitioners.

Growing out of the Women in Industry department of the federal government, a World War I entity, the Women's Bureau of the Department of Labor, worked to secure a maximum 8-hour day and 48-hour week for women, plus regular breaks and lunch hours and exclusion from night work from 10 PM to 6 AM. Demographics helped women who wanted to work. Drastic curtailment of immigration, at the same time the need for labor was increasing, stimulated the employment of more women.

Paid work was made somewhat easier for women by the tendency toward smaller families during the 1920s, as information on birth control spread. Commercial food prod-

Figure 3.2 Louis Armstrong's Hot Five, circa 1925. Armstrong is at the piano, and the band members, from left to right, are Johnny St. Cyr, Johnny Dodds, Kid Ory, and Lil Hardin (Armstrong's wife at the time. ©Bettmann/Corbis

ucts and household appliances expedited some household chores, although full-time homemakers continued to put in an average of 56 hours per week. Divorce rates continued their climb, reaching 16.5 per 100 marriages in 1929, almost double the rate recorded in 1900. Women encroached on the formerly masculine preserve of free talk about sex, partly stimulated by popularization of the writings of Sigmund Freud. Also, of course, a major masculine prerogative—the vote—was extended to American women in 1920. The League of Women Voters, a nonpartisan outgrowth of suffrage organizations, worked toward an informed electorate and general cleaning up of politics. Curiously, women's very success appeared to erode support for feminist causes. The flappers, modern, young, unmarried women who were presumed heiresses to their mothers' and grandmothers' crusade, seemed almost apolitical by contrast to earlier activism, and, until 1928, proportionately fewer women than men voted. In the opinion of older feminists, the flappers squandered their new freedoms on smoking, drinking, swearing, and wild parties.

Education

During the 1920s, education enjoyed wider support and reached increasing numbers of Americans. Free elementary education was made available in all parts of the country, and all 48 states had compulsory schooling laws. Illiteracy continued to decline, standing at 4.3 percent in 1930. High school enrollments increased fourfold between 1910 and 1930, partly sustained by the introduction of practical, job-oriented courses. The George-Deen Act provided federal matching funds for part-time and evening vocational training in retailing and product distribution (shipping and receiving).

Higher education also enjoyed increased enrollments, from 240,000 college students in 1900 to more than 1 million by 1930. Broadening access to college contributed to a democratization of higher education, with growth in colleges for women and minorities. General universities became coeducational and expanded their research by setting up research centers.

Shifting Values

Often the 1920s are portrayed as an era of cynicism and declining ideals. In part, this is true. Fundamentalist Christianity, although strong in the South and some parts of the West, was losing ground in other regions to religious liberalism in interpretation of the Bible. Evolution was starting to be taught, despite efforts to legislate against this branch of science. The 1925 Scopes Trial, fought by lawyers Clarence Darrow (pro-Evolution) and William Jennings Bryan (a biblical fundamentalist) resulted in a technical win for Bryan but a publicity disaster for the antievolution forces.

Intergenerational conflict intensified, with teens and young adults often quarreling with their parents and grandparents. The definition of the teen years as a special phase of life emerged in the early twentieth century. Adolescents increasingly identified with peers and consciously embraced behavior that conflicted with parental norms. By the post-war years, the term *flapper* encompassed not only young female adolescents but also older teens and unmarried women in their early twenties. The boys of that generation were termed *cake eaters* or *sheiks*.[4] Fast and sexy dances, including the Charleston, Black Bottom, and Tango, appealed to these youngsters. So did relatively fast cars. In fact, automobiles offered dating teens the chance to escape parental supervision and indulge in smoking, drinking (illegally), and various degrees of sexual activity. By no means did everyone engage in these behaviors, but those who did shaped the image of the entire generation.

Clothing represented another aspect of youthful assertion of independence. Cake eaters wore slicked-back hair, wide-legged oxford bag trousers (Figure 3.3), and occasionally the raccoon fur coat popularly associated with college men (Figure 3.4). Flappers sported knee-revealing skirts (but not miniskirts), rolled stockings, long beads, bright earrings, cigarette holders, and very obvious makeup. Less famously, they loved bright hats and scarves, loose coats, plaid skirts (Figure 3.5), and the unbuckled waterproof galoshes that "flapped."[5] Whatever was new, the flappers wore it, so, when some styles of evening dress became longer and fuller in the later 1920s, flappers accepted them. They also were the first to adopt an uplift bandeau, in the mid-1920s, while older adult women were still flattening their breasts with minimally contoured brassieres.[6]

Transportation and Communication

Americans of all ages enjoyed the freedom of automobile driving during this era. Twenty-three million cars were in use by 1929, with fashionable additions of color (beyond Ford's black), balloon tires (air filled for better shock absorption), and trims. New concrete roadways in some populous areas made driving more pleasurable; antifreeze additives facilitated year-round driving. Gas stations and motels popped up across the U.S. landscape, as did roadhouses, associated with drinking, dancing, and petting. In 1923, Hertz Drive-Ur-Self car rental opened for business. Fast food made an early appearance,[7] building on the success of the White Castle hamburger chain, founded in 1916. Some later commentators believed that auto driving encouraged women to wear shorter, less bulky skirts.[8]

Unlike the auto industry, aviation struggled to remain commercially viable after the end of World War I, subsisting on delivery of mail. Charles Lindbergh's nonstop transatlantic flight in 1927 helped to restore the excitement about air travel. By 1929, 25 million miles of commercial flight were scheduled per year.

Mass communication took a step forward during this decade, with the launching of the first commercial radio station, KDKA Pittsburgh, in 1920. By 1924, the National Broadcasting Company (NBC) boasted a nationwide network. Twelve million American families owned a radio by 1930. Radios became a conduit of entertainment and information, including news, sports, drama, and comedy programs and, of course music—classical, jazz, and other popular genres. Families and friends would cluster around the radio at home. A few cars featured radios by the end of the decade. Public places, such as post offices, made radio broadcasts available to people who did not own a set. Radios were comparable to the televisions that are currently ubiquitous in airport lounges, popular restaurants, and other public spaces.

Print media evolved as well, with the emergence of small-format tabloid newspapers. These made their mark with sensational journalism, centering on famous crimes and wacky stunts, of which there was no lack in a decade

Oxford Bags.

Figure 3.3 (OPPOSITE) Oxford bags and pullover sweater of the mid-1920s. *Men's Wear: 75 Years of Fashion*, New York: Fairchild, June 25, 1965, 101.

Figure 3.4 (RIGHT) Men's top-coats, raccoon fur coat, and knickers suit. *Fashions of the Hour*, Chicago: Marshall Field & Co., Exposition number, 1926 (Mary Barton Collection, Special Collections, Iowa State University Library).

Figure 3.5 (BELOW) Flapper fads, especially the plaid skirt. *Vogue*, February 15, 1921, 69.

marked by fads such as flagpole sitting and swallowing live goldfish.

Retailing and Manufacturing

Manufacturers embraced standardization, division of labor, and mass production more fully, having experienced the benefits during wartime. Apparel companies rationalized their production of fewer styles in greater depth. In part, this systemization met the large-scale demands of big retailers, including Sears, Roebuck & Co., whose wish books reached 15 million homes in 1929. Chain stores such as JC Penney and Woolworth, a group known as five-and-tens that specialized in goods at these low prices, sold many units of apparel and accessories. As a result, they chose manufacturers that could meet large orders. National Department Store of St. Louis led the way in opening branches away from the city center in 1922, the same year in which Spanish-themed Country Club Plaza brought the delights of an open mall to Kansas City, Missouri.

Traditional department stores struggled to compete with retail chains and with the door-to-door salespeople, called canvassers, who peddled a wide variety of products to householders. Women could even order a custom-fitted corset or girdle from a canvasser. To survive, department stores enhanced their customer services, partly by giving more formal training in sales. In every category of merchandise, salespeople were taught skilled selling, including product features, customer psychology, and—in the case of the corset fitters—anatomy. At the upper-end price points, department stores such as Jay Thorpe, Marshall Fields, and Lord & Taylor employed talented American designers, although their identities were usually hidden behind the store labels.

Advertising reached a new level of professionalism and sophistication during the postwar decade, crafting the mass appeals necessary to move enormous quantities of goods. Ad expenditures rose from $400 million in the early 1910s to $2.6 billion in 1929. Print ads were designed to narrate a story and to give people a reason to buy, not just delineate the features of the product. New modes of advertising emerged, from neon signs to skywriting and radio commercials. The John Powers Modeling Agency opened in 1926, testifying to the popularity of using fashion models to stimulate purchases. Models could epitomize the look of the 1920s; for Americans, one of the best was Marian Morehouse—tall, slim, with a dark, ultrashort **shingle bob** (Figure 3.6). Fashion photography also changed by mid-decade. The style of de Meyer began to be replaced by Edward Steichen's photographs, which had stylistic connections to modernism. Steichen and Morehouse worked together frequently. Of course, other role models helped move merchandise, including the celebrities of the world of arts and entertainment.

Arts and Entertainment

Americans spent some of their mid-1920s riches on recreation, which totaled $2.7 billion in 1924 alone. Spectator sports garnered $4.7 million, and European travel netted $2.3 million. Mass entertainment helped to homogenize American tastes.

Movies and Theater

Early 1920s silent movies centered on D. W. Griffith epics, such as *Orphans of the Storm*, set during the French Revolution, Cecil B. DeMille's *The Ten Commandments*, and Fred Niblo's *Ben Hur*. These and the artistically acclaimed Russian film *The Battleship Potemkin* gave audiences new thrills. Other popular genres of film included comedies, westerns, and—in keeping with the rise in crime—gangster stories. Charlie Chaplin dominated the comedy scene, with sharp observations about the lives of ordinary people. Exotic locales figured in Rudolph Valentino's vehicles, including *The Sheik* and *Blood and Sand*. Valentino and Douglas Fairbanks were major stars, whose dashing roles set a standard for masculine good looks. Movietone Newsreels, shown as preludes to feature films, pictured the news in an era before television broadcasts.[9] Not incidentally, news

films revealed what a wide range of both famous and ordinary people were wearing. Walt Disney brought out his first major cartoon, *Alice's Wonderland*, in 1924, and Mickey Mouse debuted in 1928, with Disney himself giving Mickey a voice.

Films changed radically in the late 1920s, with the development of sound, or talkies, the first of which, *The Jazz Singer*, appeared in 1927. No longer was it enough to gesture well, but one had to speak reasonable English and sound appealing, too. Some stars of silent films went into involuntary retirement when it was discovered their speaking voices were harsh, squeaky, or otherwise not a match for their appearance. European-born stars, including Pola Negri and Greta Garbo, mastered English, keeping their careers on track. Stars also had to adhere to strict codes of conduct, because any major scandal would have cost the industry dearly in lost audience. Academy Awards were given for the first time in 1927, although without the splash of current Oscar ceremonies. Janet Gaynor won the first best actress award.

Hollywood by no means overshadowed Broadway during the 1920s. In the banner year of 1927, 268 plays were presented on Broadway. Musicals enjoyed a heyday thanks to the talents of Jerome Kern, Richard Rodgers, Lorenz Hart, and Irving Berlin. They enlivened an art form that had been rather saccharine and schmaltzy even in the early 1920s. Variety shows such as *George White's Scandals* helped to turn the Charleston and the Black Bottom into dance crazes. Stars such as Humphrey Bogart, Cary Grant, Clark Gable, and Barbara Stanwyk, who ultimately gained fame in the movies, began their careers on Broadway.

Many actors who were to achieve lasting fame first appeared in films in the 1920s, including fashion figures Greta Garbo, Myrna Loy, Claudette Colbert, Gloria Swanson, and Lucille LeSueur, rechristened by fans as Joan Crawford. Gentlemen could look to Rudolph Valentino (Figure 3.7), Gary Cooper, and Ronald Coleman as exemplars of fashionability and masculine elegance. By 1928, Coleman's thin mustache replaced the brush type that adorned Charlie Chaplin. Clara Bow was designated the It Girl for her unabashed sex appeal, and Theda Bara epitomized the sultry and dangerous vamp. In short, there was a style of star for every taste. Celebrity couples included actors Mary Pickford and Douglas Fairbanks, two of the founders of United Artists studio, and the writer Scott Fitzgerald and his wife/muse Zelda. Although Charles Lindbergh was not precisely a movie star, his nonstop New York–to–Paris flight won him immediate and lasting celebrity. Fame could even touch the Girl Next Door via the competition for Miss America, who was first crowned in 1921. Celebrities were duly reported on in fan maga-

Figure 3.6 Marian Morehouse modeling gown from Frances Clyne. *Vogue*, February 15, 1925, 50.

Figure 3.7 Rudolph Valentino, Natascha Rambova (his bride), and Art Director Nazimova. May 20, 1922. ©Bettmann/Corbis.

zines, which began in the 1910s and grew explosively in the 1920s. The sensational periodical *True Confessions* won a substantial readership with its lurid stories about real people.

Music

Jazz thrived in Chicago, where it evolved from New Orleans style to include more solo performances, conferring star status on trumpeter Louis (Satchmo)[10] Armstrong (see Figure 3.2) and band leader Edward Kennedy (Duke) Ellington. Both men had a flair for dressing as well as for music. Phonograph albums and the radio spread the jazz gospel to places where no live performances were available. Harlem jazz, smoother in delivery than other versions, attracted multiracial audiences and confirmed jazz as a ma-

jor American art form. So popular was jazz that it penetrated classical music, most famously George Gershwin's "Rhapsody in Blue." Singer-dancer Josephine Baker epitomized physical beauty and sexiness. She performed on Broadway in the early 1920s and was a star by 1924. Baker went to Paris in 1925 and became famous for her dancing in the Folies Bergère braless and wearing a skirt made of a fringe of bananas. As a black performer, she was more accepted in France than in the United States, and she chose to stay there.

Sports

Boxing, baseball, tennis, and football drew large audiences and brought forth many popular champions: Jack Dempsey and Gene Tunney in boxing, Babe Ruth in baseball, Red

Figure 3.8 Helen Wills Moody on the court. Note the sleeveless dress. Late 1920s. Helen Hull Jacobs. 1993. *Modern Tennis*. Indianapolis, IN: Bobbs-Merrill.

Figure 3.9 René Lacoste on the lawn. Note the knit shirt, late 1920s. A. Wallis Myers. 1930. *Lawn Tennis: Its Principles and Practice*. Philadelphia: Lippincott.

Grange in college and professional football (and later, movies), and Helen Wills and Bill Tilden in tennis. Gertrude Ederle won international acclaim in 1926 as the first woman to swim the English Channel. Not all these stars set styles, although Wills (Figure 3.8) and Tilden did influence tennis attire, and Ederle gave a further push to body-hugging swimwear. Suzanne Lenglen, a French tennis star, popularized head scarves, two-piece dresses for the court, and wristwatches. René Lacoste, another French champion of the era, later promoted knitted polo shirts that bore a crocodile emblem representing his nickname, La Crocodile (Figure 3.9). Involvement in active sports grew also during the 1920s, in keeping with Americans' increased leisure time and health consciousness. Golf included 2 million participants during the decade, and there were enough municipal tennis courts to accommodate 1.2 million players.

Visual Arts

Abstraction and a general modernism prevailed in painting and sculpture, from Marcel Duchamp (French) through American masters Marsden Hartley, Stuart Davis, and Georgia O'Keeffe. Joseph Stella, Thomas Hart Benton, George Bellows, Lionel Feininger, and Charles Burchfield remained somewhat naturalistic in their styles, although some of these men rendered naturalistic subjects in strong patterns. Artists drew inspiration from industrial landscapes of factories as well as from more traditional scenery. Wealthy Americans collected the works of Old Masters (European) and New (American and European). Public museums sometimes received the largesse of rich patrons in the form of donations of art.

The 1925 French Exposition Internationale des Arts Décoratifs et Industriel Modernes inspired designs for furniture, interiors, architecture—including the Empire State and Chrysler buildings—and objects of daily use.[11] Even apparel borrowed linear motifs from art deco. Although the term *art deco* was not coined until 1966, it was a major design influence that continued to flourish through the 1930s. It evolved from some of the art movements discussed earlier and was more often referred to as *art moderne* in this period. There were numerous art movements, workshops, and schools that proposed to link art and technology, the functional and the aesthetic. These include the Bauhaus School in Germany, the De Stijl art movement in the Netherlands, the Russian constructivists, and the Italian futurists. All these groups of artists and designers made a connection between design and fashion and textiles. Thayaht, one of the Italian futurists, illustrated many of Madeleine Vionnet's designs and designed her logo. De Stijl artist Piet Mondrian would have a greater influence on fashion in the 1960s, when his primary colored, geometric canvases inspired Yves Saint Laurent.

Fashion illustration continued to reflect the art deco style that had begun in the 1910s, with a tendency toward geometric, bright-colored surfaces. The figures were inclined to be somewhat two-dimensional, in keeping with the modern style. Many of the artists of the previous period continued to work into the 1920s, including Barbier (Plate 3.1), Lepape, Iribe, and Erté. Illustration was still the predominant technique for showing the latest fashion, although photographs began to appear more frequently by the end of the decade. Erté continued to design covers for *Harper's Bazaar*, while American illustrator Helen Dryden created many of the *Vogue* covers. Other illustrators of the period include Americans Gordon Conway and E. M. A. Steinmetz and Frenchmen Charles Martin and Étienne Drian.

In 1922, English archaeologist Howard Carter, sponsored by Lord Carnarvon, opened the Egyptian pharaoh Tutankhamen's pristine (unlooted) tomb, which was filled with gorgeous furniture, jewelry, and other burial goods. The New York Metropolitan Museum of Art exhibited King Tut's treasures the following year. This sensational find augmented the existing taste for everything Egyptian and stimulated wide adoption of Egyptian motifs in fabrics, apparel, and jewelry, a geometric style compatible with art deco. Women used cosmetics, especially eye makeup, to create Egyptian effects.

Designers

Couture flourished in postwar Paris. In 1918–1919 new **ateliers**—major designer workshops—opened, including that of Edward Molyneux; Madeleine Vionnet and Jean Patou, closed by the war, reopened. A shopping guide to Paris listed Chanel, Vionnet, Jean-Charles Worth, Jenny, Patou, Lanvin, Louise Boulanger, Molyneux, Lelong, and Nicole Groult among the designers to be visited. Although some of these names are unfamiliar today, several designers who particularly thrived during this decade were Vionnet, master of the bias cut, Jean Patou, with his spectator sport styles, and Gabrielle (Coco) Chanel, the designer of comfortable and practical clothing that looked young and modern.

Vionnet worked for Doucet and then Callot Soeurs before opening her atelier in 1912. She closed during the war, reopening in 1918, and remained a leader in haute design until retiring in 1939. Vionnet's great contribution was her understanding of fabrics and how they could be cut and shaped to flatter a woman's body. She preferred to work with clients who had good figures, and she advocated exercise instead of body-shaping undergarments, which was revolutionary in the early 1900s. Vionnet excelled at draping, creating evening and daywear that often had intricate seaming. She became renowned for her use of the bias (diagonal) grain of the fabric to achieve a sinuous, close-to-the-body drape that would become a prevailing silhouette of 1930s evening dresses. Some of her inventive styles were asymmetrical and often had cowl or halter necklines, handkerchief (pointed) hemlines, or were dresses that simply slipped over the head, with no fasteners. She took various geometric shapes and made complex designs from them, leading *Harper's Bazar* to dub her "the Euclid of fashion"[12] (Figure 3.10). Crepes, including thin georgette and heavier charmeuse, gave her the drape she sought. Couturiers of later generations revered her skills. Although her designs were considered difficult to copy, she was a leader in the fight against design piracy of the period, putting her thumb print on her labels.

Chanel began her multigenerational career in 1909 by creating hats for women with modern taste. She added chandails or pullovers of jersey in 1914 and, after the war ended, opened an atelier on rue Cambon in Paris, which remains the House of Chanel. Her hallmarks were practicality and clean lines, often in unpretentious fabrics, including various knits and tweeds. She was especially known for her use of wool jersey for sportswear separates and dresses, a fabric that had not previously been used in high fashion attire (Figure 3.11). Her little black dress, described as a "fashion Ford" by *Vogue* in October 1926, was a slightly bloused black crepe de chine chemise with tucks, forming converging Vs on the front of the skirt and bodice. The use of Ford as a description meant that it was also easy to copy, and this unobtrusive dress sold very well and was indeed widely copied. Unlike real Fords, this model also came in Chanel's favorite red. Although not the first designer to create a perfume, she was first to market it under her name and to develop a perfume from synthetic ingredients that allowed the real perfume essences to last much longer. Chanel No. 5 perfume, although expensive, had a no-nonsense name and bottle that perfectly reflected the geometric style of the period. Chanel was her own best model and promoted her modern style as a well-known personality in Paris society. She also promoted the use of costume jewelry, casual fabrics, sportswear separates, and a look called deluxe poverty, which was actually quite expensive but was

Figure 3.10 Georgette Vionnet gown with geometric inserts. *Vogue*, October 1, 1925, 48.

designed to look modern and casual. Note the uncluttered lines of the outfits in Figure 3.11. During the early 1920s she was influenced by the many Russian exiles in Paris, integrating colorful, peasant-inspired beadwork and embroidery into her designs.

Jeanne Lanvin, a designer of fertile imagination, like Chanel began her career in millinery in 1890 and added apparel to respond to the requests of customers who admired dresses Lanvin designed for her daughter. She became famous for fine detailing, including embroidery. Lanvin's powers of imagination never flagged. In one season (Fall 1926), she presented not only tubular dresses but also offered the option of a frock with a belted natural waistline and a skirt that was gathered onto a hip yoke. Lanvin was one of the more romantic of the art deco designers and was particularly known for her *robes de style*, with a long, full skirt and dropped waist. She also developed fully coordinated ensembles of coats, jackets, skirts, and blouses and even designed ski suits, which were becoming a fashion item among those wealthy enough to frequent the Alps in the winter. Lanvin also created several well-known perfumes, including My Sin and Arpege.

Fur and leather businesses in the family helped pave the way for **Jean Patou**'s establishment of a couture atelier titled Parry in 1912. He reopened after the war under his own name. In the 1920s he was at least as well-known as Chanel for his sportswear, one of his specialties. He dressed the chic French tennis star Suzanne Lenglen in pleated skirts and pullover tops. Café society on both sides of the Atlantic wore Patou, notably his fine sweaters, bathing suits, and dressy clothes. Patou, like Chanel, was a master of publicity. He recognized not only the importance of the American customer but also that there were differences between American and French body proportions.

Lucien Lelong's father had opened a textile house in the mid-1880s, so Lelong developed his couture business from that base of knowledge. He gained a reputation especially for skillful handling of fabric and detail in streetwear and sportswear rather than for startling innovations. However, he did lead the way in diversifying into lingerie and hosiery and was one of the first to open branches in French resort towns.

Edward Molyneux, a British transplant to the French couture, got his start in the English House of Lucile. In keeping with his British heritage, Molyneux gained fame for clean-lined, well-cut, tailored suits, but he also created evening wear and frequently designed for the theater. His Paris salon had branches in London and in French resort towns.

Paul Poiret still had a well-known house, but he was no longer in the vanguard of design. Poiret seemed unable to

Figure 3.11 Chanel *tailleurs* (tailored outfits) and men's business suit. *Vogue*, November 1, 1925, 79.

Figure 3.12 Jane Régny sports costumes. *Très Parisien*, No. 10, 1926.

connect with the spare 1920s aesthetic, so different from his lavish exoticism of the 1910s. However, Poiret's younger sister, **Nicole Groult,** who had begun designing before the war, was more in tune with the styles of the time. Her designs appeared frequently in fashion publications.

The designer for the House of Worth in the 1920s was Charles Worth's grandson, **Jean-Charles.** Although overshadowed historically by his more famous uncle, Jean Philippe, Jean-Charles was considered an important designer in the period. He continued the house tradition of making high-fashion clothing for an aristocratic clientele and for well-known actresses. Sportswear designers of note were **Chantal, Jane Regny** (Figure 3.12), and **Mary Nowitzky,** who created not only daywear but also ski suits and tennis dresses in high style.

While the couture houses of Paris continued to influence fashion, they were, at the same time, influenced by their American clientele. Paris designers grew increasingly at-

tentive to the buying power of their U.S. clients, both private customers and those who mass produced, including selling models for copying. The U.S. industry concentrated on ready-to-wear production, borrowing ideas from the Paris couture but adapting these styles to American tastes and to mass-production techniques. Ready-to-wear clothing had become the standard by the 1920s, although many women continued to go to dressmakers or to sew or remodel their own clothing. However, there was a growing disdain for homemade clothing, especially among teenagers and young wage-earning women that left the impression of a widening gulf between fashionable ready-made and not so fashionable made-at-home products.[13]

Ready-to-wear manufacturers often produced hundreds of styles in a season, although most of the designers worked anonymously under manufacturers' names or department store labels. New York City was the center of the American fashion industry and of style information, but

Fields & Co., Fi-
nes and catalogs.
ustom salons that
designs to copy for
e designs at varying
to-wear departments.
fashion publications,
rt on American custom
Jessie Franklin Turner,
lara Simcox, and **E. M. A.**
Paris, some of these cus-
wn in the 1920s. Hattie
rench models but also had a
large ... designs for her customers and
manufactured ... to-wear. Many of her staff designers, such as Claire Mc ardell and, later, Norman Norell,
would become well-known in the 1930s and 1940s. Jessie
Franklin Turner opened her custom business in the 1920s,
also designing her own fabrics. Miss E. M. A. Steinmetz was
designer for Stein & Blaine, a company that produced
custom-made clothing. Steinmetz, also an illustrator, strove
to be less dependent on the French couture for her creations, using the museums of New York for inspiration. The
London designer Lucile, who had opened her New York
house in the 1910s, was also a strong supporter of American
designers and textiles.

Fashion Trends

As noted earlier, fashions of 1919–1928 stirred intense controversy. Rising hemlines, although paltry by comparison
with late twentieth-century miniskirts, raised eyebrows
and parental blood pressure. To traditionalists, everything
seemed to be shrinking in womenswear: bobbed hair, small
hats, and bare arms in dresses and swimsuits. Women's ensembles were summarized as one dress, one pair of hose,
one pair of shoes, and one **step-in** undergarment (merg-
ing a camisole with panties).[14]

Besides relative nudity, the most startling trends were increased informality and the borrowing of styles between
men and women. Schoolgirls wore **knickers** despite admin-
istrators' outcry, and not just for gym classes. Late in the
decade, pajamas became a party time fad (Figure 3.13).
What was termed the *garçonne* (boy–girl) look was in
vogue. Men, in turn, adopted wristwatches, which had
been previously for ladies only. Informality expressed itself
in bow ties and in the substitution of dark jackets and
striped pants for frock or tailcoat with matched trousers. If
top hats were worn at all, they were placed at a rakish angle, tilted over one eye. Men in knickers with **argyle** socks
cut a lively figure in golf or hunting.

Textiles and Technology

American textiles enjoyed a resurgence of color after the
war ended and U.S. dyestuff producers became fully functional. The color palette picked up unusual hues: henna (a
dull red), chartreuse, puce (dark purplish brown), and ma-
genta. Throughout the decade, just about every color was
used, including intense reds and blues, pastels, and low-
intensity black, white, cream, and beige. Rayon output increased 69-fold between 1914 and 1923, and in 1925
Celanese acetate was introduced, offering another silky but
affordable fiber option. Rayon hose became a consumer
product, and seamless stockings were tried. Textures of fabric varied: many were soft and drapy, but a few were crisp,
lending themselves to tailoring. Crepe appeared in both day
and evening dresses, in weights from georgette to heavy
wool crepes. Jersey, tweed, and velour served daytime needs;
taffeta, chiffon, lace, and silk velvet lent glamour to dressy
clothing. Geometric patterns predominated in textiles of
the later 1920s; other options included ethnic motifs from
Africa,[15] the Middle East, or South America. In the United
States, there was a fad for embroidery to personalize ready-
made dresses, sometimes with the unfortunate look of
clumsy loving-hands-at-home.

Figure 3.13 (OPPOSITE) Pajamas for a soirée. Late 1920s. *Archives of Dorothy Bickum Company*, New York. Design and Merchandising Department, Colorado State University.

Figure 3.14 (RIGHT) Boyish silhouette, in tunic dresses. *Elite Styles*, January 1925, 32.

Technology gave accessory makers new options in fasteners, specifically hookless fasteners. Developed as early as the end of the nineteenth century, hookless fasteners gradually were made more reliable and adaptable. Tailor Robert S. Ewig suggested the name zip to describe the gadget, but the name zipper, which became the standard term, was coined by Goodrich Rubber Company, maker of rubber overshoes that used the hookless technology. Although used in some military gear and soldiers' money belts during World War I, zippers were limited to accessories such as tobacco and cigarette pouches, some corsets, and women's handbags. Zippers did not appear in apparel significantly until the 1930s, when plastic or metal zippers enhanced the styling of women's day dresses.[16]

Women's Styles
Womenswear went through several style variants during this period, but a relatively loose cut remained typical.

Dresses
Dresses of 1919–1928, many of them in the straight-cut **chemise** style, could be stand-alone items, but dress–coat

combinations gradually became popular. Tailored suits adhered to a severely simple style of matching jacket and skirt. Between 1924 and 1928, overblouses provided a comfortable option, teamed with skirts and jackets or sweaters. Layered looks that used tunics, **vestees** (imitation vests or blouse fronts), and mock jackets (attached to the dress) persisted through most of the period. Such ensembles were not always acquired easily outside of large cities, because stores might sell only one component of an outfit, so the customer would have to trek from store to store, or department to department, to complete her look. Sizes of wardrobes varied considerably; some women had bulging closets, while others, even among the middle class, might wear their clothes hard and remodel them to extend their life.

During this 10-year span waistlines seldom showed indentation and were usually placed below the natural position, frequently at hip level (Figure 3.14). Sleeves tended to be very short or wrist length, rather than mid-length. Sleeveless styles remained popular for the whole period. U-shaped décolletages became chic about 1924, joined by scooped necklines in 1926 and deep V-shapes in 1927–1928. Boat necklines, straight across the collarbone, also typified this decade.

Figure 3.15 Long-waisted dress style with slight barrel shape. *Women's Institute Fashion Service*, Fall-Winter 1920–1921 (Mary Barton Collection, Special Collections, Iowa State University Library).

Figure 3.16 Narrow-hemmed silhouette and geometric motifs. *Fashions of the Hour*, Chicago: Marshall Field and Co., Spring 1928, 8.

From 1919 to 1924, fairly flat designs predominated, with bosoms suppressed, a look augmented by the fashionable slouched posture of chest in, tummy out, shoulders sloped. During the second half of the period, shoulders squared up slightly, although the hollow-chested droop persisted. Silhouettes evolved from an elongated barrel in 1919–1920 (Figure 3.15), to an oblong in the early 1920s, and then to a wedge shape, with the narrow end at the hemline, late in the decade (Figure 3.16). Although fashion illustrations continued to suggest an angular look, photographs show women in dresses that clung to the breasts and followed the waistline. By 1928, stars such as Joan Crawford, socialites, and fashion models were wearing designer dresses that revealed their curves (Figure 3.17).

Hem lengths for adult women varied from just above the ankle to a few inches below the knee, with the higher hemlines typical of 1926 to 1928. Young women, particularly young teens, dared to bare their knees, and many women's knees showed when they sat down, especially if their skirts were narrow (Figure 3.18). Only the slimmest women, especially young women, could wear the styles to advantage.

Although many dresses had plain, tubular skirts, in 1919–1921 skirts retained a few gentle gathers; flounces softened some designs. The *robes de style,* introduced by Jeanne Lanvin in 1914, and continued by Doucet and others as well, became popular about 1920 and remained so through 1928. Typically it had a plain, drop-waisted bodice and bouffant skirt that often reached the ankles (Figure 3.19; Plate 3.1). Quite a few wide skirts, and some jackets with flared peplums, associated with the seventeenth-century Spanish painter Velásquez, populated the fashion magazines in the early 1920s. In 1923–1924 the entire silhouette looked flat. Such a spare shape flattered very few wearers, so designers tried various tricks to lend grace to their styles. Pleats provided some relief to the straight skirt: knife pleats on one or both sides showed up often in 1922–1924, and

Figure 3.17 Dresses by Lucien Lelong (left) and Doeuillet (right) showing increased body definition. *Vogue*, March 1, 1928, 66.

Figure 3.18 Dancers at a marathon, 1928. Chicago History Museum.

all round pleats enjoyed a heyday in 1925–1928 (see Figure 3.14). Other devices included side gathers in 1922–1924 and godets (flared insets) and other insertions in 1925–1928 (see Figure 3.10). Flared skirts and overskirts dominated the fashion scene in 1927. Hip lines, minimally emphasized in 1922, began to be swathed in drapery as early as 1923, with the hip wraps becoming snug enough to push the bodice into a bloused line in 1924–1928. Side hip drapes and trailing panels graced some 1924 dresses and continued into 1926, with the addition of trains for evening. Pointed handkerchief hemlines came into fashion in 1927, preparing the eye for uneven hem lengths in 1928, when festive dresses featured skirts that were a few inches below the knee in front, sloping to the ankles in back. Lots of fluttering panels gave length to evening wear (see Figure 3.17). Note that this happened more than a year before the stock market crash of 1929, in contradiction to the often-stated theory that rising or falling markets correlate with hemlines.

Figure 3.19 Men in tuxedos and young women in *robes de styles*. *Fashions of the Hour*, Chicago: Marshall Field and Co., Christmas number, 1923, 13.

The curvy, flouncy, frocks for evening contrasted sharply with tailored, geometrically patterned daywear. Sporty looks, often consisting of a pleated skirt, overblouse or knit top, and knitted cardigan or jacket, gained substantial popularity between 1926 and 1928. Not limited to spectator sports, these ensembles were recommended for travel and general morning wear (see Figures 3.12 and 3.16).

Coats and Other Wraps

The most popular coat between 1919 and 1928 was the side-wrapped **clutch coat,** which had a surplice collar and fastened with a single button or not at all, hence the need to clutch it to keep it closed. Often, coats were worn several inches shorter than the dress or skirt beneath, and hip-level coats appeared in most years' array of styles (see Figure 3.1). High collars showed up in 1920 and remained popular for the remainder of the decade, offering flattery and welcome warmth, especially for riding in open autos. For evening, fringed and unfringed silk shawls, dubbed Spanish but often embroidered in China, made graceful and flirtatious wraps (Figure 3.20). Such shawls were sometimes teamed with flounced skirts and Spanish dance accessories. The favorite evening coats of the later 1920s had a cocoon shape or novelty sleeves. By 1926, fur coats and fur-trimmed cloth coats warmed the ladies. Coats sometimes had linings to match a companion dress, usually in a daytime ensemble (see Figure 3.12). Chanel claimed to have invented the look, but the House of Worth was offering this style in the 1890s.

Sportswear

Swimwear is often a barometer of acceptable body exposure in most periods of style. In 1918–1928, two styles of swimsuit coexisted: the fitted, knitted, one-piece *maillot,* useful for vigorous swimming; and the loose bathing dress, which copied the lines of streetwear dresses except for a shorter cut (Figure 3.21). Several California knit underwear companies became famous when they diversified into swimwear, including Cole of California, Catalina, and Jantzen. Although knitted wool suits did not preserve their shape well, they were often colorful and helped to popularize the sale of resort fashions in the winter.[17] Such suits also appeared in 1921 in Atlantic City, New Jersey, at the first Miss America Pageant, with its bathing beauty component. For ordinary sea bathing, cloth head-wraps or rubber bathing caps were worn, and, in 1920, there was still a tendency to don stockings and beach shoes. By 1928, bare legs prevailed among the fashionable, who were eager to acquire the desirable suntan. Beach shoes metamorphosed from ballet slippers into canvas sandals with closed toes.

Golfers and tennis players wore skirts that skimmed the knee. Golf attire usually required long sleeves, but tennis

Figure 3.20 Cocoon wrap on woman; dressy chesterfield coat, ascot, and top hat on man. *Fashions of the Hour,* Chicago: Marshall Field and Co., Christmas number, 1927, 4.

called for sleeveless tops. Players still wore hosiery and either small hats or head scarves tied band-style around their hair. Some golfers actually teed off in heels, but many wore flats or, more seriously, two-toned saddle oxfords or other tie shoes. Denim jeans, long a staple of laboring men, entered the world of fashion in the late 1920s. Hope Williams, a young actress, appeared in *Vogue* astride her horse, wearing dude ranch duds that included jeans, Southwestern-patterned vest, and white shirt (Figure 3.22). For skiing, the height of chic was a tunic jacket over matching jodhpur pants.

Underwear

During the decade, the corset continued its metamorphosis into a girdle, with few bones, often made of lightweight woven or knitted materials. Beginning with styles that often laced in back and extended above the waistline, the corset diversified in 1920 into elastic constructions that gave an uncorseted look under the chemise frocks (Figure 3.23). Not that every foundation was comfortable, with the imposition of a straight-up-and-down line in 1923–1924. One-piece **corselets,** which joined a bra top to a corset, pushed

Figure 3.21 One and two-piece bathing suits, jackets, and beach coats. *Harper's Bazar*, June 1928, 16.

Figure 3.22 Hope Williams, actress, in jeans and vest as fashionable wear for a dude ranch. *Vogue*, June 15, 1928, 49.

reluctant flesh into its mold (Figure 3.24). Gradually these progressed from totally flat to contoured in the breast area. From 1926 through 1928, low-riding and brief corsets, soft girdles (see Figure 3.23), or short garter belts kept the upper hip in check and held up stockings.

Brassieres followed a similar trajectory. Bandeau styles and full brassieres confined the breasts more or less forcefully between 1919 and late 1924, when the first signs of rebellion appeared in the form of contoured brassieres with separate cups (see Figures 3.23 and 3.24). Esseye Pollack patented the first of these in 1923, but the Maiden Form[18] Company brought a similar design to the public via ads in the trade press in fall 1924. The Model Company and G. M. Poix followed at the end of 1924 with their own uplift designs. These brassieres, with cups shaped by seams or gathers, seem too flimsy to have done more than provide a layer between the breasts and the dress.

In a period of reputed nudity, quite a few types of underwear were popular. Drawers, bloomers, knickers, or step-ins all signified divided undergarments varying from knee length for sportswear or use by more conservative women to silky, short step-ins for the young and daring. Combina-

tion and envelope chemise are two names given to undergarments that combined the camisole and knickers, removing the waistline seam and reducing bulk. A few petticoats (half slips) and slips were shown, although they receded in popularity compared with combinations. The newest fad in lingerie, pajamas of crepe-de-chine and other fancy materials, moved from the bedroom or dormitory to the informal party, where they might substitute for a dressy dress (see Figure 3.13). Some avant-garde souls wore Chinese-style pajamas to the beach.

Hats

Whether it was to accentuate made-up eyes or to look mysterious and vampish, women wore hats that skimmed their eyebrows for most of this period. Beginning the era with deep crowns and wide brims, hats reached eyebrow level in 1921, and sketches often show heads tilted back to let the wearer peek out from under her hat. Side-to-side width in hats of the early 1920s (see Figure 3.15) echoes the full-hipped skirts of high fashion. Brims almost disappeared between 1923 and 1928, when the **cloche** style predominated (Figure 3.25). As the French name sug-

gests, it approximated a bell shape, with a deep crown flowing into a tiny brim. A few styles had front brims in 1925 and higher crowns in 1926. By 1928, contoured hats began to allow the first glimpse of the forehead in seven years.

Shoes and Hosiery

At the start of the period, shoes and boots featured curved heels and needle-sharp toes. By the end of the decade, heels were straighter and higher, and toes were slightly less pointy. Instep-laced daytime shoes were shown in 1928, and various ankle-strap pumps appeared in the second half of the decade.

Hosiery for women was silky and often sheer, in pale tones that showed off the legs to advantage. Young women rolled down the tops of their stockings instead of using garters, but this lost its appeal by the late 1920s, and garter belts took over. Silk and rayon hose were much preferred to cotton lisle, except for sports use.

Other Accessories and Jewelry

Small handbags, mostly with handles but a few in envelope shape, came in varied leathers and dressy materials. Relatively short gloves were worn for daytime, but evening wear excluded gloves for most of this period.

Jewelry showed as clearly as any apparel form the influence of art deco design. Geometric designs proliferated in pendants, dangly earrings, bracelets, and clips. One typical treatment was a paving of small diamonds (or imitations) set off with a few large, colored stones (Figure 3.26). Long strands of pearls and other beads cascaded down the flat bodices of the early 1920s. Button earrings of relatively large scale were good for daytime and were a favorite of the younger set. By 1923, wristwatches were

Figure 3.23 (OPPOSITE, LEFT) Bandeau (brassiere) and lightweight girdle. Late 1920s. *Archives of the Dorothy Bickum Company*, New York. Department of Design and Merchandising, Colorado State University.

Figure 3.24 (OPPOSITE, RIGHT) Brassiere Cor-Set and Girdle and Bandeau manufactured by Bon Ton and Royal, Worcester. *Dry Good Merchants Trade Journal*, 1928, 109.

Figure 3.25 (RIGHT) Various styles of cloches. *Vogue*, August 1, 1925, 41.

self-winding. Their decorative bracelets made the watch a desired accessory.

Men's Styles
Menswear did not experience the obvious changes that womenswear underwent between the 1910s and the 1920s, but men did gain some new styles, particularly in collegiate wear.

Suits and Outerwear
Although the Paris couture was considered the epitome of women's high fashion, for men it was a custom-made suit from Savile Row in London. In 1919, the pinched-waist look remained popular with young men and was epitomized in single-breasted lounge suits with narrow, short, cuffed trousers (Figure 3.27). By 1922 the jacket line had re-

laxed into slightly straighter contours, in conservative three-button or smart two-button versions, worn with slightly longer and fuller cut trousers. Perhaps this transition became possible as prices of woolen textiles stabilized and government regulations eased with the coming of peace. Three-piece suits constituted another option and were often seen on society men. By the mid-1920s, the **Prince of Wales** style came into fashion, with padded shoulders, narrow lapels, and a straight fit at the hip (Figure 3.28). Lapels gradually widened, and peaked lapels were seen by 1925 in high fashion but did not reach mass fashion until nearly 1930. Short suit jackets of the mid-1920s earned the derisive nickname of bum freezers, because they did not cover the derrière adequately. Older men stayed with earlier styles; Calvin Coolidge (president from 1923 to 1928), regarded as conservatively well dressed, favored double-breasted coats, cuffless trousers, black shoes, and

Figure 3.26 Geometric designs in jewelry. *Fashions of the Hour,* Chicago: Marshall Field and Co., June 1928, 25.

The Ultra Lounge Suit for the Spring Season

Figure 3.27 Ultra lounge suit. Note the derby, cane, and narrow-toed oxfords. *Haberdasher,* March 1919.

stiff collars. For evening, both tuxedos and tails were worn (see Figure 3.19).

Full-cut topcoats, including the **balmacaan**, were a popular choice for adult men in the 1920s (see Figures 3.4 and 3.28) but slimmer **chesterfields** populated the fashion magazines in 1927–1928 (see Figure 3.20). Double-breasted **polo coats** were also worn (see Figure 3.4). Leather and suede jackets, some with fleece linings, gave warmth for informal outdoor use. Trench coats, first made popular in the mid-1910s by such makers as Burberry, remained in use through the period.

Young men of wealth followed a fad for **oxford bags**, trousers named for the English university where they made an appearance in 1925. High-waisted and pleated, oxford

bags could have as much as a 25-inch circumference at the knee. Bags were worn with a dark-blue or tweed blazer or with a V-neck pullover (see Figure 3.3).

In fact, blazers of navy or tweed typified informal dress; they were worn with light-colored flannel slacks, which were especially popular for summer. Linen suits with Norfolk jackets also met the need for casual dress in warm weather. Knickers and jackets appear in images of sportsmen participating in shooting or golf and were accessorized typically with cloth caps, V-neck pullovers or vests, argyle kneesocks, and low shoes (see Figure 3.2). In colder seasons, heavy sweaters and knitted vests added color and warmth to men's attire (see Figure 3.18). Bathing suits at the beginning of the period had sleeveless tops over

Figure 3.28 Knicker suit, balmacaan over jodhpurs and jacket, and business suits, including Prince of Wales style. *Fashions of the Hour*, Chicago: Marshall Field and Co., Spring 1927, 18 (Mary Barton Collection, Special Collections, Iowa State University Library).

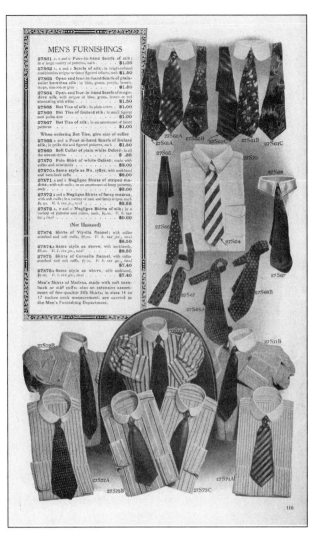

Figure 3.29 Men's shirt and necktie styles. Note the buttoned-down collar, center row. *Book of Styles*, New York: B. Altman and Co., Spring-Summer 1921, 116 (Mary Barton Collection, Special Collections, Iowa State University Library).

trunks, but by the end of the decade bare chests were revealed at the beach.

Shirts and Underwear

The Arrow Company, so successful with collars, brought out a line of shirts with attached collars. Starchless but stiff collars, often with rounded edges, were still fashionable in the early 1920s but were being superseded by pointed collars that were softer and sat lower on the neck. Striped and small-patterned shirts offered a relief from stark white (Figure 3.29).

Underwear consisted of union suits (undershirt and undershorts combined) with long-sleeved, long-legged versions for winter and sleeveless, short styles for summer. Winter materials were usually knitted blends; summer choices included thin woven cottons. Pajamas and bathrobes continued to be popular.

Accessories and Jewelry

Although **four-in-hand ties**[19] were de rigueur for business, men in the arts and letters favored open-neck shirts with spreading collars and no tie. Neckties could be very boldly patterned, but many photographs show solids or subdued patterns (see Figure 3.29).

Hats of many styles were worn; for businesswear, the snap-brim and homburg (see Figure 3.28, right) and occasional derby (see Figures 3.27 and 3.28, center) were all correct. For summer the straw boater continued in use, as did the cloth cap with small peak for sports (see Figures 3.9 and 3.28, left).

A smart top-coat is of Oxford grey herringbone woven on the reverse side in plaid; 12 to 16 years; $25. The soft felt hat is bound with ribbon; all colours; $15

Figure 3.30 Topcoat for an older girl or a young adolescent. *Vogue*, August 15, 1922, 63.

Figure 3.31 Dresses for little girls. *Vogue*, July 15, 1926, 68.

Low shoes became quite common during 1919 to 1928, with tied oxfords, plain or slightly patterned, being the preference of men of fashion. **Saddle oxfords,** with dark instep and white heel and toe, were worn for sports occasions. Socks came in varied patterns, both discreet and loud. Mufflers showed up in evening wear (in white) and for daywear, in varied colors. Men's jewelry was limited to cufflinks, studs for evening shirts, and fine watches.

Children's Styles

Little girls enjoyed pretty much untrammeled freedom in smock and chemise styles throughout this decade. Styles copied adult fashions, in a reversal of the trend in the 1910s, when children's dresses forecast maternal styles. Hem lengths varied from just covering the knee in 1919 to several inches above in the later 1920s (Figures 3.30 and 3.31). Knee-high or low socks and low tie shoes or **Mary Janes** with instep straps completed the look. Very short coats provided too little coverage for the legs, making leggings or long stockings and gaiters important for winter. Girls' headwear partly echoed that of their mothers, but also included tams, berets, and other soft, informal styles. For play, some little girls wore rompers. Union suits and slips provided under layers.

Little boys' wardrobes consisted of rompers or short pants with a tunic over it, a style that changed to shorts

Figure 3.32 Outfits for boys of different ages. *Fashions of the Hour*, Chicago: Marshall Field and Co., Spring 1928, 20.

Figure 3.33 Suits and informal clothes for preteen and teenage boys. *Book of Styles*, New York: B. Altman and Co., Spring-Summer 1921, 56 (Mary Barton Collection, Special Collections, Iowa State University Library).

buttoned onto a soft shirt by the late 1920s (Figure 3.32, center). School-age lads put on slightly longer pants—knickers as they got older—and loose jackets, collarless or in the Norfolk style (Figure 3.33). Older boys aped the style of their father's jacket, worn over knickers and kneesocks. Poorer children could be seen in overalls or loose trousers, worn with sweaters or rough-looking shirts. Boys' socks were short or long, depending on the boy's age, the season, and degree of formality. Shoes were oxford ties or short boots. Boys wore caps, rarely tailored hats. Cowboy gear, complete with chaps, bandanna, and a little version of a ten-gallon hat let small fry play at being the movie cowboys they admired in Saturday matinees. Boys' union suits approximated adult men's styles. Both

boys' and girls' fashions showed a simplification of line in 1928 compared with styles of 1919—paralleling changes in the overall look of adult styles.

Hair and Grooming

The fluffy bob of 1919–1922 gave way to the more severe shingle bob in about 1923, a trend that lasted through 1925. Very short, finger-waved coiffures (with flat, close-to–the-head waves) appeared in 1926, and by 1928 the hairdo had pronounced waves that harmonized with the more contoured hats. Permanent waves offered to remedy Nature's defect, a more compelling need at the beginning and end of the decade; in between, the shingle bob had no waves.

Figure 3.34 Tangee lipstick advertisement. *Vogue*, November 1, 1928, inside front cover.

Men styled their hair center parted and without sideburns. Slick was in, and for the most part fashionable men wore little facial hair, except for a skinny mustache. Schick marketed an injector razor in 1923 to make the job of shaving faster and easier.

Grooming became an ever more obsessive pursuit in 1920s America. Advertisements warned of acid teeth and body odor with the promise that their brand of toothpaste or deodorant could ward off social catastrophe. Kleenex celluwipes offered a hygienic, disposable alternative to linen handkerchiefs, and sanitary pads went mass market with the new advertisements by adroitly named Kotex. The discreet name and plain package eased a very personal purchase for timid women. Sunbathing for a tanned look finally lost its stigma of outdoor labor in the mid-1920s,

creating a market for lotions to prevent burns. Daytime vanishing cream and nighttime moisturizing creams with varying textures were marketed, as were complete systems of facial care.

Makeup outgrew its shy phase and boldly decked teenage girls' and women's faces. Heavy mascara and eyeliners, teamed with prominent lipstick and pancake makeup, created an unhealthy, if not debauched, appearance according to one male commentator[20] (see Figure 3.6). More than $1.8 billion was spent annually on beauty products and processes during the 1920s. Pressed powder, paste and dry rouge, and eyebrow enhancers advertised their resistance to kisses or even a dousing in water—presumably vital for rainy days. Tangee lipstick touted its ability to blend with the coloring of each wearer, giving a more natural appearance (Figure 3.34).

Beauty became part of style rather than an unchanging aspect of a woman's appearance.[21] Younger women, including teens, took more readily to visible makeup, but even middle-aged matrons began to improve upon nature and combat the signs of advancing years.

Weight control continued to be an obsession, as it had been in the previous decade. Bathroom scales appeared in fashion magazine advertisements, and rubber garments and other unproven systems of weight loss separated consumers from their dollars. The federal Pure Food and Drug legislation did not include cosmetics and beauty preparations until the mid-1930s. Some products were merely ineffective, but others posed serious dangers to skin and eyes. Many catastrophes gave ammunition to those campaigning for regulation of beauty preparations.

Summary

By the 1920s, the U.S. fashion industry had many sources of new ideas, including French designers, New York stylists, Hollywood stars, and figures from the worlds of sport and music. The physical simplification of apparel—few pieces and layers—made it possible for Americans who were not upper class to wear innovative styles and launch new fashions. There were more ways to acquire clothing; besides custom producers, there were a variety of department stores, specialty shops, mass merchants, mail-order retailers, and door-to-door salespeople. Mass fashion had arrived.

Suggested Readings

Broer, Lawrence W., and John D. Walther, eds. *Dancing Fools and Weary Blues: The Great Escape of the Twenties.* Bowling Green, OH: Bowling Green State University Popular Press, 1990.

Brown, Dorothy M. *Setting a Course: American Women in the 1920s.* Boston: Twayne Publishers/G. K. Hall & Company, 1987.

Farrell-Beck, Jane, and Colleen Gau. *Uplift: The Bra in America.* Philadelphia: University of Pennsylvania Press, 2002.

Friedel, Frank. *America in the Twentieth Century*, 4th ed. New York: Alfred A. Knopf, 1976.

Martin, Richard, and Harold Koda. *Jocks and Nerds: Men's Style in the Twentieth Century.* New York: Rizzoli, 1989.

Milbank, Caroline Rennolds. *New York Fashion: The Evolution of American Style.* New York: Harry N. Abrams, 1996 (paperback edition).

Perrett, Geoffrey. *America in the Twenties: A History.* New York: Simon & Schuster, 1982.

Reeves, Thomas C. *Twentieth-Century America: A Brief History.* New York: Oxford University Press, 2000.

Tapert, Annette. *The Power of Glamour: The Women Who Defined the Magic of Stardom.* New York: Crown Publishers, 1998.

CHAPTER 4

1929–

U.S. Events and Trends

Stock market crashes

1929

Empire State Building opens

1931

Franklin D. Roosevelt elected president

1932

Roosevelt announces New Deal Legislation

Chicago World's Fair opens

Prohibition repealed (Twenty-first Amendment)

1933

U.S. Fashions

Hemlines drop, waistlines rise

1930

Mainbocher opens Paris salon

Lastex developed by U.S. Rubber Company

Letty Lynton style introduced, based on a film design by Adrian

Dorothy Shaver at Lord & Taylor begins to promote American designers

René Lacoste opens apparel business to sell tennis shirt

1938

National Labor
Relations Board
established

Dionne quintuplets
born in Canada

1934

Shoulders become
wider

Porgy and Bess opens
on Broadway

1935

Adoption of fly
zipper for men
begins

Spanish Civil War
begins

Jesse Owens wins
four gold medals

1936

High point of
surrealist influence
on fashion and
illustration

Amelia Earhart
disappears

1937

Mainbocher designs
wedding dress for
Duchess of Windsor

Germany annexes
Austria

1938

Ferragamo
introduces platform
shoes

Fashion
on the Dole

The Great Depression dominates most accounts of the 1930s. The worst economic catastrophe in recent history, it affected people worldwide and led to significant economic, political, and social changes. In the United States, the simultaneous drought in the plains states had a devastating effect on farmers and led to a great migration westward. Franklin D. Roosevelt was the most prominent figure of this decade and into the next, because he promised a New Deal in his presidential campaign of 1932. Americans either applauded him as a national savior or criticized him as a Socialist. His time in office in the 1930s was marked by attempts to increase employment, an alphabet soup of relief programs, and other measures to aid recovery from the Great Depression.[1]

Domestic and International Politics and Economics

The Great Depression was foremost in the political and economic news of the time. Its effects were drastic and felt worldwide. In Europe, fascism was one political reaction to the economic disaster, and it, in turn, affected relations between the United States and the countries where it took hold.

The Great Depression

The boom years of the 1920s ended in October 1929. From the mid-1920s to 1929, rising prices typified the stock market. American investors enjoyed an enormous bull market, although the vast majority of Americans did not have stock market investments. The stock market slide began in September 1929, but the most significant drops were on October 24 and October 29, the latter known as Black Tuesday and usually identified as the day of the crash. Stock prices underwent dramatic rises and drops between October 29 and November 13, but, when stock prices hit their final low point, 50 percent of the value in the index had disappeared.[2]

To most people, the Great Depression seemed to come on suddenly, precipitated by the stock market crash. However, between 1923 and 1929, banks closed at an average rate of two a day. The apparent prosperity for most in the 1920s had in fact concealed serious flaws in the American banking system. Also, agriculture had suffered a general depression through most of the 1920s. America was not alone in its economic woes. The depression struck all the industrialized nations of the world, including the major European powers, Britain, France, and Germany.

There were many reasons for the economic crisis, and some debate about the causes continues today. World War I was a source of much instability in the world economy, especially through the reparation of war debts. Germany had enormous payments to make to the Allies after the war, a burden that contributed to out-of-control inflation and crippled the German economy. Both the Allies and Germany owed the United States money, although most of the debt owed was from Britain and France. These Allies were unable to pay it all back in the 1920s, and after the market crash they sank further into debt. In addition, the industrial nations still relied on the Gold Standard to support the value of currency. However, the world's gold supply was limited, and the United States controlled much of it. On the contrary, protectionism and high tariffs kept foreign goods out of the United States, making a very uneven balance of trade. Severely unequal distribution of wealth and income among Americans also worsened the length and depth of the depression.

Although most Americans did not lose their jobs or homes during the depression years, almost all were affected in some way. Initially there was optimism after the stock market crash, as President Herbert Hoover set out immediately to get business and labor leaders to keep wages and production levels steady. In an attempt to reassure the public, he chose to call this economic downturn a depression rather than a panic, because the latter was the word American economists and politicians had used to refer to previous periods of economic decline. By 1930, over 1,300 banks had failed, and many factories either cut back on production or closed, precipitating a tremendous loss of public confidence in the economy. Hoover urged voluntary actions and tried to organize private monies to rescue banks. Ultimately, he used the federal government more than any previous president to attempt to deal with the crisis. In 1932, with his support, Congress passed a bill to authorize the Reconstruction Finance Corporation to make loans to banks and farm mortgage companies. Hoover helped initiate the Glass-Steagall Act (1933) to separate banking and stock investment functions. He also tried to motivate local government and private charities to assist the poor and unemployed, but, despite increased giving, it was woefully inadequate (Figure 4.1).[3] As the economy worsened, the American public began to blame Hoover, and shanty towns grew near urban areas that were called Hoovervilles.

The economic catastrophe of the depression was intensified by the ecological devastation known as the dust bowl, centered in the Texas and Oklahoma panhandles. The dust bowl was the result of farmers continuing to produce increasingly larger crops of mostly cotton and wheat with little regard for the land. A period of drought hit in 1930, and, as the land became parched, the wind lifted huge clouds of dust that hit not only the rural areas but also the cities.

Figure 4.1 Distributing bread to the needy, October 24, 1930. ©Bettmann/Corbis.

Thousands of people began an exodus out of the devastated areas. Often called Okies, they mostly headed for California. Their plight was immortalized in John Steinbeck's *The Grapes of Wrath*, published in 1939.

Franklin Delano Roosevelt was elected president in November 1932 and took the oath of office in March 1933, stating in his inaugural address, "We have nothing to fear but fear itself." Bank failures increased again just before the inauguration. He immediately went to work to solve the banking crisis by first declaring a bank holiday. In the first few weeks of his administration, Roosevelt convened a special session of Congress to launch his New Deal. During this period, referred to as the Hundred Days, his focus was on domestic problems, deemphasizing foreign relations and putting the country in an isolationist mode. The majority of bills he proposed aimed to establish new government agencies, sometimes called the alphabet soup agencies because of their acronyms. These included the Agricultural Adjustment Act (AAA), the Civilian Conservation Corps (CCC), the Tennessee Valley Authority (TVA) and the National Industrial Recovery Act (NIRA), under which was established the National Recovery Administration (NRA). Intended to stimulate production in American industries, the NIRA was the most controversial of Roosevelt's efforts. It established codes designed to regulate prices and trade practices. It also recognized the rights of labor to organize and to have collective bargaining with management. Those who opposed it viewed it as socialistic, or even as communistic.

Roosevelt pursued not only economic reform but also more liberal social policies, including support for the immediate repeal of prohibition. The first move was legalization of beer and, with the wide support of much of the country, the ratification of the Twenty-First Amendment of the constitution—the repeal amendment.

Beginning in 1935, Congress passed a series of momentous legislative programs that are often referred to as the Second New Deal. These included the Emergency Relief Appropriation Act (ERA), The Banking Act, the Wagner National Labor Relations Act, and the Social Security Act. The largest agency created out of the ERA was the Works Progress Administration (WPA; after 1939, the Works Projects Administration) headed by Harry Hopkins. A controversial program from the start, it was designed to work at the local level and to provide jobs for thousands of the disadvantaged. The WPA projects included not only bridges and public buildings but also federal projects for the arts, music, and theater. The Federal Writers Project put writers to work on a series of guidebooks to the states and to major cities. One of their activities was to record the lives of former slaves and sharecroppers. The WPA artists' program provided work for many artists during the Depression. Numerous public buildings contain one of the over 2,500 murals painted by WPA-supported artists. This program not only put food on artists' tables but also provided excellent working experiences and opportunities to meet and support each other. Artists who benefited from the program included Willem de Kooning and Arshile Gorky, significant painters in the abstract expressionist movement of the 1940s and 1950s.

The WPA also established sewing shops in 1935 to supply clothing and household textile products to the unemployed and needy and to provide work for unskilled women unable to support themselves. The products of these factories were distributed through a number of agencies, including the Emergency Relief Bureau, the Department of Hospitals, the Department of Parks, and the Red Cross. Not all approved of the project, however, as some apparel industry manufacturers considered it in competition with their own products.

Growth of the Fascist Powers

If World War I created the environment that contributed to the Depression, it also set the stage for Adolph Hitler's rise to power in Germany. Hitler's National Socialist Democratic Party won the support of disenchanted ex-soldiers, the lower-middle class, and farmers. Germany was particularly hard hit by the depression because its economy was dependent on loans from the United States. When the economic crisis hit and loans were recalled, Germany was overwhelmed. Unemployment leapt from 8.5 percent in 1929 to 29.9 percent in 1932. At about the same time that Roosevelt became president, Adolph Hitler became chancellor of Germany, soon afterward establishing himself as absolute dictator and re-arming Germany in violation of the 1919 Versailles Treaty.

Italy invaded Ethiopia in 1935, quickly overwhelming the small country. By 1936, Mussolini joined forces with Germany to form the beginning of the Axis powers. As Europe lurched toward war, the United States tried to remain isolationist, although it was becoming more difficult, as the Spanish civil war erupted in 1936. Over 3,000 Americans joined the fighting on the Loyalist side against the Nationalists, led by Francisco Franco, who received military support from Germany and Italy. Not all sided with the Loyalists, and most Catholics and those who were opposed to communism sided with Franco. The U.S. government, however, carefully preserved its neutrality. The Loyalists were defeated in 1939, and Franco established a fascist regime in Spain.

Social Life and Culture

The history of the Great Depression often eclipses significant changes that affected everyday life in America. However, many of the innovations in technology, and in art and entertainment, were linked to the economic problems of the period as people looked to radio, films, and popular culture to provide a brief respite for their financial woes.

Technology and Communication

Communication and access to information improved, as both the sale of radios and attendance at the movies increased. In 1929, about 10 million homes had radios, rising to more than 27 million by 1939. Families gathered around the radio, much as they gather around the television today, to listen to comedian Jack Benny, a thriller called *The Shadow*, and Edgar Bergen and his ventriloquist's dummy Charlie McCarthy. There were also shows such as *Captain Midnight* aimed at younger audiences and teenagers, aired in the afterschool hours. The wide-ranging effect of radio, movie newsreels, and magazine advertising created fads and made instant celebrities out of many. The Dionne quintuplets, for example, born in Canada in1934, appeared in dozens of magazines. Child movie star Shirley Temple endorsed and inspired dozens of products from dolls to dishes. Mickey Mouse and Buck Rogers watches could be purchased from Sears, Roebuck & Co. for about a dollar (Figure 4.2). They even offered a New Deal watch, with pictures of the Capitol and President Roosevelt.

The sale of electric appliances increased, and appliances in general began to adopt a streamlined modern appearance. By the end of the 1920s, the art deco design style no longer seemed fresh, and designers embraced a sleek, streamlined, geometric style that was integrated into the form of a variety of products. A group of designers, including Raymond Loewy and Russel Wright, influenced the style of household products, from refrigerators to washing machines.[4]

Fads and brief media obsessions provided a respite from everyday concerns during the Depression years. One of the most written-about social events of the period occurred in 1936, when King Edward VIII of England, just before his coronation, stepped down from the throne, stating that it was for "the woman I love," the American divorcee Wallis Warfield Simpson. He took the title Duke of Windsor, and she became the Duchess of Windsor. The press followed their every move throughout 1935 and 1936, and both were to become fashion icons of the period (Figure 4.3). The media also followed the record-making flights of pilot Amelia Earhart, who symbolized the new adventurous woman and helped spotlight sportive clothes. She developed flying clothes for the Ninety-Nines, an international organization of licensed women pilots, and several New York garment manufacturers made an exclusive Amelia Earhart line, marketed around the country.

The depression years gave rise to an increasing recognition of teen culture, especially of girls. The fashion industry

Figure 4.2 (LEFT) Buck Rogers watch for boys or girls. Sears, Roebuck & Co. Catalog (1935). *Everyday Fashions of the Thirties as Pictured in Sears Catalogs,* New York: Dover Publications, Inc., 1986, 78.

Figure 4.3 (RIGHT) Three dresses designed by Mainbocher for the Duchess of Windsor. *Vogue,* June 15, 1937, 59.

in particular acknowledged high school girls as a distinct group and began to add teen departments. This occurred for a number of reasons. From 1930 to 1940, the proportion of 14- to 17-year-olds enrolled in high school increased from 51 percent to 71 percent as parents increasingly viewed high school as the accepted route to adulthood. In addition, as the unemployment rate rose, young people were encouraged to stay in school and out of the tight labor market. More time in school meant more time to interact with peers away from parental supervision. Manufacturers and retailers of fashions and cosmetics were quick to appeal to this market through advertising and development of specialized products. Over the course of the decade, manufacturers gradually, if sometimes sporadically, began to assess and provide for teen sizing as well as other aspects of this potential market. Teen departments bore catchy names, such as Sub Deb, Sorority Corner, and (in foundations) the Curve-Control Center.

Literature and Magazines

As the depression put millions out of work, at least some put their now free time toward reading. There were large audiences for magazines, books, and newspapers. New magazines such as *Fortune, Life, Look,* and *Esquire* began publication. They filled their pages with fiction, some news coverage and travel articles, and entertainment and high-society pages. Although not new to the depression years, confessional journals such as *True Story, Modern Screen, Photoplay,* and the pulp magazines offered popular reading distractions with titillating escapist tales. Most women's magazines also increased circulation, and new ones were added, including *Bride's Magazine* and *Woman's Day.*

Nineteen-thirties authors generated numerous literary classics, although some were not considered so until later. Conversely, some best-sellers of the day are now forgotten. Escapism, tales of exotic lands, and historic novels all sold briskly. Erskine Caldwell's *Tobacco Road* and *God's Little Acre* were widely read, but more popular were the detective novels of Ellery Queen (a pen name) and Erle Stanley Gardner, who wrote dozens of Perry Mason stories. Hollywood produced six movies between 1934 and 1937 based on this popular lawyer. *The Good Earth* (1931) by Pearl S. Buck and *Gone with the Wind* (1936) by Margaret Mitchell, two top-selling novels, also became movies. Some writers grappled with the problems of the depression or questioned the American dream. *The Grapes of Wrath* (1939) by John

Figure 4.4 Mr. and Mrs. Jesse Owens greeted by members of the press on their return home from the Olympics, August 24, 1936. ©Bettmann/Corbis.

Figure 4.5 "Monte Blue (right) and Vinnie Barnet (left) talking over the automobile situation," says the caption of this photo taken in Hollywood, CA, 1933. Note the hats and casual attire. ©Bettmann/Corbis.

Steinbeck chronicled the journey of an Oklahoma family devastated by the drought, while his novel *Tortilla Flat* (1935) described the struggles of Mexican migrant workers. John Dos Passos expressed pessimism about American capitalism in his trilogy *U.S.A.*

Sports and Recreation

Sports began to become big business, especially with the increased use of the radio to broadcast events (although the games were not actually broadcast live). Professional sports started to replace amateur sports in perceived importance as more players earned money at their sport. Baseball attendance fell during the depression years, although some teams increased attendance when they installed lights to allow night games. The biggest baseball star of the era was Babe Ruth, who made more money than any of the other players, including the also popular Lou Gehrig and Joe DiMaggio. Sports, like the rest of America, were segregated. One of the more popular entertainments for urban blacks was Negro League baseball. The Negro Leagues were also among the most successful black-owned enterprises in the United States.

Both football and basketball remained more important as collegiate rather than professional sports. The more physical football became the subject of numerous movies, including *All American* (1932), *The Big Game* (1936), and even the Marx Brothers in *Horse Feathers* (1932). There was also public interest in boxing, another popular movie subject. Over half the radio owners in the United States listened as Joe Louis defeated German boxer Max Schmeling in 1938, a fight that also had political overtones, with Schmeling as the symbol of the Nazis and the black Louis representing American honor, despite continuing problems with segregation in the United States. The 1936 summer Olympics in Berlin served to make Americans more aware of the Nazis as Hitler banned all German Jews from participating and attempted to use the games to showcase his ideologies about German supremacy. Jesse Owens, the U.S. black track star, won four gold medals and outraged Hitler, who refused to personally award his medals (Figure 4.4).

In addition to sports, and despite the Great Depression, many Americans traveled for recreation. Although car sales decreased at the beginning of the decade, Americans continued their love affair with the automobile, and after 1933, the number of cars registered continued to increase, reaching 32 million by 1940. By 1938, tourism was the third largest industry in the United States. Despite the number of automobiles, many streets were still not paved. By the end of the decade, however, the Civilian Conservation Corps and other federal groups paved more and more roads, and strip shopping developments, gas stations, and the parking meter became familiar roadside icons. Americans also used their cars for Sunday drives, a leisure activity, rather than taking only practical and purposeful trips. Advertisers quickly made a connection between fashion and automobiles, using the sleek lines of contemporary fashion to complement the style lines of the cars. Many Hollywood stars were also photographed with their automobiles (Figure 4.5). The airplane also began to be a more reliable mode of transportation for those who could afford it.

Retailing and Manufacturing

In late fall 1929, the stock market debacle seemed not to be affecting retail merchandising, but by January 1930 retail sales were 2 percent lower than they had been a year earlier. An approximately 15 percent contraction eventually occurred in retail, but this was felt unequally among stores and departments.

Fashion Retailing

Apparel, particularly at budget levels, fared relatively well, and cosmetics boomed, as did beauty parlors, spreading prosperity to the manufacturers of everything from lipsticks to permanent-wave machines. Another striking profit center in most stores was the foundations departments that purveyed bras, girdles, and corselets. Typically such units contributed about 6 percent to overall department store profits. Women who might lack the funds to buy a new wardrobe could make themselves feel and look better with new makeup, hairdo, or bra and girdle, the latter less likely to be homemade items of apparel.

Retail competition intensified tremendously because there clearly were not enough prosperous customers to go around. Because merchandise differed only slightly from store to store, service gave a competitive edge. Sales staff was trained more intensively so they could effectively persuade customers to buy. In the case of foundations saleswomen, especially the fitters, this extended to instruction in female anatomy, customer psychology, and fashion trends. Retailers and manufacturers worked together to ensure effective selling techniques, such as trading clients up to higher-priced styles and cross-selling between departments—using dresses to sell foundations or coats to sell millinery. Service extended to store amenities, including redesigned departments, more private fitting rooms, and air-conditioning. Public places such as stores and theaters were relatively quick to install air conditioning, which boosted sales and patronage during the typically hot summers of the 1930s.

Financial controls passed increasingly into the hands of general merchandise managers (GMMs), who oversaw the financial side of retail stores. Whereas formerly, decisions rested with all-powerful departmental buyers, now the GMMs had to be placated. This created additional tensions, because these statistical wizards knew little about actual products and less about customer behavior. Sometimes the GMM vetoed reorders on fast-moving merchandise, costing the store potential sales.

Aesthetics and fashion-rightness became ever more important to customers. Despite—or because of—their diminished clothing budgets, women sought the best fashion for their dollar. Product serviceability no longer compensated for dowdy styling. It was possible, however, to stretch the dollar by purchasing a semimade dress that allowed a woman to retain the factory finish on the difficult parts, such as collars or cuffs, but do final stitching at home (Figure 4.6). In 1932, *Vogue* reported that knitting your own fancy sweater was considered swank, and accessories were recommended repeatedly as inexpensive ways to vary the look of basic apparel.

Manufacturers of apparel experienced a considerable shakeout, as they grappled with economic contraction. Producers who survived typically pruned their product lines, keeping only the styles that moved well and generated profits. Some makers were able to export to countries less affected by the depression, but high U.S. tariffs discouraged imports and generally hampered bilateral trade. Stores required prompt delivery of merchandise, but producers declined to make anything until orders were received. Volume of sales, wholesale or retail, counted for little if a decent profit on each unit were not realized.

Both retailers and manufacturers confronted a changed political climate as the New Deal took hold. When the NRA came into force in 1934, it was dubbed the year of the Blue Eagle in recognition of the NRA's symbol (Figure 4.7) . In an attempt to force what was defined as fair competition, the NRA established limited work weeks of 35 to 40 hours, defined minimum age for employment at 16 years, and specified minimum wages.[5] Regulations covered everything: advertising costs, delivery charges, discounts, rebates, labeling, display charges, prices of goods, packaging, and even piracy. Compliance actually drove up consumer prices. In the face of NRA complexity, business and industry support for the act evaporated, and it was declared unconstitutional in May 1935. Not everything was eradicated, however, because work weeks did remain at about the 40-hour limit and employment stabilized, at least until a return to depression in 1937–1938.

The U.S. Apparel Manufacturing Industry

In the first year after the stock market crash, very few buyers went to Paris, and many department stores cancelled existing orders. This represented a significant loss to the French couture houses, and many cut their prices in response. It also had an impact on the U.S. apparel industry, for years dependent on the process of copying the work of Paris designers. Although the trade press continued to cover French fashion and most houses survived the economic crisis, many made significantly fewer models, even at the end of the 1930s. Stricter tariff laws also added to the expense of couture. Some French designers ventured into ready-made clothing. In addition, the Chambre Syndicale helped support

Figure 4.6 (LEFT) "Finish at Home" dress with insets on the skirt, showing the partially finished pieces. *Fifth Avenue Modes: The Magazine of Fashion*, New York: Fifth Avenue Modes, Inc., Spring, 1931, 5 (Author's collection).

Figure 4.7 (OPPOSITE, TOP) Bathing beauties in halter bathing suits and shorts, sporting the NRA symbol on their backs. ©Bettmann/Corbis.

Figure 4.8 (OPPOSITE, BOTTOM) Futuristic coat, with bright colored plastic zippers, equipped with wiring to generate heat. *Vogue*, February 1, 1939, 81.

the industry through a number of measures, including organizing the shows to make them more convenient to buyers and controlling copying through a registration process. To ensure that designers were at least nominally paid for copies, they instituted a measure that required any store buyer attending a show to purchase at least one model.

At the beginning of the depression, the dress industry was the largest of the needle trades in the United States. The economic crisis had minimal effect on the growth of the dress industry in New York, but, in the early years of the 1930s, more high-price than low-price dress companies went out of business. Retail stores began to organize stock by price and type of merchandise, creating expensive, medium, and bargain dress departments. As a result, each maker strove to work to closely defined price points, a trend that began during the 1910s and gained urgency during the depression. As the industry grew, the lower-price manufacturers copied the higher-end New York companies, many of

tors of fashions and styles against copying and piracy of styles of any trade or industry."[6] This was a brief attempt by U.S. manufacturers to register designs and control copies similar to requirements of the Chambre Syndicale in Paris. Many of these organizations sponsored fashion shows to promote American designs.

Art, Music, Theater, and the Movies

The design approach of the period was modernism, with some lingering art deco aesthetic at the beginning of the 1930s. Often called streamline moderne, the style was expressed in everything from the household to the skyscrapers that were beginning to define the skylines of major cities. The modern style that gradually replaced art deco was stripped of ornamentation—it was abstract and geometric, whereas deco had more decorative flourishes and was often representational. Chrome and stainless steel were the materials of choice. The skyscrapers that arose in both art deco and streamlined styles became the epitome of 1930s architecture. Classic examples are the Chrysler Building (1930), with its distinctive stainless steel tower, and the Empire State Building (1931). Although these were both in the more classic and decorative art deco style, architects soon created buildings in what was called the international style, an austere geometry, often of cast concrete and devoid of trim. Rockefeller Center in New York City (1933) is an early example of the trend.

Two major events bracket the period and serve as examples of the trend toward Modernism: the Chicago World's Fair (1933–1934), called the Century of Progress, and the New York World's Fair (1939–1940). Both had pavilions built and filled with streamlined art and architecture that linked modernity with industrial design. The focus was on futuristic displays and examples of the city of tomorrow. The trend toward attempting to predict the future also extended to fashion (Figure 4.8).

A group of American regionalist painters, mostly from the Midwest, came to prominence and included Thomas Hart Benton and Grant Wood. Wood's painting *American Gothic* drew attention when it was shown at the Chicago World's Fair in 1933. It became a widely copied and parodied image into the twenty-first century.

The art style known as surrealism influenced both fashion and fashion photography in the 1930s and beyond. Begun in the 1920s in France as a literary movement, it soon developed into a style of visual art, as the surrealists explored Sigmund Freud's concepts of the dream world and the unconscious in both visual and written works. In the visual arts, the concept was to create unexpected combinations of objects.

Americans were introduced to musicians, comedians,

which had begun to hire in-house designers. Numerous trade organizations arose in the late 1920s and 1930s to promote the welfare of the different market segments. These included the Popular Price Dress Group, the Garment Retailers of America, and the Fashion Group, to name only a few. The latter, established in 1931, was founded by women who would become recognized designers and retailers by the end of the decade. The Fashion Originators Guild of America, founded in 1932, protected the "origina-

Figure 4.9a (LEFT) Evening gown by Schiaparelli, inspired by the turn-of-the-century costumes she designed for Mae West; Figure 4.9b (ABOVE) a Schiaparelli perfume bottle with a similar shape. *Vogue*, June 1, 1937, 51 and December 15, 1937, 89.

and other performers on the radio and in the movies. Rudy Vallee became famous for his unique crooning singing style, projected through a megaphone, and for his radio variety show. Despite the depression, Americans flocked to the movies. By the early 1930s, most theaters were wired for sound, and films of the period provided an escape from economic and social problems. Theater managers responded to a slight decline in attendance at the beginning of the depression by lowering prices so that neighborhood theaters often charged as little as a dime. They began to show double features, two full-length films in addition to a cartoon and a newsreel. Short, one-reel, films were also sometimes shown. Some theaters gave away prizes, such as dishes, to selected lucky ticket holders. It was also the place patrons could go to escape the summer heat, as movie houses began to add air conditioning.

Films and film stars influenced fans with their lifestyle and their dress. The films of the period seemed to avoid the problems of the day. They ranged instead from musical ex-

travaganzas to westerns, gangster movies, and comedies.

Busby Berkeley choreographed some of the most elaborate musicals, such as *Gold Diggers of 1933* and *42nd Street*. Fred Astaire and Ginger Rogers set the tone for elegance and inspired both men's and women's fashions. Although Mae West had made her reputation on the stage, she became a Hollywood star in the early 1930s with her risqué comedies. When Elsa Schiaparelli designed costumes for West's movie *Every Day's a Holiday* (1938), the period-inspired styles influenced fashion silhouettes and the shape of Schiaparelli's perfume bottle (Figure 4.9a and b).

Moviegoers were also entertained by the slapstick of the Marx Brothers and what were termed screwball comedies. The screwball comedy was a genre of film that first appeared in the 1930s and was typified by modern life confusions, often including classic gender role reversals and rapid-fire dialogue.[7] One that had immediate impact on apparel was *It Happened One Night* with Clark Gable and

Figure 4.10 Dancers, including Harriett Hoddon and "Buster" Crabtree, do the latest craze: the Big Apple. ©Bettmann/Corbis.

Figure 4.11 Martin Munkacsis innovated the art of action photography for fashion. *Harper's Bazar,* December 1935, 82.

Claudette Colbert. When Gable appeared in one scene without an undershirt, men around the country promptly discarded this once-standard item of apparel, although it would be revived in later periods. Other comedies of the period included *Bringing up Baby, My Man Godfrey,* and *Mr. Deeds Goes to Town,* all optimistic and upbeat films.

The Duke Ellington song "It Don't Mean a Thing (if it Ain't Got That Swing)" is representative of both music and dancing in the 1930s, although popular songs such as "Brother, Can You Spare a Dime" also reflected the economic suffering of many. The most fashionable dances of the 1930s and well into the 1940s were the Lindy Hop, the Jitterbug, and other fast-paced dances done to the Swing music of the big bands of Benny Goodman, Glenn Miller, Duke Ellington, or Tommy Dorsey (Figure 4.10). This dancing took place in nightclubs, in dance contests, and in movies. Dance marathons, a 1920s fad, continued in popularity, but now the out-of-work could compete for cash prizes. New York ballrooms and jitterbugging contests be-

came multiracial meccas for stylish youth and provided an opportunity to spread fashion ideas.

Fashion Influences

Fashion photography began to radically change the way fashion was published and visualized. Because of both technical and artistic influences, photography might be described as falling into two distinct styles in the 1930s, realism and surrealism. The development of the small, handheld camera with high shutter speeds allowed models to be shown running, playing sports, or shopping instead of standing in static poses. Thus, if the editorial theme was resort clothing, the model could be seen running on the beach or swimming. Photographer Martin Munkacsis innovated the art of action photography for fashion (Figure 4.11). Developments in color photography also opened up possibilities. *Vogue* publisher Condé Nast supported the development of color for the magazine, hiring Anton Bruehl

Figure 4.12 Surrealist photograph of a Vionnet dress. *Vogue,* June 15, 1937, 53.

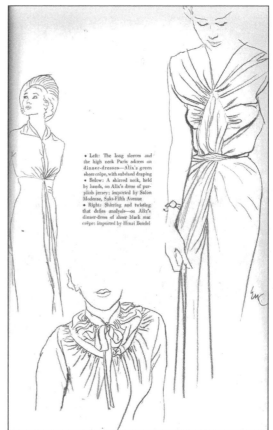

• Left: The long sleeves and the high neck Paris adorns on dinner-dresses—Alix's green sheer crêpe, with subdued draping • Below: A shirred neck, held by hands, on Alix's dress of purplish jersey; imported by Salon Moderne, Saks-Fifth Avenue • Right: Shirring and twisting that defies analysis—on Alix's dinner-dress of sheer black mat crêpe; imported by Henri Bendel

Figure 4.13 Eric illustration of Alix (Madame Grés) gown. *Vogue,* December 15, 1936, 43.

as chief color photographer to work with Ferdinand Bourges, the chief engraving technician.[8]

The counterpoint to this style was surrealism, with its theatricality and startling juxtaposition of images (Figure 4.12).[9] Photographers Cecil Beaton and Man Ray experimented with surrealist imagery. Both discarded the conventions of fashion photography of the past, creating visual compositions that not only demonstrated new ways to show fashion, but also often provided limited information about the clothing itself. Many other photographers put their own unique and creative stamp on fashion photography throughout the 1930s, including Horst P. Horst, Erwin Blumenfeld, Toni Frissell, Andre Durst, and George Hoyningen-Huene. Hoyningen-Huene often used Greek influences combined with architectural and surrealistic compositions.

Illustration remained an important technique for showcasing the latest fashion. High-quality illustrations appeared in both *Vogue* and *Harper's Bazar.* Illustrations of the first half of the 1930s accentuated and exaggerated the long, slender silhouette. Both Carl Erickson (Eric) (Figure 4.13) and René Bouet Willaumez (Plate 4.1) produced fluid

black-and-white and color illustrations for *Vogue.* Designer and painter Christian Bérard, sometimes called an expressionist romantic, also contributed illustrations, as did Cecil Beaton and surrealist artists Jean Cocteau and Marcel Vertés.

It is important not to forget the innovative and influential fashion editors of the period: Carmel Snow at *Harper's Bazar* and Edna Woolman Chase at *Vogue.* Chase began her career with *Vogue* in 1895, became an editor in her teens, and soon editor-in-chief. She worked with Condé Nast to create the fashion look and professional standards of *Vogue* until she retired in 1952. Snow began her magazine career at *Vogue,* becoming editor of the American edition in 1929. She created a furor in the fashion world when she left to become editor at *Harper's Bazar* in 1932, where she stayed until 1957.

The Designers

Paris continued to be a focus of fashion creativity in the 1930s, despite the financial impact of the depression on the

Figure 4.14 Chanel, shown here in a 1936 photo, was often her own best model. Note her bold jewelry. ©Lipnitzki/Roger Viollet/ Getty Images.

buying power of both department stores and individual customers. American designers began to exert an influence in this period in both New York and California.

Paris

Female designers seemed to dominate the Paris fashion scene in the decades between the world wars, as represented by Madeleine Vionnet, Alix (Madame Grès), Elsa Schiaparelli, Nina Ricci, Coco Chanel, Augustbernard, and Maggy Rouff. Male designers Jean Patou, Mainbocher (an American who worked in Paris), and Molyneux were also influential. Mainbocher made a name for American design when the Duchess of Windsor chose him to design her wedding dress.

The economic depression at the beginning of the 1930s had both financial and aesthetic impact on French designers. When American buyers reduced orders, designers created styles that could be sold for less money through use of either less expensive fabrics or less labor. Coco Chanel and Jean Patou, for example, created collections in cotton eyelet, pique, and organdy, not only less costly but also easier for

the ready-to-wear manufacturer to stitch in the more complicated design lines that were becoming fashionable.

Arch rivals **Chanel** and **Elsa Schiaparelli** were both influenced by and worked with some of the premier surrealist artists, but it was Schiaparelli who incorporated the motifs of surrealism more frequently and effectively into her designs. In the 1930s, Chanel was particularly known for her evening dresses in and for her innovative costume jewelry designs (Figure 4.14). Although these may not be the styles we most associate with her, it is important to remember that in each of the periods in which she designed, Chanel's clothing fit the fashions of the day.

Schiaparelli, on the contrary, set out to create fashion as art, collaborating with Salvador Dalí, Jean Cocteau, and Christian Berard. Born into an aristocratic Roman family, she turned to fashion design after a failed marriage left her with no means of support. Mentored early on by Paul Poiret, she created her first successful design in 1927—a sweater with a trompe l'oeil bow knitted into the front—a design idea that would remain popular through the 1930s. She continued to create specialty sweaters and casual sportswear, adding evening wear in the early 1930s. One of the first to develop a broad-shoulder effect through use of fullness in the upper sleeve, Schiaparelli brought a sense of humor to her designs and was never afraid to experiment with new materials such as the novel spun glass fiber or the more mundane rayon. She was one of the first designers to incorporate zippers into her collection, using plastic zips as decorations, where other designers had hidden them in plackets or under trims. Her collaborations with Dalí included a lobster dress, tear dress (with the appearance of torn sections in the fabric), and the desk suit, an interpretation of a drawing Dali created of a woman made of drawers. In 1938 she began to produce collections based on themes, such as astrology or the circus. While she experimented with art and design, she also created wearable designs for all occasions (see Plate 4.1).

Madeleine Vionnet continued her innovations with bias cut dresses throughout the 1930s, designing and cutting improvisationally on a small mannequin. Considered one of the greatest technicians of the twentieth century, she experimented not only with cut but also with lingerie stitching techniques (various special hand stitches) to allow her to keep the bias seams supple. The sinuous bias cut dresses she devised (Figure 4.15) were very representative of 1930s evening style and can be seen adapted to film costumes for stars like Jean Harlow. Vionnet also followed the trend toward more romantic lines in the mid-1930s, with back interest and slightly more structure (see Figure 4.12).

Madame Grès, another of the great women designers of the 1930s, was praised as a drapery god by *Vogue*. Born Ger-

Figure 4.15 (LEFT) Long lean line of the early thirties. Vionnet dress on the left, Hattie Carnegie on the right. *Harper's Bazar,* May 1931, 50.

Figure 4.16 (BELOW) Marlene Dietrich wearing a dress designed by Hollywood designer Travis Banton with the Letty Lynton style sleeve. *Vogue,* May 15, 1935, 55.

maine Barton, she initially wanted to be a sculptress, a career her family thought inappropriate for a woman. She then turned to sculpting in fabric, studying pattern design, cutting, and sketching only briefly before establishing herself as a couturière. In the 1930s she designed under the name Alix, but because of difficulties with business partners she reopened after World War II under the name Grès. Like Vionnet, she draped on a mannequin, creating dresses that were intricately pleated, wrapped, or draped to the body (see Figure 4.13). Although she occasionally worked on the bias, she also used wool and silk jersey where bias cut was

less important. Her later draped gowns were intricately structured and anchored to an understructure rather than taking the shape of the body underneath.

Although **Jean Patou** is often considered a designer who epitomized the style of the 1920s, he continued to be influential until his death in 1936. He is frequently credited with introducing the longer skirts and more natural waistlines in 1929.

Mainbocher was born Main Rousseau Bocher in Chicago in 1891. He studied art before World War I but went to Paris in 1917 as an ambulance driver, and decided to stay. Initially, he worked as an illustrator for both *Harper's Bazaar* and *Vogue* and eventually became an editor for *French Vogue*, creating the "Vogue's Eye View" column. He opened his own studio in 1929, aided by the many fashion connections he made while at *Vogue*. The first American designer to successfully operate a couture house in Paris, he worked with the French textile industry to create special wide fabrics. Considered a designer of elegant style, Mainbocher showed his design strengths in his evening gowns and beaded evening sweaters. One of his best-known regular customers was the Duchess of Windsor, one of the style icons of the period, whose wardrobe was frequently covered in the fashion press (see Figure 4.3).

Captain Edward Molyneux, of Anglo-Irish heritage, also made his career in Paris, initially working with Lucile. He opened his couture house in 1919, after earning the Military Cross in World War I. His use of clean lines fit well with the contemporary streamlined style, and he was known for his tailored suits and coats and for creating innovative evening pajama ensembles. His clientele included Princess Marina of Greece and the Duchess of Windsor as well as film and theater stars.

United States

The creativity of the U.S. fashion industry began to come into its own in the 1930s, despite—or perhaps even partly because of—the Great Depression. French dress imports dropped by as much as 40 percent through 1932, and U.S. manufacturers began to rely less on buying expensive Paris models to copy. Although most American designer names were still not familiar to the average customer, many began to develop a strong reputation during this period, particularly in the area of sportswear. Interestingly, many of the American designers who came to prominence were also women. These included Elizabeth Hawes, Murial King, Clare Potter, Hattie Carnegie, Nettie Rosenstein, Louise B. Gallagher, and, later into the decade, Claire McCardell. The importance of Paris design did not wane entirely, however, and many ready-to-wear manufacturers still relied on both Paris reproductions and Paris inspirations.

Many of the prominent American designers were also retail shop owners who not only had a wholesale side of the business but also imported Parisian models for resale or had retail businesses. These included Sally Milgrim, Hattie Carnegie, and E. M. A. Steinmetz. Others, such as Valentina, designed primarily made-to-order clothing, while some, such as Muriel King and Hawes, designed both custom and ready-to-wear clothing.

Hollywood and California designers in general began to exert an influence on fashion in New York City and in Europe. Costumes in the films had some impact, although most often through reproduction of one or two designs that caught the audience's eye. The *Letty Lynton* dress, designed by Adrian for the character of the same name played by Joan Crawford, was widely copied (Figure 4.16), as was the Empress Eugenie hat worn by Greta Garbo in the 1930 film *Romance*. Katharine Hepburn and Greta Garbo, among others, exerted a fashion influence at least as much for the clothing they were photographed wearing off the set as in films. When Marlene Dietrich and Katharine Hepburn appeared in public in tailored men's trousers, more women were inclined to adopt them than when the designers showed models in pants in their salon shows. It would, however, be a long time before trouser wearing was completely accepted. The casual California lifestyle, and the designers who created it, had a lasting effect on fashion. At least some were film designers who created clothing for the stars. Adrian, Howard Greer, Travis Banton, and Edith Head all made clothing for private customers. Hollywood designers and stars were frequently covered in the fashion press both in costumes and in high-fashion creations.

Promotion of American design was given a big boost in 1932 with the advertising campaign created by Dorothy Shaver, vice president of Lord & Taylor. She also set out to promote the designers in store displays. The U.S. designers were creators of wholesale, ready-to-wear and high-end, sometimes made-to-measure, clothing sold in specialty shops in New York. The first designers Shaver promoted were Elizabeth Hawes, Muriel King, and Clare Potter, followed by Tina Leser, Tom Brigance, Nettie Rosenstein, and Helen Cookman.

Elizabeth Hawes, one of the most controversial and vocal American designers, was born in 1903 in New Jersey and studied at Vassar and Parsons before going to Paris in 1925 as a sketcher at fashion shows. She subsequently worked as Paris-based stylist for Lord & Taylor and Macy's. In 1928 she returned to New York to open her own shop, specializing in simple, soft clothes that followed body proportions. Hawes expressed her philosophy in her 1938 book *Fashion Is Spinach*, decrying poorly conceived fashions. Other books followed, including *Men Can Take It* in 1939, a commentary on the restrictive nature of men's clothing. Hawes retained a commitment to design for American women's lifestyles, something she believed Paris could not do (Figure 4.17).

Muriel King studied art before choosing fashion design as a career. She did freelance fashion illustration and costumes for several Hollywood films. She had just gone into business for herself when she was featured in the Lord & Taylor promotion in 1932. Lord & Taylor sold her ready-to-wear line, but she also made exclusive dresses for her private clientele. As a trained artist, she worked initially from sketches from which customers could place orders. King de-

Figure 4.17 Two sport dresses from Elizabeth Hawes. Note the shirtwaist style on the left. *Vogue*, April 15, 1934, 117.

Figure 4.18 A Sally Milgrim design with deep armhole and the metallic cloth on top. Note the strapped shoe. *Vogue*, October 1, 1935.

signed for Katharine Hepburn both on- and off-camera. In 1937, she opened a larger salon, but she closed it in 1940.

Clare Potter, born Clare Meyer, intended to become an artist but changed to fashion design while studying at Pratt Institute. After a brief position designing embroidery and other design elements, she began work as a designer for Charles W. Nudelman, Inc. Potter epitomized the American designer, avoiding Paris as a design source and taking her inspiration from travel and her own lifestyle. Like many of the prominent American ready-to-wear designers of the period, she was known for her sports clothing and more casual day into evening dresses. Also considered an expert colorist, she often combined contrasting colors into a single outfit. Throughout the 1930s and into the 1940s, she used the lower case, elided version of her name: clarepotter.

Nettie Rosenstein was considered one of the most talented designers of the time and was among those American designers copied by other manufacturers. She started her fashion career as a private dressmaker and entered the wholesale side of the apparel business when approached to create clothing for retailer I. Magnin. She began a wholesale business in 1931 under her own name, creating as many as 400 to 500 models a year. Her high-quality clothing was sold around the country but kept exclusive by allowing only one store in an area to carry a design.

Hattie Carnegie was one of the most important names in fashion in New York. She owned a specialty store that had many separate departments and catered to the pocketbooks of many different customers, from very expensive custom clothing to more affordable styles sold in her Spectator Sports Shop. At the height of her business she had a thousand employees and trained many of the men and women who would become designers in their own right, including Norman Norell and Claire McCardell. Carnegie also had a hat-making facility and a custom-made handbag department. Her styles of the period included innovative design but also something for everyone, from suits to simple day dresses to ball gowns (see Figure 4.15).[10]

Figure 4.19 Evening dress with jacket made of rayon crepe. *Vogue*, December 1, 1933, 6.

Sally Milgrim, born Sally Noble, started her fashion career as a mannequin for Milgrim Brothers' shop. After she married the youngest of the Milgrim brothers, she began to design for the store. The business grew quickly, and the store name was changed to Milgrim. The business soon expanded to include both a custom and wholesale side. Her ready-to-wear designs were also sold at Milgrim stores in Chicago, as well as exclusively at one store in major American cities under the name Salymil. A well-known designer of evening wear (Figure 4.18), she created the inaugural gowns for first ladies Eleanor Roosevelt, Florence Harding, and Grace Coolidge.[11]

Lilly Daché was born in France but came to be one of the preeminent hat designers in America. She went into business for herself in the late 1920s and rose to fame quickly, opening a store on Madison Avenue in New York. By the mid-1930s there were Lilly Daché millinery departments in stores around the country. She frequently favored asymmetrical designs that sat tilted to one side and became

known for her turban styles. In 1938 she acquired an entire building, with seven floors to accommodate her retail shops and salons, staff, and workrooms.

Fashion Trends

The adolescent and youthful look of the 1920s began to disappear before the stock market crash, as the waistline returned to its natural position. Skirts lengthened, and there was an increasingly curvilinear silhouette for women. The ideal silhouette was long and slender in the early 1930s. Daytime fashions and evening wear become distinct, with different hem lengths for day and evening. Hems got longer through the mid-1930s and then began to rise again just before World War II. Popular color combinations included brown with red, pink, or yellow; dark red and bright green; and purple with Schiaparelli's shocking pink. New technologies changed fabrics and silhouettes, with the introduction of Lastex and the use of zippers as a fashion closure (see Figure 4.8).

Textiles and Technology

The Great Depression affected the apparel industry on many levels. As the lower-priced dress became more important, so did experimentation with less-expensive materials. American designers became adaptable in the use of more cost-effective material, and textile manufacturers such as Celanese Corporation began to promote American designers who created apparel with their manmade fibers, such as acetate, often called artificial silk. Rayon began to be used more often, and rayon manufacturers used prominent designers to promote their textiles (Figure 4.19). Even such novelties as cellophane yarns were used for embroidery.

The wonder fiber that changed style and silhouette for men's and women's undergarments and bathing suits was Lastex, which consisted of a core filament of extruded latex (synthetic rubber) covered by layers of cotton, rayon, or silk yarn. Lastex was lightweight, more stable than rubber, and washable but not as durable as the old corset standby of coutil (a firm, tightly woven herringbone twill cloth) and metal boning (Figure 4.20).

Women's Styles

The silhouette of women's clothing began to change in 1928, because, according to *Vogue*, skirts could not get any shorter or waistlines any lower. The natural waist returned at the beginning of the period and remained throughout the 1930s. By the mid-1930s, the emphasis began to be on a broader shoulder line, initially developed through fuller

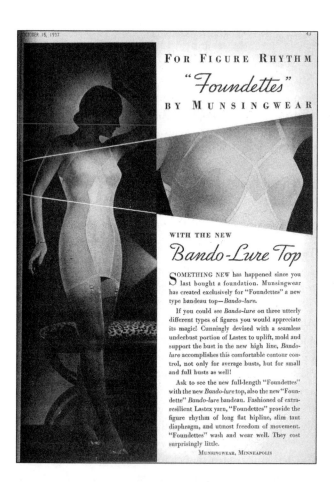

sleeve shapes, and later with introduction of shoulder pads, a style that would remain through World War II.

Dresses

A slender silhouette dominated dresses at the start of the period. These slim styles also demanded trim bodies, so exercises such as cycling were recommended in the early 1930s. Hemlines dropped, and a natural, fitted waistline returned to dresses and suits. Although the new silhouettes were accepted rather rapidly, there was a very brief period of transition in 1929 and 1930 when the accent was on both a higher waistline and on the hips, with insets or pleats (Figure 4.21). A narrow silhouette continued until mid-decade, with increased emphasis on the shoulder through use of wide or full sleeve caps. The wide shoulders were influenced in part by Schiaparelli's use of sleeves with fullness at the top and by the designs of Adrian for Joan Crawford. His full, ruffled sleeve Letty Lynton dress continued to be copied for years after the film was released (see Figure 4.16). Adrian created numerous designs for Crawford, intended to make her hips appear smaller by widening the shoulder line. These included wide collars and, later in the decade, shoulder pads.[12] Cape sleeves (extremely flared at the hem) and capelets on all types of dresses all served to widen the silhouette across the shoulders. The wide shoulder continued not only throughout the 1930s but also through the World War II period. Deep-cut, **dolman**-style sleeves appeared on both dresses and jackets (see Figures 4.18 and 4.19).

Figure 4.20 (OPPOSITE, LEFT) Munsingwear Foundettes of Lastex. *Vogue*, October 15, 1937, 43.

Figure 4.21 (OPPOSITE, RIGHT) College student wearing a dress designed and made in apparel class at Iowa State University, 1930. Department of Apparel, Education Studies, and Hospitality Management [AESHM], Iowa State University.

Figure 4.22 (RIGHT) Maternity dress designed in the style of the period with adjustable belted waist. *Lane Bryant Catalog*, 1932. (Department of Apparel, Education Studies, and Hospitality Management [AESHM], Iowa State University.)

Almost all dresses, suits, and coats were accented with a belt. Some suggested that the ubiquitous belt, often in fabric matching the dress, was a technique used by the ready-to-wear industry to provide a fit for various figure types, as women could take a slightly unfitted dress and cinch it into their own waistline. This belted style also included maternity wear, designed as wrap dresses that fit close to the body but expanded through a series of graduated closures (Figure 4.22). Many dresses and suits, both day and evening, had intricate design lines with insets and **godets** (see Figure 4.6).[13] In contrast to these detailed cuts was the shirtwaist dress, introduced in 1932 (see Figure 4.17). Shirtwaist blouses also appeared in styles reminiscent of shirts 30 years earlier.

In the first half of the period, evening dresses were long and narrow and often featured a low back or halter-style neckline. The backless evening dress remained popular throughout the 1930s and could now show off a suntanned back. Close-to-the-body, bias-cut dresses, influenced by Vionnet, emphasized the long, slender silhouette (see Figures 4.15 and 4.19). Some also had a decorative, fitted seam, accenting a high empire waist but still retaining a fitted, natural waist (see Figure 4.3).

As the decade progressed, designers, perhaps tiring of the streamlined mode, took inspiration from the past or at least from the period costumes seen in films such as *The Barretts of Wimpole Street* (1934), *Little Women* (1933), and *The Scarlet Empress* (1934). Dresses, especially for evening wear, began to be a mix of the modern and the historic. A

Figure 4.23 Dress and jacket combination, peplum suit, and deep sleeve, wide shouldered coat. Note the hats and shoes that accessorize these ensembles. *McCall's Magazine,* February 1937, 117.

Figure 4.24 Casual sportswear: trousers, halter top, and short jackets for women. *Vogue,* June 1, 1937, 45. Illustration by René Bouet-Willaumez.

long tunic top worn over a skirt appeared mid-decade for both day and evening (see Figure 4.3). The new romanticism continued to develop gradually until the beginning of World War II, with fuller skirts (see Figures 4.10 and 4.12) or an occasional bustle-like fullness in the back. Both Vionnet and the always-modern Coco Chanel were affected by the trend toward historic inspiration with gowns in an eighteenth- or nineteenth-century mode (see Figure 4.12). By 1938, Paris designers began to show the small-waist, full-skirted silhouette that anticipated Dior's New Look by about a decade.

Suits and Outerwear

Ensemble dressing was a standard for daywear, with matching jackets for both suits and dresses. Jackets at the beginning of the 1930s were longer and more loosely belted, but,

by mid-decade, shorter **peplum** jackets with emphasis on the shoulder and wider belts were the mode (Figure 4.23).[14] Skirts remained long and narrow in the first half of the 1930s, creeping up slightly after 1935. By 1938–1939, lengths were definitely shorter, and more fullness crept in from the waist down, not just at the hem edge.

The slim silhouette was also standard in coats through the mid-1930s, sometimes with a dolman sleeve or a full gathered leg-of-mutton sleeve top. Coats were both single and double breasted and by 1931 also firmly anchored at the waist. Wide and sometime elaborate collars are seen on coats until the end of the period. A boxy silhouette joined the slim belted style from mid-decade on. In the film *The Scarlet Empress*, designer Travis Banton wrapped the cast in furs at the request of producer Adolph Zukor, a former furrier, in an effort to boost the trade. The trend for fur stoles,

Figure 4.25a (LEFT) Accessories: Gauntlet glove; Figure 4.25b (RIGHT) ghillie tie shoes. *Vogue*, April 1, 1935, 132; *Harper's Bazar*, October 1938, 17.

Sportswear

Sport clothing, for both spectator and active participation, was an important part of the 1930s wardrobe. The sport of the period was skiing, inspired by the 1932 Winter Olympics in Lake Placid, New York. Like other styles, the ski silhouette was long and slender, with waists accented by a belt. Jackets were either single or double breasted, usually with a wide collar, worn with trousers that bloused slightly at the ankle, sometimes held in place with knitted bands, sometimes made with Lastex. The beach pajama had gained popularity in the late 1920s, with a loose, full pant. Trousers also became acceptable for other sporting occasions (Figure 4.24), seen in a number of variations, including jodhpurs,

divided skirts, and plus-fours. For tennis, the white dress was still the standard, but styles followed the trends of the day, with longer lengths and a natural waistline. Skirt fullness was achieved with gores and insets in addition to pleats. Some backless styles even appeared. Shorts gradually began to be accepted in mid-decade, even at Wimbledon.

Bathing suits also followed the general style trends. In the late 1920s, the bathing suit was still made primarily of wool or cotton but was closer to the body in a one-piece tank style. Swimwear was rapidly becoming a style intended to promote standards of beauty by beauty pageant organizers and by Hollywood. The studios often posed starlets in bathing attire, and California manufacturers took the lead in ready-to-wear production. The introduction of Lastex revolutionized fit and style. When woven into a satin fabric, Lastex gave suits a sleek appearance that increasingly revealed the body. New swim attire included lower-cut necklines, halter tops, and backless styles, not unlike evening dresses (see Figures 4.7 and 4.11). Women could also choose from numerous other style variations, including two-piece suits with brassiere-style tops and shorts. As more and more women actually swam in their suits, swim fashion included rubber swim caps to keep the hair dry. The popularity of suntans grew out of the enthusiasm for sports and swimming, with the accompanying lotions and other beauty products to encourage a deep-brown shade or to prevent sunburn.

Accessories

Hats and gloves were considered essential accessories, worn for both day and evening. The close-to-the-head cloche style hat began to shrink in size and develop a small brim by the late 1920s and was soon replaced by smaller, jauntier hats. Hats remained relatively small throughout the period, often worn at a stylish angle. There were seemingly infinite variations on style and trim, including pillbox shapes, turbans, berets, platter shapes, and even sailor styles, with trims of feathers, bows, beads, artificial flowers and netting and veils (see Figures 4.4, 4.9, 4.18, and 4.23 and Plate 4.1). Some resembled a man's fedora, again influenced by styles worn by movie stars, whereas others took inspiration from the surrealists, including Schiaparelli's shoe hat and Chanel's shell-shaped hat. The importance of the hat is illustrated by Irving Berlin's 1933 song Easter Parade, as women displayed their Easter bonnets. Gloves were worn for both day and evening, often with a flared, gauntlet style cuff for day (Figure 4.25a) but long and close fitted for evening.

The most frequently worn shoes were pumps, sometimes in two-toned spectator styles. Most sat high on the arch of the foot, and many had straps. T-strap sandals, most often with a heel, were popular for summer wear (see Figure 4.18). **Ghillie** ties and Oxfords were also worn, sometimes with rubber soles for sport dress (see Figure 4.25b). Platform shoes began to be introduced by the end of the 1930s, particularly from shoe designer Salvatore Ferragamo.

The vogue for costume jewelry that began as a fad in the late 1920s continued unabated, still largely in imitation of real stones and jewels. Semiprecious stones and use of nontraditional objects in the surrealist manner also gained popularity, frequently in bold, substantial pieces (see Figure 4.14). The American jewelry designer Miriam Haskell achieved a reputation for her intricate filigree, rhinestone, and large faux pearl creations.

Underwear: Foundations

For many manufacturers of girdles, corselets, and bras, the 1930s were a period of opportunity. Some firms failed, but many new and existing companies thrived, especially if they managed to control costs and continue to update their products. Technology gave foundations companies Lastex, which, according to *Women's Wear Daily,* "wiped out the Depression for the foundation garment industry."[15] Lastex foundations had to be replaced more often, compensating for their somewhat lower costs.

Fashion also favored the sale of girdles, corselets, and bras. A trim silhouette, with increasingly prominent curves, could not be achieved for most women without some controlling undergarments. All-in-one corselets, reaching from breast to thigh, provided the greatest continuity of line. Beginning with slight breast curves in 1929, corselets continued to gain contour until significant waist indentation and a curvaceous breast were achieved in the late 1930s (see Figure 4.20). Girdles plus bras offered similar shaping, with greater comfort and flexibility. Two-way-stretch Lastex girdles offered comfort that persuaded even young women to buy (Figure 4.26). As trousers for women gained gradual acceptance, panty girdles became an option, starting about 1934.

Brassieres had Lastex, too, mostly for the back band, although one popular line, Munsingwear Foundettes, cleverly employed the tensioning of Lastex to achieve a comfortable uplift (see Figure 4.20). Lightweight knitted fabrics were also employed in bras for youthful customers: full-fashioned, knit-to-shape styles and also tricot for cut-and-sewn styles. The growing acceptance of brassieres among college women gave rise to the abbreviated term bra, starting as student slang about 1934. Besides Lastex and comfortable knits, after about 1932 bras of the 1930s boasted cup sizing. Adjustable straps added to the possibility of a satisfactory fit. Spiral stitching, patented by the Hollywood–Maxwell Company in 1935, gave a more stable shape to cotton bra cups and persisted as a feature into the 1960s. The forerunner of the training bra came on the market in the 1930s in the form of the Mouldette for girls 10 to 15 years of age. Although previously most bras had been made on the East Coast or in the Chicago area, by the 1930s there were numerous producers in southern California. They traded on Hollywood glamour, as reflected in company names such as Mabs of Hollywood, Heléne of Hollywood, and Renée of Hollywood. Other lingerie included clinging slips, cut on the bias, and shortie sleepwear, shown for summer 1936.

Men's Styles

The silhouette of men's clothing developed along similar lines to that of women's, getting narrower initially and then becoming broad shouldered through additional padding. Casual and sport clothing were increasingly important elements in a man's wardrobe.

Suits and Outerwear

Men's suits came in variations from a simple, conservative two- or three-button cut to the more exaggerated peaked lapel style that had gained popularity by the late 1920s. The elongated and broad-shoulder silhouette popular in women's clothing also describes the masculine silhouette of the period. The broad chest and inverted V were perhaps reminiscent of the moderne style but also of the highly defined masculine images seen in fascist art and sculpture. The trend setters in men's suits were the Prince of Wales and Hollywood actors. *Esquire*, which began publication 1933, was influential in promoting sophisticated menswear and lifestyles.

The **English Drape** suit, developed by Savile Row tailors, was adopted by the Prince of Wales and then widely accepted. It persisted until the beginning of the war and textile restrictions. The cut produced a broad-chested silhouette and had wide shoulders with fabric that draped on either side at the front and along the shoulder blades in the back. It was fitted in the waist and worn with a higher-cut, pleated trouser that tapered slightly, ending in a cuff. Double-breasted suits also became stylish (Figure 4.27; see also Figure 4.4 and 4.30). In the mid-1930s, there was a fad among young men for trousers with high and wide waistbands and wide, cuffed pant bottoms (Figure 4.28). One of the significant changes in men's trousers was the adoption of a zipper fly around 1935–1936.

The Duke of Windsor influenced the trend toward casual elegance and is credited with making lighter-weight fabrics more acceptable for summer wear and popularizing less-structured clothing. Summer suiting fabrics included linens, seersucker, and new lightweight tropical wools (see Figure 4.27, upper left). Hollywood stars such as Fred Astaire, Clark Gable, and Cary Grant became fashion icons. Astaire also had suits made on London's Savile Row but softened up the tailoring with button-down shirts and a scarf or tie as a belt instead of suspenders.

As suit coats became broader, outerwear also became oversized and with a broad-shouldered silhouette. They came in both single-breasted, chesterfield style and double-breasted, and, like women's coats, many had a belt. Short jackets, sometimes with a belted waist, were also worn for more casual occasions, as were **bush jackets**, borrowed from the styles of hunters and explorers. In the later 1930s, a sport jacket with side vents and a belt in back became the favored coat for more casual occasions. It usually had lapels in the same styles as suit coats but with patch pockets in front. By the mid-1930s, jackets often had a zipper closure (Figure 4.29). There was a brief fad for white painters' jackets, called **beer jackets,** among college boys.

For evening attire, coats followed the broad-shoulder, narrow-waist silhouette with either a shawl collar or the popular

Figure 4.26 Lastex "singlettes." *Vogue,* March 1, 1934, p. 72.

peaked lapel. Despite the fact that Fred Astaire often danced in a tailcoat, it was seen less frequently than the dinner jacket tuxedo, in either black or white, worn with black trousers, a cummerbund, and a bow tie (see Figure 4.27, upper right).

With the new 40-hour work week and more leisure time, sport clothing became just as important a component of men's wardrobes as it was for women's. Also like women's clothing, some of the more casual styles, such as the collarless **cardigan coat,** originated in California. The more casual jacket style also might be worn with an open neck shirt with long collar points (see Figure 4.5) . Knitted polo shirts and tennis shirts with placket necklines were made in a variety of patterns, and boat-neck shirts and casual **dishrag**

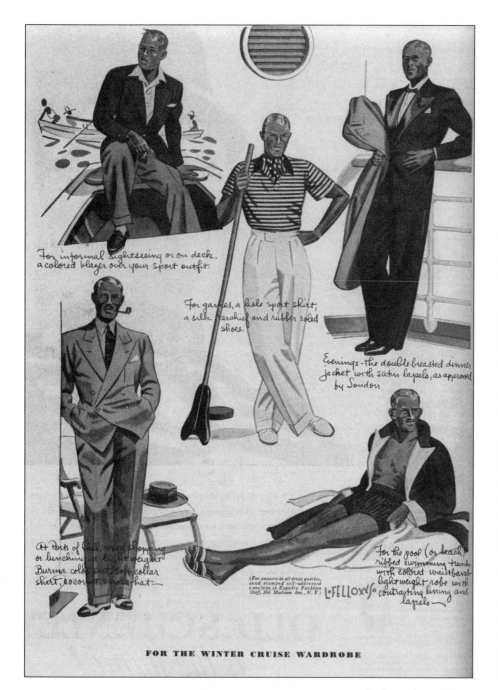

For informal sightseeing or on deck, a colored blazer over your sport outfit.

For games, a lisle sport shirt, a silk kerchief and rubber soled shoes.

Evenings—the double breasted dinner jacket with satin lapels, as approved by London

At Ports of Call, when shopping or lunching a lightweight Burma color suit, soft collar shirt, coconut straw hat.

For the pool (or beach) ribbed swimming trunks with colored waistband, lightweight robe with contrasting lining and lapels.

(For answers to all dress queries, send stamped self-addressed envelope to Esquire Fashion Staff, 366 Madison Ave., N.Y.)

L•FELLOWS

FOR THE WINTER CRUISE WARDROBE

Figure 4.27 (LEFT) Selection of men's styles from formal to casual. *Esquire*, February 1937, 136.

Figure 4.28 (OPPOSITE, TOP LEFT) Wide-leg style pants for younger men. Sears, Roebuck & Co. Catalog (1933). *Everyday Fashions of the Thirties* as pictured in *Sears Catalogs* (New York: Dover Publications, Inc., 1986), 56.

Figure 4.29 (OPPOSITE, BOTTOM LEFT) Men's short jackets with zip front, worn with fedora style hat. *Sears, Roebuck & Co. Catalog* (1936). *Everyday Fashions of the Thirties* as pictured in *Sears Catalogs* (New York: Dover Publications, Inc., 1986), 88.

Figure 4.30 (OPPOSITE, RIGHT) Lastex support garment for men, shown with sport dress, business attire, and formal wear. *Esquire*, March 1937, 155.

shirts made of open-weave, net-like fabrics appeared. Tennis player René Lacoste began producing the now familiar polo shirt with the crocodile emblem in 1933. Sweaters, both cardigan and pullover were also worn for casual occasions. The 1932 winter Olympics created interest in ski clothing for men, including **anorak**-style jackets. Trousers and, gradually, shorts began to be worn more often than knickers for sport. Men's bathing suits were also made sleeker with the use of Lastex satin fabrics. By mid-decade they no longer wore tank-style tops with their trunks (see Figure 4.24 and 4.27).

Shirts and Undergarments

Lastex gave manufacturers an opportunity to experiment with other products. One example is the support-type garment shown in Figure 4.30. Intended to provide a smoother, more toned shape, it is unclear whether it was widely worn. However, Lastex did change men's dress practices, as they began wearing socks reinforced at the top with the stretch fiber, making the previously necessary garters obsolete. Socks also came in a variety of patterns, including argyle and chevron. Men's undergarments lightened up considerably when Jockey introduced men's cotton briefs in 1934,

allowing men to dispense with more cumbersome union suits or wool undergarments, although they continued to be worn by some.

Shoes and Accessories

High-top shoes generally went out of style at the beginning of the period, with Oxford-style shoes, sometimes two-toned, worn with suits. Moccasin shoes, nicknamed **weejuns**, and borrowed from the style of Norwegian fishermen, were worn for casual occasions. Sandals and cloth or canvas **espadrille** styles appeared for summer or casual wear.[16] Hat

styles included felt fedoras and panamas in the summer. For casual wear, boaters and soft hats with a snap brim were worn (see Figures 4.29 and 4.30).

Children's Styles

Children's fashions were subject to style changes, although more so for girls than for boys. The most significant style influences came from two sources: Shirley Temple and the English princesses Elizabeth and Margaret (Figure 4.31). Youngsters dressed in uniquely children's clothing, al-

Figure 4.31 Shirley Temple clothing for young girls. Note the ski wear, similar to adult styles. *Sears, Roebuck & Co. Catalog* (1935). *Everyday Fashions of the Thirties* as pictured in *Sears Catalogs* (New York: Dover Publications, Inc., 1986), 77.

Figure 4.32 Selection of styles for children from youth to adolescence. *Delineator*, July 1936, 42.

though young boys might wear versions of men's suits for dress, but with shorts rather than trousers. Knickers and hats were common for boys, and sailor styles continued to be popular for both boys and girls (Figure 4.32).

Young girl's dresses were generally short, often with full puffed sleeves, and smocking placed on a high yoke. Toddlers wore rompers or **creepers**, one-piece play clothing that buttoned at the back or between the legs for changing diapers. Both boys and girls also donned a variety of sweater styles—pullover, cardigan, or sleeveless vests—for play or casual wear along with jeans. Children continued to play dress-up as cowboys, aviators, or other cartoon figures and also in the costumes of their favorite movie or radio stars, such as Buck Rogers.

By adolescence, styles were variations on adult clothing despite a focus on the teen years in other aspects of popular culture. For girls, waistline emphasis followed the styles of women's clothing, as did the hemline and skirt fullness, getting fuller by the end of the 1930s (see Figure 4.32). In 1935, skirt lengths for coeds began to inch upward. For adolescent boys, long pants were worn with jacket styles similar

to those worn by men. The exception for boys was a tendency toward a trouser with wider flare at the hem.

Oxfords or saddle shoes were worn by both boys and girls and high-top tennis shoes for play. Strapped Mary Janes were popularly worn with dresses for girls. The newly emerging teen market offered loafers or saddle shoes with socks.

Hair and Grooming

Despite the Great Depression, style, product, and technology changes meant that beauty shops thrived. Longer hairstyles began to replace the short, bobbed hair of the 1920s. Even with longer hair, women curled their hair or created deeply sculpted, even, close-to-the-head **marcelled** waves with the assistance of permanents or electric curling irons (see Figures 4.17 and 4.21). Platinum blonde became a popular shade, influenced by actress Jean Harlow. In 1933, John Breck revolutionized the marketing of shampoo by introducing products for different hair types: dry, normal, and oily.

Women began to adopt dark-red lipstick and nail polish,

applying powder and rouge in the style of their favorite film stars. Some adopted a thin, arched eyebrow, achieved by plucking out most of the natural hair and replacing it with a thin, penciled line (see Figure 4.16). New products included tape depilatories, cream mascara, and liquid or semiliquid foundations. False eyelashes were advertised in *Vogue* in 1931. Not all cosmetics were harmless; indeed, some caused blindness or serious skin eruptions. Public outcry precipitated the inclusion of cosmetics in the Food and Drug Act in 1938. In addition to forbidding hazardous materials, the legislation prohibited adulteration or false and misleading claims in advertising.

Clean-shaven faces were the rule for men throughout the 1930s, a style supported by the introduction of the first electric razor in 1931 by Schick. Despite the cost (at least $15—a significant amount in the 1930s), it was an immediate success and served to changed more than just grooming habits. Hotels now had to provide an electrical outlet in the bathroom, as did trains and planes. By the end of the 1930s, women could also shave with electric razors marketed directly for them, saving the mess of waxing or depilatory creams.

Women's oldest grooming problem, management of menstruation, became a bit easier with the introduction of tampons in 1935, under the Wix and Tampax brands. Long-used therapeutically, tampons helped to make the wearing of clinging dresses easier. Makers of sanitary pads also responded to the new dress styles by creating pads with tapered ends.

Summary

The worldwide depression of the 1930s dramatically affected the lives of most people in some way, and it changed the course of twentieth-century history. As investment in the U.S. economy shrank, jobs disappeared, with an average of one out of five people unemployed. Sometimes because and sometimes despite the economic crisis, there were significant changes that affected everyday life in America. The movies, a frequent escape from the reality of everyday life, influenced fashions in both the United States and Paris. Although it may appear at first glance that lengthened hemlines occurred simultaneously with the stock market crash, longer lengths along with a natural waistline began to evolve in late 1928 through 1929. The economic problems also provided the impetus for the American fashion industry to begin to support and promote its own designers. As the decade drew to a close, this set the stage for the U.S. industry to rise to the challenge when put center stage during World War II.

Suggested Readings

Chierichetti, David. *Hollywood Costume Design*. New York: Harmony Books, 1976.

Friedel, Robert. *Zipper: An Exploration in Novelty*. New York: W.W. Norton & Co., Inc., 1994.

Kennedy David M. *Freedom from Fear: The American People in Depression and War, 1929–1945*. Oxford: Oxford University Press, 1999.

Kirke, Betty. Madeleine *Vionnet*. Toyko: Kyuryudo Art Publishing Co., Ltd., 1991.

Liberman, Alexander, and Polly Devlin. *Vogue Book of Fashion Photography: 1919–1979*. New York: The Condé Nast Publications, Ltd., 1979.

Marketti, Sara and Parsons, Jean, "Design Piracy and Self Regulation: The Fashion Originators Guild of America, 1932 to 1941," *Clothing and Textiles Research Journal*, 24 (3), 214–228, 2006.

Martin, Richard. *Surrealism and Fashion*. New York: Rizzoli, 1990.

McElvaine, Robert S. *The Great Depression: America, 1929–1941*. New York: Random House, 1993.

Milbank, Caroline Rennolds. *New York Fashion: The Evolution of American Style*. New York: Harry N. Abrams, 1989.

Steele, Valerie. *Women of Fashion: Twentieth-Century Designers*. New York: Rizzoli, 1991.

Young, William H., and Nancy K. Young. *The 1930s*. Westport, CT: Greenwood Press, 2002.

CHAPTER 5

1939 -

	1939	1940	1941	1942
U.S. Events and Trends	World War II breaks out in Europe	Franklin D. Roosevelt elected president for a third term Nazis occupy Paris	United States enters war	WPB Limitation Orders regulate apparel and many other products

U.S. Fashions	Nylon hosiery on the market Women: full-skirt silhouette, introduced in Paris	Nylon bras and girdles on the market Many French couture houses close American designers come to fore	Women: clingy silhouettes	Men: narrow, plain suits Zoot suits for some young men Women: slim suits, broad shoulders Surge in slacks sold to women

-1946

U.S. birthrate regains
pre-1930 level

1943

D-day Normandy

Roosevelt reelected
for a fourth term

1944

Roosevelt dies; Harry
S. Truman becomes
president

1945

Nylon available in
small amounts

War ends in Europe,
then Japan

Wartime consumer
controls end

Deemed start of
"baby boom"

1946

Softer shapes,
narrower shoulders

Theatre de la Mode
comes to America

Fashion on Duty

World War II dominated life, including fashion, between 1939 and 1946, even in the United States, which was spared attack on its mainland. Europe, however, suffered extensive devastation and depopulation. Most countries of Asia and parts of North Africa also endured the agonies of warfare.

War came on gradually. The rise of Adolph Hitler brought Germany under a totalitarian regime, one that persecuted and killed minorities: Jews, Gypsies, and anyone who protested the curtailment of human rights. Having consolidated power at home by 1934, Hitler built up Germany's military might and proceeded to take over neighboring countries, including Austria and Czechoslovakia in 1938–1939. England, France, and other free European countries dithered until Germany marched into Poland on September 1, 1939, precipitating war. Italy, under dictator Benito Mussolini, had invaded Ethiopia in 1935 and allied itself with Germany the following year. Japan, which overran northern China in 1937, continued its expansionist warfare in southeast Asia and formally joined the Axis powers in 1940.

At first, the United States held back, as it had done in World War I, because isolationist sentiments were strong. President Franklin Roosevelt and other alert leaders became increasingly disturbed by political and military developments in Europe, but they hesitated to call for rearming the country. Once war actually broke out in Europe in 1939, English Prime Minister Winston Churchill relentlessly campaigned for American assistance. The beleaguered British, holding out against the German armed forces after the Continent had been conquered, urgently needed arms from America. By 1940, German bombing had begun to demolish large parts of English cities, so food, clothing, and other relief materials were sent, as well as ships, antiaircraft guns, and planes under a Lend–Lease bill that relieved Britain of paying immediately for all supplies. The Germans marched into Paris in June 1940, occupying the city and, particularly critical for the U.S. fashion industry, cutting off any information from the Paris couture.

Preparedness became the new watchword in the United States, too. Military buildup began in August 1939,[1] accelerating through 1940. The first-ever peacetime draft was passed in September 1940, by which time 70 Reserve Officers' Training Corps units were in operation on Land Grant college campuses.[2] Ultimately, 15 million Americans, both volunteers and draftees, served in the armed forces. Even fashion magazines showed most of the men at social gatherings in uniform, beginning well before America's declaration of war and continuing throughout the war years (Figure 5.1). Preparedness efforts paled beside the vast expansion of rearmament in fall 1941, when the federal gov-

Figure 5.1 Men in uniform at a wedding. *Vogue*, January 1, 1943, inside front cover.

ernment was spending $42 million *per day* on defense.[3] Note that this occurred *before* Japan bombed the American fleet anchored in Pearl Harbor, Hawaii. From that day, December 7, 1941, through August 15, 1945, when Japan surrendered, the American economy and much of U.S. society was dedicated to the war effort.

Americans fought the war on two fronts: in Asia and the Pacific Islands and in Europe, in alliance with the British, Canadians, Australians, New Zealanders, Free French, and members of other European resistance movements.[4] At first, there were more defeats than victories, but breakthroughs came with success in the battles of Coral Sea and Midway in the Pacific in spring 1942. Hard campaigns were fought against the Germans in North Africa in 1942–1943, after which the fighting continued into Sicily and Italy. In June 1944, Allied armed forces under the supreme command of General Dwight Eisenhower succeeded in invading the European mainland in Normandy, driving back the Germans. However, the fighting was far from over, extending for almost another year in Europe. Victory in Europe (V-E Day) came on May 8, 1945. Bloody battles in the Pacific Islands continued. Only with the dropping of two atomic bombs on the cities of Hiroshima and Nagasaki was Japan forced to surrender on V-J Day. Franklin D. Roosevelt did not live to see that victory, dying from a cerebral hemorrhage on April 12, 1945. Vice President Harry S Truman succeeded to the presidency and carried forward the wartime leadership of his predecessor.

The Wartime Economy

As soon as American factories started to supply England and the other Allied countries with guns, ships, and tanks, the Great Depression began to recede. The idle factories and workers probably made the rapid conversion to military production possible. Accelerating the manufacture of arms for the United States as well as for Europe meant that work was available to almost anyone who wanted it. About 2 million women took jobs in factories, welding battleships, tanks, and airplanes. Another 17 million worked in offices, on farms, and in service occupations. Minorities, who had had little access to well-paying jobs in manufacturing, gained new opportunities in armaments plants, partly due to a presidential executive order, issued on June 25, 1941, outlawing segregation in defense industries and government. Wages often rose to large multiples of what African American women and men had previously earned in service work, farming, or unskilled labor. Teenagers also found employment, often part-time jobs after school, at tasks left undone by those who entered full-time factory work or the armed services. Some 14- to 19-year-olds dropped out of school indefinitely to earn full-time wages. Many men of all races took blue-collar positions; some white men left office jobs for factory labor. The average hours worked lengthened from 40.6 hours in 1941 to 45.2 hours in 1944, and unemployment dropped to 1.2 percent.

To an extent unimaginable today, the federal government regulated what was manufactured, for whom, and at what price. The War Production Board (WPB) took control of all strategic materials in 1942, including most types of metal, natural and synthetic rubber, most textile fibers, other chemicals, and plastics. President Roosevelt's 1942 "shopping list" for arms included 45,000 tanks, 60,000 aircraft, and similar numbers of trucks and guns. Each tank, for example, had 30,000 parts—placing unprecedented pressure on the supply of both raw material and labor. The WPB struggled to balance the needs of the military with requirements to keep at least a basic civilian economy functioning.

Trains, trucks, and ships all came under government control at the start of hostilities to ensure that troops and civilian government business were served first. This complicated the already difficult situation for manufacturers, who could not count on receiving supplies when needed or shipping their products to retailers on schedule. To add to the stress, consumers flush with wartime wages besieged retailers for apparel because there were no civilian hard goods, such as autos or washing machines, to buy. Gross weekly wages averaged $25.20 in 1940 and rose to $43.39 in 1945. Recognizing that the pressure of too many dollars chasing too few goods could precipitate dangerous inflation, the Office of Price Administration set prices for each type of item manufactured. Patriotic appeals to buy war bonds or war stamps to help finance the fight were also designed to nudge Americans to save their new-found wealth. As the costs of war mounted, corporate taxes rose steeply, and tax money was withheld from wages for the first time.

Farmers, who had suffered cruelly from the depression and the extreme drought of the 1930s Dust Bowl, enjoyed rapid improvement of their fortunes. Once more the market for crops was stimulated by a needy Europe; huge numbers of soldiers, sailors, and airmen; and a prospering civilian population. Military exemptions for farmers allowed many to stay on the land to bring in the sorely needed crops. Women who were not already participants in family farming joined the Land Army to assist with agricultural tasks and to free able-bodied and willing men for war work in the military or support services.

With consumer incomes far above depression-era levels, scarce foods came under pressure. To contain the problem, the WPB rationed canned goods, coffee, sugar, meat, butter, and all fats, which were used in explosives as well as for food. Gasoline and fuel oils likewise were in short supply relative to demand, so everything possible was done to curb unnecessary driving. Gas and fuel oil were both rationed, as were rubber tires. Use of personal vehicles was restricted, and the speed limit was set at 35 miles per hour nationwide. This draconian measure was needed because tires in the early 1940s wore out far more quickly than do twenty-first-century versions. People simply had to stay at home or in their neighborhoods more, helping local stores prosper more than supermarkets. Families often deferred their vacations for the duration.

War's Impact on Social Trends

Traditionally, the Baby Boom is said to have begun in 1946, as the soldiers returned home and began families. However, a notable up-tick in the birth rate actually began in 1940, because returning prosperity encouraged Americans to have families. In 1943, the birth rate reached a level not attained since 1927.[5] Besides the growth in numbers, the U.S. population shifted location to centers of factory production. California experienced a major boom, growing by 72 percent during the 1940s. The states of Washington and Oregon grew strongly, too, as did Detroit, Chicago, and Pittsburgh. Communities expanded in those parts of the South with military bases or camps, but, for the most part, the population shifts were from South to North and from East to West. Suburban development can be traced to the early 1940s, clustered around defense plants.[6] Willow Run,

Figure 5.2 Bobby soxers in sweaters, skirts, slacks, and lumberjack shirts. *Life*, December 11, 1944, 97, ©Time & Life Pictures/Getty Images.

Figure 5.3 Zoot suit with high-waist trousers and oversize jacket and tie. *Life*, September 21, 1942, 44, ©Time & Life Pictures/Getty Images.

near Detroit, became the fastest-growing city in the nation. By the war's end, about 20 percent of Americans had moved to another state or region, many of them permanently.

Wartime marriages were often conducted in haste, on a brief furlough or before the groom shipped out. The marriage rate for 1942 was the highest it had been since 1920. Women struggled to keep up a home, often in fairly cramped quarters, and sometimes to care for an infant. Most women with small children did not enter paid work, but eked out a living on their soldier-husband's paychecks. Some soldiers never returned, and their wives coped with widowhood or remarried. In other cases, reunited couples could not adjust, and marriages failed. Physical separation eroded some unions; others dissolved because men who had experienced combat changed in ways not easily accommodated by women insulated from the warfront. Divorces, difficult to arrange or finance during the war, were deferred until peacetime, causing the divorce rate to spike as soon as peace arrived. Americans of Japanese origin were forced into internment camps.

Teenagers became a major force in U.S. society. Their sheer numbers and growing economic power helped propel teen preferences in dress, music, dance, and movies into the mainstream of American style. Fashions that appealed to teenagers included denim dungarees, thick bobby socks, and oversize shirts, the latter items popular with girls and boys (Figure 5.2). Walter Annenberg introduced *Seventeen* magazine in 1944 both to track and shape adolescent girls' tastes. Slumber parties, beach parties, soda-shop dates, and pep rallies all became part of teen socializing. Not all teenage trends were equally innocuous: juvenile crime burgeoned (including girls and some preteen boys), partly due to the disruption of family life in wartime and lessened supervision by adults.

Some teenage and older boys, especially blacks and Hispanics, adopted **zoot suits** (Figure 5.3). The zoot suit was, however, more than just a fashion statement. The term probably evolved out of urban jazz culture in the late 1930s. The style consisted of an exaggerated jacket with oversize padded shoulders, loose trousers sharply tapered at the ankle, and dangling chains, described in the slang of the day as "a killer diller coat with a drape shape, reat-pleats, and shoulders padded like a lunatic's cell."[7] In 1942, the WPB banned the manufacture of zoot suits, because of the excess amount of

Figure 5.4 Coeds at Howard University, showing more dignified campus trends. *Life*, November 18, 1946, 111, ©Time & Life Pictures/Getty Images.

fabric used. Riots broke out in Los Angeles in the summer of 1943 as servicemen from local military bases attacked Latino males who wore zoot suits. For some, the suit had come to represent the juvenile delinquency that was on the increase during the war years. A central issue in the riots was patriotism, but they also had racial implications.

Literature of the era mirrored the stresses of the times, with major works by Ernest Hemingway (*For Whom the Bell Tolls*) and Katherine Anne Porter (*Pale Horse, Pale Rider*). James Hilton published the poignant *Random Harvest*, which neatly bridged the years between World Wars I and II in England. Pearl S. Buck produced *Dragon Seed* about China. Thrillers in the fiction realm included Daphne Du-Maurier's *Rebecca* and *Green Dolphin Street*. Playwrights often turned successful novels into theater scripts or movies.

Nonfiction was dominated by firsthand accounts of the war, written by newspaper reporters, military officers, and other observers. War correspondent Ernie Pyle, in particular, won acclaim for his columns detailing the daily lives of frontline soldiers. Two influential works on sociopolitical topics include Frederick Hayek's *The Road to Serfdom*, a treatise promoting democracy and free markets; and Gun-

nar Myrdal's *An American Dilemma*, unsparingly evaluating the racial divide in the United States. Recognizing perhaps an ideal time to offer advice to millions of new parents, Dr. Benjamin Spock issued the first edition of his classic *Baby and Child Care* in 1946.

Science, Technology, and Medicine in Wartime

Americans directed their powers of invention largely to the war effort, for armaments and other gear needed by troops and support personnel. The United States was the first to develop a nuclear bomb, and it belatedly but effectively collaborated with the British in improving radar. Civilian inventions did not cease, but were definitely delayed in commercial development. Television, which had emerged as a viable medium in the late 1930s, had begun to carry commercial programming (including occasional fashion shows) in July 1941. Commercial schedules were canceled in 1942, and television was dedicated to defense uses, such as training programs for air-raid wardens. Food technology improved, but this, too, was centered on feeding the troops. Spam became a staple meat,[8] and foods were freeze-dried. Frozen foods—orange juice, vegetables, and poultry—came on the civilian market by the end of 1945.

Major trends for the future grew from wartime efforts to shrink electronic components, harness the atom, and apply radar, which eventually yielded microwave cooking. To meet wartime needs for storing data and running mathematical calculations, scientists developed the first huge, cumbersome versions of the computer. The war affected university programs of research even more broadly, because collaboration with the federal government on priority projects built a foundation for the expansion of science and technology on postwar campuses. This was further promoted by the peacetime influx of former soldiers, sailors, and pilots into colleges, made possible by educational grants provided in the 1944 GI Bill. The war disrupted college life, and even the Ivy League schools found it expedient to run classes around the calendar in order to shorten a degree program from 4 to 3 years. Both men and women took advantage of accelerated college courses to enter technical fields vital to defense.

Once hostilities ended, college populations began to swell with GI-Bill scholars. Young women on campus dressed up more to win the attention of male collegians. Various styles of tailored pants provided an alternative to skirts for casual occasions, as noted on the young woman at Howard University, an elite African American institution (Figure 5.4).

Medicine took major leaps forward between 1939 and

1946, notably in the development of antibiotics. Penicillin, discovered in England and first tested in 1929, the sulfa drugs (1935, Germany), and Aureomycin (1944, United States) were used to quell infections from wounds and battleground living conditions. These became available to combat scarlet fever, rheumatic fever, and tuberculosis when peace arrived. Improvements in the transfusion of whole blood and plasma saved not only soldiers' lives but also those of people far from the fighting. Local anesthesia likewise translated from battlefront to dental and civilian medical use postwar. Wartime pressures on hospital capacity brought changes in practice, notably shortening hospital stays after childbirth and surgery, sometimes helping to speed recovery times.

Nylon, released in late 1939 for women's hosiery and applied to bras and girdles in 1940–1941 (Figure 5.5), was largely withdrawn from civilian apparel to be used for parachute canopies, cordage, and bagging for food and ammunition. The few companies that had acquired a significant supply of nylon yarns or fabrics before America entered the war managed to produce a small number of nylon bras through 1943 and 1944. People who had nylon hosiery and underwear were asked to sacrifice it for reuse in military products, but not everyone complied, even when movie stars such as the pinup-girl Betty Grable set an example by publicly donating stockings.

Retailing and Manufacturing

With millions of men and women in arms, the federal government required vast quantities of uniforms, undergarments, and boots, not to mention tents, rucksacks, mosquito netting, and the myriads of other textile products that soldiers and sailors needed in wartime. To preserve both materials and factory capacity to make such products, the WPB issued regulations in April 1942 governing the styling of factory-made outerwear (L-85) and underwear (L-90).[9] Men's suits could not be made with vests, double-breasted styling, cuffs, or patch pockets. Women's dresses and suits were regulated in length, circumference (sweep) of the skirt, types of trims, lengths of jackets for suits, and many other details (Figure 5.6).

The WPB rationed shoes, meaning that they issued to civilians coupons to purchase a maximum of three pairs of shoes per year, regardless of their clothing budget. Athletic shoes—called sneakers at the time—became almost unobtainable because of the shortage of rubber. Most people adhered to these regulations out of a sense of patriotism, but there was a minority who circumvented the law and bought them on the black market. Americans who sewed their own clothes were not covered by limitation orders, but they were

AND NOW, FOUNDATIONS OF NYLON

Nylies BY Formfit

GIRDLES $5 · GIRDLEIERES $7.50

The miracle yarn Lastex plus the magical thread Nylon now combined by Formfit in girdle and Girdleiere styles which you will be proud to wear. They're lighter, softer, firmer and will wear longer. Ask for Nylies by Formfit. At the better stores.

still exhorted to make-do and mend, meaning recycle old clothing in order to conserve materials for the war effort. Compared with the utility garments imposed by the British government on its people[10] and the severe deprivations of the French and other continental Europeans, American apparel sacrifices were minimal.

Manufacturing and retailing adapted to the crisis as best they could. Producers learned how to manage a limited supply of labor and cope with shortages of materials; how

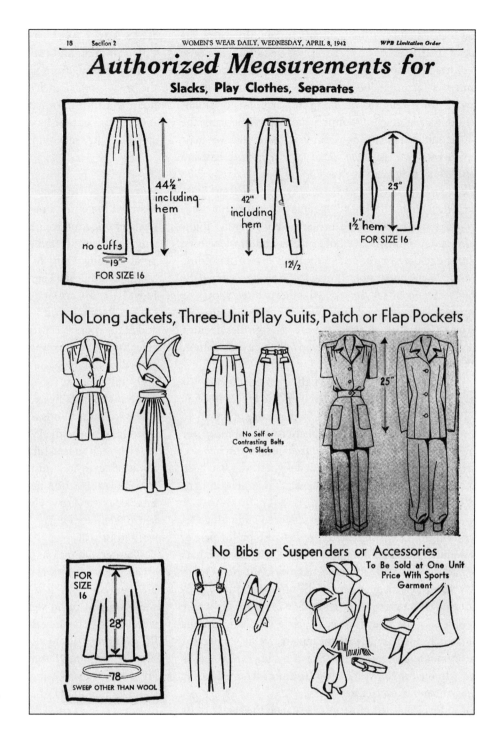

Figure 5.5 (OPPOSITE) Nylon girdle and bra. *Mademoiselle*, October 1940, 195.

Figure 5.6 (RIGHT) L-85 images of permitted and forbidden features. *Women's Wear Daily*, April 8, 1942. Courtesy of Fairchild Archives.

to do each job efficiently; and how to meet government specifications on contract goods. The latter technique carried over into the practice of manufacturing according to technical design specs after the war ended.

Companies that made soft goods found it difficult to recruit and retain labor because workers could get much higher wages in munitions factories. Working directly in companies that supported the war effort also provided a feeling of contributing directly to victory, no small con-

sideration for people who had loved ones on active duty in Europe and Asia. One strategy that helped some apparel producers survive was to obtain a government contract, making products for the armed services in lieu of civilian goods. This took interesting forms, such as the production of paratroopers' carriers for messenger pigeons, which the bra company Maiden Form designed and made in the shape of a small, laced sling.[11]

Retail advertising took up patriotic themes and messages

that focused on the store itself rather than promoting the sale of specific goods. In part, this was a necessary response to shortages of apparel. No retailer wanted to promise customers what might be impossible to obtain. Most ads carried some plug for investing in war bonds or small-denomination defense stamps, which gave Americans the opportunity to lend their government money that would be repaid with interest once victory was achieved. Fashion copy in elite magazines such as *Esquire* prompted readers to give blood—so necessary to saving lives on the front lines. Retailers with insufficient salespeople resorted to more self-service options, even in the formerly labor-intensive foundations departments that sold girdles and bras. Women working in defense industries took advantage of evening hours in department stores and in some cases welcomed the greater degree of self-service, which expedited shopping errands. A few astute retailers even sent fitters into the factories to help women select the bras and girdles deemed necessary to good posture and to avoiding physical fatigue in production jobs.

One group in apparel undeniably benefited when war enveloped Europe: American designers. No longer in thrall to Paris, U.S. designers emerged from relative obscurity to become symbols of American creativity triumphing over adversity.[12] *Vogue* and *Harper's Bazaar* initially carried features on American collections and designers who had been active in the industry prior to the war. Other new designers debuted during the war years.

Original apparel styles had to adhere to Limitation Orders, but this only stimulated inventiveness on the part of new and established designers (Figure 5.7). Because hats and accessories were not subjected to a Limitation Order, they were often the mediums of the utmost creativity, substituting straw, cloth, and cellophane for relatively scarce wool felt. In the face of the crisis, New York labor unions and management undertook the remarkable step of pooling their funds to promote New York as a fashion capital. Labels proclaiming the New York Dress Institute identified locally designed and manufactured dresses.

California gained impetus to broaden the extent of its apparel industry, which had begun in response to the needs of film stars for off-screen wardrobes and the widespread desire among Californians for clothing that accommodated the Sunshine State's outdoorsy, informal lifestyle (Figure 5.8). European fashion was so alien to the West Coast milieu that its designers were quite willing to strike out on their own, becoming especially successful with swimwear and casual fashions. Smaller apparel industries thrived in Boston, Philadelphia, Cleveland, Kansas City, St. Louis, Dallas, and Chicago. Chicago-native Mainbocher resettled in New York after closing his successful Paris atelier at the start of the war.

Arts and Entertainment

Entertainment and the arts served war aims, sometimes with prompting from the Office of Wartime Information, the propaganda branch of the federal government. The Office of Wartime Information endeavored to keep up civilian morale, discourage loose talk that could be used by Axis spies, and generally support the troops.

Movies and Theater

Many of the entertainers who flourished during this period became American icons, enjoying long-lived or recurring popularity. Notable examples are the crooners Frank Sinatra, Bing Crosby, and Perry Como; songbirds Jo Stafford and Peggy Lee; and Hollywood stars Bette Davis, Judy Garland, Cary Grant, Gary Cooper, Humphrey Bogart, Lauren Bacall, Ingrid Bergman, Gene Kelly, John Wayne, and many more. Numerous male stars volunteered for service; Jimmy Stewart was a decorated pilot. Others, such as comedian Bob Hope and actress Marlene Dietrich (Figure 5.9), did their bit for the war effort by entertaining the troops, even in camps very near to the frontline fighting.[13] A few sold war bonds, including Carole Lombard, a very chic film star who died when her plane crashed on a return flight from a successful tour promoting bonds. President Roosevelt gave her a posthumous medal as "the first woman to be killed in action in the defense of her country. . . ."[14] English-born Cary Grant (Figure 5.10) devoted his $137,000 salary for *The Man Who Came to Dinner* to relief work in Britain.

Theater and film stars of this era were strong individuals and very often style setters. Marlene Dietrich and Carole Lombard, as well as Katharine Hepburn, showed that some women could wear slacks effectively. Trendsetters with varying signature styles were Latin beauty Dolores Del Rio, southern sophisticate Tallulah Bankhead, polished blonde Constance Bennett, girlish Claudette Colbert, and European woman-of-mystery Greta Garbo. The younger set could look to Judy Garland and Elizabeth Taylor as images of beauty. Men copied Fred Astaire and Cary Grant for debonair style, Jimmy Stewart for clean-cut boyish looks, and Clark Gable or John Wayne for rugged, outdoorsy panache. Among society elites, the Duke and Duchess of Windsor retained their image of international sophistication, but their popularity lost its luster due to their open tolerance of German Nazism.

Films, as well as their actors, resonated with the public. Understandably, many movies centered on wartime themes, including the masterpiece *Casablanca*. Lighter subjects included the comic *Road*[15] pictures of Crosby, Hope, and Dorothy Lamour; Bing Crosby's *Bells of St. Mary*; and Dis-

Figure 5.7 (RIGHT, TOP) Claire
McCardell tailoring a dress, July
26, 1940. © Bettmann/Corbis.

Figure 5.8 (ABOVE) California style
for men: contrasting jacket with
wide-legged slacks and boldly
patterned tie. *Men's Wear:
75 Years of Fashion*, New York:
Fairchild, June 1965, 133.

Figure 5.9 (RIGHT, BOTTOM) Marlene
Dietrich in "uniform." Everett
Collection.

Figure 5.10 Cary Grant and Joan Fontaine in *Suspicion*, 1941. Note the back fullness in her jacket. Everett Collection.

Figure 5.11 Dizzy Gillespie's All Stars. Note the zoot suits on these musicians. Frank Driggs Collection.

ney classics, including *Pinocchio* and *Song of the South*. Thrillers by Alfred Hitchcock (*Notorious, Suspicion*—see Figure 5.10) vied with feel-good flicks (*It's a Wonderful Life*). Of course the biggest movie in cost, length, and fame was *Gone with the Wind*, completed in 1939, recalling a traumatic war for Americans as they stood on the brink of an even more sweeping conflict. To a modest extent *Gone with the Wind* confirmed fashions for full-skirted ball gowns and wide-brimmed hats. On the contrary, the notionally 1860s costumes bore strong traces of late 1930s aesthetic. At the end of the war the acclaimed film *The Best Years of Our Lives* (1946) detailed the trauma experienced by many veterans as they attempted to readjust to civilian life.

Music

Many creative streams fed popular music during this period—jazz, big bands, theater and movie music, ballads, and Latin American dance. Vocal jazz flourished with exponents such as Sarah Vaughn, Dinah Washington, and Billie Holiday, many of whom sang with bands led by Lionel Hampton and Duke Ellington. Star instrumentalists included the lightening-fingered pianist Art Tatum, saxophonist Charlie Parker (Figure 5.11), pianist Thelonious

Monk, and drummer Gene Krupa. The New York Metropolitan Opera House staged its first jazz concert in 1944. Americans swayed to the melodies of big bands headed by Glenn Miller, Jimmy and Tommy Dorsey, Bennie Goodman, and Artie Shaw. At the peak of his career, Miller joined the army in 1942 and died in a plane crash in 1944.

Popular vocalists such as the Andrews Sisters, Dinah Shore, Jo Stafford, Peggy Lee, Bing Crosby, and Frank Sinatra got started singing with bands and then launched solo careers. Much of the repertoire was romantic, tinged with the sadness of wartime separations, but cowboy ballads and humorous novelties enlivened the mix, with upbeat selections emphasized in shows for servicemen. Given the giants of lyrics and score working in the American theater in these years, it is no surprise that songs from *Oklahoma* and *Annie Get Your Gun* topped the pop charts, along with "Over the Rainbow" from the film *The Wizard of Oz*. Classical music emphasized American composers and themes, many of which became patriotic standards, such as Aaron Copland's "Fanfare for the Common Man." Dance during the war years became eclectic—standards like the fox trot; Latin styles, including the rumba and samba; and the jitterbug (Figure 5.12), a variant of the Lindy hop. These fast dances traced their origins to the late 1920s and early 1930s.

Figure 5.12 Jitterbugging couple. Note his jacket and wide pants. ©Time Life Pictures/Getty Images.

Figure 5.13 Golfers in slacks and T-shirts and sport shirt, New Jersey, circa 1940. Author's collection.

Sports

In the run-up to World War II, major popular spectator sports included boxing, whose reigning star was Joe Lewis, the youngest heavyweight champion in history. Baseball commanded a huge following and made celebrities of Joe DiMaggio and Ted Williams. Many professional sports went into cold storage during the war years because players enlisted in the military, allowing college football to achieve ascendancy. Baseball revived strongly after the war, with the colorful talents of Yogi Berra, Bob Feller, and Warren Spahn. In 1946, Jackie Robinson broke the color line in baseball when he joined a Montreal team that fed talent to the Brooklyn Dodgers, a National League team. Robinson soon became the first African American on a major-league team. Golf had a postwar revival, too, and a hero in Ben Hogan. Golf attire changed from knickers and knitted vests to sport shirts or T-shirts and slacks (Figure 5.13).

Visual Arts and Design

Defying the antimodern artistic tastes of the dictators, American arts embraced abstraction and expressionism during the 1940s. Sculpture was dominated by Alexander Calder—famous for mobiles and "stabiles"—Isamu Nogu-

chi, and Jacques Lipschitz. Louise Nevelson began to achieve prominence in 1946. Painting embraced the geometrics of Mark Rothko; recent European immigrants Piet Mondrian and Fernand Léger also received substantial publicity. A freeform, expressive, nonrepresentational style called abstract expressionism had powerful exponents in Jackson Pollock, Arshile Gorky, and Willem de Kooning. It is now considered to be the first truly American art movement of worldwide importance. Museums held numerous exhibitions of recent artists, sprinkled among shows featuring Americana, victory themes, and celebrations of the arts of Allied countries.

New York's 1939 world's fair World of Tomorrow projected modernism in domestic life, but the war sadly put those dreams on a seven-year hold. Nonetheless, major architects of the twentieth century designed landmark buildings over those eight years: Walter Gropius, Marcel Breuer, Eero and Eliel Saarinen, Ludwig Mies Van der Rohe, Richard Neutra, and Albert Kahn all had major successes. Many of these men had left Europe in anticipation of the outbreak of war and applied their talents in their adopted country.

Fashion photographer Louise Dahl-Wolfe captured the lean look of the era. Fashion photography during the war tended to be more restrained, and fashion magazines frequently published articles on women's wartime roles. Conditions differed in each major fashion center. *French Vogue* studios closed in 1940, but things were less restrictive for publishers and fashion artists in the United States, where the editorial mood was somewhat less restrained. Dahl-Wolfe was one of the most influential photographers of the period. She did her first black-and-white photos for *Harper's Bazaar* in 1936 and first color photos in 1937. She was a master of contrast and lighting in black and white and an innovator in the use of color photography for fashion. Other influential photographers of the time were John Rawlings and Horst P. Horst at *Vogue*, although Horst spent part of the war years as a photographer for the army.

Fashion Influences

Wartime disruptions shifted the balance of influence in U.S. fashion from the formerly dominant French designers to a group of emerging creators of a distinctly American style, as seen in Traina-Norell's creations, shown in Figure 5.14.

France

The Germans entered and occupied Paris beginning in June 1940, which created the initial perception that there would be a creative vacuum in the entire fashion industry. The haute couture had been the center of fashion for decades, and, at the end of the 1930s, the couture houses became more commercial as some even began to produce less expensive ready-to-wear styles or to authorize more designs for direct copying. When the Nazis arrived in Paris, they chose to protect the luxury trades but attempted to move the industry to Berlin or Vienna. Lucien Lelong, president of the Chambre Syndicale, managed to intercede to keep the couture industry in Paris, but it was forced to operate in a very different way and for different customers.

Unable to produce clothing for their foreign clients, French designers retained a few of their French and German customers, wives and mistresses of fascist leaders, and some who made their money on the black market. More than a hundred couture houses managed to stay open to some degree. Jacques Fath, Nina Ricci, Lelong, Patou, Lanvin, and Marcel Rochas, to name a few, continued to do business in Paris. Mme. Grès remained open, although the authorities closed her house temporarily after she showed her entire line in patriotic French tricolor. Molyneux returned to England, and Schiaparelli came to the United States, although both houses remained open in Paris. Chanel closed her house and spent the duration of the war

in the Ritz hotel, much of the time as the companion of a Nazi secret-service man.

The evolution of French fashion during the war years was very different from styles in Britain or the United States. Although textile and other supplies were rationed, French designers continued to evolve the silhouette that was shown in 1939 and 1940 with a fuller skirt, wider hips, and smaller waist. The Victorian influences prevalent in Paris just before occupation continued, especially with bustles and other back interest. News of Paris fashion leaked out only once during the occupation, in 1943. The first real fashion reports began in August 1944, shortly after the liberation of Paris. The elaborateness of French fashion surprised and shocked British and American readers, and the French designers quickly began to adapt styles to reflect the constraints of rationing and other restrictions. However, these styles were not particularly successful. In an attempt to publicize their designs and reestablish their reputation, in 1945 couture designers created a touring exhibition of fashion dolls called the Théatre de la Mode. The show consisted of 12 scenes designed by famous artists, with wire dolls dressed in fashions, shoes, and jewelry from the couture houses.[16] It opened in Paris in March 1945 and traveled to major European cities and the United States when the war ended. The exhibit was enormously successful and was widely covered by the U.S. fashion press.[17]

U.S. Industry and Designers

U.S. designers gained an opportunity to display their talents and their particularly American approach to design after Paris was occupied by the Germans. Many of these designers had been working unheralded for years and were well prepared to step into the limelight. A few Americans designed for the custom market, but the majority worked in the ready-to-wear industry and could quickly meet the challenges of working within the L-85 limits. For many, their strength was in what we now define as classic American sportswear, clothing that was easy to wear and modern. Designers who best represent this style include Claire McCardell, Tina Leser, Mildred Orrick, and Tom Brigance, who will be discussed along with other designers of the period.

Claire McCardell's tragically early death in 1958 cut off the career of one of the most original American designers. She began her design studies in 1927 at the Parsons School of Design, first in New York and then in Paris, and worked initially as both a model and sketcher. Designer Richard Turk hired McCardell as his design assistant in 1929, and, when he sold his business to Townley Frocks in 1931, McCardell went with him. Turk died soon afterward, and Mc-

Figure 5.14 Traina-Norell dress showing end-of-war waist cinching, predating Dior's New Look. *Vogue*, February 1, 1945, 149, John Rawlings/*Vogue* ©1945 Condé Nast Publications Inc.

Figure 5.15 Claire McCardell suit. Note the curvy silhouette and use of stripes. *Vogue*, September 1, 1946, 67.

Cardell assumed his job as head designer. She had her first big design hit with a simple and easy-to-wear dress dubbed The Monastic. Unfortunately, it was also easy to copy. When Townley went out of business shortly thereafter, McCardell worked for Hattie Carnegie for two years, returning to Townley when he reopened in 1940, this time with her name on the label with Townley.

Her trademark was simplicity of shape, informal fabrics, and practical solutions to the problems of everyday dressing. In the war years she focused on play clothes and dresses rather than on the more masculine suits of the period. McCardell converted denim, mattress ticking, gingham, and jersey into impressive shapes. Her **popover dress**, a wrap style intended for busy women faced with extra household duties during the war, was a major hit in 1942 and remained a classic. A one-piece "diaper-style" bathing suit, bloomer-like playsuits, **dirndl skirts**, **tube tops**, and bareback summer dresses all gained lasting popularity. McCardell was also an exponent of **ballerina slippers** and wool tights—the

latter a boon to women faced with a dearth of nylon and silk hosiery during the war years. Her L-85–conforming styles still managed to look soft. McCardell designed the Civil Defense[18] uniforms used during the war. With the return of peace, McCardell experimented with fuller silhouettes (Figure 5.15).

Philadelphia-born **Tina Leser** began her fashion career with her own retail shop in Honolulu, selling her original designs. In 1940 she went to New York on a buying trip, where she showed her design for a playsuit to Saks Fifth Avenue, whose buyer responded with a large order. During the 1940s she designed sportswear and separates, often ethnically influenced, both for her own New York business (1941–1943) and for the New York manufacturer Edwin H. Foreman. She was also known for her bathing suits and other beach clothing. She received a Coty Award in 1945 for her "originality in the design of playclothes."[19] Coty, a fragrance company, sponsored awards to talented American designers as chosen by the Council of Fashion Critics. The first such award, in 1943, went to another emerging talent, **Norman Norell,** who is profiled in Chapter 6.

Mildred Orrick was another designer known for her skill in creating easy-to-wear sportswear. She was born in Virginia and studied at Parsons School of Design in New York. During the war, Orrick created the idea of leotard styles, an idea that was subsequently credited to McCardell. By 1945 she was designing under her own name and creating a variety of inventive sportswear styles, including shirtwaists, sundresses, and bathing suits.

Tom Brigance migrated from his native Texas to New York and Paris to study fashion. He began his career selling freelance sketches to French and English fashion houses. In 1939, he went to work as the house designer for Lord & Taylor department store; then he enlisted for service in counterintelligence in World War II. After discharge from the army, he returned to active designing and opened his own business in New York in 1949, specializing in sportswear, including beachwear. Brigance draped sarong-style skirts and wrapped and midriff-baring tops. His fabrics and combinations were often unusual: drapy with crisp; rough with delicate. Informality was a hallmark, very different from the prevailing mood of the late 1940s.

B. H. Wragge (Sydney Wragge) became an especially skillful purveyor of wardrobes with interchangeable components at modest prices. His collections of tops, skirts, pants, two-piece dresses, and coats retained similar shapes from season to season but illustrated different color themes as a way to encourage purchases. He used primarily natural fabrics and interesting prints keyed to his current theme.

Philip Mangone ran a large New York company in the mid-1940s, specializing in wool suits and coats of his own design (Figure 5.16) with fabrics he either created himself or were designed by Pola Stout. His wartime fame was secured by his design of the uniform for the Women's Army Corps (WACs). Dressmaker styles, capes, and **topper**-coats were specialties of Mangone, as was use of fur in trim or linings.

Jo Copeland, the designer for **Patullo,** like many designers who had begun their careers a decade earlier**,** gained recognition in the 1940s. She charted a course independent of the wartime silhouette, keeping to a fitted bodice or short jacket and flaring or draped skirt. She used both natural and manufactured materials skillfully. Her fortés were after-five apparel for dinner or theater and suits for every occasion, but she also designed hats, separates, and evening gowns.

Sophie Gimbel (Sophie of Saks) designed for Saks Fifth Avenue department store, where the Salon Moderne sold only her designs during the war. They remained a core of that department even after the French couture began sending styles to the United States. Gimbel's style tended to for-

Figure 5.16 (LEFT) Dressy coat with fur trim by Philip Mangone. *Vogue,* October 1, 1947, 3.

Figure 5.17 (OPPOSITE, LEFT) Clare Potter halter top and draped skirt. *Vogue,* March 15, 1944, 115, John Rawlings / *Vogue* ©1945 Condé Nast Publications Inc.

Figure 5.18 (OPPOSITE, RIGHT) Adrían suit with geometric details. *Vogue,* March 15, 1944, 8.

mality and often to curvaceous shapes, although not to the exclusion of the broad-shouldered look of the early 1940s.

Designers from earlier decades continued to produce imaginative styles during the war years. **Hattie Carnegie** employed a thousand people in ready-to-wear and custom work during the 1940s. Among the more celebrated members of her design team were Jean Louis and future socialite Pauline Potter. Although little black dresses and simple suits were her specialty, she could also design imaginative daytime and evening wear, such as the wartime pairing of a gold-paillette–trimmed peasant blouse with black velvet skirt or a sequined jumper with an organdy and lace blouse.

A cosmetics innovator, **Germaine Monteil** designed dinner suits, ballerina-length evening dresses, and tailored evening suits.[20] She used prints and beading for decorative effect. Monteil's silhouettes most frequently had fitted bodices and full skirts, although slim skirts were not unknown in her collections.

Clare Potter specialized in sports clothes but ones that could be adapted to dressier occasions by interesting use of materials, as shown in Figure 5.17. Well-cut pants, multicolored outfits, and creative sweaters became Potter trademarks. Like Claire McCardell, she managed a fluid look despite wartime restrictions on yardage in dresses (see Figure 5.17).

After concluding his work for MGM in 1941, **Gilbert Adrían** opened a shop in Beverly Hills, California, where he

Brilliant bars of vermilion on a muted taupe wool suit, with matching helmet

the Wm. H. Block Co.

INDIANAPOLIS

showed both custom-made and ready-to-wear clothing. Adrían proved ingenious at cutting intricate suit designs from geometrically patterned fabrics by Pola Stout; these became signatures of his clothing business (Figure 5.18). He also excelled at cocktail dresses, full-length dinner dresses, and evening gowns. Adrían often designed his own prints, frequently based on animal motifs or with trompe-l'oeil effects. He frequently incorporated into his collections gingham, a fabric he considered quintessentially American. He loved the wide-shouldered look and retained it even after 1946, when most other designers shifted gears. After suffering a heart attack in 1952, Adrían retired.

Fashion Trends

Wartime necessity proved a stimulus to creativity in use of textiles and in apparel design solutions, developments that would continue to affect textiles and fashions after the war.

Textiles

The war created shortages of many textiles, including wool (for uniforms), cotton (for tenting, sacking, all sorts of military uses), nylon (new and valued for strength and durability in cordage, parachute canopies, mosquito netting, and bomber noses), and silk (supplies from Asia cut off). Rayon and cotton blends were used in 1941, even for winter clothes, to take pressure off the supplies of wool. Rubber, both natural and synthetic, remained in tight supply due to its use in jeep and truck tires, parts of tanks, aircraft, and ships.

Nylon yarn first became available in 1939, creating a sensation when used in hosiery; by 1940, bras and girdles made of nylon powernet were marketed (see Figure 5.5). Supplies were curtailed after 1942 but reemerged in 1945, although in quantities far too small to meet demand. Lastex, a synthetic rubber, came in handy for things like belts.

In 1939, Guatemalan and Polynesian prints were in style. In fact, prints assumed prominence throughout the war years, perhaps as a way to stretch supplies of scarce dyestuffs, or as a mask for the flimsy quality of materials. By 1942, shortages of dyes were predicted: only 15 shades of textiles, and also fewer colors of leathers, were to be offered to apparel manufacturers. Beiges and grays became staple colors, and in January 1944 *Vogue* featured ways to use small colorful accessories to enliven black and white outfits.

Women's Styles

In the patriotic mood of the times, magazines urged women to spend carefully and to buy with thought, not wastefully or timidly.[21] Pre–L-85 styles were deemed acceptable to buy as long as they remained available.[22]

Figure 5.19 (LEFT) Balenciaga red satin gown, showing late 1930s full silhouette. *Vogue*, September 15, 1939, 58.

Figure 5.20 (BELOW) Welder in overalls, work boots, gloves, and safety helmet. National Archives.

Dresses and Suits

From 1939 to 1941, the prevailing look was crisp—snugly fitted jackets or bodices and full, often flared skirts. Bustle-like back fullness had a brief spurt of popularity, along with other forms of artful drapery (see Figure 5.10). Daytime skirts just covered the knees, but evening dresses remained long and full, sometimes with knife-pleats or overdrapes. Once war broke out in Europe and defense became an American theme, military motifs gained popularity. A clingier, less crisp look came into fashion in 1941 (Plate 5.1). This incipient softness remained an occasional style, but in general the looks of 1941 to 1946 were structured (Figure 5.18). Square shoulders, slim skirts with slight fullness, and lengths just below the knee represented 1942 style. Various styles of **shirtwaist dresses** were worn. Separates became popular because of their versatility. Women teamed a skirt and blouse with a sweater or jacket. Short jackets proved especially popular.

By 1943, suits were very trim and short; **weskit suits** paired a vest-like component with a long-sleeved dress or a skirt and blouse (see Plate 5.2). Blouses enjoyed a vogue as a means to vary the look of a basic suit, and first-rate designers developed high-style blouses (see Plate 5.1). The pronounced T shapes of 1943—broad shoulders and slim

torsos—remained in fashion through 1945. By 1946, the padded-shoulder look was sharing some of the limelight with more natural shoulder lines, particularly in garments for young women.

Partly inspired by couture examples from the late 1930s, such as the Balenciaga gown shown in Figure 5.19, American designers embraced fuller skirts once L-85 was rescinded in late 1945, although lengths remained just below the knee. Knife-pleats, gathers, and flare returned to daytime dresses and skirts (Figure 5.15). Evening and cocktail styles had not been severely restricted during the war and had been embellished by drapery. One Hattie Carnegie dress with a detachable **"ballet skirt"** had all the elements soon to be crystallized in Christian Dior's "New Look."[23] Similar shapes appeared in various 1946 issues of *Mademoiselle*, a magazine devoted to college students, young marrieds, and career women. Evening dresses of 1946 showed full skirts, with décolletage in back or front. Strapless gowns also made an appearance.

Coats and Other Wraps

Belted coats with slight flare remained in favor throughout the period, but the most typical shape was boxy in both short jackets and full-length **polo coats**. If anything,

Figure 5.21 (BELOW) Two-piece swimsuit in red, white, and blue. *Life*, July 7, 1941, 8, ©Time & Life Pictures/Getty Images.

Figure 5.22 (RIGHT) Girdle and bra. ©Getty Images.

coats became more squared off in 1946. Fur coats and trims on cloth coats took the fashion spotlight as soon as peace arrived.

Sportswear

In 1939, the fashion press featured slacks, both full-length and shortened versions similar to the present-day "Capri" style. By 1942, slacks came into heavy demand, and stage star Jinx Falkenburg was shown in *Vogue* in a slacks suit retailing at $44—not exactly a low-budget purchase for the times, considering that a felt jacket could be obtained for under $10. Less costly slacks sold briskly, with the demand in 1942 up 5- to 10-fold over 1941 levels. Pant wearing was not, however, without controversy. Many college women considered them acceptable for day wear (see Figure 5.4) but not for more formal occasions (see Plate 5.2). Pants were taboo on some college campuses, but on others women students adopted dungarees for comfort, along with other traditionally masculine clothing.[24] **Coveralls** remained largely in the realm of on-the-job attire, required in some armaments factories for safety reasons. **Bib overalls** were the choice for farm work and for some factory workers, such as the trainee welder shown in Figure 5.20.

"Floating," built-in bras offered improved fit in 1939

swimsuits. June 1942 brought swimsuits knitted of spun nylon yarn, costing $6.95 and available in a half-dozen colors. Skirted suits provided options for mature figures. Nylon swimwear, much like nylon undergarments, almost disappeared during the height of the war. An acetate jersey two-piece suit of patriotic red, white, and blue is shown in Figure 5.21. In 1946, a French designer showed the very bare two-piece suit dubbed the **bikini** after the island where the first atomic bomb was tested. This style, however, did not gain wide acceptance in America until the early 1960s.

Throughout the period, **play clothes** were a fashionable category among those who could afford occasion-specific clothing. Cotton shorts with bare midriff tops or halters and one-piece sunsuits populated the back yards and parks of summertime America. Ocean beaches, an obvious place for such styles, carried a measure of menace because there had been several submarine attacks on American oil tankers and merchant ships that were anchored just offshore.

Underwear

Corseting made a bid for return to fashion, to conform women's bodies to the narrow waist and slim hip popular in dresses. Corselets, fairly popular in the 1920s and 1930s, proved less effective than a high-waist corset and uplift bra

(Figure 5.22) in creating this new fashion, sometimes called the Princess or Eugenie silhouette. Foundations of lightweight, drip-dry nylon enjoyed a vogue in 1940–1942; Carter showed a style of girdle made of nylon powernet. After Pearl Harbor, both nylon and Lastex were withdrawn from use in consumer products, halting further innovations in foundation garments. L-90, passed in April 1942 and active by the following autumn, drastically reduced the amount of elastic that could be put into a girdle or bra. Once the elastic supplies on hand ran out, in about 1943, nothing more could be obtained until after the war. In fact, the WPB suspended L-90 in 1944 at the pleading of corset and bra makers, but elastic supplies remained tight. Canceling an L-order did not change the fact that 150,000 pounds of rubber were required in the construction of *one* battleship. Civilian products stood little chance.

Heavy, inflexible synthetic materials continued to be used in girdles until about 1947, when companies were able to obtain supplies of Lastex. Postwar girdles became lighter, more flexible, and more colorful, with pastel pinks, blues, and snowy white coming into fashion in place of the dull peach tones that predominated earlier. Black, which had enjoyed a brief vogue in the later 1930s, returned postwar.

When the average adult American woman got a view of herself in slacks, she hurried to purchase a **panty girdle**, a style introduced in the mid-1930s that surged in popularity during the war. Wartime bras showed strong uplift and a rather pointy silhouette. Some support features wittily incorporated V shapes, which had become an advertising cliché related to the struggle for Victory.

Pajamas remained a popular form of sleepwear, but nightgowns continued to be favorites with some women; both styles were limited in yardage by L-119. Once this restriction was lifted, nightgowns blossomed with fuller skirts.

Hats
Whimsy and a forward tilt typified 1939 hats. Some had flat crowns and small brims; others featured tall, tapered crowns or turban drapery. By 1943, small hats were frequently shown with high or low crowns and net veils (Figure 5.23; see also Plate 5.1). Simple **berets** and miniature **fedoras** shared the hat scene with a few dramatic tall or wide-brimmed styles (see Figure 5.23). Pillboxes came into fashion in 1944; berets continued in favor. Because hats were not subject to a Limitation Order, they could be made with whatever materials could be found, including wood and other odds and ends. As soon as peace arrived, hats celebrated with rich materials and striking shapes, from **turbans** to cloches to roll-brimmed **Bretons**. In contrast to the early 1940s, the hat was typically placed off the forehead, sometimes on the back of the head. Styles were con-sciously designed to harmonize with hairdos, which favored a pulled-back arrangement.

Shoes and Hosiery
Wedgies were not exactly new, but they became popular in 1940. Espadrilles, ballet slippers, **sling-back pumps** with open toes, and some **platform pumps** were featured in 1942. Practical shoes predominated from 1942 through 1945 to encourage walking, thereby saving scarce tires. Much consideration was given to the tight ration of three pairs per year per person. Unrationed raffia (palm straw) and cotton shoes became a fashion in spring–summer 1944; sandals and espadrilles came in bright woven raffia (including the soles), duck, mesh, and denim. The more typical **moccasins** (such as loafers), pumps, step-ins, and a few ankle boots had low or medium heels, which were not only easier to walk in but harmonized more readily with the omnipresent slacks (Figure 5.24). After the war ended, shoes retained a somewhat chunky look, although heels became higher.

"Silk is certainly on its last legs" quipped *Vogue* editorial staff in May 1, 1942, as the war in the Pacific cut off supplies from Asia.[25] Nylon still appeared in a Belle Sharmeer hosiery ad in 1942, but it was destined to dwindle. Occasionally, nylons could be obtained at military base "exchanges."[26] The fashion for knee socks with shorts, and the substitution of woolen tights for winter, resulted from diminished options in sheer leg coverings. Lacy cotton hose had been mentioned in prewar fashion magazines, and these augmented the choices for leg coverings. The Summer of '42 brought out such products as Elizabeth Arden's "Velva Leg Film" to smooth on legs in imitation of the look of stockings. Some women drew a "seam" with black pencil up the back of the leg to enhance the illusion of hosiery and in the belief that seams made the legs look slimmer. High-twist rayon seamless stockings were marketed but could not compete with the shape retention of thermoplastic nylon in the estimation of consumers.

Other Accessories and Jewelry
During the war years, the shoulder bag enjoyed great popularity, because it freed the hands for carrying packages and other tasks. Gasoline rationing reduced the use of autos for errands and curtailed deliveries of purchases; cash-and-carry became the norm.

Jewelry of all types, bracelets, necklaces, brooches, and earrings, was styled on a bold scale in 1939. By 1942, fashion reporters contemplated wood, glass, plastic, and shell jewelry in lieu of scarce metals. Some precious metals remained available at elevated prices.

Bold, cuff-style bracelets encircled wrists for day and

Figure 5.23 Various shapes of hats, c. 1943. ©Condé Nast Archive/ Corbis, photograph by Horst P. Horst.

Figure 5.24 Assorted shoes, including practical shoes for walking. ©Condé Nast Archive/Corbis, photograph by Horst P. Horst.

evening wear. Imitation pearl necklaces, in single or multiple strands, constituted a wartime staple. Brooches perched on hats and decked dresses and suits (see Plate 5.1 and Figure 5.23), generally featuring floral and plant themes, including wreaths, sprigs, the stylized fleur de lys, and a humorous palm tree. Coin shapes were shown in brooches and dangling from belts. One B. H. Wragge dress featured a giant safety pin as a neck closure.

Men's Styles
With many men in uniform and with L-85 in effect for menswear as well as for womenswear, civilian men's attire remained relatively static from 1939 through 1945.

Suits and Outerwear
Men's suits changed slightly from 1930s styles, in response to L-85 restrictions. Vests, patch pockets, and cuffs were deemed wasteful and were relinquished for the remainder of the war. Jackets, including suit coats and informal jackets, were cut relatively short, and trousers became narrow. Double-breasted styles with peaked lapels continued to be produced (Figure 5.25). Solid gray, blue, and pin stripes were prominent colors; brown was less accepted until the later

1940s. Tweed suits could be worn for somewhat casual dress.

After the arrival of peace, suits temporarily continued a wartime shape, but by fall 1946 advertisements showed a three-piece suit with rounded lapels and slightly less tapered hips. Formal events decreased in wartime, and the WPB banned production of formal clothes. "White tie and tails" gave way to the single-breasted dinner jacket or to a dark blue suit for daytime events. Trench coats remained in fashion, helped no doubt by Humphrey Bogart's élan in *The Maltese Falcon* and *Casablanca*. Boxy short coats, called **British Warms**, had a vogue during the war years, and other topcoats retained a straight line (Figure 5.26).

Sporty styles included jodhpurs and plaid jackets for riding (Figure 5.27); belted, hip-length **bush jackets** with expandable bellows pockets for all round casual wear; tweed blazers; and civilian versions of the waist-length, fly-front battle jacket. California style was credited with some of the casual innovations, including blazers with contrasting pants. Ski pants and coordinated jackets were worn on the slopes. Having waged war in cold places, Americans learned to layer lightweight, porous garments under a wind- and water-resistant outer garment, a trend that curbed enthusiasm for heavy wool coats. Brown leather, fleece-lined jackets gained cachet from associa-

Figure 5.25 (LEFT) Men's single- and double-breasted suits. The Advertising Archives.

Figure 5.26 (OPPOSITE, TOP) Men in business attire, including topcoats and snap-brim hats. ©*Time*, November 24, 1941, 53.

Figure 5.27 (opposite, bottom) Military and civilian riding attire. Note the jodhpurs and plaid sports jacket. *Esquire*, June 1943.

tion with bomber pilots and continued to be worn in peacetime. Pullover sweaters served for chilly fall and spring sports. When mild weather came, golfers chose slacks and sport shirts or T-shirts instead of the knickers and sweater-vests that had been typical in the 1920s and 1930s (see Figure 5.13). Shorts appeared at resorts and at informal events in warm weather, sometimes accompanied by polo shirts.

Shirts and Underwear

Shirts with spread collars maintained conservative styling during the period. White and pastels colors continued to

be popular, but some dark tones were teamed with light-colored suits. Flannel shirts satisfied informal needs and helped men to keep warm with thermostats set lower for fuel conservation. The prominence of Hawaii at the outset of the war made **Aloha shirts** a casual fad, reinforced later by President Harry Truman's fondness for these.

Pajamas largely replaced nightshirts. Belted robes were the rule. Not all men wore undershirts, but manufacturers made both sleeved and sleeveless styles. Sleeved T-shirts were issued as part of the military uniform, acclimating young men to wearing them. Jockey shorts, introduced in 1934, continued to be popular, but boxers were also made, although with button waistbands in-

shared a vogue with tied oxfords. New styles were not introduced in part because of WPB restrictions.

Teen Apparel

Adolescents of the early 1940s adopted quasi-unisex dungarees, although girls usually wore casual skirts, except for outdoor activities. They preferred faded and straight-cut jeans. Baggy sweaters, **saddle oxfords,** moccasins, thick **bobby sox,** and loose shirts had a vogue among the young, who were sometimes labeled bobby-soxers (see Figure 5.2).

Loose tweed jackets were shown for teens in June 1942. In the classroom and on dates, girls chose a conservative look based on blouses and skirts, topped with a cardigan or boxy wool jacket (see Figure 5.4). Long coats might be straight cut or contoured in princess style, the latter for dress-up. Cotton and rayon dresses with varying degrees of embellishment satisfied the needs for church and parties (see Plate 5.2).

Early 1940s style on small-town campuses tended to relative formality for social occasions, as seen in the "Y" group from Iowa State University in 1942 (see Plate 5.2). Girls typically wore dresses or skirts and blouses with sweaters; boys sported suits or blazers and slacks. Coed collegians tended to slip into baggy styles during the height of the war, but with the return of peace and the GIs[27] in 1946, they resumed more figure-revealing apparel, including trim skirts and sweaters, accessorized with belts, bags, and gloves (see Figure 5.4). Vassar College permitted shorts and slacks in the classroom in 1946, but this was not a universal norm; skirts were more typical, and men students often wore sport jackets and even suits to class.

Teen boys imitated adult styles of suit for dress-up or put a blazer with contrasting slacks (see Figure 5.12). For classes, shirt, slacks, and cardigan or pullover sweater sufficed. Daring teen boys, including many minority youths, wore the zoot suit (see Figure 5.3).

stead of snaps or elastic, both of which required priority materials.

Accessories and Jewelry

Knitted vests became popular substitutes for tailored ones, particularly to combine with a tweed blazer and slacks. Hats included the snap-brim, sometimes with a decorative band for casual wear (see Figures 5.26 and 5.27). Another casual option was the **Tyrolean** style, with brush-like trim, and the soft cloth cap with small brim.

Ties came in conventional stripes and all-over patterns, some in decidedly unconventional bright colors. Ascots lent high style to informal outfits. **Monk-strap** style shoes

Children's Styles

Girls from toddlers to school-agers regularly wore cotton dresses, with puffed sleeves, attached sashes, and back buttoning (Figure 5.28). Also popular with the grade-school set were jumpers with blouses. Skirts and blouses were more typically chosen by preteens, although they, too, wore dresses. Girls' coats came in loose cuts or fitted styles, similar to those shown for teens. Ankle socks appear on all young girls, with both oxfords and patent-leather Mary Janes for dress-up. Dressy shoes had instep straps (see Figure 5.28) or ankle straps, which had extra glamour. Pants and jeans rarely appeared on small girls until about 1942, although overalls were worn, as they had been since the

Figure 5.28 Note the little boy's short pants and the little girl's cotton dress and Mary Jane shoes. ©H. Armstrong Roberts/ Getty Images.

Figure 5.29 Family-like group in dressy daywear. *Time*, October 28, 1940, 87.

early twentieth century. Because adult women adopted slacks, they could hardly be withheld from children. Shorts and T-shirts or tailored blouses met warm-weather needs; overalls and long-sleeved shirts accommodated cooler days. Cardigan sweaters provided the outer layer.

Snowsuits for girls and boys consisted of one or two pieces, made of tightly woven cotton and closed with zippers, to the decided relief of mothers trying to dress wiggly small fry. Sleepwear still included nightgowns, but pajamas were very popular, and bathrobes resembled those worn by adults. Underwear still included full length slips and panties, sometimes frilled with lace.

Small boys most typically dressed in overalls or shorts and T-shirts (Figure 5.28). Shorts replaced knickers as small-boy wear. Saddle oxfords and other tie shoes were the norm, worn with low socks or knee-highs. Even in flannel suits, young boys wore short pants. Older boys went into long pants, worn as part of a suit or with shirt, tie, and sweater (Figure 5.29).

Hair and Grooming

Permanent waves helped ensure that popular styles could still be worn by those with straight-as-pins hair. Upsweeps enjoyed popularity (see Plate 5.1), as did long curls, worn loose or in a more controlled pageboy cut, with the hair flipped under. Sausage-shaped curls were another option.

Fluffy bangs accompanied some coiffures. Unconfined, long hair was firmly prohibited in wartime factories as a major threat to life and limb, helping to popularize nets, bandannas, and barrettes. The welder trainee shown in Figure 5.20 goes the whole way with a protective helmet. Movie star Veronica Lake was asked to alter her hairstyle, which included a wave swooping over one eye. When women around the country attempted to copy it, it was deemed too dangerous for the assembly line. Hair pins and bobby pins became like gold because they were considered "inessential" compared with bullets and were not being manufactured. Stories were told of women keeping a sharp eye out for lost hairpins, which they would gladly scoop up from the sidewalk.

Little girls sported soft curls and some corkscrew curls. Braids helped to keep unruly hair in check. Preteens and teenage girls loved pageboy cuts and fluffy, medium-length styles.

In keeping with military discipline, safety, and health, men's hairstyles were very short; ultrashort crew cuts and other close-cropped styles predominated. A few younger men adopted a full-topped front, called the **pompadour** (see Figure 5.3). Some men wore mustaches but it was more typical for men to be clean-shaven.

As for makeup, the war did not curtail its use. If anything, young women working in mixed-sex factories or offices more regularly applied face, lip, and eye makeup. Lip

Figure 5.30 Matching nail polish and lipstick. Note the hat and gloves in this surrealist photograph. *Vogue*, March 15, 1943, 49, John Rawlings/*Vogue* ©1943 Condé Nast Publications Inc.

and nail colors coordinated, often in deep red or rose shades (Figure 5.30). In fact, cosmetics were judged essential during the conflict to keep up women's morale and the spirits of the men who worked and lived around them.[28]

Summary

A quick glance at women's and men's apparel from 1939 and 1946 would reveal considerable continuity, but underneath the very subtle changes in styles lay more significant and fundamental shifts. Dress lost much of its formality to the exigencies of war, launching a long-term trend that still reverberates in American fashion.

Women's wider adoption of pants for wartime jobs or volunteer activities accustomed them to the convenience of this style. After the war, slacks remained a staple, at least for recreation. Slacks and hats did not go well together, accustoming at least some young women to hatlessness, a trend that spread in later decades.

This shift to informality was fostered by the casual, colorful fashions emanating from California and from the design houses in New York and other metropolitan areas. American designers enjoyed a heyday, as they tested their abilities to design for Americans free of the influence of Paris, although the reviving couture in Paris and London,

plus the 1950s emergence of the Italian fashion industry, would offer serious competition for American design that never shrank to its prewar scope. Instead, it kept on evolving methods of meshing creativity with the demands of mass production, eventually creating businesses that would gain worldwide recognition and patronage.

Technical change also carried long-term implications for U.S. apparel. Nylon moved from a fiber just for hosiery and foundation garments to a staple of sleepwear and then outerwear, including dresses for women and (briefly) shirts for men. Nylon and the other synthetics that came on the market in the 1950s drastically altered garment care and established new standards of convenience—drip drying and packability, to mention just two. At the level of industry, adherence to government-mandated specifications carried over to precision in civilian apparel production after the end of hostilities.

America, relatively unscathed by the war and greatly increased in power, prestige, and know-how, would become a major source of fashion ideas for the rest of the world in the ensuing decades.

Suggested Readings

Callan, Georgina O'Hara. *The Thames & Hudson Dictionary of Fashion and Fashion Designers*. New York: Thames & Hudson, 1998 (paperback edition).

Fisher, David E., and Marshall Jon Fisher. *Tube: The Invention of Television*. Washington, DC: Counterpoint, 1996.

Friedel, Frank. *America in the Twentieth Century*, 4th ed. New York: Alfred A. Knopf, 1976.

Kennedy, David M. *Freedom From Fear: The American People in Depression and War, 1929–1945*. New York: Oxford University Press, 1999.

Milbank, Caroline Rennolds. *New York Fashion: The Evolution of American Style*. New York: Harry N. Abrams, 1996 (paperback edition)

O'Brien, Kenneth Paul, and Lynn Hudson Parsons. *The Home-Front War: World War II and American Society*. Westport, CT: Greenwood Press, 1995.

Perrett, Geoffrey. *Days of Sadness, Years of Triumph: The American People, 1939–1945*. New York: Coward, McCann, & Geoghegan, 1973.

Reeves, Thomas C. *Twentieth-Century America: A Brief History*. New York: Oxford University Press, 2000.

Tapert, Annette. *The Power of Glamour: The Women Who Defined the Magic of Stardom*. New York: Crown Publishers, 1998.

Train, Susan. *Theatre de la Mode*. New York: Rizzoli International Publications, 1991.

CHAPTER 6

1947-

U.S. Events
and Trends

U.S. House
Committee on
Un-American
Activities begins
hearings regarding
Communism

1947

U.S.
Fashions

Dior introduces the
New Look

The Marshall Plan is
implemented

Harry S. Truman
defeats Thomas E.
Dewey for president

1948

Velcro invented

NATO is created

1949

President Truman
sends ground forces
to Korea

1950

DuPont begins
production of the
newly named acrylic
fiber Orlon

Disneyland opens

1955

Semifitted styles
dominate the shows;
Dior introduces the
"A-line"

1956

Act to protect voting
rights

1957

Dior dies

Yves Saint Laurent
becomes designer for
House of Dior

1958

1958

I Love Lucy show premieres

1951

DuPont launches "Dacron" polyester

Eisenhower wins presidency

1952

Fad for "beanies" with propeller top

Crick and Watson discover the structure of DNA

1953

Fad for felt circle skirts

Jonas Salk begins testing polio vaccine in Pittsburgh

The U.S. Supreme Court rules segregation in education unconstitutional

1954

Dior introduces the "H" look, a straighter silhouette with hip emphasis

Chanel reopens her couture house

New Wealth, New Looks

The decade of the 1950s really starts with the end of World War II and the return home of thousands of GIs. The ratification of the United Nations Charter by the U.S. Senate in 1945 permanently ended U.S. isolation and ushered in a period of American domination in world politics. As soldiers settled into civilian life, they married and began to raise families, marking the beginning of a boom in the birthrate that peaked in 1957. This baby boom affected social life and culture in myriad ways.

Domestic and International Politics and Economics

The end of the war brought peace but also a long Cold War as the United States tried to contain Communism and the Soviet Union in particular. Although the United States and the Soviet Union were allies during the war, long-standing disagreements surfaced during the peace negotiations. Ultimately Germany was divided into a western zone jointly occupied by British, French, and Americans and a Soviet-occupied eastern zone. When the Soviets sealed off West Berlin in 1948, the free world responded with a massive airlift of food and fuel. The cutting off of Eastern Europe was described by British Prime Minister Winston Churchill as an iron curtain, and containment of Communism and the Soviet Union became the prevailing American policy in the postwar years, led by two presidents, Harry S Truman and Dwight D. Eisenhower.

An initial focus of containment and a step in the onset of the cold war was the 1947 Truman Doctrine, intended to provide aid to national governments in conflict with communist factions and to restrict the influence of the Soviet Union. Containment also entailed extensive economic aid for the recovery of war-ravaged western Europe. Under the direction of U.S. Secretary of State George Marshall, an aid program was developed with the western European nations known as the Marshall Plan. Marshall also offered to include the Soviet Union in the plan, but Soviet dictator Joseph Stalin refused to participate. The plan was beneficial to the U.S. economy, as it provided a market for U.S. goods.

Determination to contain communism led to U.S. intervention in Asian affairs, initially in Korea and later in Vietnam. The proclamation of the People's Republic of China in 1949 by Communist party leader Mao Zedong sparked fear of a domino effect—that one nation after another might fall to Communist forces. The Korean War (1950–1953) brought armed conflict between the United States and China, when the Chinese army crossed the Yalu River into Korea in 1950, entering the war on the side of the North Korean Communists.

Arms control and the atomic bomb became integral factors in U.S. national security policy and also entered into popular culture. Although at first Americans were excited about, rather than afraid of, the bomb, when the Soviets developed the capability to produce atomic weapons in 1949 anxiety mounted over a potential nuclear attack. The arms race escalated, with development of the new hydrogen bomb, which was much more powerful than the atomic bomb. As the population was warned about radioactive fallout and contamination of food products, many undertook the building of bomb shelters. By 1960, it was estimated that one million families had built shelters.

The Cold War affected domestic affairs in other ways. A combination of espionage scandals and the establishment by Truman of a Federal Employee Loyalty Program in 1947 contributed to anticommunist feelings—a red scare.[1] The initial government anticommunist action was establishment of the House Un-American Activities Committee, intended to investigate alleged communistic activities in Hollywood. Witnesses called before the committee became subject to blacklisting, effectively ending the careers of many. The most vocal anticommunist was Senator Joseph McCarthy. He accused numerous government officials of being Communists or Communist sympathizers, gaining visibility through extensive coverage on television, newly available to many Americans. McCarthy's extreme tactics led to a climate of paranoia among Americans. However, when televised hearings in 1954 visibly demonstrated his bullying tactics, his public support waned and the Senate condemned his conduct.

The Postwar Economy

The end of the war brought a surge of prosperity to the United States, despite a brief recession and some fears of a reversion to the prewar depression. The 1944 GI Bill provided benefits for returning veterans, giving them priority for many jobs, low-interest mortgages, and educational support. This resulted in a tremendous wave of building on college campuses. More women also attended college, although they were still concentrated in traditional programs such as teaching and nursing, and many dropped out to get married.

The postwar economy was soon booming, and as incomes rose more people could own their own homes and more could consider themselves part of the middle class. In the mid-1950s, almost 60 percent of Americans enjoyed a middle-class level of living compared with 31 percent in 1928. Despite the appearance in popular magazines and television that most women stayed at home as wives and homemakers, working wives contributed substantially to family income.

Figure 6.1 Three of the young women who were among the first black students to attend Little Rock Central High, pictured after the first day of school, September 9, 1957. ©Bettmann/Corbis.

Figure 6.2 A family in the suburbs. Note the trim suit and hat on mother, and the plain suit on father. ©H. Armstrong Roberts/Corbis.

The Civil Rights Movement

Although the economy improved dramatically, blacks became increasingly impatient with inequities and discrimination. The army was still segregated during World War II, and, despite Roosevelt's signing of a Fair Employment order in 1941 and a ban against whites-only voting primaries in 1944, racism and discrimination continued to be widespread. A migration of blacks out of the South accelerated, with most moving to cities in the North. The civil rights struggle gained momentum rapidly throughout the 1950s. Truman desegregated the army in 1948, and a series of judicial challenges to segregation began slowly to bring change. In 1954, the Supreme Court issued a ruling in *Brown v. Board of Education* that the policies of separate but equal schools were unconstitutional, and the slow and sometimes violent desegregation of schools began.

The most decisive confrontation occurred in 1957 when governor Orval Faubus of Arkansas stated that it would be impossible to integrate the schools peacefully. President Eisenhower used federal troops to protect black citizens and children entering the schools in Little Rock (Figure 6.1). In 1955, Rosa Parks was arrested in Montgomery, Alabama, because she refused to surrender her bus seat to a white passenger. Her arrest sparked a successful boycott of public transportation. Black leaders, led by Martin Luther King Jr., organized civil rights protests, and within a year the Supreme Court ruled that bus segregation was also illegal. The Civil Rights Act of 1957 authorized the Justice Department to protect the civil rights

of blacks who were denied the opportunity to vote. With the many court rulings and other changes, the civil rights struggle was underway but would continue into the next decade and beyond.

Social Life and Culture

As soldiers returned home after the war, they went back to school for new training, got married, and started families. Rapid population growth was an indicator of the increased economic prosperity of the period. The birth rate rose dramatically after the war, peaking in 1957, when a baby was born every seven seconds in the United States.

The Move to Suburbia and the Baby Boom

The returning soldiers and the baby boom had an impact on every aspect of society, from schools to clothing to housing. It put particular stress on the housing market, giving rise to a series of suburban housing developments of affordable, although small, homes. The first of these was Levittown on Long Island, New York, developed by William J. Levitt, a pioneer in mass-produced components for housing. Many more developments quickly followed, often with homes in the increasingly popular ranch style. Ultimately, 85 percent of the new homes built in the 1950s were suburban, and, by the early 1960s, almost every city was surrounded by suburban development. The design uniformity of these developments added to the sense of conformity that pervades ideas about the 1950s (Figure 6.2). Popular culture images of the time present an impression of comfort and stability and a general unwillingness to challenge the status quo.

The growth of the suburbs meant that travel and the automobile came to define American life both for commuting to work and for leisure. New highways began to link the suburbs to urban areas as well as joining cities across the nation; between 1945 and 1955, car ownership doubled.[2] Mass transit was available in the largest cities, but in many cities and towns a move to the suburbs usually meant a drive to work. Although the cost of a car rose, auto manufacturers made significant improvements. New cars had larger engines, tires that lasted longer, automatic transmissions, and fewer mechanical problems. Auto body styles also took flights of fancy often inspired by streamlined rockets and jet wings, and new models were introduced with the same fanfare as new fashion collections. Fashion even became an integral supplement to many car advertisements (Figure 6.3). In addition to suburban development, there was a strong migration of population to the West and the South. The populations of cities such as Phoenix, Houston, Dallas, and Atlanta swelled, helped by federal highway construction and the accessibility of affordable air-conditioning.

Interstate highways and auto improvements combined to create a dramatic increase in vacation travel. More Americans received at least some paid vacation time, and the new and growing young families became enthusiastic about affordable automobile holidays. Recognizing that families needed a clean and reliable place to stay while on the road, Kemmons Wilson opened the first Holiday Inn in 1954, and by the end of the 1950s there were more than 200 across the country. Competitors such as Ramada and Howard Johnson, eager to cash in on the travel boom, also opened.[3]

Figure 6.3 Five American ready-to-wear designs in an advertisement for a Chrysler Imperial car. Designs by (left to right) Estevez for Grenelle, Brigance, Ben Reig, Claire McCardell, and Adele Simpson. *Vogue*, December 1955, 17.

Travel along the new highways also brought the rise of other roadside services, frequently identified by imposing signs inspired by the space race or atomic imagery, such as rockets, satellites, or large rotating atoms with neutrons. Many of these signs, intended to be seen from a distance by drivers, became iconic symbols of new motels and restaurants. One of the most universal signs of this more mobile society became the fast-food restaurant. Ray Kroc acquired a franchise for the hamburger stands owned by the McDonald brothers in California. He added the trademark golden arches, opening his first franchised McDonald's in Des Plaines, Illinois, in 1955. In 1961, Kroc bought the company from the McDonald brothers and by the early 1960s had stands all over the country. McDonald's success led to competition—Kentucky Fried Chicken opened in 1954 and Pizza Hut in 1958.

Technology and Communication

Technology changed quickly, sometimes radically, during the postwar period with the rapid development of computers, atomic energy, and rocketry. The 1950s was also the decade when the television became a major social presence.

New Technology

Computer development had begun before the war but was limited until the production of the faster and more reliable transistor in 1948. The computer and transistors both transformed business and allowed for more advanced levels of space exploration. The tiny transistor also affected everyday objects such as radios and hearing aids. Space exploration and advances in aeronautics attracted the public's attention throughout the 1950s and into the 1960s. When the Russians launched the first Sputnik rocket into space in 1957, it sparked a race for control of space, and by mid-decade the United States was developing space satellites and unmanned, self-guided missiles, in addition to exploring alternate sources of energy. Other inventions of the period include Edwin Land's Polaroid camera, made available to the public in 1948, and, after the mid-1950s, the rapid advance of fiber optical technology.

Medicine

There were numerous medical advances in the decade after World War II that had lasting effects on both the health and the behavior of the general public. In 1951, the U.S. Public Health Service announced that fluoridation of water could significantly reduce tooth decay. In a few years much of the nation's water supply was fluoridated. Not everyone approved, and a few suspected it was a Communist plot to poison the water supply.

A significant medical advance was the development of the polio vaccine. Polio was one of the most terrifying and debilitating diseases of the time, striking mostly children and young adults. A polio epidemic in the United States peaked in 1952, creating national anxiety. The disease damaged the heart, muscles, and lungs, leaving some confined to a mechanical ventilator or iron lung to aid breathing and leaving others crippled for life. The first breakthrough in eradicating the disease is credited to Dr. Jonas Salk. After extensive testing of a vaccine in 1954, it was approved for public use in 1955 with a nationwide immunization program for children. Among scientific advances, most notable was the 1953 discovery of the structure of the DNA molecule, the result of years of research by numerous scientists. American James Watson and Englishman Francis H. C. Crick were the first to publish the research in the journal *Nature*.[4]

Communication

The first television broadcasts were made in the late 1920s, but it was in the first decade after World War II that television began to have a profound impact, as ownership rates increased dramatically. At the beginning of the period fewer than 10 percent of Americans owned a television, but, by 1960, more than 80 percent owned a set. Early televisions had small 11- to 12-inch screens, and, although there were many local television stations, most of the population could get only limited reception. Stations were affiliated with three major networks: NBC, CBS, and ABC. Some immediate effects of increased television ownership were a drop in attendance at movies and sporting events, lowered radio listening, and even a reduction in library usage (Figure 6.4). It also meant that people began to make decisions based on television images, something that ultimately had an impact on politics. The Democratic and Republican conventions were first broadcast in 1952, affecting the way delegates negotiated the process. One of the first politicians to use television to his advantage was Richard Nixon, when he broadcast his famous Checkers speech in 1952, denying improper acceptance of gifts.[5]

General Electric introduced the first portable television in 1955, and, by the late 1950s, limited color broadcasting had begun, although television sets were expensive. Drama, comedy, and variety shows dominated the period. Milton Berle's *Texaco Star Theater* on NBC was one of the most popular, relying on visual comedy and a revue-style format. At the same time CBS introduced a show called *Toast of the Town* with host Ed Sullivan, which became an early hit. Renamed *The Ed Sullivan Show* in 1955, it continued to be the premiere variety show on television until 1971. Other hit comedy/variety shows included *Your Show of Shows, The Colgate Comedy Hour,* and *The Jack Benny Show.*

Figure 6.4 Family watching television. The Advertising Archives.

The situation comedy, or sitcom, became a staple of television programming from the beginning, taking its format from similar radio shows. Premiering in 1951, *I Love Lucy* with Lucille Ball and husband Desi Arnaz dominated the genre. Although only 39 episodes were made, Jackie Gleason's *The Honeymooners* is also considered one of the best sitcom shows of the time. In addition to Lucille Ball, television portrayed an endless series of extremely well-dressed mothers and housewives throughout the decade, stressing traditional home roles for women. These women included Donna Reed in the *Donna Reed Show* and Jane Wyatt in *Father Knows Best*. The young baby boom generation grew up watching *The Mickey Mouse Club* and *The Howdy Doody Show*, while teenagers watched *American Bandstand*, featuring that new music genre rock and roll.

Soap operas entered afternoon programming in the 1950s and included long-running shows such as *The Edge of Night* and *The Guiding Light*. Television quiz shows such as *The $64,000 Question*, developed from a show called *Take It or Leave It*, attracted big audiences, lured by the idea of substantial financial jackpots and instant celebrity. Producers created shows with increasingly larger jackpots as the decade progressed. They continued to be successful until 1958, when a series of scandals revealed that many of the games were rigged and that contestants were sometimes given answers before the show. Almost overnight, popularity faded. Quiz shows such as *What's My Line?* and *To Tell the Truth*, which relied less on large winnings, survived into the next decade.

Literature and Magazines

Literature was an eclectic mix in the 1950s and ranged from religious topics, to the improvisational style of the Beat Generation, to paperback mysteries and romance novels, often with lurid covers. The paperbacks dominated sales, although many other best-sellers continued to appear first in hardback editions. Norman Vincent Peale's *The Power of Positive Thinking* was a best-seller for several years, while evangelist Billy Graham became an admired figure both through his writing and his television and radio broadcasts. Novels about loneliness or teen angst included John Steinbeck's *East of Eden* and J. D. Salinger's *Catcher in the Rye,* a novel about a lonely young antihero that was soon required reading in high school and college literature courses.

More sexually explicit novels marked the end of American sexual innocence. Grace Metalious's *Peyton Place,* a novel filled with sexual details about a small town, became not only a best-seller but also a movie in 1957. The Mickey Spillane novels about detective Mike Hammer often blended violence with anticommunist themes. As a counterpoint, one of the best-selling books of the period was *The Common Sense Book of Baby and Child Care* (1946) by Dr. Benjamin Spock. With more than 76 million Americans in the baby boom generation, the book sold approximately 1 million copies a year in the 1950s as families grew and parents searched for information on raising children. With the increase in suburban development, these new, young parents were no longer in close proximity to grandparents, a traditional source of information and child-rearing support.

A new literary style was spawned by the Beat writers and poets, who first appeared on the West Coast of the United States. These writers rejected contemporary mass culture and created a bohemian subculture, much of it centered initially in San Francisco. Advocates of a nonconformist style, Beat writers included novelists William S. Burroughs and Jack Kerouac and poets Allen Ginsberg and Gregory Corso. Kerouac especially seemed to characterize the genre in his 1957 novel *On the Road,* which was written in a stream-of-consciousness style and symbolized the free-spirited existence of the Beats. After 1957, the suffix *nik* was added and a new term—beatnik—entered the language. The beatniks were disaffected youth, frequently identified by their apparel. They congregated in coffee houses and wore unconventional dress for the time, usually black clothing, dark glasses, sandals, and, for men, beards.

Magazines remained popular reading. New titles on the market catered to more specialized audiences, as some that aimed at a general readership ceased publication. *Collier's, Woman's Home Companion,* and the *American Magazine* failed, at least in part because of decreased advertising revenue. Four that entered the popular culture lexicon were *Sports Illustrated* (1954), *Playboy* (1953), *Ebony* (1945), and *TV Guide* (1953). The popularity of cars spawned several car magazines, including *Motor Trend* (1949). With teenagers as an important and more affluent group, many

publications targeted them. First issued in 1944, *Seventeen* came into its own as a pivotal magazine for high school girls. It was joined in 1955 by *Young Miss.*

Sports and Leisure

The consumer buying spree of the 1950s extended to toys and other leisure-time games, including a succession of fads that often seem silly in retrospect. Many of the new games and fads were product tie-ins to television shows and movies and to screen personalities. The *Hopalong Cassidy* show and Walt Disney's *Davy Crockett* series produced an abundance of associated merchandise (Figure 6.5). Other fads included the Slinky, Silly Putty, propeller beanies from the *Beany and Cecil* show, and hula hoops. Wham-O, manufacturer of the hula hoop, also introduced the Frisbee in 1957.

Baseball and football continued to be popular spectator sports, especially with the growth of professional football, and were enhanced by the increased use of television to broadcast games, including the World Series, first televised in 1950. New York seemed to dominate baseball, with the Giants, the Yankees, and the Brooklyn Dodgers. Improvements in commercial air travel, however, allowed for more national competitions, and, by 1957, the Dodgers were in Los Angeles and the Giants relocated to San Francisco.

Other leisure activities can be attributed to the move to suburbia. Bowling became a principal sport for many, encouraged by construction of modern bowling alleys with automatic pin-setting machines and formation of local leagues. Perhaps the most popular leisure activity for the new group of suburbanite homeowners was to do-it-yourself. The home-improvement industry encouraged the family togetherness of home-improvement projects, and women's magazines published numerous articles devoted to home projects.

Art, Music, Theater, and the Movies

Music and film had a unique visual effect on the viewing public in terms of dress and fads. With drops in attendance, movie producers experimented with gimmicks and films aimed at the youth market to attract patrons. Radio, also floundering with decreasing numbers of listeners, found new markets in Top 40 pop music aimed at teens and an increasing number of people with car radios.

Art and Painting

Abstract expressionism, sometimes called The New York School, continued to be the most influential modern art style of the period. Jackson Pollock, Willem de Kooning, and

Figure 6.5 Davy Crockett costumes for boys or girls, 1955. *Butterick pattern counter catalog.* Author's collection.

Figure 6.6 Marlon Brando as Johnny Stabler with his gang in *The Wild One* (1954). ©John Springer Collection/Corbis.

Franz Kline, among others, were officially recognized at the New York Museum of Modern Art. Pollock, sometimes call Jack the Dripper for his splatter style of painting, received much positive and negative media attention. The abstract movement of the period falls into two broad groups—the action painters such as Pollock, de Kooning, and Kline, who focused on the physical action used in painting, and the color-field painters such as Mark Rothko, Morris Louis, and

Kenneth Noland, who explored the effect of expanses of color on the canvas. Rothko, for example, used large-scale color blocks to create a sense of visual impact.

For the general public, the experimental abstract artists of the period had less appeal than more traditional, representational artists. Immensely popular illustrator Norman Rockwell continued to represent recognizable and folksy American scenes throughout the period. Technically and stylistically proficient, he was best known for his numerous cover illustrations for the *Saturday Evening Post.* Other realist artists such as Edward Hopper and Georgia O'Keefe continued to produce exemplary work throughout the period.

The Movies

To bolster attendance, Hollywood looked for ways to lure back the audience from television with technical innovations and gimmicks, such as three-dimensional imagery, in which the audience wore cardboard glasses that gave the illusion of three-dimensional depth to science fiction and horror films such as *The Creature From the Black Lagoon* (1954). This fad, along with smellorama, which produced odors in the theater, and ShockoVision which gave the audience a mild electrical shock, had very brief popularity. In 1953, CinemaScope created wider screen images and a panoramic display. This soon became the standard technology for big-budget spectacles such as *The Robe* and some of the other religious epics popular during the decade.

Although drive-in theaters had been around since the 1930s, they became popular in the 1950s with the growth of the suburbs. While the drive-in was a hit with families, it also became the ideal spot for teenagers to be alone in a reasonably safe and private location. Many films of the era appealed to the new teen audience by showing disaffected teenagers alienated from mainstream culture. James Dean epitomized this in *Rebel Without a Cause.* Others such as *Rock Around the Clock* and *Rock, Rock, Rock!* (1956) capitalized on the popularity of rock and roll. The youthful stars who emerged in these films also had an impact on fashion, with teen idols who demonstrated rebellion in their dress style. Both Dean and Marlon Brando, in films such as *A Streetcar Named Desire* and *The Wild One,* represent this antiestablishment image (Figure 6.6). Other big-screen themes of the period included dramas, westerns, war epics such as *The Bridge on the River Kwai,* science fiction, and pessimistic commentaries on Communism. *The Man in the Grey Flannel Suit,* from the novel by Sloan Wilson, depicted contemporary society's conformism and made a statement about the uniformity of male fashion.

Music

The 1950s were the last hurrah for big-budget film musicals. Both *Singin' in the Rain* and *An American in Paris* won Academy Awards. Broadway musicals dominated the live theater scene, with enduring favorites such as *South Pacific*, *My Fair Lady*, *The King and I*, *The Music Man*, and *West Side Story*. Many theatrical hits were also eventually translated to film, and individual songs topped the popularity charts.

At the end of the war, American popular music was in a state of change. The popular big-band style of the 1930s and 1940s declined, but the pop music that would characterize the 1950s had not yet emerged. The turning point came in 1953 and 1954 with several hits by the band Bill Haley and the Comets (Figure 6.7). Their 1955 hit song "Rock Around the Clock" solidified the place of rock and roll as the music of teens, as Haley became the first white musician to bring traditional black rhythm and blues to a larger audience. Although up to this point radio stations had segregated music, by the end of the decade, rock and roll and rhythm and blues by both black and white performers were played on the now-popular rock radio stations.

The musician who best personified this assimilation of black music by a white performer was Elvis Presley, who blended country or hillbilly music with black rhythm and blues and an animated beat. Presley created a sensation with a string of hits in the mid-1950s, including "Heartbreak Hotel" and "Hound Dog." His legendary career as a teen idol with a controversial image is best characterized by his appearances on *The Ed Sullivan Show*, when his hip gyrations were deemed too suggestive for the viewing audience and he was filmed only from the waist up. Just behind Elvis Presley in popularity was Pat Boone, whose smoother versions of rhythm and blues songs also had an impact on rock

Figure 6.7 Bill Haley and the Comets in plaid dinner jackets (1957). ©Hulton-Deutsch Collection/Corbis.

music. His trademark was his white bucks, a shoe style that became fashionable with teenagers.

Retailing and Manufacturing

During the war years, retailers had struggled to find the merchandise that newly prosperous Americans demanded. Once peace came, the reverse problem set in: an abundance of goods was for sale at many types of retail outlets. Americans could splurge on new cars, new appliances, and of course new apparel. Young families, of which there were millions, had to budget carefully, enhancing the appeal of discounters such as E. J. Korvette, which opened in 1948 and by 1959 enjoyed $157.7 million in sales.[6] Foresighted department store merchants anticipated that supermarkets and the super drugstores emergent by 1958 would begin selling apparel, providing another source of stressful competition.

What made this revolution in shopping possible was the growing practice, through the 1950s, of putting apparel in packages, with detailed information. This made self-service of some degree possible in infants' wear, men's furnishings, hosiery, boys' apparel, bras, girdles, and household textiles. Besides speed and convenience, packaging (which had begun in a tentative way in 1941) offered cleanliness to the customer. Retailers gained by efficient stock handling and control, fewer markdowns, and a lower selling cost, the last of which counted significantly in an era of rising wages and resulting higher costs of staff. Customers were found to spend more on packaged versus bulk (loose, unpackaged) purchases, another inducement for stores to switch wherever possible.

To compete with discounters and supermarts, department stores streamlined and updated their departments. Newer styles of counters were installed in the blond woods so popular in the 1950s. Colors were soft, with an emphasis on pinks, grays, and touches of black. Modern amenities included air-conditioning, soft lighting, and light boxes for the display of selected goods. A few self-service counter displays appeared, such as for bras and soft girdles, although for the most part merchandise was placed on the tops of storage units.

Stores not only looked different but also functioned differently. Various services were offered, from educational programs to entertainment, especially for teen girls, a demographic group whose importance merchants were beginning to recognize. Saturday morning clubs, teen advisory boards, and special fashion shows were held. Some foundations departments even sent representatives into the schools to coach the teens on how to select and wear a bra and garter belt[7] or brief girdle. Education reached the adult woman, too, notably in the form of a 1952 film about breast self-examination, which was part of the emerging campaign against cancer. Some services were withdrawn, however: gift wrapping and delivery were no longer free, if offered at all.

Night openings for stores, experimented with in the early 1940s, returned gradually during the 1950s—usually for one or two nights a week, Fridays and Mondays being the most popular choices except in the New York metro area, where Mondays and Thursdays were the choices. These later hours responded to women's complicated daytime routines, access to cars—presumably after husbands returned from work—and availability of babysitters. Branch stores multiplied, reaching into the suburbs where the population was growing much faster than in downtown areas, but gradually eroding the sales of center-city stores.

Manufacturers grappled with their own postwar, boom-time challenges. They switched quite nimbly from munitions and military supplies to consumer goods once peace arrived. With demand for goods rising rapidly and old machinery reaching the limit of its usefulness, manufacturers spent heavily on new buildings and equipment, to the tune of $26.9 billion just in 1952. Unions, which had cooperated with management during the war years, demanded wage increases, employment guarantees, and better benefits, backing up their demands with frequent strikes. The merger between two mega-unions, American Federation of Labor and Congress of Industrial Organizations (AFL-CIO) created a powerful labor combination.

Regulations constrained producers, too. Fair trade practices were passed during the mid-1950s to prohibit selling at different prices to two wholesale customers. Rebates, discounts, and refunds could not be used to sweeten the deal with one outlet over another. Services like advertising allowances could not be discriminatory, either. Fair Trade required informative labeling about fiber content and the origin of imported products. Warranties had to disclose their limitations, and terms of the warranty had to be observed. Advertising could not make unjustified claims when none existed. Emerging business trends included streamlining, automation, forecasting, and market analysis.

Fashion Influences

Images of women and fashion throughout the decade after World War II kept to a tradition of showing very lady-like models, presenting an often exaggerated and untouchable image of fashion photographed in distant and exotic locales. A younger group of models and photographers, influenced by an increasingly prominent teen population, began to exert an influence by mid-decade with a younger and more casual style.

The wedding of England's Elizabeth II in 1947 and her coronation in 1953 were fashion as well as media events. The fashion press covered the queen's dresses, both created by British designer Norman Hartnell, and the attire of her attendants and guests and offered articles on elaborate special occasion dressing. Many film stars were style icons and trendsetters. Audrey Hepburn epitomized an innocent but sophisticated persona both in film and in her personal dressing style. Although Hepburn was often dressed by her favorite couturier Hubert de Givenchy, the simplicity and clean lines of her clothing are often identified as representing an American look, and her elegant style continues to be imitated. Givenchy opened his couture house in 1952 and quickly became known for impeccable separates and refined designs intended for a relatively conservative, unostentatious clientele. Grace Kelly presented an elegant and classic beauty in films such as *High Society* and *Rear Window*. In addition to her film career, her marriage to Prince Rainier of Monaco in 1956 made her a constantly photographed fashion figure. Marilyn Monroe and Jayne Mansfield, on the contrary, used both film costume and personal dress to create a seductive image, often with low-cut gowns and very tight fits.

There were many excellent fashion illustrators and photographers in the decade after the war, but it was the photographer who increasingly defined the representation of fashion and style. Numerous talented photographers, each with a recognizable style, filled the pages of fashion publications during the 1950s. Some, such as John Rawlings (Figure 6.8) continued to be influential, but two relative newcomers dominated the world of fashion photography for the remainder of the century—Irving Penn and Richard Avedon.[8] Penn was originally a painter but began working for *Vogue* magazine in 1943. Known for his fashion work, he was also a master of still life, and often these images appeared in fashion layouts. He explored detail, texture, and pattern in his glamorous, formal, and often stylized images, and he used models in sometimes slouched or exaggerated poses. Avedon was a staff photographer for both *Harper's Bazaar* (1945–1965) and *Vogue* (1966–1990), who considered fashion photography an art form. He created glamorous images that by the end of the decade incorporated more action into photos that mixed realism with fantasy. Later in his career he became known for his striking celebrity portraiture.

Modeling became a highly paid profession, and models such as Suzy Parker (Figure 6.9), Sunny Harnett, and Lisa Fonssagrives Penn (wife of Irving Penn) became celebrities and created an aura of glamour that made modeling a dream occupation for young girls. Expanding numbers of modeling schools and agencies attracted young aspirants

Figure 6.8 A slim cocktail coat photographed by John Rawlings, c. 1957. ©Condé Nast Archive/Corbis.

Figure 6.9 Model Suzy Parker in a Chanel suit behind the camera, c. 1954. The model she is photographing is wearing a suit by Fath. ©Condé Nast Archive/Corbis.

despite the rigors and the often short-lived nature of the career.

Notwithstanding the increased dominance of photography in the fashion press, illustrators continued to impart their own unique perspective on style. Although shown with less frequency, several artists from previous periods continued to contribute work to fashion publications, and several new names emerged. René Bouché continued to illustrate for *Vogue* through the 1950s, as did Eric, with his distinctive style, until his death in 1958 (Figure 6.10). Newcomers included American Tom Keogh and René Gruau, of French and Italian heritage, who illustrated for *Vogue* but who is best known for his advertising illustrations for the Paris couture houses, particularly that of Dior.

The Designers

Women's fashions began to change in subtle ways immediately after World War II ended. Both American and French designers showed lower hems and skirts with added flare and narrower waistlines. It was not until the introduction of

Dior's first couture line in 1947, however, that the changes seemed to coalesce into the distinctive silhouette that would be called the New Look.[9]

Paris

The French couture houses attempted to reestablish their style leadership at the end of the German occupation with promotional measures such as the Théatre de la Mode, but it was a single designer who appeared to restore the prestige and power of Paris. When **Christian Dior** introduced his first line in February 1947, it was dubbed The New Look by *Harper's Bazaar* editor Carmel Snow. It was not until his second collection, however, that the name New Look became permanently attached to the silhouettes he presented. Dior took inspiration from mid- to late-nineteenth-century styles and exaggerated the trends that had been evolving both before the war and just after. His collection of designs had narrow waists, extremely full and long skirts, often with padded hips, and sloping shoulders (Figure 6.11). Some had very long and narrow skirts with the very fitted bodice. To ob-

Figure 6.10 Eric's illustration of Italian fashions by Fabiani (LEFT) and Simonetta (RIGHT) (1955). *Vogue*, March 1, 1955, 138, Carl Erickson/*Vogue* ©1955 Condé Nast Publications Inc.

Figure 6.11 Christian Dior New Look dress, 1947. *Vogue*, October 1, 1947, 181, Erwin Blumenfeld/*Vogue* ©1947 Condé Nast Publications Inc.

servers it appeared to be the antithesis of the boxier and broad-shouldered look of the war years. Most seemed to forget that designers had gradually started to adopt a more romantic and full-skirted silhouette in the years just before the war. Indeed, during the occupation years in Paris, the French designers had never completely abandoned the fuller silhouette of the late 1930s. Not everyone accepted the long, full skirts, and some in the United States even protested or formed clubs they called the Little Below the Knee clubs.

Much hyperbole surrounds the introduction of the New Look, and some fashion writers have suggested that it was Dior who single-handedly saved French couture. Certainly the House of Dior and Paris fashion made a dramatic comeback after the war, and it dominated the fashion press for much of the 1950s despite the significant advances made by American designers during the war years.

Born in 1905 in Normandy, France, Dior demonstrated artistic creativity at a young age. Against his father's wishes, he initially chose a career as an art dealer. Forced to sell his gallery during the Great Depression, he took fashion drawing lessons and began to work freelance for many of the

Paris couturières. In 1938 he went to work at the design house of Robert Piguet where he learned the details of garment construction. Called up for military service in 1939, he left the army when the German occupation began in 1940. During World War II he designed for the house of Lucien Lelong. After the war, he was set up in his own business with the backing of the textile house of Marcel Boussac, who was swayed by Dior's plan to create dresses that would use many yards of fabric, an obvious benefit to the French textile industry. After the success of Dior's first two collections, his atelier became the premier house watched by the fashion press throughout the 1950s. It soon was the largest couture house in Paris, producing and selling more models of clothing than any other—more than half of the couture's foreign exports. After Dior's death in 1957, Yves Saint Laurent became head designer.[10]

Other couture designers also exerted an influence on fashion, despite the seeming preeminence of Dior. **Jacques Fath**, **Pierre Balmain**, and **Nina Ricci** each created a unique slant on the New Look and captured a significant portion of the couture business of the 1950s. Fath opened his first design house in 1937, expanding to a larger couture house in 1944. He was best known for creating glamorous styles that were imbued with angles and movement and often had dramatically pointed collars (Figure 6.12). Fath also recognized early on the importance of the American market, contracting to create a ready-to-wear line with a Seventh Avenue manufacturer. He died in 1954 at the peak of his career.

Pierre Balmain claimed to have created the New Look with his first collections in 1946. Indeed his first designs had many elements of the style, with long full skirts and small waistlines. Also like Dior, he worked as a designer for Lucien LeLong, leaving a year earlier than Dior to open his own couture house. Balmain sketched his designs rather than draping them, creating simple but elegant day dresses and often extensively embroidered evening gowns

Nina Ricci, born in Turin, opened her design house in 1932, showing a style distinctly different from the style of the day. Her customers were wealthy, elegant women who did not want to be dressed at the cutting edge of fashion. She instead created sophisticated, classic styles. In 1951, she chose Jules-François Crahay to codesign the collection with her.

Spaniard **Cristobal Balenciaga** is considered one of the most creative and technically talented of the couture designers. Unlike many designers, he could draw, cut intricate patterns, and sew. A master of creating flattering shapes for women of all ages, he was fascinated by the structure of a garment. His designs did not follow as closely as other designers the New Look silhouette, and he tended to be less connected to the annual changes of silhouette or hemline. Balenciaga was always more occupied with a perfection of cut and fit intended to complement his customers' figures. He moved to Paris from Spain in 1937 during the Spanish civil war to open his couture house. Often inspired by his Spanish heritage, his clothing was architectural without the layers and understructure of Dior's models. Although he shied away from publicity, Balenciaga was most influential for his ability to create styles that were both comfortable and high fashion (Plate 6.1).

Coco Chanel left France to live in Switzerland immediately after the war, having spent the war years with a German officer, something many of her fellow citizens refused to forgive. She returned in 1954 at the age of 70 to reestablish her couture house, claiming to be disgusted with the exaggerated boned and padded silhouette of the New Look and asserting that men could not design for women. Her highly anticipated first collection was not particularly well received in Paris but gained an almost immediate following in the United States. She chose to create styles that were simple and less constructed than the current mode, returning to many of her original ideas about practicality with

Figure 6.12 A 1955 ensemble by Jacques Fath features his signature large-pointed collar and an A-line silhouette based on Dior's design. ©Picture Post/Getty Images.

style. These styles had an immediate influence on U.S. designers and were deemed an "American way of dressing (Figure 6.13)."[11] She is perhaps best remembered for the collarless wool tweed suits trimmed with braid that she created during this second phase of her career. She certainly seemed to anticipate a desire by women to have less complex alternatives in their wardrobes and was soon back at the top of the couture. Her influence waned during the turbulent 1960s when she refused to support the short skirt fad. Chanel died in 1971, but her couture house continues to be influential.

Paris remained a fashion center, with dozens of couture houses officially registered with the Chambre Syndicale de la Couture Parisienne. The organization wielded even more power than before the war, controlling press release dates, registering designs, and setting show dates. French couture was only available to the wealthiest, but officially sanctioned copies were available through many higher end stores, and store openings showed the reproductions with great fanfare (Figure 6.14).

Figure 6.13 Chanel suit interpreted by U.S. company Davidow. *Vogue*, January 1, 1957, 84, Frances McLaughlin-Gill/*Vogue* ©1957 Condé Nast Publications Inc.

Figure 6.14 American copy of Dior's "A" line suit, described as "A little gentled for America." *Vogue*, April 1, 1955, 128, Horst/*Vogue* ©1955 Condé Nast Publications Inc.

Italy

Italian fashion finally began to come into its own in the early 1950s, helped in part by American machinery and know-how in ready-to-wear. The Fascist government of the 1930s had encouraged and even compelled Italians to do original designs, training a skilled group of artisans who would be important after the war ended. Immediately after the war, Italian designers tended to follow the Paris designers but soon began to put their own unique stamp on their designs. The first collective shows for Italian designers occurred in 1951 in Florence and became an immediate success. Buyers and the press began to attend in growing numbers, copying or buying to copy from the couture. Designers who emerged from these shows included some dressmakers who had been in business for years, such as **Germana Marucelli**, the **Fontana Sisters**, **Simonetta**, and **Alberto Fabiani** (see Figure 6.10), as well as a group of newcomers, such as **Roberto Capucci**, who made his debut in 1952, and **Princess Irene Galitzine**, whose first designs were shown in 1949. Other well-known Italian design companies would become international names in the 1950s and

1960s, including the long-established **House of Gucci**, which became the Guccio Gucci Limited Company in 1939. Hollywood stars such as Grace Kelly and Audrey Hepburn helped to make the Gucci signature leather bags and accessories glamorous.

United States

By the 1940s and 1950s American women were developing their own version of fashion, and, although still influenced by Paris designers, it was a more casual and less structured version of Parisian style. The United States now had a significant group of both New York and California designers who were establishing a sportswear-oriented approach to dressing. Initially the most influential designers continued to be Claire McCardell, Jo Copeland, Adrian, and the other designers who became recognized names during World War II, but many more soon entered the ready-to-wear arena. The fashion press continued (or returned to) significant coverage of French fashion but now added editions that focused on the New York collections.

McCardell continued to design until her death in 1958, creating a postwar look that was long and full but softer and without the padding and understructure that characterized French couture. Both easier to wear and easier to make, her designs were suited to ready-to-wear production processes. Adrian also adopted some of the New Look silhouette, continuing to design ready-to-wear until he had a heart attack in 1952. Both Jo Copeland and Tom Brigance created the American sport and dress styles they had become known for in the 1940s, each expanding their designs into more diversity of styles and categories (see Figure 6.3).

Other U.S. designers entered the market, mostly in ready-to-wear, although some created custom clothing, and a few did both. **Charles James** was one of the limited number of American designers to focus almost exclusively on high-end custom design. Considered a gifted designer both technically and creatively, he worked in Paris until the war began, returning to New York in 1940. Throughout his career, James created his own distinctive approach to structure and shape, and his evening dresses were especially consistent with the structured styles of the 1950s (Figure 6.15). His forté was one-of-a-kind creations for private clients. In the mid-1950s he experimented with ready-to-wear but found it difficult to simplify the structure of his designs for mass production. He also created suits, coats, and daytime dresses, constantly striving for perfection of shape, viewing fabric as a sculptural medium.

Another custom designer, Arnold Isaacs worked in Paris as an apprentice before returning to New York, where he spent two years working with Charles James. He opened his own business under the name **Scaasi**—a reversal of his last name—that operated like a couture house in that he showed collections twice a year for potential customers. The influence of Charles James is sometimes evident in his use of sculptural shapes. His specialty was dramatic evening clothing that relied on intricate cuts in beautiful fabrics.

Norman Norell's first collection was shown in 1941 for the company Traina-Norell. He became known for well-made tailored clothing, often with the kind of design details expected in custom clothing, although he worked exclusively in ready-to-wear. His design premise was that fashion was a logical progression, one style leading into the next, with no dramatic changes. Norell did not design for just one apparel category, as many ready-to-wear designers did, but rather he showed entire collections, from day dresses and suits to evening wear. He was famous for his all-over sequined dresses, dubbed mermaid styles because of their sinuous fit and slight flare at the hem.

Pauline Trigère, one of the influential ready-to-wear designers of the postwar era, began her business in 1942 with a group of 12 dresses. Successful almost from the start, she re-

Figure 6.15 Charles James sculptural evening gown. *Life*, October 23, 1950, 130, ©Time & Life Pictures/Getty Images.

ceived attention from the fashion press with well-made clothing characterized by clean tailoring and elegant simplicity.

Like many of the female designers of the period, Trigère did not sketch, preferring to drape directly in the fabric. From the beginning her specialty was coats in various styles, but she also created wool day dresses, dramatic evening wear, and even wool styles for evening (Figure 6.16).[12]

Bonnie Cashin was one of several California designers to come to prominence after the war. During the war she worked as a costume designer in Hollywood, but she returned to New York in 1949 as designer for the company Adler and Adler. She started her own company with a business partner in 1953. Her design style was geared toward active women and what she called layered dressing, always aspiring to comfort and function in her clothing.[13] Some of her signature looks included capes and ponchos, often with leather edgings, and wool jersey dresses and tops.

James Galanos, another Californian, opened his fashion company in 1951 in Los Angeles. He began to show in New York two years later. As a young man, Galanos worked both in Hollywood as a costume designer and in

Plate 1.1 The Empire waistline (LEFT) would eventually replace the long-waisted, bloused silhouette (RIGHT) starting about 1908. *The Delineator*, August 1900.

Plate 4.1 René Bouet-Willaumez illustration of autumn suits and coats by Schiaparelli, 1932. Note the leg-of mutton sleeve (LEFT), use of fur trim (CENTER). © Condé Nast Archive/Corbis.

Plate 2.1 (OPPOSITE, TOP) Designs from Georges Lepape, 1911. © Historical Picture Archive/Corbis.

Plate 3.1 (OPPOSITE, BOTTOM) Evening wear from the 1920s in *robe de style* and slim silhouettes, illustrated by Georges Barbier. © Stapleton Collection/Corbis.

Plate 5.1 Three suits by Hattie Carnegie. Note the print blouses, adjustment to using less wool, and whimsical hats for a lift. *Vogue*, March 1, 1942, 42. John Rawlings/*Vogue* © 1942 Condé Nast Publications, Inc.

Plate 5.2 Students at a meeting of the Y Center of Humanities. *The Bomb.* Iowa State College, 1942, 149.

Plate 7.2 Yves Saint Laurent's Mondrian dress, as seen here in the designer's 2002 show. © Reuters/Corbis.

Plate 6.1 (TOP) Cristobal Balenciaga red linen suit, circa 1952. © Condé Nast Archive/Corbis.

Plate 7.1 (BOTTOM) Cover-up by Emilio Pucci showing optical-art motifs. © Condé Nast Archive/Corbis.

Plate 8.1 Deborah Turbeville photograph of Scott Barrie dress made of Qiana, silk-like nylon fiber, (LEFT), Stavropoulos dress (CENTER). *Vogue*, October 1975, 195. Deborah Turbeville/*Vogue* © 1975 Condé Nast Publications, Inc.

Plate 8.2 Stephen Burrows red-panne velvet dress with ruffled edges. *Vogue*, October 1974, 112. Photo by Helmut Newton/*Vogue* © 1974 Condé Nast Publications, Inc.

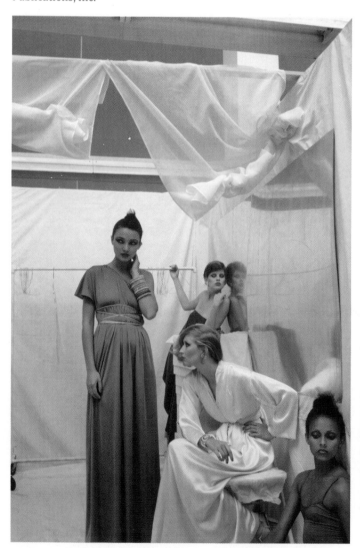

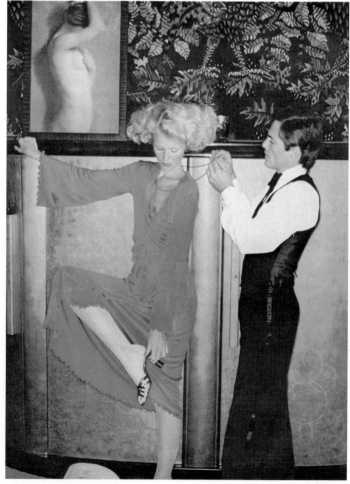

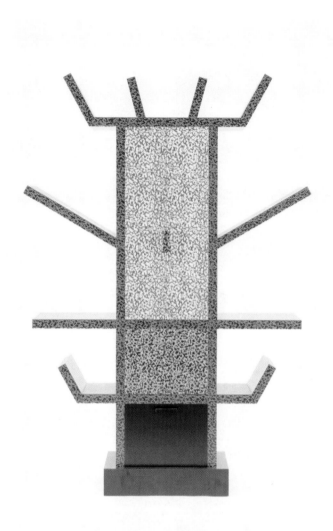

Plate 9.1a Brightly colored, geometric Casablanca sideboard by Ettore Sottsass, the lead designer of the Memphis Design Collective. © Philadelphia Museum of Art/Corbis.

Plate 9.1b Bright colors in a design from Thierry Mugler's 1985–86 fall/winter runway show demonstrate the impact of Memphis design on color trends in the fashions of the period. © Pierre Vauthey/Corbis Sygma.

OVERLEAF

Plate 9.2 (TOP) Designer Christian Lacroix with models wearing designs from spring/summer 1988, the second collection under his own fashion house. © Julio Donoso/Corbis Sygma.

Plate 10.1 (LEFT) Dress from John Galliano's couture collection for the House of Dior, with historic, Asian, and Masai inspirations. © Condé Nast Archive/Corbis.

Plate 11.1 (RIGHT) A silk chiffon dress from BCBG Max Azria, worn with Manolo Blahnik shoes. *Women's Wear Daily,* September 22, 2004, 16.

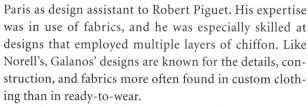

Figure 6.16 Pauline Trigère coat. ©Gjon Mili/Time & Life Pictures/Getty Images.

Figure 6.17 Anne Fogarty in a princess styled, full-skirted satin dress she designed. ©Martha Holmes/Time & Life Pictures/Getty Images.

Paris as design assistant to Robert Piguet. His expertise was in use of fabrics, and he was especially skilled at designs that employed multiple layers of chiffon. Like Norell's, Galanos' designs are known for the details, construction, and fabrics more often found in custom clothing than in ready-to-wear.

Molly Parnis is perhaps best known for dressing First Lady Mamie Eisenhower. Her design specialties in the 1950s were very full-skirted shirtwaist-style dresses and narrow-skirted suits. **Anne Klein** also got her start in this period as designer for a company called Junior Sophisticates. She created uniquely tasteful clothing in a junior size range, targeted to a more sophisticated market than most junior clothing.[14] Klein went on to open her own design company in the early 1960s, with a focus on separates and sportswear. **Anne Fogarty** embarked on her apparel design career creating clothing for teens for a company called Youth Guild. She then moved to Margot Inc., a junior dress company. She initially designed dresses in the full-skirted New Look silhouette but with simpler construction and lines. Fogarty was best known for her **crinoline**-supported skirts—crisp

full layers of underskirts intended to hold the skirt away from the body (Figure 6.17).

Fashion Trends

The decade after World War II is often considered a time of conformity and of conservative fashion. Women's overall looks were polished and mature, with a trend for matching accessories. Fashion publications tended to make dictatorial pronouncements each season about what was or was not the latest fashion rule. Men's clothing was inclined to a uniform appearance, with neutral, often somber colors. Suburban living in America gradually encouraged a tendency toward less formality.

Textiles and Technology

When the war ended, textile materials slowly but surely began to return to store shelves, and experimentation occurred with both new and established fibers. The mobile, consumer-oriented society of the 1950s provided ready markets for a profusion of new, easy-care synthetic fibers. After at least eight years without silk, a younger generation was largely unfamiliar with this traditional fiber and more than ready to embrace synthetic fibers. The DuPont Corporation accelerated the postwar production of nylon so that, by 1947, the customer queues to purchase nylon hose that had existed just after the war had mostly disappeared. DuPont, along with its British competitor Imperial Chemical Industries (ICI), initially developed polyester, introducing Dacron (DuPont) and Terylene (ICI). Polyester was promoted as a fiber that consumers could wash and wear, required little or no ironing, and consequently reduced time and money spent in garment care. In fact so much clothing was now wash-and-wear that sale of washing machines also rose.[15]

DuPont commercially produced acrylic (the first brand name was Orlon) in 1950. Acrylic was a fiber that lent itself to use in fabrics that had the loftiness of wool, but were washable, fast-drying, and resistant to moth damage (Figure 6.18). Celanese Corporation commercially produced the first triacetate fiber in the United States in 1954. In 1948 Swiss inventor George de Mestral, while investigating the reason burrs stuck to his clothing, came upon a starting place for developing a two-sided hook and loop fastener. He named the invention Velcro, for the French words *velour* and *crochet*, hoping the tape would become a fastener to rival the zipper.

Figure 6.18 Hubert De Givenchy's sleeveless cardigan sweater made from black Orlon and worn over a white Orlon pique skirt. ©Bettmann/Corbis.

Women's Styles

Two silhouettes dominated for all categories of women's clothing until the mid-1950s—either pencil slim or very full, bouffant skirts, almost always with a narrow, pronounced waistline. By mid-decade, Dior introduced a series of silhouette variations, including what were termed the A-line and the H-line (see Figure 6.14). These filtered down into ready-to-wear and helped create a trend for slightly less fitted silhouettes. However, some variety in silhouette for both suits and dresses was shown throughout the period. Fashion tended to be occasion specific, defined by event and time of day.

Dresses

Dior's first New Look dresses used remarkable amounts of fabric in the skirts, sometimes as much as 25 to 30 yards. At the same time he also showed an extremely narrow silhouette. Both skirt shapes were topped with a close-fitted bodice, small waist, and sloping shoulder devoid of the shoulder padding of the previous decade (see Figures 6.9 and 6.11). As counterpoint to the Paris designers, a relatively simple and conservative style of dress more accurately epitomized the majority of American women's fashions. By

the mid-1950s shapes for some dresses were slightly less constricted in the waist, and some had an accent on the hip, through either seaming or trim placement.

Daytime

Daytime dresses came in both narrow and full silhouettes, and whereas the Paris couture style was often padded in the hip and had complexly layered and boned inner structures, the ready-to-wear versions were less intricate while retaining the overall shape. The cotton **shirtwaist dress** became a fashion standard, usually buttoned up the front, with fitted waist and a variety of collar styles (see Figure 6.1). In response to the active American lifestyle, some ready-to-wear dresses were actually a separate skirt and blouse, to help extend the wardrobe. Lengths remained long through most of the period and shortened gradually after mid-decade, continuing to do so into the 1960s. Hem length, however, varied to some degree almost yearly and was a frequent topic of the fashion press.

For summer, dresses were sleeveless or halter style, often in cotton or linen. In 1956 and 1957 the sack dress was introduced by Balenciaga and Givenchy to the consterna-

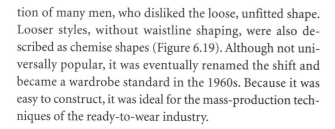

Figure 6.19 Chemise dresses. ©Thomas D. Mcavoy/Time & Life Pictures/Getty Images.

Figure 6.20 Mother and daughter in matching cardigans. ©Hulton Archive/Getty Images.

tion of many men, who disliked the loose, unfitted shape. Looser styles, without waistline shaping, were also described as chemise shapes (Figure 6.19). Although not universally popular, it was eventually renamed the shift and became a wardrobe standard in the 1960s. Because it was easy to construct, it was ideal for the mass-production techniques of the ready-to-wear industry.

Cocktail and Evening

Cocktails such as martinis and manhattans were the popular alcoholic drinks of the 1950s, and cocktail hour was the time of day to serve drinks, sometimes at home, sometimes in cocktail lounges. For this a special dress style came into fashion just after the war in the same silhouettes that dominated the period (see Figures 6.8 and 6.17). The cocktail dress was usually similar in length to a day dress, but in more decorative fabrics such as taffeta or intricately pleated silk chiffons. Some narrow silhouettes had elaborate back draping, reminiscent of the bustles of the nineteenth century. There was a brief vogue for a balloon-shaped skirt in 1957.

Evening gowns were often complicated and elaborate constructions, frequently boned and strapless. To wear the style required a strapless bra and often even a corselet or **merry widow**, essentially a long-line bra extending slightly below the waist. For dinner parties ballerina length (below midcalf but above the ankle) was popular, often with lace or tulle overskirts that gave the appearance of ballet costumes. Full-length gowns were worn for formal occasions. Some had **fishtail** hems, narrow skirts with fullness at the lower back, while others were defined as mermaid styles, fitted with fullness all around the hem. The elaborate back draping also appeared in evening dresses (see Figure 6.15).

Suits and Outerwear

Suits and dresses with matching jackets were a wardrobe standard, with very fitted shapes dominant in the first half of the period, and slightly boxier shapes by mid-decade. Both silhouettes appeared simultaneously, however, through much of the decade (see Figures 6.2 and 6.14 and Plate 6.1). Suits were crisply tailored until Chanel introduced her now-famous collarless jacket in a less fitted, more relaxed silhouette. Although not widely accepted at first, it became a staple by the end of the decade (see Figure 6.13). A few suit skirts were full, but most were narrow. Jackets had a variety of collar and pocket styles, usually with narrow sleeves and high-set armholes. Raglan and kimono

sleeves with an inset gusset were also a frequent jacket detail, and three-quarter-length or bracelet length sleeves became fashionable with the New Look (see Figure 6.12 and Plate 6.1).

The vogue for cashmere, wool, and even acrylic sweaters (see Figure 6.20) and sweater sets provided a more relaxed but still polished alternative to a suit. The sweater set or **twin set** consisted of a waist-length or slightly longer cardigan sweater, with a matching sleeveless or short-sleeved shell. Often decorated with pearls, jewels, or fur collars, the style originated in Mainbocher's World War II evening sweaters but hit its stride in the 1950s.

Coat design was the antithesis of the tightly fitted silhouettes in dresses. Often in large and oversized tent shapes, some stood away from the body in firmly woven wools or thick boucles, mohair, or curly **astrakhan cloth** (see Figures 6.10 and 6.16). Fur was popular not only in a full coat, but also in stoles and wraps or as decorative collar additions.

Sportswear, Separates, and Active Sport Clothing

The American ready-to-wear industry pioneered the concept of sportswear and mix-and-match separates, and U.S. sportswear designers were among the most recognized. The press may have covered the Paris couture, but the U.S. industry, centered on Seventh Avenue in New York City and geared to efficient mass production, dominated ready-to-wear design and manufacture. American women came to love the idea of separates that could be combined in numerous ways to extend the wardrobe. Perhaps part of the do-it-yourself culture,

it also allowed women to create their own version of style, whether French or uniquely American. Pieces included skirts in the dominant silhouettes of the period, a variety of jacket shapes and pullover tops, blouses and sweater blouses, and pants or shorts (see Figure 6.21). Stripes and dots were particularly popular, along with crisp but comfortable fabrics such as denim, seersucker, poplin, and jersey.

Although pants were still not generally considered appropriate for professional or dress occasions, a variety of narrow-legged trouser styles became popular for casual wear or for at-home entertaining. Slim **toreador** and cropped-length **capri pants** were worn with dressy and casual blouses (Figure 6.22). There was a brief vogue for narrow trousers worn under full skirts, usually split up the front, for home entertaining. Shorts also were popular for both casual summer dressing and for actual sport activities. Bermuda shorts were worn by both men and women, and short shorts gained popularity toward the end of the period, although not without some controversy.

Bathing suits, on the contrary, often tended to constructions that looked like the elaborate evening dresses of the day, at least in the bodice (Figure 6.23). The advent of synthetic fabrics and wash-and-wear finishes meant a new level of easy care, in addition to the ability to create permanent pleating for skirts, whether for more formal occasions or for tennis dresses.

The baby boom also brought the need for well-designed maternity clothing. Shown in catalogs, maternity clothing was only occasionally seen in fashion publications. Maternity styles, however, were no longer designed to hide the

Figure 6.21 (OPPOSITE, LEFT) Jantzen
sportswear. The Advertising
Archives.

Figure 6.22 (OPPOSITE, RIGHT) Audrey
Hepburn in black sweater, black
Capri pants, and flats. ©Hulton
Archive/Getty Images.

Figure 6.23 (BOTTOM, LEFT) One piece
structured, nylon, satin bathing
suit. ©Genevieve Naylor/Corbis.

Figure 6.24 (RIGHT) Patterns for
maternity blouses and skirts from
a Butterick counter book. Author's
collection.

Figure 6.25 (BOTTOM, RIGHT) Styles for
a family outing. ©Retrofile/Getty
Images, photograph by H.
Armstrong Roberts.

Figure 6.26 Costume jewelry. ©Condé Nast Archive/Corbis.

Figure 6.27 Bra and panty girdle designed to create the contoured silhouette that the fitted suits demanded. ©Peter Sickles/ Superstock.

pregnancy as much as in earlier periods, and most had very full smock tops (Figure 6.24). Another offshoot of the baby boom was a vogue for matching mother–daughter dresses or the presentation of clothing designed to epitomize an attractive family on an outing together (Figure 6.25).

Accessories

Hats were an essential accessory for most occasions, including cocktail and evening wear, and ranged widely in both style and size. Some were quite small (see Figure 6.10), often with a veil in the front, but wide-brimmed **picture hats** were also worn (see Figure 6.19). Other styles included turbans and straw hats for summer. By the end of the period, most hats were relatively small in scale.

Popular jewelry included multiple strands of pearls, beads, and rhinestones in an array of colors (see Figure 6.18). Two or three small pins, sometimes called scatter pins, might also be worn together on sweaters. Jewelry often came in matching sets that included necklace, bracelet, and earrings and there was also a diverse selection of other costume jewelry (Figure 6.26).

In the first half of the period, round-toe shoes were the standard, usually a medium or high heel pump for dress oc-

casions (see Figure 6.14). Some also had ankle straps or were sling backs. By the mid-1950s, shoes developed increasingly pointed toes, still with a high but much narrower heel. By the very end of the decade **stiletto heels** (resembling a stiletto blade) were popular, most with extremely pointed toes. Casual shoe styles included ballet and other styles of flats (see Figure 6.22) often worn with narrow pants or more casual full skirts. Espadrilles, loafers, sandals, and canvas tennis shoes were also commonly worn and, for teens, saddle shoes or white bucks, a lace-up style made from white buckskin were popular.

Foundations, Lingerie, and Sleepwear

After the restrictions and shortages of the war years, lingerie blossomed during the late 1940s and 1950s, helped by new fibers and stimulated by successive changes in the fashionable silhouette.

Nylon and Lastex returned to full use in 1946, once the industry switched from military to consumer goods and the last of the wartime government controls ended. Girdles, which had been made of heavy synthetic elastic in dull peach tones, now were shown in lighter weight Lastex in appealing whites and powder blues. Bras, although structured,

Figure 6.28 Beaumond Lingerie peignoir set. ©Hulton Archive/ Getty Images.

reverted to white nylon marquisette or fine cotton broadcloth, abandoning coarser cotton except for a few plaids and checks for young customers. More variety was to come. As the 1950s progressed, the color range in girdles, bras, slips, and sleepwear expanded to include soft pink, mint green, yellow, amber, red, black, navy, and brown. Foundation and lingerie departments were located near each other and showed the first glimpses of the color coordination that would typify the 1960s. Woven nylon gave girdle panels firmness with light weight, and permanent pleating created appealing styles of nightgowns and slips.

When Christian Dior launched his New Look, he did the foundations manufacturers a huge favor. Suddenly, cinched waistlines, full hips, and prominent breasts were in vogue. Most women could not wear the new silhouette well without a high-waist girdle and bra (Figure 6.27) or corselet. Later styles of sheath dress put figures even more on display and required firm girdling. The merry widow foundation worked well with the long-torso styles that Dior presented in 1954. During the later 1950s, when sheath styles shared the fashion scene with chemise dresses, girdles became less constricting, and dipped waistlines were offered. Panty girdles remained popular from the end of the war through-

out the 1950s, because women—especially teens and young women—wore slacks and shorts for informal occasions, although rarely for school or at work.

Bras came in a wide array of types during this period. Low necklines guaranteed a market for strapless bras made with under-wires or over-wires, which ran through the tops of the cups instead of under the breasts. Once the military requisition of metal supplies ended, many companies produced wired bras. Foam rubber padding offered help to those who wanted more than nature had bestowed. Unfortunately, foam turned dry and brittle over time and had to be laundered with care and air dried. Styles proliferated: convertible straps made it easier to wear halters, backless dresses, or strapless dresses. For the really daring, there were stick-on bras that consisted of two half-cups, period. Functional styles met the needs of some customers, including maternity bras, pullover bras for the comfort-seeking wearer, and bras with pads for women who had had mastectomies. Cup styles changed subtly with time; the long-torso, high bosom look in style in 1954–1955 encouraged bra makers to soften the cone-shaped cup into a rounder, less aggressive contour.

Slips went through various style changes, too, from stiff, bouffant crinolines popular during the late 1940s and early 1950s to slim cuts when the sheath silhouette became popular. Crinolines of taffeta, netting, and other crisp materials might be worn in multiples, a fad with teenagers. Bra slips came on the scene to create a smooth line under the close-fitting sheaths. Availability of nylon tricot encouraged women to buy fancy slips and other decorative intimates such as peignoir sets (Figure 6.28) because they were relatively easy to wash and required little ironing.

Men's Styles

Men, like women, presented a polished appearance in the decade after World War II, with suits or sport coats and trousers, but there was now greater attention to separates and casual attire. The American ready-to-wear industry was again the leader in creating sportswear for the casual lifestyle engendered by suburban living.

Suits and Outerwear

Unlike women's fashion with the New Look, men's styles changed less dramatically after the war. Undoubtedly tired of uniforms, men quickly adopted civilian dress and perhaps looked for a change from the war and prewar years. When wartime fabric regulations were lifted, suit trousers could again have a cuff. Although double-breasted suits continued to be worn into the 1950s, the single-breasted style with narrow lapels and a softer shoulder was more common. The suit shape that dominates impressions of the

Figure 6.29 Gregory Peck in a traditional slim style suit in *The Man in the Gray Flannel Suit*. ©20th Century Fox/The Kobal Collection.

That made-for-you look...

HART SCHAFFNER & MARX

Figure 6.30 Ivy League style with vest. The Advertising Archives.

1950s is perhaps best represented by the book and subsequent film *The Man in the Gray Flannel Suit* (Figure 6.29). This boxy, sack-suit silhouette was the essential style of the midfifties. Trousers were generally styled without pleats.

Suits or sport jackets were standard attire even for young men, including some of the early rock and roll performers. The development of synthetic fabrics led to the wash-and-wear suit, first introduced in 1952 with a flurry of ads showing men leaping into pools or exiting the shower in a Dacron polyester suit. Regardless of whether polyester suits were actually tossed into the laundry or not, they did need to be cleaned regularly in the early years, because the fiber could take on an unpleasant odor. For those who did not like the appearance and hand of 100 percent polyester, many wool and polyester blends began to appear.

Younger men wore what was considered an Ivy League look, based on styles popularized by Brooks Brothers on East Coast campuses. The look consisted of a three-button sport jacket, often in softer fabrics such as corduroy or tweeds, a button-down collar shirt, basic tie, and sometimes **chinos** and loafers. Some also wore vests in plaids or paisley, or V-neck sweaters with the sport jacket (Figure 6.30).

At the other end of the dressing spectrum from the Ivy

League look was the greaser look, sometimes associated with working-class adolescents instead of collegiate or college-bound young men. The look represented a rebellion against the more conservative styles of dress and usually consisted of blue jeans, T-shirts, leather motorcycle jackets, and slicked-back hair. Sometimes banned in high schools, its most likely inspiration was Marlon Brando in *The Wild One* or James Dean in *Rebel Without a Cause* (see Figure 6.6).

Dinner jackets and tuxedos continued to be the evening wear of choice, depending on the formality of the occasion (see Figure 6.7). For warm-weather wear, a white dinner jacket, usually with a shawl collar, was preferred.

Casual Dress

The popularity of separates that permeated women's fashions also extended to men. The American ready-to-wear industry produced casual pants, sport shirts, and outerwear for relaxed suburban dressing for evenings and weekends at home. Hawaiian-print shirts were popular, and even President Harry Truman sported one. Both Bermuda shorts and jeans were worn with knit shirts or plaid, button-down collar sport shirts. Some sport shirts were designed with a

Figure 6.31 Men's dress trousers with casual shirts. The Advertising Archives.

Figure 6.32 Casual clothing styles, including Bermuda shorts and sports shirts. ©Bettmann/Corbis.

spread collar, to be worn open at the neck (Figure 6.31).

Outerwear came in a variety of styles, including short, zipper-front jackets, cardigan sweaters, and topcoats and overcoats for wear over suits. President Eisenhower gave his name to a waist-length, front-buttoned jacket for casual wear. Although he began to wear the style during the war, it continued to be popular well into the 1950s. Eisenhower was also given credit for further reinforcing the trend toward more casual dress when he chose a standard suit jacket and homburg hat over the more traditional cut-away coat and top hat for his 1953 inauguration.

Shirts, Shoes, and Accessories

Although most suits were gray or other neutral shades, there was at least some color in shirts, most often blue or pink. Collars were either button-down or fastened with a collar pin under the tie. Brooks Brothers experimented with some of the first polyester-and-cotton blend shirts, reinforcing the easy-care lifestyle of the period. Narrow ties and sometimes bowties were the most common accessory with a suit. Patterns were usually simple stripes or small geometrics (see Figure 6.32). The occasional ascot was worn, but these never became widely popular. There was little

change in men's undergarments, with boxers, cotton jockey briefs, and T-shirts the standard.

Hats were considered an essential accessory for the properly dressed man and were offered in a variety of styles, again usually restrained and not ostentatious. **Snap-brim hats,** with a small brim, and fedoras were worn year-round, and in the summer men might sport a straw Panama hat. Some men might wear a more continental cap, but, like the ascot, it was a less widespread style. Shoe styles for men varied with the occasion, oxfords, and brogues for wear with suits and loafers and moccasins and sandals for summer casual dressing.

Teen Styles

The teenager as a targeted market truly came of age in the 1950s, and many styles were now offered just for teens. Magazines such as *Seventeen* and *Young Miss* presented a whole new opportunity for girls to see clothing styles designed for them. Teen fashions ranged from very specific youth styles to clothing that was in close imitation of adult dress. For both boys and girls, dungarees or jeans, frequently rolled up at the hem to give a cuffed appearance, were the standard for casual after school dress (see Figure

Figure 6.33 Felt circle skirt with felt appliqués. Private collection.

Figure 6.34 Children in jeans and play clothes (1954). ©Bettmann/Corbis.

6.6 for dungarees). Girls often wore oversize shirts or jackets, bobby sox, and loafers or saddle shoes with their jeans.

A popular style for teen girls was the preppy look—a very full skirt often held out with crinoline skirts or slips underneath, which served to emphasize a narrow waist. This was topped with decorative sweater blouses. One variation of this was the poodle skirt, a full-circle skirt often made of wool felt with poodles appliquéd at the hem. Although later 1950s nostalgia associated the poodle motif almost exclusively with this style, the skirt could also be purchased with a variety of other images, from telephones to geometric designs, and was easy to make at home and personalize (Figure 6.33).

Some teen boys also adopted the preppy look, while the more rebellious chose the styles associated with teen rebels portrayed in movies or rock and roll. The **white buck,** the style popularized by singer Pat Boone, was popular with both teen boys and girls.

Children's Styles

Children's clothing ranged from durable, comfortable, and washable play clothing, to fad clothing inspired by televi-

sion or movie characters, to dress styles for church, parties, or other special occasions. With the rapidly increasing number of children, merchandising of children's clothing increased exponentially. Girls of all ages wore cotton dresses in what could be considered a New Look style but were in fact the typical dress style of young girls for decades—a fitted bodice with full gathered skirt and often puffed and gathered sleeves. This basic silhouette offered a seemingly infinite variety of details, yoke, pocket, and collar variations, and usually buttoned up the back. Little boys wore dress-up clothing that closely resembled men's suits or sport coats, sometimes with shorts for the youngest (see Figure 6.25).

Play clothing was sometimes unisex, with similar denim pants, overalls, and T-shirts for both boys and girls. Cardigan sweaters could be layered with knit shirts to be worn with elastic waist, pull-on pants for boy or girls or a skirt with suspenders for girls (Figure 6.34; see also Figure 6.2). Creepers with a snap crotch for easy diaper changing were still usual for babies and toddlers.

Coats for children came in many styles that were similar to adult clothing, both dress and casual. There were front-zippered jackets, parkas, and a variety of single- and double-breasted wool coats (Figure 6.35).

Figure 6.35 Children's winter coats, jackets, and one piece snow suit. *Little Golden Book*, image courtesy of The Advertising Archives.

Hair and Grooming

Hairstyles for adult women were controlled, in keeping with the overall polished style of the period. Toni home permanents and home hair-coloring products such as those of Miss Clairol reflected the trend toward do-it-yourself, and blond was an especially popular shade, inspired in part by Marilyn Monroe. Other styles included medium-length pageboys or, alternatively, with the lower rolled curl flipped up, both sometimes with bangs (see Figures 6.13 and 6.24). Mamie Eisenhower's short, evenly trimmed front bangs also inspired numerous imitations. For younger girls and teens, the ponytail and short, curly poodle cut were popular. It was not until late in the decade that a more bouffant style began to be popular, held in place by back-combing (teasing) the hair and prodigious amounts of hair spray. This style would continue into the early 1960s, contributing to the decline in hat wearing.

Women's makeup was also designed to create a mature, polished, and refined appearance. Dramatic, arched eyebrows accented eyes outlined with eyeliner and by mid-decade, a variety of eye shadow shades. The lip colors of choice were bright reds.

Men's hair was almost uniformly short throughout the 1950s (see Figure 6.29). Styles such as the crew cut and flat top were popular, and, although they gave the appearance of an easy and carefree cut, many, like the flat-top, were held stiff, with hair straight up, through use of hair waxes and others products.[16] Brylcreme, a product that had been around since the 1930s, became popular again with the television advertising campaign slogan: "Brylcreem—A Little Dab'll Do Ya!" An alternative to the short style was the **ducktail**, associated with rebels and rock and rollers, worn by teenagers and popularized by stars such as Elvis Presley.[17] It was longer than other styles, with a curly high pompadour in front and parted in the back with a long length, suggestive of the tail feathers of a duck.

Summary

The Dior New Look in 1947 signaled a change in styles distinct from the austerity of the war years. There was actually a tremendous amount of diversity in silhouette and in fashion details over a 10-year period, despite the tendency to view it as a time of conformity and conservatism. By 1958, skirts were getting shorter, the impact of rock and roll on fashion was increasing, and the baby boom generation was entering its teen years, heralding dramatic changes for the next 10 years and beyond.

Suggested Readings

Cawthorne, Nigel. *The New Look: The Dior Revolution*. London: Reed International Books Limited, 1996.

Coleman, Elizabeth Ann. *The Genius of Charles James*. New York: The Brooklyn Museum, 1982.

Halberstam, David. *The Fifties*. New York: Villard Books, 1993.

Handley, Susannah. *Nylon: The Story of a Fashion Revolution*. Baltimore: The Johns Hopkins University Press, 1999.

Liberman, Alexander, and Polly Devlin. *Vogue Book of Fashion Photography: 1919–1979*. New York: The Condé Nast Publications, Ltd., 1979.

Milbank, Caroline Rennolds. *New York Fashion: The Evolution of American Style*. New York: Harry N. Abrams, 1989.

Palmer, Alexandra. *Couture & Commerce: The Transatlantic Fashion Trade in the 1950s*. Vancouver: UBC Press, 2001

Schreier, Barbara. *Mystique and Identity: Women's Fashions of the 1950s*. Norfolk, VA: The Chrysler Museum, 1984.

White, Nicola. *Reconstructing Italian Fashion: America and the Development of the Italian Fashion Industry*. Oxford: Berg, 2000.

Young, William H., and Nancy K. Young. *The 1950s*. Westport, CN: Greenwood Press, 2004.

CHAPTER 7

1959–

U.S. Events and Trends	Russian lunar space probe American Football League founded	John F. Kennedy elected president		Cuban missile crisis First overseas television broadcast First industrial "robots" marketed	John F. Kennedy assassinated; Lyndon B. Johnson becomes President *Feminine Mystique* published
	1959 	**1960** 	**1961** 	**1962** 	**1963**
U.S. Fashions	Slim bodice, full or slim skirt	Jacqueline Kennedy's style becomes influential Bodice shapes ease Norell culotte suit			Courrèges pantsuits

Tripping

1968

Beatles come to United States

Lyndon B. Johnson elected President

Inner-city riots begin

Civil Rights Act of 1964 passed

Baby boom officially ends

Hippie culture coalesces

National Organization for Women founded

First Super Bowl

American Basketball Association founded

LBJ's youth fitness initiative

Antiwar protests increase

Assassinations of Robert Kennedy and Martin Luther King, Jr.

Europe torn by student riots

Organ transplants

Arthur Ashe wins first U.S. Tennis Open

 1964

 1965

 1966

 1967

 1968

"Beatle" fashions spread

First flared pants

Gernreich's "no-bra" bra

High-waist styles

Saint Laurent's "Le Smoking" tuxedo for women

Miniskirts

Shift dresses become popular

Apparel $15 billion industry

"Op art" influences dress

Paper dress fad

Twiggy tours United States

Warnings about dangers of sun tanning

India influences styles

Athletic shoes for jogging introduced

Out on Fashion

Much like the 1920s, the 1960s carry a heavy freight of memories for those who experienced them and bear a similar burden of stereotypes for people born after that momentous decade. Words associated with that era often include protest, revolt, black power, feminism, youthquake, generation gap, space age, mod, Beatles, and, of course, miniskirt, love beads, and bell-bottomed hip huggers. Probe beyond these words and you will find as complex a period as any in modern history, fraught with turmoil but also yielding marvelous technical and scientific progress; frenetic, but also introspective; beset with crises, from assassinations to Cold War brinksmanship, but also full of creative energy in music, film, and the visual arts. Americans explored their world more fully during that decade, sampling the cultures of Asia, Africa, and Latin America even as they competed with the Soviet Union to reach worlds beyond this globe.[1] Many of the conveniences taken for granted in the twenty-first century came into use between 1959 and 1968: satellites, lasers, microwave ovens, robots and, most pervasive, offshoots of the early mainframe computer. The 1960s deserve a careful look, for they yield many surprises.

Political and Military Situation
International Politics

Between 1959 and 1968, the Cold War raged between the western free world and the Soviet Union and other Communist states. The United States worked with allies in Europe to confront Soviet and Communist aggression. The North Atlantic Treaty Organization (NATO) represented the military arm of the western democracies. Threats to freedom loomed not just in Europe, where Soviet troops moved into Berlin, partitioning the city with a wall, but also in the Americas and Asia. Cuba fell to Castro's Communists in 1959, and Vietnam's simmering civil war between Communist and anti-Communist forces escalated. With communism as the real and present danger to freedom, it is understandable that American leaders, including Presidents Dwight Eisenhower, John Kennedy, and Lyndon Johnson—all strongly anti-communist—engaged in or backed military actions in Cuba and Vietnam. Neither fight succeeded, although Communism was held in check elsewhere. Russian missiles were removed from Cuba only after a hair-raising confrontation between Premier Nikita Khrushchev and President Kennedy in 1962. Real fear of a nuclear war prompted some U.S. families to continue to build and stock fallout shelters in or adjacent to their homes.

The so-called space race embodied another front in the war between democracy and Communism. American and European efforts to launch satellites and human beings into space were driven by the need to prevent the initially successful Russians from dominating what President Kennedy termed the New Frontier.

Europe, like the United States, endured a turbulent period in the 1960s, with the year 1968 being wracked by violent student protests in many countries (Figure 7.1). Anticapitalist, antiwar, and antiestablishment, these protests spoke of an alienated young generation. On the whole, however, Europe progressed economically. The Treaty of Rome (1957) had created an integrated market, without tariffs, in a few major commodities; this entity grew gradually into the Common Market[2] free of trade barriers for a wider range of goods. The destruction from World War II was gradually repaired in western Europe, and cooperation flourished among its countries, led, significantly, by the old adversaries Germany and France.

Domestic Politics

President Eisenhower devoted his last year in office to efforts to conclude a nuclear test-ban treaty with the Soviets, but Khrushchev used a U.S. spy plane incident to derail the talks. In 1960, John F. Kennedy gained a quite narrow presidential victory over Richard Nixon, which may have persuaded him to proceed slowly with his domestic political agenda. Democrats controlled Congress, but within the party the southern legislators hewed to a very conservative line, especially on racial integration. Kennedy backed civil rights legislation, which was stalled in Congress at the time of his assassination in November 1963. Vice President Johnson, sworn in as president within hours of Kennedy's death, pursued many aspects of Kennedy's program and did his best to bring a sense of stability to a shocked nation.

Fear that communism would spread from North Vietnam and Laos into all of southeast Asia persuaded Eisenhower, Kennedy, and Johnson to back the South Vietnamese government against invasion by Communist leader Ho Chi Minh's forces from the North. The analogy of falling dominoes was used: topple one domino and each one in the stack would fall in sequence. South Vietnam's leader, a corrupt strong-man, nonetheless was supported as preferable to Uncle Ho. Through the 1960s, material support for the South Vietnamese army gradually metamorphosed into sending military advisers to train native troops and then to committing U.S. service personnel to combat. Chinese and Russian backing for Ho Chi Minh's forces ensured that the defeat of the Communists would prove very difficult.

Military stalemate and mounting American casualties hardened opposition to the war. "Hell, no. We won't go!" became the cry of some potential draftees. Although earliest opposition to the war came from the nation's youth, by

Figure 7.1 Protester arrested in Brooklyn, N.Y., 1967. ©Bettmann/ Corbis.

Figure 7.2 Julian Bond as a young activist, in Ivy-League casual dress, 1966. ©Bettmann/Corbis.

the end of the decade they were joined by an increasing number of adults. Students seized buildings on college campuses and generally disrupted campus life. By the end of his administration in 1968, President Johnson began to limit the bombing of North Vietnam to encourage peace talks. The war, however, would continue for another seven years. Hostilities in Vietnam dominated and fragmented American politics; antiwar riots disrupted the Democrats' 1968 presidential convention in Chicago. Endless violence seemed to be the nation's fate in that year, with the assassinations of presidential candidate Robert Kennedy and civil rights leader Martin Luther King Jr.

Although the Supreme Court ruled racial segregation in U.S. schools illegal in 1954, progress on civil rights moved at a glacial pace. By 1957, fewer than one-fourth of schools in southern states were even partially integrated. Under Presidents Truman and Eisenhower, the army and a few southern schools desegregated, but the races remained mostly separated in civilian life. Access to voting rights improved slightly as the Civil Rights Act went into effect in early 1960. Sit-ins to protest refusal of service to young blacks in a Greensboro, North Carolina, restaurant sparked hundreds of sit-ins and demonstrations in 1964. Desegregation began to progress in about 100 cities, bringing integrated public transportation, restaurants, restrooms, and hotels.

Two strands of black leadership dominated the 1960s: the nonviolent stream, led by Martin Luther King Jr., and the militant variety, led by Stokely Carmichael, Floyd McKissick, and Malcolm X, who preached black power. Civil rights legislation in 1964 and 1965 began to thwart the intimidation of would-be black voters, but continuing economic disadvantage and general frustration boiled over into riots in hundreds of large and small American cities between 1964 and 1968—especially in the wake of the as-

sassination of Dr. King in 1968. Business journals counseled readers about coping with a riot by backing up records, arranging physical security, and reducing inventory of desirable items during periods of local unrest. Peace was eventually established, although some downtown areas recovered slowly, if at all. A sweeping reform act in 1968 outlawed discrimination in housing, affecting about 80 percent of all housing. The Equal Employment Opportunity Commission (EEOC) worked to eradicate racial discrimination in the workplace. Politically, there was some progress, with Julian Bond (Figure 7.2) nominated as vice president, although he withdrew his candidacy because of insufficient delegate support.

Under the banner of a Great Society, President Johnson's administration tackled the problems of poverty in the United States. The federal government established several hundred agencies and launched programs such as Medicare, Medicaid, and federal aid to education. Federally subsidized public-housing complexes, built to replace slum housing, did not prove to be a panacea: crime, vandalism, and drug sales all flourished in these vertical ghettoes.

Social Context

The United States comprised 176 million people in 1960, rising to 203 million by the end of the decade, thus sparking alarm about overpopulation. Immigration, legal and illegal, contributed to the swelling numbers of Americans. As it turned out, America's birth rate declined during the 1960s, reaching a level lower than that of the Great Depression years. The baby boom, which began officially in 1946, tailed out in 1964 and turned to a baby bust. The first of the boomer cohort reached their teens in 1959, giving them considerable power to shape taste in fashion, music, and other forms of recreation. They rejected parental standards of dress and entertainment, coining the late 1960s slogan "Don't trust anyone over 30." A substantial number of teens embraced the newest forms of rock and roll, long hair on males, ultrashort skirts, unisex styles, and drugs. Alcohol had long been a party staple, but marijuana and mind-altering hallucinogenic drugs, such as LSD, were used by hippies and other youthful subcultures. *Hippie,* a termed derived from the hipster or beatnik of the previous decade, rejected mainstream values and espoused peace and love as a solution to the problems of the day.

The roots of 1960s feminism reached back to the 1940s, when women were displaced from industrial jobs by returning veterans. Women had discovered that they could do all kinds of work, and they enjoyed the independence conferred by a paycheck. Some, but by no means all, women accepted a return to domestic life in 1946. Educated women chafed at being consigned to spend their days at home, with limited intellectual stimulation. Undoubtedly, some marriages that foundered after the war did so because the woman would not relinquish her autonomy.

Published in 1963, Betty Friedan's *The Feminine Mystique* became the manifesto of feminists. She and like-minded activists founded the National Organization for Women (NOW) in 1966 to spearhead agitation for equal pay, full access to employment options and advancement, and an end to social stereotyping of women. They demanded favorable divorce laws, tougher sanctions against rape, access to abortion, and better daycare for children. In the mid-1960s, women constituted only 7 percent of U.S. physicians and fewer than 4 percent of lawyers. Those who had demanding careers resented the expectation that they would carry the full burden of household work and child care.

Socially, feminists objected to what they termed the objectification of women, including expectations for physical beauty. The more radical members of the movement ceased to shave their legs, wear bras or girdles, or apply makeup. Others, including Helen Gurley Brown (Figure 7.3) and Gloria Steinham, two advocates of sexual liberation, maintained an outward image of physical attractiveness. At the end of the 1960s, Steinham embraced a more complete version of feminism.

Nascent environmentalism emerged in the 1960s, with publication of Rachel Carson's *Silent Spring* (1962). Smog in California prompted new state standards for auto emissions, to become effective in 1969. By 1970, 109 million cars were registered, so automotive contributions to pollution were noticeable. Ralph Nader published a tract—*Unsafe at Any Speed*—against the American auto companies in 1965, condemning their lack of safety and reliability. An equally strong challenge to Detroit came from the Volkswagen bug,

Figure 7.3 Helen Gurley Brown, editor of *Cosmopolitan* and author of *Sex and the Single Girl*, at her typewriter, January 1965. ©Bettmann/ Corbis.

an inexpensive, gas-thrifty alternative to Detroit's big cars. As the decade progressed, Volkswagen minivans became the chosen vehicles of the hip—and hippie—crowd.

Science and Technology

One *Time* cartoon of the early 1960s showed a gathering of extraterrestrials declaring: "If they keep throwing hardware up here, we'll keep buzzing their swamps!" America and the Soviet Union devoted vast amounts of public money and talent to putting machines, animals, and finally humans into space during this period. In 1959, Russian space probes photographed the dark side of the moon, and, in 1962, the Bell Telephone communications satellite Telstar permitted brief transatlantic television broadcasts. Russian animals, then Russian cosmonauts, and later American astronauts broke through the atmosphere to orbit in space. Views of Mars reached Earth from the commercial satellite Mariner IV in 1965. United States astronauts circled the moon 10 times in 1968, paving the way for the dramatic moon landing in the following year.

Back on Earth, medicine made striking advances during this decade. Livers and lungs were transplanted and, in

1968, the South African Dr. Christiaan Barnard performed the first heart transplant. New surgeries affected relatively few people, but innovations with wide impact included synthesis of penicillin, linkages of cholesterol with heart disease and smoking with lung cancer, decipherment of the code of DNA, and production of an oral contraceptive, known popularly as the Pill and hailed as a cornerstone of the sexual revolution.[3] Amniocentesis monitored prenatal health, reassuring expectant parents.

Revolutionary, too, was the laser (light amplified by stimulated emission of radiation), which found uses in industry and even in surgery on the retina of the eye. Jersey Central Power Company launched the first commercial nuclear reactor. Dolby eliminated background hiss in music recordings to the satisfaction of music lovers of all tastes.

Computers continued their march into every aspect of life in the 1960s. Industrial robots were marketed for the first time in 1962, the same year in which Digital, Inc. unveiled its minicomputer, with a whopping 15 kilobytes of memory.[4] Minicomputers were essentially scaled-down offshoots of mainframes and, as such, useful to businesses. In 1964, IBM demonstrated a word processor that would store, correct, and retype text. Silicon chips, carrying tiny circuits, hit the market, and words such as printout and program began to come into popular use.

Manufacturing and Retailing

Although the period 1959–1968 was largely prosperous, with a generally rising stock market, gradually declining unemployment, and fairly quiescent inflation, the basis of U.S. prosperity had already begun to shift from manufacturing to service businesses. These included professional services, such as law and medicine, and humbler jobs in fast food chains. Competition from Europe and Asia challenged American durable goods—such as cars and small appliances—crimping profits. However, U.S. soft goods, including bras and girdles, were successfully exported to western Europe, Japan, India, and parts of South America. American companies sometimes expanded overseas by teaming up with licensees, working closely with local owners to set up factories and to source materials for products. The United States boasted a $15 billion apparel industry in 1966.[5]

One area of growth in domestic hard goods manufacturing was production of computers. Mainframes, the large computers capable of the number-crunching needed by government and large institutions, dominated the electronics industry, although minicomputers had made an appearance for small-scale business use late in the period. Applied to the scheduling of work flow in factories, minicomputers gave company executives data for decision making. Resulting economies helped American companies compete with foreign rivals. Automation came into factories, too, starting with imitations of the functions of the human hand.

Manufacturers and retailers had to contend with emerging consumerism, a form of activism that issued complaints about high prices, unsafe or defective products, poor durability, and deceptive advertising. *Consumer Reports* and *Consumer Bulletin* compared different brands of product, including apparel. One way for producers to cope with consumer demands was to do more thorough market research, conducting interviews of potential customers in scientifically identified geographic areas. Two groups that riveted business people's attention were teens and blacks.[6] The former, long studied by manufacturers and retailers, were becoming ever more numerous and powerful, driving the selection of products for sale, presentation in stores and ads, and development of the images of products and departments. The latter group, newly recognized as a growing minority with varied income, background, and lifestyles, were wooed with improved service, greater respect, and better representation among employees and in advertising. Fashion models Donyale Luna and Naomi Sims broke the color barrier in the mid-1960s, as blacks slowly began to appear in fashion and other women's publications (Figure 7.4). Sims was also the first black woman on the cover of the *Ladies' Home Journal* in 1968.[7]

Retailing, a major component of the service economy, flourished during the 1960s. Shopping malls, with roots in early twentieth-century centers in Oak Park, Illinois, and Country Club Plaza, Kansas City, Missouri, and 1950s enclosed malls, continued to spread rapidly into the burgeoning suburbs that surrounded every American city. Department stores, fleeing the riot-ridden, decaying central cities, eagerly anchored the new malls. Retail stores stayed open longer hours, six nights a week in suburban branches, to accommodate women who held paid jobs, along with running their households. In the interest of time savings, self-service became more common in stores, with displays and garment hang-tags dispensing the information once imparted by sales staff. Counters went out, and special display fixtures came in, a long-term change in the look of departments.

The credit card brought a significant and long-term change in the way people shopped. Bank of America introduced its first Bank Americard (later Visa) in 1958. Computers allowed tracking of transactions, and people no longer had to purchase only what they could afford. Although time payments had been used earlier for expensive items, now they could be extended to everyday purchases.

Discounters, the bane of traditional stores, had begun to converge toward conventional retailing, adding services

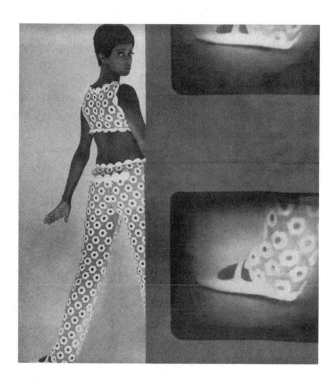

Figure 7.4 African American model in a Courrèges outfit. *Vogue*, March 15, 1967, Bert Stern/*Vogue* ©1967 Condé Nast Publications Inc.

and improving the looks of their premises. More challenging to department and specialty stores were the new boutiques springing up to cater to the teen and young adult markets. The boutiques in London and New York adopted a fashion-of-the-moment approach rather than the more traditional seasonal buying in order to react quickly to the ephemeral styles of the youth market. The first was Mary Quant's Bazaar boutique, opened in 1955 with husband Alexander Plunket Greene and lawyer Archie McNair. They filled the store with nontraditional clothing that was geared to the burgeoning youth market. Others quickly followed, many acting as laboratories for new designers and design ideas, partly stimulated by the interaction of customers/hangers-on with the designer-owners. Some boutiques catered to both men and women, espousing the idea of unisex clothing. Others, such as the influential Paraphernalia in New York, with its in-house designer Betsey Johnson, offered the sort of do-it-yourself clothing that appealed to a young customer who wanted to put her own unique design stamp on her clothing.

The influence of London youth also appeared in a craze for secondhand clothing. There was much borrowing of 1920s flapper styles, among others, that appealed to the new young fashion shopper looking for an eclectic and original look. By the 1970s, many of the London boutiques were fading, partly because of mass-produced imitations of their original styles, partly undermined by poor management and stock control.

Arts and Entertainment

A huge youthful cohort—the baby boom generation—propelled their styles of music, dance, and films to prominence.

Movies, Theater, and Television

Films of 1959 through 1968 presented a smorgasbord of fare. Biblical epics such as *Ben Hur* and the classical themes of *Spartacus* and *Cleopatra* shared the box office with mysteries, including *Anatomy of a Murder*, and horror films, famously Alfred Hitchcock's *Psycho* and *The Birds*. To compete with television, movies purveyed sexier material than had previously been sanctioned: *The Apartment*, *Tom Jones*, and *Lolita* pushed into new erotic territory. Films such as *Guess Who's Coming to Dinner* confronted racial prejudices. Intellectuals could look to European cinema for offerings such as *Hiroshima, Mon Amour*, and *Black Orpheus*. Social issues emerged in *To Kill a Mockingbird* and *Days of Wine and Roses*; intergenerational tensions were explored in *The Graduate*. Given their huge following, the Beatles quite naturally tried their hands at movies, completing *A Hard Day's Night*, *Help!*, and *The Yellow Submarine* between 1964 and 1968. Fashions influenced by film included makeup and jewelry imitating *Cleopatra* and hats and coats derived from the Russian styles in *Dr. Zhivago*.

The film approach of the period had a broader effect, as directors and producers introduced themes related to drug use and increased sexual freedom. To counteract the resulting problems with getting pictures approved by the Production Code Administration, the movie rating system was introduced in 1966.

Films borrowed freely from the stage, with musicals often translated into celluloid. *The Sound of Music*; *Gypsy*; *Camelot*; *The Unsinkable Molly Brown*; *Hello, Dolly!*; *My Fair Lady*; and *Mame* all succeeded onscreen as well as onstage. In some assessments, this era was the last great period of musicals. Nonmusical theater continued to feature challenging topics of homosexuality, mental retardation, and family alienation. The musical *Hair*, subtitled *The American Tribal Love/Rock Musical*, opened on Broadway in 1968 and challenged many of the norms of the time. A musical about drugs, music, and peace-promoting hippies, it became famous for a nude scene at the end of the play.

Television clung to its infatuation with the Wild West, airing huge hits in *Bonanza*, *Rawhide*, *Gunsmoke*, and *Have Gun, Will Travel*. By the later 1960s, crime dramas, spy series, and science fiction challenged the preeminence of the horse opera. *The Man From U.N.C.L.E.*, *Hawaii Five-O*, and *NYPD* all did well, although, for cult status, few offerings could rival *Star Trek*. *The Avengers*, hugely popular in England, succeeded also in the United States; Emma Peel (Diana Rigg), one of the two main characters, exemplified feminist modernity in her catsuit outfits. *I Spy* broke new ground by pairing Bill Cosby with Robert Culp in a biracial partnership. *Julia* starred Diahann Carroll as a black American woman with a small son. Comedy hits included *Laugh-In,* a sometimes controversial show that added a number of slang phrases, such as *sock it to me* and *ring my chimes,* to 1960s vocabulary. Dance shows were popular, including, *Bandstand, Shindig,* and *Hullabaloo.* Television quiz shows remained under investigation, and payola scandals tarnished radio disk jockeys who accepted bribes to promote certain songs.

Music

Rock and roll ruled a large swath of the musical world in the 1960s. Elvis Presley continued his reign, and surfer music by the Beach Boys had a huge audience early in the period. Both of these were challenged after 1964 by the biggest names in all of rock—John, Paul, George, and Ringo—The Beatles (Figure 7.5). Beatlemania and all things British shook the teenage generation, moving the rock concert from a neighborhood affair (as conducted by an East Coast disc jockey Murray the K) to a vast performance. The Fab Four's dress evolved from rather clean-cut, band-collared suits to velvet jackets and Maharishi-inspired Indian threads, including **Nehru jackets,** as the decade advanced. Naturally, whatever the Beatles wore, teens copied it. Beatle mop-top hairstyles, considered too long by many parents and school districts, became the rage for boys. Some chose Beatle wigs instead of growing their own hair, and they became a hot item in 1964. Mania for British music raised the fortunes of soft-rock duos, such as Chad and Jeremy or Peter and Gordon, and of the Rolling Stones, who offered music with a harder edge and a rhythm and blues orientation.

Rock grew out of African American rhythm and blues, emerging as a multiracial art form in the 1950s and continuing with soul music in the early 1960s. Berry Gordy's Motown Records, centered in Detroit, carried forward the pulsating black sound, with such stars as Diana Ross and the Supremes (Figure 7.6), Stevie Wonder, Smoky Robinson and the Miracles, the Temptations, and Martha and the Vandellas. The Motown sound reverberated through the whole decade, and beyond.

Folk music appealed to a relatively educated group—older high school students, collegians, and young adults. Building on gritty protest songs from Woody Guthrie and the Weavers, groups such as the Kingston Trio, Peter, Paul, and Mary, and Simon and Garfunkel harmonized on ballads about love, social injustice, and the vicissitudes of everyday life, past and present. Bob Dylan, who began his career singing in Greenwich Village coffee houses, became perhaps the most poetic protest singer-songwriter of the era. Other performers, including politically active Joan Baez, also sang many of his hugely popular songs. Baez and Dylan both toured and participated in protests together.

The hootenanny became the folk equivalent of the rock concert, with the audience joining in on songs such as the folk anthem *This Land Is Your Land.* There was even a short-lived television show, *Hootenanny,* airing on Saturday nights. Later in the decade, the Mamas and the Papas mixed folk themes with rock rhythms, creating their own brand of California sound.

The Kingston Trio and their imitators presented a very clean-cut look, all neat slacks and crisp button-down shirts, a look also popular with college students (Figure 7.7). In contrast, folk singers like Dylan dressed in drab working class clothing, and Joan Baez popularized loose dark shifts and long, center-parted hair. Folk rockers dressed in a hybrid style that echoed their blend of music.

No end of variations on folk and rock proliferated through the period, fed by hippie culture, surfer lifestyle, and such technical innovations as the Moog synthesizer[8] and Jimi Hendrix's electric guitar. In 1967, the Monterey Pop Festival was the starting point for large rock and roll festivals and heralded what became know as the Summer of Love.

Adults over age 30—the untrustworthy generation—had to make do with jazz, as purveyed by Sinatra, Ray Charles, and Nat King Cole, or theater and film music, including themes from *Breakfast at Tiffany's, Cabaret,* and *Al-*

Figure 7.5 The Beatles with pop shirt motif and ruffles. ©Hulton Archive/Getty Images.

Figure 7.6 The Supremes in dresses with high waistlines (Florence Ballard, Diana Ross, and Mary Wilson), 1965. ©Bettmann/Corbis.

Figure 7.7 Collegiate men dressed in neat slacks and button-down shirts debating about the Peace Corps. *Life,* March 17, 1961, 34, ©Time & Life Pictures/Getty Images.

fie. Harry Belafonte's Calypso music provided a Caribbean flavor early in the decade; sitar music by Ravi Shankar gave an Indian touch in the late 1960s.

Those 10 years brought a heyday for popular dance. In 1959, the twist struck, ruining more than one spinal column. By 1964, a whole array of energetic choreography fed on youthful energy and flexible bodies: the watusi, frug, monkey and swim, some of these performed by minimally clad go-go girls in clubs and all enjoyed by young couples. Limbo contests required participants to lean back far enough to slide under a pole, which got lower at each pass, until the performer was parallel to and at the level of the ground. Not exactly a dance, the limbo demanded a certain physical prowess and skill, making it very popular with the teen crowd.

Sports

In this decade sports figures achieved new heights of celebrity, as even non-fans knew names such as Joe Namath (football), Wilt Chamberlain (basketball), and Cassius Clay (boxing). These big names appeared in advertising and made news outside the sport realm, as when Clay converted to Islam and took the name Muhammad Ali in 1964. Willie Mays, a longtime baseball star, even had a theme song written for him, "Say Hey, Say Willie." Women sports stars included Billie Jean King in tennis and Peggy Fleming, gold medallist in figure skating.

New sports groupings emerged from 1959 through 1968. The American Football League (AFL) was founded by Lamar Hunt in 1959 and played its first season in 1960. Beginning with eight teams, the AFL expanded to 10 members in 1962. Five years later, the first Super Bowl was played between the NFL and the AFL champs, resulting in a win for legendary Green Bay Packers, coached by Vince Lombardi, a star in his own right. The American Basketball Association came into being in 1967. Although the sportscaster was a sideline figure in earlier periods, Howard Cosell made news himself, with his blunt speech and disputatious personality. Another first was achieved when Jackie Robinson became the first black American to be initiated into the Baseball Hall of Fame. Arthur Ashe won the first U.S. Tennis Open in 1968.

President Johnson launched an effort to improve fitness among children in 1967, issuing badges to those who were able to show competence in a range of activities.

signs and became an apparel fad in 1966–1967 (Figure 7.8 and Plate 7.1).

Sculpture thrived, including Louise Nevelson's metal constructions, George Segal's super-realistic people, Alexander Calder's mobiles and stabiles, and Marisol's wooden people. In 1968, Christo packed the Museum of Modern Art in a foretaste of his later fabric wrappings of large structures. David Smith did construction-sculpture of welded metal, and Robert Morris and others brought minimalism to the fore. Claes Oldenburg turned the idea of hard sculpture on its head with his inflated telephones, bathtubs, and other everyday objects.

Architecture made grand gestures, too, from the Verazano Narrows Bridge, longest single-span suspension bridge in the world, to the initiation of the World Trade Center, begun in 1966. Curvilinear shapes demonstrated the technical possibilities of modern materials in apartment and office buildings, the Guggenheim Museum in New York (Frank Lloyd Wright), and airport terminals at Kennedy and Dulles in Northern Virginia, and the Gateway Arch, St. Louis, all by Eero Saarinen and Associates.

Art exhibits became blockbusters, including the 34-piece Treasures of Tutankhamen (1962), which traveled to raise funds to rescue Nile Valley temples threatened by flooding. A definite Egyptiana pervaded early 1960s dress and adornment, including jewelry and cosmetics à la Cleopatra. Never mind that she was of Greek, not Egyptian, lineage; only the bedizened film image of Elizabeth Taylor lingered in the minds of average Americans.

Clean-lined and organic shapes dominated domestic design in this decade. Marimekko textiles, a fashion among intellectuals, thrived especially in the neighborhood of university campuses. Armi Rattia, a Finnish designer, originated the Marimekko cottons with their bold, vivid prints. These made up easily into simple shifts, worn with tights or pantyhose and low shoes (Figure 7.9). Panels of Marimekko decorated walls as well as bodies and symbolized the new informality in urban life.[9]

Fashion photography gained ascendancy over illustration and developed an eclectic style that both influenced and was influenced by new visual trends of pop and op art. Irving Penn continued to create exotic photographs on location, while Helmut Newton, Richard Avedon, and David Bailey forged a young and energetic style. Bailey embodied the newly glamorized and sexually charged lifestyle of fashion photographers—a lifestyle that was loosely captured in the movie *Blow-Up*. Avedon also developed new approaches in the 1960s that reflected the sexual revolution, creating controversy with his nude photo of socialite Christina Paolozzi for *Harper's Bazaar*. From 1965 onward, crazy action shots became the norm for showing fashion. At the same

Figure 7.8 Sonny and Cher in matching op-art, supermod suits. ©Bettmann/Corbis.

Visual Arts and Design

Abstract expressionism continued to be a leading style, still influenced by the work of Willem de Kooning and Robert Motherwell. In the early 1960s, it began to be replaced by a style that emphasized bright color and bold geometry, sometimes called hard-edge painting. This geometry played a prominent role in 1960s painting, including Josef Albers's many renderings of The Square. Apparel drew on geometry, too, notably in Yves Saint Laurent's shift dress with block design taken from a Piet Mondrian painting (Plate 7.2). Broad movements included pop art, represented by Andy Warhol's soup cans and multiple images of Marilyn Monroe, Roy Lichtenstein's comic-strip–based canvases, and Robert Indiana's LOVE graphics. Pop drew upon earlier work by Jaspar Johns and Robert Rauchenberg. Pop artists sometimes sponsored events called happenings, intended to draw on a sense of improvisational, experienced art. The pop trend also translated into designs printed on plain shifts: for example, a humorous vest or necktie might be plastered onto a solid color shift or shirt. Optical (op) art, rooted in the 1950s work of Victor Vasarely and influenced by science and technology, created dizzying patterns of wavy or geometric lines that translated well into textile de-

Figure 7.9 Marimekko shifts for adult and child. Famous Barr advertisement. *Vogue,* September 15, 1966, 18, courtesy of Famous Barr.

Figure 7.10 Twiggy in typical minidress. ©Bettmann/Corbis.

time, photographers worked with a new range of models who represented another 1960s rebellion, this time against the more traditional standards of beauty of the past. Best known perhaps was Twiggy (Leslie Hornby), a model famed for her big eyes and spindly, immature frame, representative of the adolescent figure (Figure 7.10). Others included the 6-foot, 2-inch German countess Verushka; Jean Shrimpton, whose long-maned, youthful looks were widely copied; and Penelope Tree. Rudi Gernreich's model and muse, Peggy Moffitt, created a sensation with her pale face, heavy dark eyes, and geometric haircut by Vidal Sassoon.

Illustration styles responded to the free-flowing art associated with psychedelic drugs and harkening back to the art nouveau illustrator Aubrey Beardsley. The psychedelic art form often contained kaleidoscopic patterns and bright colors and became popular for rock concert posters and music album covers. In fashion illustration, models often sported long swirling locks that streamed behind or above them. The illustrator Antonio, who first came to prominence in the 1960s, created fashion art in this style (Figure 7.11). Bodies received minimal delineation and generally had the stalky proportions that paid homage to the undeveloped figures of young girls. Psychedelic debuted as an

expression in 1966, just after flower power.[10] By 1967, guru[11] and be-in[12] joined the lexicon. Many expressions and images arising from the drug scene and counterculture were appropriated to describe fashion.

Fashion Influences

More than previous periods of the twentieth century, the 1960s produced several levels of fashion. High-fashion magazines such as *Vogue* and *Harper's Bazaar* set up fashion shoots with fantastic confections of cloth devised explicitly to generate dramatic photos and never offered for sale as actual apparel. Next came fashion-forward garments shown in runway presentations of couture and upper-level ready-to-wear. Then there were the youth styles embraced by such groups as hippies, Anglophile mods, black power advocates, and surfers. Finally came adult middle- and lower-income Americans who followed trends quite distantly and modified their long-standing habits of dress very slowly. For instance, while the youthful avant-garde embraced miniskirts, ordinary adults showed just a bit of knee and continued to prefer skirts to trendier pants. The youth market seemed to embrace a new style every week, emphasizing the tempo-

Figure 7.11 Baby-doll dress and hip-hugger shorts illustrated by Antonio. Courtesy of Paul Caranicas.

Figure 7.12 Gloria Guinness in a Mainbocher couture dress. *Vogue,* April 15, 1966, 128, Horst/*Vogue* ©1966 Condé Nast Publications Inc.

rary nature of fashion. The plurality of fashionable skirt lengths evident from 1959 to 1968 signaled the demise of a single skirt length as an essential component of high style.

Technology periodically inspires designers, and did so in the 1960s. Space-age explorations gave rise to bubble-helmet hats, plastic apparel, and metallic-embellished ensembles from both European and American designers. Even light-colored, calf-length **go-go boots** and thigh-high versions owed something to the ultramodernism represented by space exploits.

Style Models

Stars of stage, screen, and the recording studio continued to epitomize style for their fans. Except for Sean Connery in his James Bond 007 roles, and perhaps Paul Newman and Robert Redford, few actors represented a look to imitate. Women had more exemplars in youthful Debbie Reynolds, lavish Elizabeth Taylor, petite and perky Sandra Dee, and European gamine Audrey Hepburn. Lauren Bacall represented adult sophistication, while Julie Christie appealed to the young woman. Television personalities, including talk show hosts (Jack Parr, Johnny Carson), and *American Band-*

stand participants helped disseminate their brand of style. Most significant, however, were singers, as noted previously, and models, who epitomized the little-mod-girl look.

For the period 1960–1963, First Lady Jacqueline Kennedy set the tone for worldly fashion. Before becoming First Lady, her fashions of choice came from the French couture. Under pressure after the election to showcase American designers, she effectively blended French and American styles. She began her period in the White House favoring the American Oleg Cassini, but patronized Hubert de Givenchy, a French couturier, as well. Her crisp suits and coats, pillbox hats, trim pumps, and perfect hair represented an adult woman's chic ideal. After President Kennedy's death, Jackie continued to be admired and to claim the spotlight intermittently, as when she married shipping magnate Aristotle Onassis in 1968. Other socialites dependably represented up-to-date elegance: Babe Paley, Gloria Guinness (Figure 7.12), C. Z. Guest, and Amanda Burden appeared on sundry best-dressed lists and showed up regularly in the fashion press. "Baby" Jane Holzer enjoyed a few years of fashion fame in the mid-1960s and became a symbol of the swinging sixties when she starred in Andy Warhol films.

Inspired by a sexy, grown-up German doll named Lilli,

the Barbie doll appeared in 1959 and within 6 months had become a huge hit. Barbie embodied high fashion and the independent young woman, whose up-to-date outfits referred to different career options and who seemed largely independent of family or romantic ties (notwithstanding the 1960 introduction of boyfriend Ken). Little girls loved to dress Barbie and experience her lifestyle vicariously. Late 1960s feminists decried the unrealistic body ideal represented by Barbie, but that did little to blunt her appeal.[13]

European Designers

Europe had many design centers in the years from 1959 through 1968, as the Continent and England developed design as a way to stimulate their economies and move away from a complete dependence on heavy manufacturing. London became a potent center of youthful fashions.

Paris

The Paris couture industry underwent monumental and permanent changes by the mid-1960s, particularly as silhouettes became simpler and hence easier to copy or knock off. No longer was fashion following the couture lead, but rather styles emerged from the street. Although French fashion was eclipsed by the popularity of London style, innovative designs still came from Paris. There emerged a group of young designers who could adapt the traditions of couture to the new customer, who demanded contemporary looks and did not want to spend the time in fittings required of

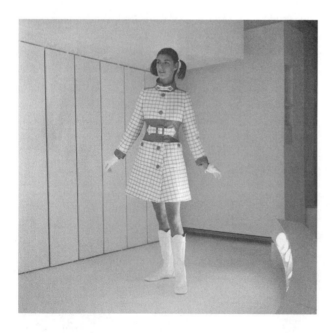

Figure 7.13 Courrèges-inspired ensemble, including boots. ©Bettmann/Corbis.

couture styles. French designers slowly attempted to respond to the demand for convenient fashion with prêt-à-porter (ready-to-wear). One of the first to do so was **Yves Saint Laurent**, who was responsive to the youth movement, blending couture with contemporary fashion inspirations. He forged a link with the art world with designs influenced by contemporary art movements. His Mondrian dress, created for his fall 1965 collection, was widely copied (see Plate 7.2). He went on to create Warhol-inspired pop art dresses. In 1966, recognizing the fashion revolution occurring around him, he entered into the world of ready-to-wear with his prêt-à-porter shop Rive Gauche. Much of the Saint Laurent design vocabulary of the 1960s has now passed into the world of classic and recognized styles, including safari-inspired jackets and menswear-inspired pants suits. In the 1960s he also designed mod-inspired ensembles that borrowed from abstract art styles, see-through blouses, and an African collection made of beads.

Several of the new couture designers looked to technology and the space age for inspiration. **Andre Courrèges, Emanuel Ungaro, Pierre Cardin**, and **Paco Rabanne** all responded to change by designing contemporary and youth-oriented collections in the mid-1960s. Courrèges, originally trained as an engineer, began his fashion career as a cutter for Balenciaga and opened his own house in 1961. His most influential years were 1964–1965 when he made headlines with a space-age look, a collection of mostly white and silver, shown to loud music. Also included were narrow pants for day and evening, square, geometric lines on everything, short white boots, and helmet-like hats. His initial orders were huge, but the lines were also easy to copy, and copies were often cheap. Frustrated, he closed his business for two years, returning in 1967 to show cat suits and cosmonaut suits, adding some black to his all-white theme (Figure 7.13).

Ungaro worked for both Balenciaga and Courrèges before opening his own business in 1965. Unlike Courrèges, he preferred bright and undulating colors, but he also worked in the youth mode, creating some of the shortest skirts in Paris.

Although Cardin established his house in 1950, his modern and sometimes pop and op art designs of the mid-1960s place him as a leader of the new wave of Paris designers. He created looks inspired by space technology, and his pinafore jumpers worn over ribbed sweaters and matching tights were also widely copied.

Rabanne, who began by designing accessories, created a stir with the futuristic looking plastic disk dresses he introduced in 1966. He went on to create chain-mail style garments made from aluminum, leather, and wire rings.

Givenchy continued to be prominent as the favorite designer of celebrities such as Mrs. Kennedy and movie star Audrey Hepburn. Chaste lines and glorious materials in suits and evening dresses were Givenchy's specialties. Possibly because of the problems of the modern couture system and of changing approaches to fashion, Balenciaga closed his house in 1968. Other Paris designers such as **Emmanuelle Khanh** began to rebel against the constraints of couture, creating a less structured and more individual approach to fashion.

Italy

Notable Italian names included **Emilio Pucci**, famed for bold prints on silk knits, perfect for travel. Although he had been designing them in the 1950s, Pucci's silk prints in bright swirling colors struck a chord in the psychedelic 1960s (see Plate 7.1). **Valentino (Garavani),** who showed his collection in Florence for the first time in 1962, gained greater prominence in later decades.

London

London, dubbed swinging in 1966 by *Time*, was the center of the latest fashions for much of the 1960s and drew young patrons to Carnaby Street (also known as peacock alley) shops for mod men and Chelsea for mod girls (so called birds). Chelsea represented an elegant bohemian neighborhood, but Carnaby Street had a lower-price image until fame struck. **Mary Quant**, Alexander Plunket Greene, and Archie McNair opened Bazaar in 1955, initially stocking it with ready-mades by other designers. Unable to find the young, inexpensive, and classless clothing that fitted her aesthetic, Quant began designing and producing clothes herself. A huge hit in the United States and elsewhere, her designs featured ribbed poor-boy sweaters (Figure 7.14), bright print dresses, macramé vests, hipster belts, plastic raincoats, and miniskirts, of which Quant has been called the mother.[14] So great was the appeal of these clothes that usually cautious JC Penney stocked Quant styles to draw teen and twenty-something customers into its stores.

Other British designers of note included Barbara Hulanicki, founder of the boutique **Biba**, **Jean Muir**, and **Foale and Tuffin**. Biba was pivotal in the popularization of boutique shopping. The store grew out of a mail-order business, becoming a source for brown smocks, floppy felt hats, vampish dresses, trouser suits, and later, the new romantic look, at prices even the poorest young shopper could afford. Wildly successful in the 1960s, Biba was considered as much a tourist attraction as other London sights. Jean Muir, who originally worked for Jaeger (a wool specialist), began to produce her own designs in 1961 under the Jane & Jane label. Jersey and suede, handled with controlled fluidity, represented Muir's strengths. Avoiding the stiff lines typical of the 1960s, Muir turned out smocks, smock-like peasant dresses, shawls, and two-piece suits with timeless appeal.

Foale and Tuffin (**Marion Foale** and **Sally Tuffin**) began

Figure 7.14 American version of Mary Quant's poor-boy sweater; British-inspired accessories. *Vogue,* February 1, 1965, 165, Franco Rubartelli/*Vogue* ©1965 Condé Nast Publications Inc.

designing in 1961, soon after graduating from the new fashion department at the Royal College of Art. Starting with the philosophy of many of the young designers of the period—that no one was designing for the new generation of young people—they became especially known for their trouser suits with hipster pants. Customers included socialite and Warhol star Jane Holzer. The new Paraphernalia boutique in New York City also carried Foale and Tuffin designs.

New York and California Designers

"[Today] everyone influences everyone else, and spectacular new ideas can spring up anywhere" opined *Time* in fall 1966.[15] With this pronouncement, the writer attempted to appease those who believed American fashion was original while placating those who claimed Paris or London set the pace. Clearly, fashion had more than one fountainhead, even though French couture enjoyed prestige among a slowly dwindling number of customers. American design was alive and well, appealing to a range of tastes from traditional to ultra modern. What U.S., British, and (to some extent) Italian fashion offered was very lively styling without the laborious fittings typical of French originals.

New York fashion, at least in the first half of the 1960s, was divided between the more traditional ready-to-wear designers and the younger and more outrageous innovators who were beginning to appear on the scene. The more with-it clothing appeared in boutiques, where experimentation and change were the rule. Much that was new came from these small, hidden-away shops, giving the impression that style was coming from the streets. *Vogue*, led by Diana Vreeland, who became editor in 1962, responded to the new and experimental approach to fashion. She is credited with coining the term *youthquake* and for creating imaginative layouts with models in body paint, enormous hair, and quantities of large jewelry.[16]

Betsey Johnson was one of the most important young designers of the era and the leader in the United States of youth-oriented fashions. Not bound by the traditions of Seventh Avenue, she was an in-house designer for Paraphernalia. She offered young wearers chalk-striped gangster suits, clear vinyl dresses with do-it-yourself decals, silvery motorcycle suits, and T-shirt dresses. She showed minidresses with thigh-high leather boots and what she called noise dresses—with grommets and rings that jangled. By 1969, she had left Paraphernalia to design clothing for the Alley Cat label and to start her own boutique with two friends, calling the shop Betsey Bunky and Nini.

Rudi Gernreich (gurn'rick), a California designer, was another tradition breaker in the U.S. fashion ranks. Gernreich loved to shock. A major advocate of the miniskirt and sexy swimwear, he really made news with his 1964 topless swimsuit, and in 1965 he patented the unstructured, transparent **no-bra** for Exquisite Form (Figure 7.15). Gernreich appeared on the cover of *Time*, in December 1967, significant of a decade when fashion gave reporters all the headlines their hearts could desire. In no earlier period had fashion so unfailingly created major news.

Youthful but adult fashions had several New York exponents, including **Donald Brooks, Oscar de la Renta,** and **Bill Blass**, along with established designers such as Norman Norell. Brooks gained a reputation for relaxed silhouettes, unusual prints and vivid colors, and fine detail. He devised hooded evening dresses, gowns with handkerchief and uneven hemlines, and caftans paired with draped loincloth-like pants. De la Renta offered newness with a touch of ladylike grace. He was designing for Jane Derby's company at the time of her death, so he took control of the company and gave it his

Figure 7.15 Model Veruscka wearing Rudi Gernreich's bra. *Vogue,* March 1, 1966, 178–179, Gianni Penati/*Vogue* ©1966 Condé Nast Publications Inc.

own name. He borrowed youthful themes, especially for evening wear, which drew on his experience in Paris working with Antonio del Castillo. De la Renta's daytime ensembles featured firm fabrics, seam-line emphasis, and curving shapes, these influenced by Balenciaga. Bill Blass (Figure 7.16) kept his daytime lengths in the vicinity of the knee while creating shorter dresses for evening, sometimes in lace. His women's daywear used man-tailoring, and indeed Blass embarked on designing menswear, too. Blass experimented with suits in which the jacket, skirt, and blouse were different colors.

Both **Anne Klein** and **Anne Fogarty** began as designers for junior lines and then set up their own companies. Fogarty did girlish styles such as Empire waistlines, ruffled skirts and blouses, and knits and was also among the first U.S. designers to produce bikinis. Klein specialized in sportswear, such as dresses with matching jackets, blazers, battle jackets, blouson dresses, and slinky jersey dresses.

California also counted other designers of note, especially **James Galanos** and **Bonnie Cashin**. Galanos remained true to his own style during the turbulent 1960s, working in soft chiffons and creating wool day and evening clothes, often in vivid colors. Superb details of structure and

Figure 7.16 Designer Bill Blass with a model wearing one of his creations. ©Bettmann/Corbis.

intricate beading were hallmarks of Galanos' apparel. He was an expensive ready-to-wear designer, unlike the New Yorker Mainbocher, who was the one, well-known couturier—custom designer—working in the United States.

Bonnie Cashin designed like no other 1960s creator, developing wearable suits, coats, and tunics in leather, suede, and tweed. Also, unlike other ready-to-wear designers, she worked as a freelance designer. She shunned contrived shapes and miniskirts, although her tunics could be adapted to be worn with tights as a mini equivalent. What Cashin prescribed for the woman with an active lifestyle— her target customer—were shorts, culottes, and puffy bloomers. She loved turtleneck sweaters and helped make them classics.

Fashion Trends
Textiles
This decade became the heyday of synthetics and finishes on naturals, because wrinkles were taboo except among countercultural groups, such as hippies and some folk enthusiasts. Fabrics often had stiff texture, especially suited to the crisp shapes that characterized the decade. Polyester may be best (or worst) remembered, but double-knits also came in wool. Loopy-textured bouclé of wool and mohair, wrinkle-resistant linens, silk gazar, cotton organdy, and denim all supported the look of the era. Textile technology generated such novelties as mylar, which created a metallic look without the weight or tarnish-proneness of metal. Textured nylon helped make pantyhose a huge hit, and these, in turn, contributed to the popularity of ultrashort skirts. Dupont introduced Fiber K in 1958; later christened Spandex, this lightweight elastic fiber helped bras and girdles to respond to demands for greater comfort and easier care. Unusual combinations of fabric were explored during the period: a glossy plastic with wool knit, or lace with tweed.

Colors ran riot, singly, paired, and in psychedelic prints that mixed several high-intensity hues (see Plates 7.1 and 7.2). Favorites included shocking pink, orange, lime green, purple, and canary yellow. Almost every color in the palette was used at one time or another, and, of course, white was appreciated alone or with black in eye-dazzling op art prints (see Figure 7.8). By 1968, couturiers weary of the color wheel offered black or black-and-white ensembles. Also a softer, ethnically inspired color palette began to appear. Ornamentation included sequins, beloved of Norman Norell, and tiny beads. Embroidery appeared more sparingly, often in amateur efforts by hippies on smocks and blue jeans. Youth culture generated an enthusiasm for the visual component of flower power. Besides floral prints on fabric, accessories and even makeup blossomed with daisies and other posies.

Any account of this decade must include the paper dresses that became a fad in 1966. These sold for as little as $1.25 or as much as $1,000, depending on complexity and who designed them. Many had lively prints, were laminated to metallics, or were reinforced with a grid of filament yarn. Some were spun-bonded sheets of fibers. Although they could be trimmed easily to establish a new hemline, these little dresses could neither be dry cleaned nor (obviously) washed, so they were a new step toward disposable fashion.

Women's Styles
Despite the period's reputation for wild, kicky dressing, it began in a fairly sedate way, with most skirts skimming the knees and most waistlines firmly defined and girdled (Figure 7.17). Despite late 1950s efforts to introduce the free-swinging trapeze and sack-style dresses, fitted shapes remained prominent in advertising. Some skirts were full, and the bell silhouette continued to be offered, even in metropolitan areas, until almost mid-decade. Only by about 1964 did a revolutionary high fashion reveal itself—and more of women's bodies. Change became ever more fre-

netic, with new fashions offered several times a year as wholesale designers strove to keep up with the boutiques. Some women switched styles from day to day, drawing on ethnic, historical, or space age designs.

Dresses and Suits

In 1959, some designers offered waistlines just below the breast, releasing the natural waist from the tight embrace of the still-prevalent sheath. A few bloused bodices gave ease to the torso and retained popularity through 1962. Shifts with dropped waistlines, or overblouses with skirts, were beginning to be shown in 1960–1961. By 1963, Galanos presented a tent-shaped **smock dress** that featured much greater width than Saint Laurent's 1958 flared-from-the-shoulder **trapeze dress.** Intricate seams, including yokes and princess lines, gave interest to the simple silhouette.

By 1966, **shifts** dominated the dress racks (Figure 7.18; see also Figure 7.9), with color-keyed shapes in the so-called **puzzle dresses.** Skirts rose higher each season (see Figure 7.10), and a **micromini** was introduced in 1968–1969. As hemlines climbed, controversy followed. Schools, workplaces, and houses of worship attempted to legislate acceptable skirt lengths, with little success. Informality predominated, in **polo-shirt shifts** and various minidresses with matching panties, to accommodate the likelihood of undergarments showing. Waistlines were reintroduced from time to time, with greater acceptance in 1968. Some full skirts appeared at the end of the decade, mostly in short versions.

Evening dresses generally had fitted waistlines early in the period but became more diverse as the years passed. High waistlines (see Figure 7.6), including Norell's kimono styles, were presented in 1965. Most gowns offered crisp shapes, with a few exceptions, such as French couturière Mme. Grès's drapy chiffons. One long dress style for young Californians blended the **granny** look with the Hawaiian *muumuu.*[17] This was not acceptable for school wear at the time and appealed mostly to teenagers. Shifts and high-waisted designs dominated evening fashions in 1967–1968.

Suits of the era came in a quick succession of silhouettes, from fitted to shift style. Skirted suits began the decade with skinny belts defining the waist (Figure 7.19) and progressed to waist-skimming styles, consisting of short jackets paired with slim or slightly gathered skirts. Plaids and pastel tweeds were popular fabrics. Skirts often touched the knees, but by 1964 there were more obvious displays of kneecap. One 1965 suit cleared the knees by several inches and was teamed with matching kneesocks, as if to announce its informality. Marc Bohan and the House of Patou in Paris, Fabiani in Rome, and Victor Joris and Jacques Tiffeau in the United States all tried unsuccessfully to launch calf-length skirts in 1966. Three years later, some lower hemlines were accepted, espe-

Figure 7.17 Tightly waisted dress of the early 1960s. Note the covered knee. ©Hulton Archive/Getty Images.

cially in cocktail dresses, but the mini retained its grip on women's imaginations into the early 1970s.

Pantsuits represented an avant-garde fashion, which gained notoriety as early as 1960, when Norman Norell presented short-pant or culotte suits for street wear. In 1963, André Courrèges showed pantsuits with stovepipe legs, worn over boots. By 1964, lacy pants and tunics were the latest for evening events, and, in 1965 these ensembles were billed as dinner pajamas, hinting that they constituted at-home wear and loungewear (see Figure 7.4). Saint Laurent's Le Smoking was a tuxedo-style pantsuit appropriate to dressy events. Despite fierce controversy, and bans in certain restaurants, clubs, and other public places, women's pantsuits marched slowly but inexorably onward, perhaps supported by—or supporting—the feminist movement. Schools and offices remained holdouts in acceptance of pants. Designers teamed pants with short jackets, thigh-length coats (Figure 7.20), and, in 1968, with tunic looks,

All you feel
in a Bali bra
is beautiful.

Just five minutes in a fitting room will prove it.

THE BALI COMPANY, INC., 16 EAST 34TH STREET, NEW YORK, N.Y. 10016

Figure 7.18 Shift typical of mid to late 1960s, by Cuddlecoat. Note the accessories and mesh hosiery. Bali advertisement, *The New Yorker*, June 3, 1967, 11.

Figure 7.19 Ben Zuckerman suit for late day wear with matching cap and white pigskin gloves. *Vogue* February 1, 1961, cover, Herbert Matter/*Vogue* ©1961 Condé Nast Publications Inc.

such as one model by Yves Saint Laurent. Tunics could convert into minidresses, adding to their appeal. Pant legs were usually stove-pipe straight, but flared legged pants and **bell-bottoms**—narrow in the thigh, wide at the hem—offered another option, starting about 1964. Pucci offered a palazzo pantalon with wide legs in 1967, a look other designers followed.

Coats and Other Wraps

Early 1960s coats often had a straight-cut or barrel shape (Figure 7.21), crisply tailored and often with raglan sleeves. Wide coats, tent-like in shape, appeared in 1966, sharing the scene with capes of equal capaciousness. By 1968, many coats had wide lapels and collars, after a period of narrow wedding ring collars or breast-plate-like **plastron** fronts. One trick used by designers to put across a new hem level was to team a mini- or above-knee length dress with a below-knee coat. These combinations appeared often in 1968. Furs coats

of all lengths were sold throughout the decade in both long and thigh lengths. Fur trims enhanced late 1960s long coats inspired by the film *Dr. Zhivago*. At the synthetic end of the continuum, shiny materials enlivened basic rain slickers, sold in electrified hues of chrome, red, and lilac.

Casual Separates and Clothes for Active Sport

As American life grew steadily more casual in the 1960s, separates became a growth category, especially in pants. During the early 1960s, tight pants were the prevailing style. By 1964, flared **flamenco pants** arrived, heralding bell-bottoms with a low rise, originally called **hip-hangers** and later renamed **hip-huggers**. Tapered legs did not vanish, but flares retained the spotlight. Body suits with snap crotches provided a smooth, tucked-in transition to the low waist, covering unchic love handles. Skiwear pants retained a smooth, stretchable shape. Jeans, increasingly popular with young women, remained in the category of housework attire for

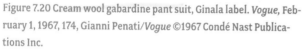

Figure 7.20 Cream wool gabardine pant suit, Ginala label. *Vogue*, February 1, 1967, 174, Gianni Penati/*Vogue* ©1967 Condé Nast Publications Inc.

Figure 7.21 Sarmi coat from the early 1960s. ©Bettmann/Corbis.

adults. In fact, some women avoided wearing pants for general purposes while accepting denim skirts as a casual alternative. These were often worn with a button-down shirt or round-collar blouse with floral print. T-shirts remained largely the province of children, teens, and some men.

Bikinis, which debuted in France in 1946, finally become popular in the United States (Figure 7.22), making the song about the "Itsy-Bitsy, Teeny-Weeney, Yellow Polka-Dot Bikini" a hit in 1960. Various styles of maillot satisfied the more modest swimmer, but even those could be gotten with plunging necklines, sometimes filled in with netting. Most shocking of all swimsuits were Rudi Gernreich's topless styles of 1964. These gained extensive coverage, even in the general press, and sold a surprising 3,000 units. Rear cleavage and side-baring styles followed in 1967–1968. At a less sensational level, peek-a-boo suits with strategic cut outs or excisions revealed the side waist, derriere, navel or coin-sized glimpses of breast. **Baby-doll suits** with high-waist, skirted tops came down over brief panties for those with demure taste or strict parents.

Underwear

One of the great misconceptions about 1959–1968 is that underwear practically disappeared. Quite the contrary, undergarments diversified and became highly fashion-driven, with groovy[18] new colors and patterns in bras, panties, and half-slips or **petti-pants**, like a half-slip but covering the crotch for wear with ever-shorter skirts or culottes. These were also practical as liners under pants to prevent cling.

Despite its image, the no-bra decade brought forth a profusion of bra styles.[19] Highly structured, slightly pointy bras of 1959–1964 included strapless models (Figure 7.23) and strap versions (Figure 7.24) with front or back plunges. Décolletage, especially popular in 1964, allegedly drew inspiration from the movie *Tom Jones*. From about 1965 onward, firm engineering gave way to not-all-that-bra[20] comfort—seamless cups to harmonize with knit outerwear, stretch straps, and, in 1965, Rudi Gernreich's no-bra (see Figure 7.15). One small dart or heat-set shape created cups in a nearly transparent garment, which worked well under very sheer clothes, including transparent blouses from Saint Laurent. Padding, for those wishing it, came in the form of polyester fiberfill, which over-

Figure 7.22 Moderate bikinis and bathing suits. ©Hulton Archive/Getty Images.

Figure 7.23 High-waisted girdle and strapless bra. Treo advertisement, *New York Times Magazine*, September 10, 1961, 64.

came foam rubber's tendency to turn rigid or powdery with age or ignite in an overly hot dryer.

Given the need for a small waist in some styles in the early 1960s, high-waist girdles were in vogue (see Figure 7.23). These gave way to low-waist panty girdles with elongated legs to smooth wearers of low-slung, snug pants even for teens (Figure 7.24). One girdle took the trend to naturalism to its veritable foundations, outlining the buttocks rather than masking their shape.

Spandex, being lighter weight and thinner than previous elastic materials, made foundation garments more acceptable to comfort-loving women. Garter belts sufficed for stocking support among younger or slimmer women. Eventually, pantyhose brought notable decline in sales of girdles and garter belts.

Coordination of foundations and other lingerie, to each other and to outerwear, marked the mid-1960s. Color had been around since the 1930s, but was fully exploited in this era, with offerings in red, toast, blue, acid green, hot pink, purple, wine, chrome yellow, and prints of every variety—animal fur, paisley, whirlpools, Japanese motifs, and bias

plaid. Loungewear became a significant category for increasingly informal home entertaining. The colorful lingerie looks of the decade also extended to evening pajamas, culottes, and hostess robes. Sexy nightgowns came in long and shorter lengths.

Headwear

Hats enjoyed their last period of popularity before fading from the fashion scene. Like most apparel of the decade, hat shapes were plain and stiff. **Pillboxes,** derbies, **helmets,** and **mushroom** shapes fitted well with crisply tailored suits and coats (see Figures 7.18 and 7.21). A few turbans made a showing. For those who disliked conventional hats, **whimsies**—little velvet circlets with wisps of veil—served the need for head covering in houses of worship and other formal situations. **Chapel veils**, triangles of lace, could be donned in church and then folded away in purse or pocket. From the mid-1960s onward, hats went into decline among most age groups, killed by informality, feminism, and the reign of Majestic Hair, teased, piled high, or long and flowing. Hats looked awkward with pants, which were increas-

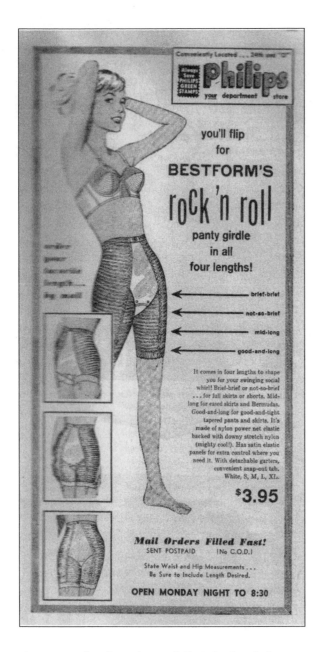

Figure 7.24 Push-up bra and panty girdles in four lengths by Bestform. *Merchants Trade Journal*, February 1960, 83.

ingly popular for many occasions. Mods wore British style caps (see Figure 7.14), and some women took to the broad-brimmed hats featured in 1968, but serious chapeau-wearing seemed, well, old-hat. Small kerchiefs were a teen fad (Figure 7.22).

Shoes and Hosiery

Clearly, legs and feet were the locus of fashionable fervor, as skirts rose and more leg was revealed. Textured nylon hose in the early 1960s yielded a better fit, but pantyhose

become popular after 1965. Plain or patterned tights harmonized with tunic-like shifts in the second half of the decade. Fishnet panty hose enjoyed a vogue in 1966–1967 (see Figure 7.18), and so did kneesocks coordinated to the color or pattern of the main outfit (see Figure 7.14). Knee-highs were even teamed with chunky heels, although most shoes paired with knee-highs were flat. Despite stocking-makers' efforts to devise separate hose with narrow top welts for wear with short skirts, sales of pantyhose rose continuously.

Shoes began the period with either high stiletto or stacked heels and pointed toes (see Figure 7.17), but by the close of the decade heels were low and toes broad and rounded or very slightly tapered, to harmonize with the little-girl look of dresses (see Figure 7.10). New materials won popularity, including corfam, a synthetic leather that could hold a shine much better than traditional patent leather. Shoes, like other parts of the ensemble, glowed with bright color, with doodads on the instep. **Go-go boots** had low heels and initially were just above ankle high but later came to mid-calf or knee level, in shiny white (see Figure 7.13). Other boot colors included yellow, lilac, and metallics. Color-coordinated boots were worn with city suits. Microminis for cool weather begged for some functional leg covering, making way for black thigh-high boots of soft leather.

Other Accessories and Jewelry

During the 1960s, handbags appeared sporadically in fashion photos, often in the form of small clutch purses, belt purses, and shoulder bags (see Figures 7.14 and 7.20). Although it is doubtful that women stopped carrying bags, they seem not to have looked good with the free-swinging style of fashion presentation.

Belts and sashes marked the upper margin of hip-hugging pants or delineated a low waistline on a jumpsuit or dress. Chain-link belts were a fad of 1967–1969. Gloves came in all lengths and colors, usually in suede or cotton. No longer, however, were gloves automatically included with every dress and suit, in another concession to casual dressing.

Jewelry took on a big and bold scale, the better to complement the unbroken expanses of shift dresses and tailored suits. Brooches had large, imitation stones in symmetrical or irregular shapes. Pendants, in geometric or kitschy realistic styles, such as oaks became a fad. Pearls, a classic given a new look by enlarging their scale, were popularized by Jacqueline Kennedy and other ladies of her social set. Up-swept or beehive hair, and even streaming curls, drew attention to the ears, making impressive earrings an important part of the jewelry scene.

Men's Styles

The period began with relatively conventional apparel for men but ended with highly unconventional looks in apparel and hair, particularly popular with some young men.

Suits and Casual Separates

Like women, men wore rather traditionally styled suits in 1959–1963, with narrow lapels, gently fitted jackets, and lean pant shapes (Figure 7.25). Crispness was valued, making lightweight tropical suitings and wool-polyester blends popular. Slacks had finishes to banish wrinkles and low rises to emphasize a lean body look.

Between 1964 and 1968, many new options for suits came on the market. **Continental fit** offered a snug chest, high sleeve mounting, less shoulder padding, and a longish jacket with slight flare. Pierre Cardin promoted this look, especially after 1966; Mr. Steed, a character in the television show *The Avengers*, helped lend cachet to the look. Young men aped the Beatles' 1964 style of collarless suits, which became a badge of Anglo singing groups for a couple of years. Semi-Edwardian styles offered nipped waistlines and slightly flared pants. Peacock finery enlivened young men's clothing, with dramatic shirt styles and even some pop art touches (see Figure 7.5).

When the Beatles and other singers became devotees of Indian mysticism and sitar music, **Nehru-collar jackets** won a following (Figure 7.26). The style bore the name of Indian Prime Minister Jawaharlal Nehru and had a small standing collar, no lapels, and a longish buttoned front. Men of sharp but strictly Euro-American style could choose a double-breasted, peaked lapel suit or sport coat, often in navy for wear with contrasting slacks of gray or white (Figure 7.27). Double-breasted jackets had been out of favor since the end of the 1940s, so there was a whole new generation of wearers to entice.

Tuxedos and other formal wear abandoned the strict black and white penguin suit look to blossom in burgundy, blue, and a wide, wild assortment of pastels. Velvet collars enjoyed a run in fashion. Shirts that began the period with discreet tucks exploded with vivid patterns and a few ruffles.

Young men's casuals included hip pants with flared legs in denim or other sporty materials (Figure 7.28). Casual blazers appeared in wild plaids and polyester seersucker, for the wrinkle-free look, without cotton seersucker's comfort. Men in Vogue showed **tunics** with trousers in 1968, and there are even hints of the leisure suit of the next decade in loose jackets with pleated bellows pockets.

Coats and Wraps

Leather jackets became identified with folk singers, but many other informal styles came into fashion during the period, including shirt-jackets, pullovers, cardigan sweaters, and knitted jackets (more structured than cardigans). For really cold weather and winter sports, quilted jackets entered fashion in 1967. In the heyday of English singing groups, navy **pea jackets** held sway. Vests with fringe covered the chest (often otherwise bare) of young hipsters in the late 1960s. Full-length coats were shorter than at previous periods, with hems just above the knee. Collars tended to spread widely, a trend that continued into the early 1970s.

Shirts and Underwear

Shirts enjoyed some of the action in 1960s menswear. Snug fit predominated in shirts with loud prints and flashy tuxedo shirts with tucks and frills. Even conservative ads showed glen plaid shirts with coordinating bias-plaid ties. Patterns were often mixed, with decidedly unsubtle results. Proportioned to the tapered cut, moderately sized collars came in spread or button-down styles. Chambray work shirts and knit sport shirts were teamed with casual slacks. Some men attempted a fashion coup by teaming white turtle-necked sweaters with evening wear jackets, but this never became a major formal fashion. Neither did cotton eyelet overshirts, Russian-styled shirts, or borrowings from other countries although worn by some younger

Figure 7.25 Botany suit by Daroff. Note the slim tie and buttoned-down shirt. The Advertising Archives.

Figure 7.26 (LEFT) Bob Gibson, pitcher for the St. Louis Cardinals, in a Nehru suit, 1968. ©Bettmann/Corbis.

Figure 7.27 (BELOW) Single-breasted and double-breasted blazers with turtlenecks and trousers, 1969. ©Bettmann/Corbis.

Figure 7.28 (OPPOSITE, LEFT) Three young photographers working for *Vogue*. Note their hip-hugger slacks and the longer swim trunks. *Vogue*, November 15, 1968, 107, Elisabetta Catalano/*Vogue* ©1968 Condé Nast Publications Inc.

men. Turtlenecks did penetrate the casual market, to wear with V-necked pullovers or cardigans, or with blazers (see Figure 7.27). By 1968, **caftans** were promoted as at-home wear for fashion-forward men.

Accessories and Jewelry

Narrow snap-brim hats were worn for business in the early 1960s but gradually disappeared toward the end of the decade. Hip men were as likely to wear a braided leather or plain cloth band around their heads as a hat. Neckties traced the pathway of men's fashion in this era, beginning skinny and small-patterned but ending wide and bold in color and design. Carnaby Street influence touched even mature business types. Ascots had a vogue at the end of the decade (see Figure 7.28). Much of the point of Nehru jackets, turtlenecks, and exotic shirts was to avoid wearing a tie.

Shoes and boots were often shiny. Oxfords and slip-ons were prevailing styles, some with chain decoration on the vamp. Athletic shoes for jogging appeared by 1968. Low boots combined well with casual, young styles, initially made popular by the Beatles. Belts were wide, for use with low-hip pants; leather and later chain belts were seen, as were scarves tied like belts. Jewelry, comprising inconspicuous watches and rings in the early 1960s, went bold among the young, with hip beads, chains, and pendants by the end of the decade (see Figure 7.28).

Rock stars, such as Jimi Hendrix, sported satin pants, beaded vests, and buccaneer sashes. While few men followed such dramatic styles, the efforts of many to break out of dull convention helped to give the name Peacock Revolution to the end of this period of style.

Youth and Ethnic Styles

Group styles defined an important aspect of young men's and women's fashion during this decade, and deserve separate mention.[21]

Clean-cut, collegiate style for men in the early 1960s comprised khakis, corduroys, and other well-pressed pants, worn with button-down shirts, crewneck sweaters, and loafers (see Figures 7.2 and 7.7). Bermuda shorts were popular for summer. Collegiate women favored wool skirts or pants and women's versions of the shirts, sweaters, kneesocks and loafers

Figure 7.29 (BELOW) Students in campus attire. ©Bettmann/ Corbis.

or tights and flats (Figure 7.29). Circle pins on round-collared shirts were a cliché. Small-patterned prints and solids predominated in college shops around the United States. Later in the decade more shift-like dresses and jumpers became favorites. Collegiate men of the early 1960s wore crew cuts or short hair and shaved daily. Their female counterparts loved short, feathery cuts or pouffy styles supported by setting on huge rollers.

Surfer style embraced longish hair, bleached, like their eyebrows. A permanent tan was mandatory, as were **baggies**—long swim trunks—and Pendleton shirts. Chino pants and striped windbreakers provided a streetwear alternative. **Flip-flops** and **huarache sandals** were standard footwear. Surfer girls dressed in bikinis and other beachwear.

Young men who followed folk style preferred jeans, work shirts, battered leather jackets, and boots. Mature folk enthusiasts—such as college faculty—wore cords and dark-colored shirts. Women center-parted their hair and donned Mexican peasant garb, shifts, wraparound corduroy skirts, and leotards or tights (see Figure 7.29). Sandals were a mark of folkhood, as was turquoise and silver jewelry.

Hippie style enjoyed a profusion of influences, from sec-

ondhand finery to India-inspired guru garb that emphasized white or beige and natural fibers. Sandals or bare feet and "peace symbol" jewelry, an accessory that continued into the early 1970s, completed the look.

African-American/black pride style embraced natural hair, free of straighteners. Apparel emphasized African-inspired prints, notably in loose tunics called **dashikis** (Figure 7.30). Women wore turbans and tunics. Dappled furs and various ethnic pendants added deluxe touches.

Children's Styles

Although at various periods of fashion history little children have worn the newest styles, during the years 1959–1968 they fell into the role of imitators, specifically of teenagers. Most fashions on little kids echoed those of their elder siblings. One possible exception was the collarless jacket for little boys (Figure 7.31), which later turned up on the Beatles and was imitated by teens and young adults.

In a largely affluent period, some parents spent lavishly on their children. The *New York Times Magazine* explored and deplored the prices some were willing to pay for infants'

and children's' clothes, especially dresses for little girls.[21] Upper East Side Manhattanites may have been atypical in their devotion to status consumption, including kiddy-couture dresses ranging from $200 to $500. However, the use of children as accessories to a chic mother and natty father persisted beyond this decade and outside of New York.

Little girls' dresses of about 1959–1963 showed the full skirts and fitted waistlines typical of some adult dresses (see Figure 7.31). Later in the period, shift shapes, with or without sleeves, were worn as dresses or jumpers (see Figure 7.9). Often shirt-style blouses or turtlenecks teamed with the jumpers. Mini lengths became obvious on preteen school girls. Sweaters, kneesocks, and loafers or tie shoes completed the school look. Pants were not yet accepted in many schools. Hair was worn long and mostly straight, except for a few pageboy styles. Other hairdos included ponytails, side-tails, and bobs.

Boys' staples included slacks and jeans, worn with soft shirts or turtlenecks. Summer brought out T-shirts and shorts (Figure 7.32). Hair on little guys followed adult and teen looks, short at the outset, but fuller and longer later in the decade.

Hair and Grooming: A Generation Gap

The very fact that a play could be called *Hair* speaks eloquently of the emotional charge in styling of locks. The adult man wore short hair, even a buzz cut; many younger men sported Dutch-boy cuts and other slightly longer locks. The hippies espoused wearing hair as long, uncombed, and sometimes as unwashed as possible. There were many gradations in between. Curly hair, left uncut, formed **Afros** on black men and on men of other races with curly hair. Facial hair on the hirsute young (or middle-aged) included sideburns, moustaches, and beards, short and neat or long and matted.

Women began the decade wearing curly styles, backcombed much or little, depending on taste. This coiffure shared spotlight with short, wispy cuts in the early years. By 1962, hair was bouffant, and many towering styles depended on augmentation with purchased switches and extenders. Great manes of hair, for which socialite Jane Holzer was famous, typified 1964–1965. Blunt, asymmetrical cuts were popular, too, thanks to celebrity London stylist Vidal Sassoon, who continued variations on the blunt cut until almost the end of the decade. Flips, with the bottom of hair turned up; kid-like ponytails; exotic pigtails; and bunches of false curls decked the models in magazine shoots. Long, flowing tresses—sometimes achieved with false hair—came into fashion by 1966, and pixie cuts returned in 1967. Smooth, tie-back styles appeared in 1968. Older, more conservative women continued to wear tight curls or carefully controlled waves for most of the decade.

Figure 7.32 Boys in casual dress. *Life*, September 29, 1967, 66, ©Time & Life Pictures/Getty Images.

altered for the long term. Hatlessness became common, except in certain black churches and among conservative women outside of metropolitan areas. A hat became a practical matter in cold climates, no longer an indispensable fashion accessory. Gloves likewise reverted to use in inclement weather instead of being an everyday accompaniment to a dress or suit. Jeans, once relegated to strictly casual and utilitarian wear, became staples of everyday dress, particularly in later decades when designer jeans and continuous tweaking of style kept denim in the fashion limelight. Men gained more color in their wardrobes and greater latitude in length of hair and choice of facial hair, even after the 1960s ended.

Much has been written about the meaning of 1960s fashion, with its themes of liberation, breakdown of conventions, and youth orientation. Styles of the era created major news beyond its reportage in the fashion press. No doubt, youth set many of the fads of the decade. Fashion fragmented into a plurality of *fashions*. Older people, middle-aged adults, and teens and young adults dressed differently. Within age groups, politics, lifestyle, ethnicity, and musical taste all helped shape variant apparel fashions, while casualization occurred in most groups. Niche marketing became a clear necessity for apparel makers, because no one style was going to win general acceptance.

Aside from the culture of hippiedom, plenty of grooming aids were sold, for men as well as for women. Yardley of London became a big purveyor of scents and cosmetics, an example of a stodgy company finding its second youth during the era of England Swings. Big eyes, shadowed in many shades, with false eyelashes by the yard, marked the face of the 1960s. Lashes looked painted on, as one observer noted, in imitation of dolls. Lips bloomed in medium-red or rose colors at the beginning of the decade, fading to pales about 1964. Healthy skin began to be a serious worry, sparking appeals to limit sun tanning as early as 1967. Ads warned of wrinkles, age spots, and incipient skin cancer.

With the emphasis on youth, slimness became an ever more pressing obsession among Americans, especially women. Weight-control products, including liquid-diet concoctions, and calorie counting appeared in magazines and were promoted on television. Diet pills came under government scrutiny about 1968 because of problems of safety and effectiveness. Sport and fitness, just emerging as an American enthusiasm, had the added appeal of controlling weight.

Summary

At the beginning of the next decade, minis, wild colors, and some of the manifestations of the Peacock Revolution gradually dwindled away, but styles of dressing had been

Suggested Readings

Callan, Georgina O'Hara. *The Thames & Hudson Dictionary of Fashion and Fashion Designers.* New York: Thames & Hudson, 1998 (paperback edition).

Devlin, Polly. *Vogue Book of Photography: 1919–1979* New York: Simon & Schuster, 1979.

Farrell-Beck, Jane, and Colleen Gau. *Uplift: The Bra in America.* Philadelphia: University of Pennsylvania Press, 2002.

Fogg, Marnie. *Boutique: A '60s Cultural Phenomenon.* London: Mitchell Beazley, 2003.

Friedel, Frank. *America in the Twentieth Century,* 4th ed. New York: Alfred A. Knopf, 1976.

Lobenthal, Joel. *Radical Rags: Fashions of the Sixties.* New York: Abbeville Press, Inc., 1990.

Lord, M. G. *Forever Barbie: The Unauthorized Biography of a Real Doll.* New York: William Morrow and Co., 1994.

Milbank, Caroline Rennolds. *New York Fashion: The Evolution of American Style.* New York: Harry N. Abrams, 1996 (paperback edition).

Quant, Mary. *Quant by Quant.* New York: G.P. Putnam's Sons, 1966.

Reeves, Thomas C. *Twentieth-Century America: A Brief History.* New York: Oxford University Press, 2000. Jane Stern and Michael Stern. *Sixties People.* New York: Alfred A. Knopf, 1990.

CHAPTER 8

1969

U.S. Events and Trends	Woodstock Festival in New York State	First Earth Day Four students killed at Kent State University	Two huge antiwar marches in Washington, D.C.	Richard Nixon elected president for a second term	Cease-fire in Vietnam Arab oil embargo
	 **1969**	 **1970**	 **1971**	 **1972**	 **1973**
U.S. Fashions	Eclectic year in fashion	Fairchild launches *W* Midi/miniskirt controversy Beginnings of platform shoe style	Hot pants fad	Revival of 1930s and 1940s styles	Wrap dress style becomes popular

1978

Nixon resigns,
Gerald Ford becomes
president

Economy in worst
recession in 40 years

Americans celebrate
the U.S. Bicentennial

Jimmy Carter elected

U.S. space shuttle
makes first test
flight

100,000 march in
support of ERA

1974

1975

1976

1977

1978

Giorgio Armani
opens womenswear
salon

Punk clothing begins
to be seen

The "Annie Hall" look
becomes popular, as
does fashion from
Saturday Night Fever

The "Dress for
Success" look
takes off

Retrenchment and Reaction

The years from 1969 to 1978, sometimes characterized as the Me Decade, are often regarded as a dismal time, with inflation, gas shortages, and the Watergate scandal.[1] Viewed from the distance of several decades, many also see it as a time of bad fashion (leisure suits, synthetic dresses) and bad music (disco, punk). In the wake of the dramatic and turbulent events of 1968, the subsequent years were a continuation of, reaction to, and sometimes reaction against the events of the 1960s. It was a decade that witnessed the wider acceptance of many ideas considered extreme during the 1960s, with advances in civil rights, environmental activism, and women's equality.

Domestic and International Politics and Economics

The year 1968, one of the most tumultuous in U.S. history, is an appropriate end to the decade of the 1960s and a beginning point for the next decade. It was a year of violent confrontation between students and either governments or universities not only in the United States but also in France and Germany. Racially motivated rioting in many U.S. cities followed the assassination of Martin Luther King Jr. There were riots during the Democratic convention in Chicago, and a presidential candidate, Robert Kennedy, was assassinated. The Tet Offensive, a surprise attack by the North Vietnamese on the America embassy in Saigon, left many more Americans opposed to the continuation of the war than previously. These chaotic events led to disenchantment with government for many and a continuation of many of the social movements that began in the last years of the 1960s.

The decade began with inauguration of a new president, Richard M. Nixon, after a close and often contentious election.[2] He would remain president for six years marked by an often perplexingly ambiguous approach to both domestic and international politics. A seemingly humorless man, Nixon appeared to manipulate others and engage in contradictory strategies that earned him the nickname Tricky Dick. Although his presidency is often excoriated for abuse of power and the undermining of many federal agencies and programs, it also witnessed significant achievements in foreign diplomacy. Nixon was followed by Gerald Ford and then Jimmy Carter. All dealt with stressful domestic and foreign policy issues.

When Nixon took office in 1969, he inherited a country that was divided by the Vietnam War, civil rights problems, and what was termed the generation gap. Although Nixon had campaigned on a promise to "bring the American people together," much of the fragmentation continued to grow. Nixon viewed the many very vocal antiwar groups as a mi-

nority and aimed his policies at what he termed the silent majority.

Bringing an end to the Vietnam War proved a formidable task. The antiwar movement was becoming larger, more visible, and more vocal. Early in his presidency, Nixon set a goal of ending the war through Vietnamization, a gradual reduction in troops with the idea of turning the conclusion of the war over to the South Vietnamese. At the same time, however, he increased bombing of North Vietnam and secretly began bombing neutral Cambodia because Cambodia's Ho Chi Minh Trail had become a route for North Vietnamese soldiers to invade South Vietnam.

When the bombings were publicly revealed, anger mounted on college campuses. One tragic event was the 1970 shooting of four students at Kent State University, Ohio, by National Guardsmen attempting to halt an antiwar demonstration. This led to student strikes on campuses across the United States, the killing of two more students at Jackson State College in Mississippi, and a significant antiwar rally in Washington, DC (Figure 8.1). By 1972, peace talks began in Paris, and, after a series of very slow and tedious negotiations, an agreement was reached to end American participation in the war in January 1973. More than two years later, the South Vietnamese government in Saigon fell to the Communists, as shocked Americans watched the horrifying evacuation of the U.S. embassy.

In addition to problems with finding a way to end the Vietnam War, Nixon inherited an unsettled economic situation. The long economic boom of the post–World War II era was at an end. Inflation was rising, in part because of the war, and did not subside during a mild recession in 1969 and 1970. Agricultural problems led to a dramatic rise in farm prices at least in part because of a miscalculated sale of wheat to Russia in 1972 that left no grain surpluses. How-

Figure 8.1 Protesters at an antiwar rally in Washington, D.C., 1970. ©Wally McNamee/Corbis.

ever, the most significant impact on the economy was the Arab oil embargo. A 1973 war that pitted Israel against Egypt and Syria led Saudi Arabia to impose an embargo on oil shipped to the United States, an ally of Israel. Dramatic price increases resulted in a significant increase in wealth in oil-producing countries. Americans were soon facing both shortages and high prices, with inflation reaching 11 percent in 1974 and unemployment jumping to 9 percent—the highest since the Great Depression of the 1930s. Gas shortages caused lines to form, and some factories laid off workers to save fuel costs, with an immediate effect on the economy. In the United States, younger workers, marginalized social groups, and the unemployed suffered most.

The energy shortage continued through both the Ford and Carter presidencies, with another gas crisis in 1979. To emphasize the need to conserve, Carter addressed the nation in 1977 wearing a cardigan sweater rather than the usual suit. Throughout the 1970s, the term used to describe the economy was stagflation—a combination of high interest rates, high unemployment, slow growth, and decreased productivity.[3]

Two of the successes of the Nixon administration were the relaxation of tensions with the Soviet Union and the opening up of relations with China. By 1969, U.S. domination as a world power was beginning to decline, and Nixon determined the need to improve relationships between East and West, particularly establishing friendliness with Communist countries and an easing of Cold War tensions. He moved toward détente (defined as a relaxation of strained relationships) with the Soviet Union. Nixon and his National Security Advisor Henry Kissinger arranged a summit in Moscow in 1972 that produced the basic principles of U.S.–Soviet relations and the Strategic Arms Limitation Talks (SALT) treaty, which prohibited the testing of antiballistic missile systems (ABMs).[4]

Following on the heels of his success in Moscow, Nixon opened up relations with China in 1972, making the historic first visit of an American president to China. In the course of a week-long summit he took the first steps in establishing diplomatic relations, including removal of at least some trade restrictions. Interest in China and everything Chinese pervaded the popular press and the fashion world.

Despite Nixon's success in China and the Soviet Union, his presidency will be forever tainted by the Watergate scandal that began with the break-in at the Democratic headquarters in the Watergate hotel in Washington, DC, during the 1972 election campaign and ended with his resignation in 1974. When Nixon resigned, Vice President Gerald Ford became president, inheriting many of the problems that plagued Nixon.[5] Ford focused particularly on improving the economy, with some success. By the end of his two-year presidency, inflation had been cut in half and the unemployment rate had dropped. However, he also inherited a legacy of distrust of the presidency, making it difficult to accomplish other domestic and foreign policy goals.

A positive event in the mid-seventies was the huge celebration of the nation's bicentennial in 1976. Planning had begun years before, but the political divisions of the previous decade led to more subdued celebrations than originally planned. Rather than one single all-inclusive event, there were thousands of separate events across the country that ranged from simple to extremely elaborate. It also provided an opportunity for a host of businesses to market bicentennial-themed products.

Social Life and Culture

The years from 1969 to 1978 were about adjustments and reactions to changes begun in the 1960s and are characterized by the continuation of many social movements. The antiwar movement, most notably visible on college campuses, continued until the end of American involvement in Vietnam. Modern behaviors began to be replaced by what was defined as postmodern.[6] American family life changed, as traditional family structures eroded from a rising divorce rate and declining birth rate. More women pursued careers, and there was an increase in the number of single-parent families. The baby boom generation, no longer teenagers, was instrumental in growth of a singles culture, with more openness about sex and sexual relationships and a loosening of sexual mores that included awareness if not acceptance of the gay and lesbian community. Coed residence halls became common at many colleges and universities. The Twenty-Sixth Amendment to the Constitution was passed in 1971, giving the right to vote to 18-year-olds.

Social Movements

The civil rights movement continued from earlier decades, as activists fought against the many inequalities that continued to exist, especially in the form of housing and education discrimination, and against broader institutionalized racism. The Supreme Court addressed the issue of school segregation that resulted from the existence of neighborhood schools, a situation that effectively isolated black students. Mandatory busing was used to achieve integration, which sometimes led to violence, particularly in South Boston and several other northeastern cities (Figure 8.2). Other ethnic minorities also joined the fight to end discrimination. Mexican Americans began to use the term Chicano(a) to express their distinctive identity as separate

Figure 8.2 To achieve integration, mandatory busing was implemented in September 1971. ©Bettmann/Corbis.

from a more general U.S. culture. The American Indian Movement was founded in 1968 as an alternative to other Indian Rights organizations. During the 1970s, a number of federally funded cultural, welfare, and political programs were created.

The feminist movement (also called the women's liberation movement) that began in the 1960s gained momentum in the 1970s, although not every woman supported it. Evidence that women were excluded from many positions as well as from equal access to housing led movement leaders to work for change through a variety of successful publications and through governmental processes. In 1971, feminist Gloria Steinem, along with several others, founded *Ms. Magazine* and the National Women's Political Caucus.

Many women, from a variety of backgrounds, worked for legal reform through the Equal Rights Amendment (ERA). Although it appeared to be moving toward ratification by the required 38 states, the ERA never achieved final approval. One change that feminists supported was the legalization of abortion, obtained through the still divisive 1973 *Roe v. Wade* decision by the Supreme Court.

Other transformations occurred, however, and, by the mid-1970s, more women entered business, medicine, and engineering fields in college, and, by the end of the decade, more than half of all college graduates were women. Many more began to aim for middle- and upper-management positions, and the proportion of women in state legislatures tripled. In general, however, women continued to earn significantly less than their male counterparts.

One of the more visible events that epitomized the women's movement was a 1973 tennis match between Billie Jean King, top ranking in women's tennis, and Bobby Riggs, an ex-Wimbledon champ. Billed as the Battle of the Sexes, the match drew a television audience of more than 45 million Americans. King won the battle in straight sets, and, despite media exaggeration of the event, it effectively marked the beginning of a broad expansion of women's athletics in the United States. The passage of Title IX as part of the 1972 Education Amendment expanded women's participation by prohibiting sex discrimination in educational programs that received federal funds.

The environmental movement also began to take shape in the mid-1960s, gaining momentum in the 1970s, aided in part by gasoline shortages and a number of ecological crises. Americans became aware of and concerned about air and water pollution with discoveries such as the thermal pollution from nuclear power plants, the threat of the chemical DDT to wildlife, and an oil spill in California. During the Nixon presidency, Congress passed the Clean Air Act and a Water Quality Improvement Act and authorized establishment of the Environmental Protection Agency. The first Earth Day was celebrated in April 1970.

Older Americans also became advocates for the rights of the elderly. Life expectancy had increased, and Medicare and an expansion of Social Security meant more financial security for retirees, but there was a perceived insensitivity to the needs of Americans over age 65 years. An organization called the Gray Panthers was formed in 1971 to fight for—among other benefits—better health care and living centers better suited to the needs of the aging. By 1980, the American Association of Retired People (AARP) had more than 12 million members and wielded economic and political power.

The consumer movement gained momentum in the 1970s, led by consumer advocate Ralph Nader, who made a splash in 1965 with the publication of *Unsafe at Any Speed*, decrying the safety problems of the Chevy Corvair. Inspired by Nader, many volunteers, called "Nader's Raiders," established consumer protection offices. The first Consumer Actions office was opened in 1971 in a San Francisco church, organized to respond to consumer complaints via the first Consumer Action hotline. Nader took on many products that presented real or perceived dangers to the American public, including the recently fashionable platform shoes (Figure 8.3).[7]

Rise of the Sunbelt

Both population and political power began to shift to the southern, or Sunbelt, states in the 1970s. Southern cities were the fastest growing in the United States, as rising oil prices brought more hardships to the industrial north, sometimes called the Rustbelt. The election of Georgian Jimmy Carter to the presidency in 1976 was evidence of the growing power of southern voters. The South was attractive to business and industrial development for many reasons, not least its warm weather. Low labor costs, muted civil rights protests, and lower levels of union membership also contributed to the appeal for industry. As these shifts occurred, political power also shifted, and the traditionally Democratic South began to vote Republican.

Technology and Communication

There were many advances in technology in the decade of the 1970s, but perhaps none so dramatic in the potential to change work and communication habits as the debut of the personal computer late in the decade. Various types of digital technologies captured the public's imagination and dollars. In the early 1970s, the pocket calculator became affordable, and digital watches became the rage in mid-decade. Video gaming also entered popular culture, particularly with the introduction by Atari of low-priced integrated circuits for use with a television. Video game arcades became a standard in shopping centers. The first floppy disk appeared in 1970; the following year Intel introduced the microprocessor. Early personal computers were cumbersome, and, with no keyboard and no screen, not very useful to the general public. The Apple II, intro-

duced in 1977 and the Tandy TRS-80 with a keyboard and screen were influential, but it was the development of word processing and spreadsheet programs in 1978 that enticed Americans into computer ownership.[8]

The climax of the space race came in July 1969 when Apollo 11 became the first manned mission to the moon and Neil Armstrong the first man to set foot on the lunar surface. More trips to the moon followed; the second, Apollo 12, occurred only a few months later. By the time Apollo 13 was launched, space travel had begun to seem commonplace to Americans. However, an explosion on the spacecraft caused a near disaster and brought the country back to view the harrowing but safe return of the astronauts. The last moon mission was in 1972. The National Aeronautics and Space Administration (NASA) next began development of a space shuttle program, successfully launching the first shuttle in 1977.

Medical advances included the use of ultrasound as a diagnostic technique. In 1978, the first test tube baby was born in England, developed in a Petri dish from an artificially inseminated egg implanted into the mother's womb. The sites of DNA production on genes were discovered in 1972, and genetic engineering began development. In the mid-1970s magnetic imaging techniques were also developed.

Literature

In this period of social unrest and a pervasive sense of alienation and volatility, literature reflected many of these sentiments. Popular reading included themes of alienation, the search for spiritual meaning, and responses to the political situation. A wave of psychology books and articles appeared, much of it asserting the priority of personal fulfillment and self-expression.

Figure 8.3 Balancing in platform shoes, New York, 1973. ©Bettmann/ Corbis.

The Culture of Narcissism: American Life in an Age of Diminishing Expectations (1979) by Christopher Lasch seemed to define the period. Books such as I'm OK, You're OK and How to Be Your Own Best Friend focused on the interest in finding one's self. A surprise hit was Jonathan Livingston Seagull, a parable about a seagull not content with an ordinary life. It seemed to strike a chord in the 1970s exploration of self. Other sometimes graphic books addressed the new sexual awareness. These included The Joy of Sex, The Hite Report: A Nationwide Study of Female Sexuality, Everything You Always Wanted to Know About Sex: But Were Afraid to Ask and Fear of Flying. The jogging craze brought The Complete Book of Running and The Joy of Running. A number of feminist books also were widely read, including The Female Eunuch and Against Our Will, and the women's health book, Our Bodies, Ourselves. In a backlash against the women's movement, The Total Woman suggested women surrender totally to their husbands.

Toni Morrison began her writing career in the 1970s, examining the black American experience, and becoming one of the strongest literary voices of the time. All the President's Men (1974) by Carl Bernstein and Bob Woodward detailed the Watergate investigation and was also made into a film in 1976.

Sports and Leisure

Some remember the 1970s as an era of bizarre fads that included everything from mood rings (a ring that supposedly changed color to match the wearer's mood) and Rubik's cubes to smiley face stickers and pet rocks. One of the more outrageous fads was "streaking"—racing nude through very public places.

By the early 1970s, Americans ate more fast food meals and more meals away from home than ever before. Many prepackaged foods were full of fat, sugar, and artificial flavoring—often ambiguously labeled. A counter-trend promoted more healthful eating, raising and eating organic foods, and getting more exercise. In 1973, the Food and Drug Administration began to require nutritional information on food labels, and many Americans took up bicycling, running, and jogging, a craze that also led to new jogging-related apparel.

One of the best-selling books of 1978 was The Complete Book of Running by Jim Fixx, and sales of running shoes skyrocketed to 50 percent of all shoes sold. The Nike Company was founded in 1972 and soon became a major source of athletic shoes and apparel. From the start, the company sought athletes' endorsements, first from runner Steve Prefontaine. Other individual sports became or remained popular, including golf, tennis, bicycling, and for the young,

skateboarding. However, by 1978, the average American weight was at least 14 pounds higher than in 1963.

Americans continued to be ardent viewers of spectator sports, especially as more were broadcast on television. The 1972 Munich Olympics enjoyed popularity, as U.S. swimmer Mark Spitz won seven gold medals.[9] Both professional and collegiate athletics had large followings, although the tight-fitting and revealing attire worn by cheerleaders for the Dallas Cowboys attracted perhaps as much attention as the game at the 1976 Super Bowl.

Art, Television, Music, and the Movies

The various social movements of the 1960s and 1970s, including the sexual revolution, the women's movement, and the ecology movement, were reflected in all forms of the arts, from fine art to the entertainment industry.

Art and Architecture

Art and artists in the 1970s continued some of the trends of the 1960s but also explored new areas. The environmental movement led to earth art, a style that challenged ideas about time, size, and space, and was created by artists such as Robert Smithson, Michael Heizer, Alice Aycock, and Alan Sonfist. Smithson's Spiral Jetty, for example, was a massive earthwork created at Great Salt Lake. Feminist art moved away from the abstraction of earlier periods and strove to convey information. Miriam Schapiro and Judy Chicago were in the vanguard of the women's movement. Chicago's Dinner Party Project, which evolved into a group work, became one of the most significant pieces of the time. Other notable schools of art included concept art, photo-realism, and political art.

By the early 1970s, the uniformity of the modern school of design had been overcopied, and architects envisioned a new approach that allowed for creating buildings and houses that fit into their surroundings. Many looked to the past, creating a style that blended disparate ideas together, with a more ornamental approach than modernism. Postmodernism became the term applied to this style. This borrowing from the past and the mixing of styles is evident in the Piazza d'Italia in New Orleans, which includes classical Roman details. Other notable buildings of the decade include the Sears Tower in Chicago and I. M. Pei's East Wing of the National Gallery in Washington, DC.

The wearable art movement began in the early 1970s, combining clothing and various types of fiber art: weaving, painting, embroidery, and dyeing. It was most likely an outgrowth of the do-it-yourself/self-expressive clothing decoration practiced by 1960s hippies (Figure 8.4).

Television

Television became the dominant entertainment medium in the 1960s but perhaps truly came of age in the 1970s. The number of hours people spent watching television increased, and by 1978, 98 percent of U.S. households had at least one television. Much programming was in direct response to events of the period, reflecting racial problems, women's issues, and even war. Television had, from the beginning, brought Americans directly in contact with news events, including presidential campaigns and the Vietnam War, and by the 1970s many people acquired all their news from the television. In fact, *TV Guide* became the most widely read publication.

Television series programming rarely connected with the dramatic events of the late 1960s, but, by the early 1970s, a number of shows directly or indirectly reflected social and cultural events and problems. Situation comedy took a sharp turn toward social commentary with *All in the Family*, featuring Archie Bunker (Carroll O'Connor) as the bigoted but

Figure 8.4 Young man adding patches to his denim jeans for self-expression, 1974. ©Bettmann/Corbis.

lovable blue-collar star and his well-meaning, often befuddled wife Edith (Jean Stapleton). The show tackled racial issues, the women's movement, and the sexual revolution, opening up topics never before discussed on prime-time television. *The Mary Tyler Moore* show also debuted in 1970, with Moore as a single, 30ish, and independent career woman. This show, along with *Saturday Night Live*, made Saturdays a stay-at-home-and-watch-television night.

Other classic shows of the decade included *M*A*S*H* (1972), based on the movie. Although set during the Korean War, it accurately reflected the antiwar sensibilities of this post-Vietnam decade. Ethnic sitcoms also made in-roads into prime-time television's programming. *Sanford & Son* (1972) starred Redd Foxx as a Watts junk dealer, *Good Times* (1974) depicted a working-class black family in Chicago, *Chico and the Man* (1974) starred Puerto Rican comic Freddie Prinze, and *The Jeffersons* (1975) depicted an upwardly mobile black family. Shows such as *The Brady Bunch*, on the contrary, avoided any political or cultural commentary. There was also a craze for 1950s nostalgia on television with shows such as *Happy Days* and *Laverne & Shirley*.

Also popular was *Charlie's Angels*, an odd blend that depicted three career police women whose main attraction was their (obviously braless) sex appeal. Feminists complained, but *Charlie's Angels* made a star of Farrah Fawcett-Majors, who posed in a bathing suit for one of the most popular posters of the late 1970s, and helped create a mania for her loose, curled hairstyle (Figure 8.5).

Alex Haley's *Roots*, a miniseries that ran in 1977, became a national phenomenon. It chronicled Haley's search for his family roots from the early days of slavery up to their post–Civil War freedom. It depicted the harsh conditions of slavery in the United States and forced many white Americans to face this period of history for the first time. It also led many families to explore their own heritage.

Television viewing was permanently altered with the introduction of the Sony Betamax video-recording system in 1975. With a longer recording time and lower price, JVS's Video Home System (VHS) soon became the dominant technology in the industry for home recording.

Movies

Movie attendance lost out to television in the 1960s but made a dramatic come-back in the 1970s with the birth of what was called the new Hollywood and the decline of the old studio system.[10] Movies also mirrored the trauma of current events and problems, particularly in the first half of the period, but also saw directors freed from the constraints of the studio's process. A new group of filmmakers explored more challenging subject matter or dealt with top-

Figure 8.5 Charlie's Angels: Jaclyn Smith, Kate Jackson, and Farrah Fawcett-Majors posed in menswear-inspired three-piece suits, with wide collars and open necks, 1976. ©Bettmann/Corbis.

Figure 8.6 Diane Keaton and Woody Allen in a scene from *Annie Hall*, with Diane Keaton dressed in the character's signature menswear look, 1977. ©Bettmann/Corbis.

ical issues. These included Robert Altman's *M*A*S*H* (1970), Stanley Kubricks's *A Clockwork Orange*, Francis Ford Coppola's *The Godfather* and *The Godfather II*, and Martin Scorcese's *Taxi Driver*. Sex and drugs and the counterculture also became film topics in *Easy Rider* and *Midnight Cowboy*, both released in 1969. George Lucas created nostalgia for what seemed like a less complicated time with *American Graffiti* (1973), set in 1962. A later movie, *Animal House* (1978), was set in the same time period but celebrated the debauchery of college life rather than innocence. *The Exorcist* (1973) fed into a popular interest in the occult. Looking for new heroes, America flocked to see *Rocky* in 1976, perhaps as an escape from all the disaster films of 1974 (*Airport*, *The Towering Inferno*, *Earthquake*).

By 1975, Hollywood discovered the blockbuster, with Steven Spielberg's *Jaws*. Released during the mid-1970s recession, it set box office records as a summer escape movie. In 1977, George Lucas's *Star Wars* became another summer blockbuster, launching hundreds of merchandising tie-ins, soon a standard of film major releases. Woody Allen's comic and often slapstick films of the early 1970s (*Bananas*, *Sleeper*) changed pace and created a fashion phenomenon in 1977 with the release of *Annie Hall*. The heroine, played by Diane Keaton, wore loose, unconstructed, menswear-inspired clothing designed by both Ralph Lauren and costume designer Ruth Morley, which spawned a wave of imitations (Figure 8.6).

Filmmakers also began to recognize the importance of the black audience. The huge success of *Shaft* (1971), about a black private detective, ushered in dozens of imitators in what were termed blaxploitation films, including *Superfly* (1972), *Cleopatra Jones* (1973), and *Blacula* (1972). These films generated controversy, as the NAACP argued that black males were portrayed as drug users, pimps, and gangsters. The film style lasted only a few years, until about 1974, but did create clothing fads that evolved into the hip-hop styles of the 1980s.

Hollywood actresses reflected the general tendency toward casual dressing in the 1970s, posing in jeans and blazers and opting out of the elaborate evening dress for special events.

Music

A diversity of music styles pervade this decade, but the dominant music of AM radio was rock and roll. Two pivotal events of 1969–1970 symbolized the end of the 1960s: Woodstock and the breakup of the Beatles. Several of the rock music styles of the 1970s became at least as much about the clothing as about the music.

The Woodstock Music and Art Fair occurred in August 1969 in New York State with a lineup of the most important stars of the late 1960s, including Jimi Hendrix, Janis Joplin, Joan Baez, the Who, and the Grateful Dead. Despite rain,

Figure 8.7 John Travolta and his dance partner in *Saturday Night Fever*, 1977. ©Bettmann/Corbis.

overcrowding, and insufficient amenities, it was a peaceful event that captured viewers (either with fascination or shock) with images of nudity, drugs, and sexual freedom. For the youthful audience it seemed to promise an idealized and classless new America. By the end of 1970, however, Joplin and Hendrix would both be dead, victims of drug and alcohol use. By the early 1970s, the counterculture of the 1960s began to look inward and to develop some of the me generation traits. Popular music moved from protest to introspection, especially as sung by vocalists such as James Taylor, Carol King, Carly Simon, and Joni Mitchell.

The early 1970s were characterized by an eclectic mix of rock and roll, from heavy metal to southern rock to funk. There was a short-lived vogue for glitter or glam rock bands such as the New York Dolls and David Bowie, all known for their outrageous dress. Bowie took on numerous personas, all tied to elaborate stage sets and frequently androgynous costume and makeup styles often copied by fans. By the mid-1970s, a new music style—disco—was dominating the club scene. With a dance beat that blended Latin rhythm with an electronic synthesized dance beat, disco represented the ultimate seventies statement, with the hedonism of becoming a temporary star of the dance floor and an entry code to many clubs that required elaborate dressing up. The opening of Studio 54 in New York in early 1977 lent disco snob appeal, as owners carefully guarded the doors to allow in only the famous or the most fashionable. The 1977 release

of *Saturday Night Fever*, with a musical score by the Bee Gees, brought disco to a broad audience and popularized floral knit shirts and three-piece white suits like the one worn by star John Travolta (Figure 8.7). The disco beat and the lifestyle of those who frequented the clubs inspired a vogue for shiny, fluid dance attire and spandex, body conscious clothing that included heat transfer prints on synthetic fabrics. By 1980, however, disco was in rapid decline, and an anti-disco culture had emerged.

The other rock music style that was intimately connected to fashion was punk. Although punk was most often associated with bands that came out of London, one of the first punk groups was the Ramones, from Queens, New York. Punk music rejected the more concept-oriented and commercial albums of the late 1960s, substituting short, fast songs with a loud and often chaotic style intended to be offensive. The outrageous British band the Sex Pistols embodied the alienation that was a product of the economic problems in England. Malcolm McLaren, along with designer Vivienne Westwood, created the fashion style of the band, at the same time promoting their clothing boutique SEX in London's Kings Road area. The punk style, with torn shirts and jackets decorated with heavy chains and safety pins, had an enduring influence on the fashion world and brought London designers a popularity they had not enjoyed since the mid-1960s.

Unlike previous decades, 1970s songs from Broadway generally did not receive much AM radio airplay, although several musicals had noteworthy effects on popular culture. These included *Jesus Christ Superstar* (1971), *A Chorus Line* (1975), nostalgic *Grease* (1972), and a series of musicals by Stephen Sondheim (*Company, Follies, A Little Night Music*).

Manufacturing and Retailing

The boundaries between production and retailing became more permeable between 1969 and 1978, hence the overlap of the two functions in this discussion. Manufacturing and retailing rose or fell along with the economy, creating a whiplash effect for businesses. Styles could generate radically different responses: knit suits for men were a bonanza; the midiskirt, a calamity.

In 1971, the women's fashion apparel business was valued at more than $13 billion wholesale, and this branch of the industry had 1.4 million employees.[11] Such large enterprises as Jonathan Logan, Bobbie Brooks, Russ Togs, and Originala remained rarities in an industry still typified by small firms. Many manufacturers specialized in one classification of goods (e.g., coats or evening dresses), in a specific price zone (better vs. moderate). A few makers diversified into related lines. Villager, for example, began as a producer of shirts but added sweaters, dresses, and hosiery to their lines. Some companies branched out from menswear to womenswear and vice versa. Seasonal lines began to blur because of population shifts southward and because new styles were introduced continuously to match customers' habits of shopping more frequently. Some of the tilt away from fixed seasons arose from manufacturers' desire to spread production throughout the year and thus avoid the rush seasons that necessitated the payment of overtime, which eroded already-slim profits.

Menswear continued to be produced by large companies (Cluett Peabody and Hart Schaffner Marx), as had been true through most of the twentieth century. Their product mix changed, however; for example, staple white shirts lost ground to versions in fashion colors. In 1965, 80 percent of the shirts made by Arrow were white; by 1970, the same proportion were colored or patterned. Between 1950 and 1974, strictly tailored suits declined in sales compared to less-constructed sports coats and slacks. Fewer sizes were offered in an effort to control costs. Men's increasing interest in fashion led many designers to enter the menswear business. These included Bill Blass, John Weitz, Calvin Klein, Geoffrey Beene, Oscar de la Renta, Yves Saint Laurent, Giorgio Armani, and Ralph Lauren.

Apparel manufacturers formed various combinations for desired economies of scale. Horizontal integration entailed diversification of the types of products made, whereas vertical integration involved making the textiles and other components as well as the finished apparel under the umbrella of a single company.

The industry's locus changed, too, from northeast and north central states to the southeast, west, and southwest. Dallas achieved third-rank status as an apparel production and marketing center after New York City and Los Angeles. By moving away from Manhattan, companies could build sprawling modern plants, with easier access and lower operating costs. Companies that were prepared to sell apparel overseas made use of production facilities in the importing country. Some Europeans seemed eager to buy better sportswear: American expertise in fitting, coordination, and merchandising lent allure to U.S. products. In other cases, offshore production helped save manufacturers money while providing American customers with appealing goods. Conversely, imports grew fast, especially from Hong Kong, Japan, and South Korea, eroding domestic makers' sales of shirts, blouses, and childrenswear.

Technology assisted the producers to keep up with the hectic pace of the industry. Laser-beam cutting of pattern pieces, which began in menswear, spread to women's and children's apparel. Computer-aided pattern making debuted in the mid-1970s with automated pattern layout and guidance of sewing machines, plus electronic storage of patterns. A few firms tested automated pattern and marker making during this period, although not yet widely adopted. In the wake of the 1973 Arab oil embargo, the cost of energy and petrochemicals rose steeply, forcing economy in all industries.

The rise of consumerism during the 1960s prompted anxious manufacturers and retailers to assess consumer opinion and demand. Electronic data processing at the point of sale gave retailers a precise picture of the products that were most popular. Not only was the assortment of merchandise calculated carefully, but also the dates when specific quantities of particular styles, sizes, and colors were needed to use promotion and display schedules advantageously, maximize sales, and support the store's cash flow. Retailers also deployed computers to match the number of staff on the selling floor with volume of traffic in specific departments at particular times of day and week.

From Diners' Card's modest beginnings in 1950, use of credit cards spread, first to cards usable in the local area and then in 1966 to cards with nationwide acceptance. United States consumers owned 275 million credit cards of various types in 1971. Total sales charged on cards rose from under $1 billion in 1967 to more than $7 billion in 1970. Improved computer records and security processes helped to curb early problems with theft and fraud.

Faced with competition from grocery and drug stores, especially in the sale of utilitarian apparel such as hosiery and underwear, department stores struggled to maintain a fashion-right image. Warehouse stores and factory outlets took some of the market share from department and specialty stores. Store hours continued to expand, making seven-day selling weeks common. The nature of selling also evolved to include more catalog sales and an ever-increasing amount of self-service.[12] By the mid-1970s, menswear, manufacturers were distributing their products through regular retail stores and via their own wholesale outlets, a practice called dual distribution, which undercut conventional retailers. Discounters of all types and sizes flourished, offering various price cuts on everything from designer apparel to more staple goods.[13] E. J. Korvette and Great Eastern cut into sales at traditional department stores. Specialty shops, including the Talbot's chain, prospered and multiplied. Struggling to survive, some big-name stores fell under the control of conglomerates, including Carter-Hawley-Hale and Federated Department Stores.

As branch stores and chain stores proliferated, the buying and selling functions diverged. Individual stores no longer selected the merchandise; that function shifted to the main office of the chain or group. Buyers increasingly concentrated their market visits on regional trade shows held in New York City, Chicago, Los Angeles, and Dallas. Denver, Miami, and Charlotte, North Carolina, acquired markets by the mid-1970s.

Department stores dropped some of their long-standing departments, including custom or couture departments, fabric and home-sewing areas, and millinery. Some began to seek out and cultivate new American designers as a way to create a distinctive or exclusive product mix. The elite store Henri Bendel, for example, created an opportunity on Friday mornings for design directors and buyers to see what was new and interesting, as aspiring designers lined up at the doors. Bloomingdale's also supported young design talent and reconfigured itself as the trendy place to shop and to be seen, adding individual designer boutiques within the store.

Advertising and promotional departments flourished. Publicity campaigns included appearances by celebrities to promote certain styles or brands. More U.S. homes had colored television, which helped to expand television advertising of fashion goods. Deluxe retailer Neiman-Marcus began to test ads on cable television in 1974.

Some retailers carefully targeted mailings of catalogs, especially before Christmas and Hanukkah, to generate better return on advertising investment.

Fashion Influences

Fashion influences and directions ran the gamut from health and fitness to the ease of synthetics, and from nostalgia and retro styles to disco and punk. Although mainstream clothing was relatively subdued, it was a period when styles splintered and subcultural trends further influenced fashion.

Photography and Illustration

The combination of economic problems and the effects of the Vietnam War, among other things, led to a more sober, less fanciful approach to fashion. Clothing was generally more muted, with easy-to-wear dresses and coordinated, layered looks. To create excitement in the fashion pages, photographers turned to a variety of styles and techniques. Much photography seemed to suggest either a sexually charged atmosphere or hint at violence. There was often a sense of unease in the settings that created the feeling of an underlying message that readers sometimes found disturbing (Plate 8.1).

Dozens of excellent photographers worked for the major fashion publications, although several in particular set the tone for the decade. Helmut Newton, who had been photographing fashion since the 1960s, created harder edged images of women and often showed the models in sexual poses (Plate 8.2). Guy Bourdin, one of the more controversial photographers of the decade, often used suggestive poses and settings. Deborah Turbeville became one of the most successful and imitated of a new group of women photographers. Her photographs were softer, sometimes with a sense of alienation or sadness in models posed in a mysterious or even ominous environment (Plate 8.1). Despite the sometimes dark overtones of fashion photography, models, although still tall and slim, adopted a more natural look, with the idea that a toned body was achieved through exercise and diet rather than through support garments. One of the most representative of the period was Lauren Hutton, but other models included Naomi Sims and Ali McGraw.

Fashion illustration took a back seat to photography in fashion magazines, although there were many excellent illustrators who created dramatic images for *Women's Wear Daily*, advertising, and catalogs. These included Steven Stipelman, Steven Meisel, and Kenneth Paul Block (Figure 8.8).[14] Antonio Lopez's energetic and graphic style, often with a sense of fantasy, could now be seen more often in Eu-

Figure 8.8 Knit and ultrasuede separates from Halston, illustrated by Kenneth Paul Block, November 14, 1975. Fairchild archives.

ropean fashion magazines but set the stage for a resurgence of illustration in the 1980s.

The Designers

In general, the New York ready-to-wear industry thrived in the 1970s despite the recession. As part of this Me Decade, personal lifestyle choices and ambitions began to be reflected in clothing choices. Mixing and matching elements became more the norm, while the haute couture seemed less relevant to the times. In fact, by 1975, Kennedy Fraser of the *New Yorker* declared the haute couture a "degenerate institution propped up by a sycophantic press."[15] For the Paris design houses, the prêt-à-porter (ready-to-wear) was becoming the creative and profitable side of the business. The combination of recession and inflation meant women were more cautious about their clothing purchases as prices rose. In this atmosphere, American designers truly came of age in the 1970s, and were finally front and center in fashion publications. Almost all made their name with ready-to-wear and most with the clean design lines of contemporary sports wear. When several U.S. designers were invited to show their work at Versailles in 1973, the designs looked modern and wearable, receiving more press acclaim than the French designers' offerings.[16]

United States

Many American sportswear designers became household names, even stars, in the 1970s, launching fashion power houses. Others were significant contributors to the fashion of the times but did not last long into the next decade. Both **Ralph Lauren** and **Calvin Klein** launched their women's wear businesses in the early 1970s, becoming the rising stars of New York fashion. Klein started his own business in 1968 designing coats, but, by 1971, he was creating elegant but easy-to-wear sportswear and working with the concept of wardrobe dressing. He created his designs with expensive and graceful fabrics such as silk charmeuse and cashmere. Relatively simply cut, and usually in a neutral color palette centered on beige, his clothing represented a new minimalism in fashion. A design strong point was the concept of layering separates (Figure 8.9). He hired some of the best photographers of the time, including Turbeville and Bourdin, for his advertisements. Klein won his first Coty award in 1973 and by the mid-1970s was becoming a fashion celebrity.

Lauren began his menswear company Polo in 1967, designing wide neckties. By 1971, he added a line of men's-style shirts for women and soon expanded his women's collections to include other categories, all based on a menswear style of dressing, often with a retro feeling (Figure 8.10). His designs for two films, *The Great Gatsby* (1974) and *Annie Hall,* influenced the ready-to-wear world, particularly the adaptations of menswear for women. Lauren persuaded Bloomingdale's to create a small boutique within the store, concentrating all his apparel and accessories in one area and leading to very strong sales.

Halston provided a fashion alternative to the masculine styling of Lauren, with soft and unstructured styles. Born Roy Halston Frowick, he started as a milliner for Lilly Daché and Bergdorf Goodman, designing Jacqueline Kennedy's pillbox hat for the inauguration of her husband. By the late 1960s, he began to design clothing, and he opened a salon for private customers in 1968. He soon expanded his business into ready-to-wear, with a focus on luxury fabrics cut into simple shapes (see Figure 8.8). Making a reputation as a designer of clean-lined and elegant American clothing, Halston was soon considered one of the top New York designers. Halston pioneered the use of the new Ultrasuede fabric, which he made into shirtdresses and coats. His designs ranged from fitted cashmere sweaters to jersey knits in simple but very body-conscious shapes, often halter styles. Seen at the popular Studio 54 disco with other New York celebrities, he created a personality for himself that turned

Figure 8.9 Calvin Klein layered separates. *Vogue,* August 1975, 104, Arthur Elgort/*Vogue* ©1975 Condé Nast Publications Inc.

Figure 8.10 Menswear inspired separates from Ralph Lauren. *Vogue*, September 1, 1975, 242, Daniel Michaels/*Vogue* ©1975 Condé Nast Publications Inc.

Figure 8.11 Diane Von Furstenberg wearing her signature wrap dress, 1976. ©Burt Glinn/Magnum Photos.

fashion design into a glamorous profession, his impact perhaps best characterized by an article in *Esquire* titled "Will Halston Take Over the World?"[17]

Diane von Furstenberg was born Diane Halfin in Belgium. She married Prince Egon von Furstenberg at age 18 years and immediately became a member of the international jet set. She began her designing career soon after, working initially as an apprentice to fabric manufacturer Angelo Ferretti. When she moved to New York in 1970, she arrived with several silk jersey dresses, showing them to Diana Vreeland, who chose to run one of them in an issue of *Vogue*. Faced with more orders than she could fill, von Furstenberg opened a showroom in New York with a financial backer. In 1973, she introduced the wrap dress, a one-piece, body-hugging style that sold immediately.[18] She continued to make moderately price dresses, including shirt dresses and separates styled as dresses until 1977, and expanded into cosmetics, accessories, and other licenses that continue under her name (Figure 8.11).

Anne Klein continued to create high-quality classic sportswear until her death in 1974. Considered an influential New York designer, she was one of the five designers invited to the fashion presentation at Versailles. The company continued under the design direction of **Louis Dell'Olio** and **Donna Karan.**

Stephen Burrows had one of the most fashionable boutiques in New York, Stephen Burrow's World at Henri Bendel. He created clothing that relied on nontraditional sewing and finishing techniques for the time. Closures were snaps or laces instead of buttons, and the seaming was sometimes on the outside. Many of his styles were made in synthetic jersey and stretched when sewn to create a rippled effect. He

also went against the trend toward neutral colors, designing with bright colors and trims (see Plate 8.2). He opened his own business in 1973, winning a Coty award in 1974. Burrows also showed his collection at Versailles in 1973.

Scott Barrie, one of the few black designers of the period, opened his company in 1969 designing sexy clothing, mostly for evening, using mainly synthetic jerseys and chiffons (see Plate 8.1). Other styles included jumpsuits, tunics, and knit dresses for daywear. His clothing was carried at both Bendel's and Bloomingdale's and was often worn by model Naomi Sims.

Clovis Ruffin founded his own company in 1972 and created a name designing high fashion but affordable clothing. He began designing T-shirt dresses and other wearable knit styles intended to be a backdrop for the wearer to accessorize and personalize.

Europe

British designers **Vivienne Westwood** and **Zandra Rhodes** put London fashion back on the map with their interpretations of punk style in the mid-1970s. Westwood is considered the originator of punk fashion, symbolized by ripped clothing made of cheap fabrics, safety-pin closures and piercings, and elements of bondage (Figure 8.12). Her early designs were sometimes described as decadent or unwearable, but they were also influential. She opened a boutique with partner Malcolm McLaren on King's Road, London, called Let It Rock, changing the name to SEX in 1974, and then to Seditionaries in 1977, as the punk movement took on political overtones. By the early 1980s she and McLaren had abandoned the punk style and introduced what was defined as the New Romantics movement.

Figure 8.12 (LEFT) Vivienne Westwood and models in her punk creations, April 1977. Photograph by Tim Jenkins, courtesy of Fairchild archives.

Rhodes began producing inventive clothing in the late 1960s, often hand-screened with her own designs. She experimented with novel ways to construct garments, including pinked seams turned to the outside in an early collection of coats. Always innovative, she smoothed the rough edges of punk and made it more glamorous, using unfinished and torn edges fastened together with jeweled safety pins. Rhodes considers herself an artist who works with apparel.[19]

In Paris, **Yves Saint Laurent** continued to be a pivotal, often-copied designer. His collections in the early 1970s, although often not well received, soon entered mainstream fashion. He introduced the longuette collection in 1970—an initial attempt at lengthening skirt hems—and a 1940s-inspired collection in 1971. The latter was so poorly reviewed that he declared it would be his last couture collection, stating that "couture cannot be modernized." In a short time, however, elements of 1940s styles were everywhere, including wedge and platform shoes. Yves Saint Laurent continued to design and show couture, creating exotic themed collections that would set it clearly apart from ready-to-wear by the end of the decade (Figure 8.13).

Missoni knits, designed by Italians Tai and Rosita Missoni, were expensive but also considered works of art. Their complex knitwear in distinctive patterns and colors were made in limited numbers and have also been included in museum exhibits.

Fashion Trends

From 1969 through the beginning of the 1970s, the hippie style continued to be popular with the young. However, as the baby boom generation began to grow up, they no longer wanted to look like adolescents, and generally designers began to direct designs toward a more mature audience. As the number of career women increased, they looked for more polished career fashions that were easy to manage and could be worn in a variety of ways and for numerous occasions. The ultimate statement of this was the success of John T. Molloy's 1975 book *Dress for Success* and the 1977 sequel *The Woman's Dress for Success Book*. The first book was aimed at professional men, and the second provided advice for women who aspired to climb the corporate ladder. It led many women to adopt an antifashion look intended as a feminization of the men's business suit.

In 1970 a debate over skirt length raged, but by the end of the decade a multiplicity of lengths made it fade away,

and the real style winner was pants for women. By the mid-1970s, mainstream fashion presented versatile and easy-to-wear clothing that was generally slim and minimalist. The simple styling of ready-to-wear clothing meant that American designers began to focus on image and marketing more than on design, putting money into advertising and, for the first time, late in the decade, placing logos and initials on the outside of clothes.

Textiles and Technology

Fashion designers and textile scientists continued to experiment with synthetic fibers throughout the 1970s, although there was also interest in a return to natural fibers that grew out of the ecology movement. Several fiber innovations became synonymous with the 1970s. Qiana nylon was developed in the late 1960s by DuPont. Initially DuPont tried to promote Qiana through the Paris couture houses as a luxury fiber that simulated the drape of expensive silks. When that was not successful, they reached out to home couturiers, and numerous patterns recommended Qiana as the appropriate fabric. Unfortunately, it scorched at a relatively low temperature and tended to develop static, and it was

discontinued in the early 1980s. In 1970 Toray Industries' scientist Dr. Miyoshi Okamoto created the first ultramicrofiber. Along with his colleague Dr. Toyohiko Hikota, they developed a technique for transforming it into a new, nonwoven fabric. This fabric was trademarked as Ultrasuede, a synthetic suede with an excellent hand that was also washable (Figure 8.14). By the end of the decade there was a backlash against synthetics, many of which had developed objectionable culture associations, particularly polyester leisure suits and Qiana knit dresses and the synthetic shirts so popular in discos.

There were several important legislative acts in the 1970s that affected the apparel industry. The first was an addition to the Flammable Fabrics Act that set standards for children's sleepwear. The second, the Permanent-Care Labeling ruling of the Federal Trade Commission, required all wearing apparel to carry a permanent label with care instructions.

Women's Styles

Throughout most of the 1970s there were two distinct directions in fashion: coordinated tailored pieces, frequently menswear inspired, and fluid, close-to-the-body dresses.

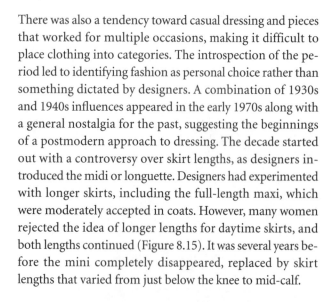

Figure 8.16 Layered skirt with ethnic influences designed by Giorgio Sant'Angelo. ©Condé Nast Archive/Corbis.

Figure 8.17 Knit, T-shirt dresses are at knee length. Spiegel spring/summer 1976 catalog, 15.

There was also a tendency toward casual dressing and pieces that worked for multiple occasions, making it difficult to place clothing into categories. The introspection of the period led to identifying fashion as personal choice rather than something dictated by designers. A combination of 1930s and 1940s influences appeared in the early 1970s along with a general nostalgia for the past, suggesting the beginnings of a postmodern approach to dressing. The decade started out with a controversy over skirt lengths, as designers introduced the midi or longuette. Designers had experimented with longer skirts, including the full-length maxi, which were moderately accepted in coats. However, many women rejected the idea of longer lengths for daytime skirts, and both lengths continued (Figure 8.15). It was several years before the mini completely disappeared, replaced by skirt lengths that varied from just below the knee to mid-calf.

Dresses

Dresses of the late 1960s and the first years of the 1970s were most often inspired by hippie styles, some with long full skirts or a hem ruffle. Other early inspirations came from ethnic influences, also borrowed from the counterculture (Figure 8.16).

The shirtdress style appeared in the late 1960s in short versions and became one of the standards of the decade, shown in a variety of fabrics and design detail modifications. The Ultrasuede version introduced by Halston was widely copied. The introduction of the wrap dress in 1973 by Diane von Furstenberg helped to create a vogue for comfortable, easy-to-wear dresses (Figure 8.11). Numerous designers created a variety of soft, fluid, usually relatively slim silhouettes, including halter, T-shirt, and softly bloused styles (Figure 8.17). Typical fabrics were matte jersey, cotton knit, chiffon, and crepe de chine.

The tendency toward casual dressing eroded the differences between daytime and cocktail dresses, and women relished the ability to wear the same dress to work and then out to dinner or a party. There was generally less formal dressing for evening, although some evening dresses were longer than day dresses. In fact, in 1976, *Vogue* stated that there were no

Figure 8.18 Oscar de la Renta ensemble, to wear at home or out to a dinner party. ©Bettmann/Corbis.

Figure 8.19 Ann Margaret and Roger Smith wear period-inspired suits with similar styling (1972). ©Photo by Keystone/Hulton Archive/Getty Images.

longer "rules of P.M. dressing" and recommended styles that included everything from gold lurex dresses with fur coats to pyjama-styled outfits to evening suits.[20] The casual style trend was seen in caftans, robes, and "at home" clothing for entertaining (Figure 8.18). By the end of the period, fashion based on costume from cultures all over the globe began to appear. Yves Saint Laurent created couture lines inspired by Russian and Chinese dress, ideas that quickly filtered into mainstream styles, particularly evening wear.

Suits and Coats

Pantsuits began to appear in the mid-1960s and became a standard for all occasions—casual wear, work, or evening. The tendency toward menswear inspirations that began in the late 1960s became full blown in the 1970s. For example, in 1970, Yves Saint Laurent introduced safari suits for both men and women, while American designers turned to blazers and other elements from men's closets. Although there was also a brief popularity for knickers, trousers tended to be wide legged, often with a broad cuff in the first

half of the decade, inspired in part by the suits seen in movies such as *The Godfather* (1972) and *The Sting* (1973) (Figure 8.19). By the later 1970s, tapered pants began to be shown. Another variation on pantsuit dressing was the tunic-over-pant style. By the end of the decade, narrower trousers began to return to fashion.

Skirted suits were also worn, still with masculine overtones, and blazers became a standard in women's wardrobes. *Dress for Success* condemned pant suits as inappropriate for women who wanted to climb the corporate ladder, and the widely adopted style for career women became a skirt suit worn with a shirt with a wide loose tie or bow and low-heeled shoes, all in neutral colors.

Coats followed the general trends of the period, with tailored lines that followed the body. Some were belted or wrapped, following the fashion in dresses, and trench coats were also worn. With the popularity of knits, heavy knitted coats, some with the appearance of hand knits, became popular (Figure 8.20), and, late in the 1970s, down- and fiber-filled coats and jackets also appeared.

Figure 8.20 Knitted ensemble. ©Hulton Archive/Getty Images.

Figure 8.22 A panty shirt, a combination of shirt with body suit. Spiegel fall/winter 1973 catalog, 61.

Figure 8.21 Woman wearing hot pants and full cape, ca. 1971. ©Condé Nast Archive/Corbis.

Sportswear, Separates, and Active Sport Clothing

Separates were an important component of women's wardrobes and tended to follow the general silhouette of dresses and suits. Both skirts and tops came in wrap styles. Flare-legged pants remained popular through the early 1970s (see Figure 8.4), but the waistline moved up from the hip to a natural position. One-piece jumpsuits were also briefly popular. Although women chose not to adopt the midiskirt when introduced in 1970, many did wear the new short shorts, dubbed **hot pants** (Figure 8.21). Some shirts, trousers, and other separates had elements borrowed from the men's department, although it often was done with the retro styling of the 1930s.

Jeans remained a wardrobe standard and became increasingly fitted by the end of the 1970s, when designer jeans took center stage sporting labels that identified the designer's name on one of the pockets. The designer jean craze would reach its peak in the next period. Enthusiasm for running, jogging, and other sports meant new active wear styles designed for specific activities. Track suits and other active sport clothing cut in a variety of stretch fab-

Figure 8.23 Knit separates. *Vogue,* February 1974, 110, Francesco Scavullo/*Vogue* ©1974 Condé Nast Publications Inc.

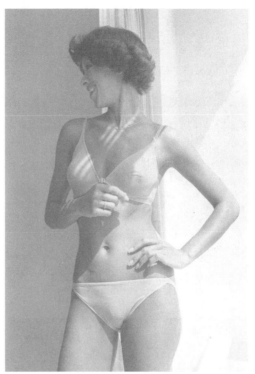

Figure 8.24 Soft-cup bra and bikini panty. Photograph by Peter Simins, August 29, 1975, courtesy of Fairchild archives.

rics began to influence daywear and casual evening wear. Leotards, bodysuits, and shirts that were cut like a bodysuit, with snaps in the crotch, appeared, worn with active sportswear, daywear, or even to the disco (Figure 8.22).

Women's Wear Daily declared 1973 the year of the sweater, and sweater dressing became an important component of casual clothing throughout the 1970s, helped along by lowered thermostats during the energy crisis.[21] This included heavy knits over trousers, T-shirt knits, knit suits, and stretchy synthetics in everything from dresses to body stockings to separates. Knit tops and coordinated knit tunics and other separates that were **space dyed,** dyed to create irregular horizontal lines, became popular in a variety of markets (Figure 8.23).

Foundations and Underwear

Bras came in many styles during this period, even a few pointy shapes, but the most popular bras featured smooth, rounded contours that would be inconspicuous under knitted or sheer dresses and separates. Soft looks were prevalent in both full-cup and demi-cup styles (Figure 8.24). Specialty styles included stick-ons, push-ups, pullovers, and adjustable front-fastening models. Stretch straps became common, and side panels with extra give were offered. Flat underwires replaced round ones for improved comfort. Lace was applied to cups and straps, and an alluring shine was achieved in nylon. Padding of polyester fiberfill continued to be sold, although most silhouettes of the decade did not require prominent curves, except for plunging necklines.

Color coordination, so much a hallmark of the 1960s, continued into the 1970s with matching bras, smoothers (elasticized, seamless undergarments intended to create a smooth figure under knits), and slips in taupe, navy, red, lime green, sun yellow, rose, and orange. Nude, white, and black adapted best to many wardrobes, however. Throughout this decade clothing had a close-to-the-body cut. Flat-front pants were particularly unforgiving. All of this contributed to the survival of foundations garments, purged of the dreaded moniker girdle and euphemistically marketed as slimwear or form persuaders. Panty girdles ranged from briefs to long-legged styles that almost reached the knees. Advertisements played up sheerness and

Figure 8.25 Figure smoothing pantyhose to be worn under flat-front, fitted trousers. The Advertising Archives.

Figure 8.26 Elsa Peretti wearing her cuff and belt. The belt can also be worn as a necklace. Photograph by Mo Becker, November 15, 1973, courtesy of Fairchild archives.

light weight, touting the two-ounce girdle. Spandex blended with nylon was the fiber combination preferred for foundations. For many women, however, control-top panty hose were all they needed or wanted in body shaping (Figure 8.25).

Panties themselves featured hip-hugging lines, with some bikinis, including the string style that was hardly bigger than a present-day thong. Prints and bright colors were offered in knits blended of cotton and rayon. Full slips and petticoats were shown in ultrashort models. **Petti-shorts**—ultrashort petticoat substitutes—for wear under short pants and skirts blurred into the short-lived fashion for **teddy pants** or **tap pants**, underpants evocative of 1930s buttoned styles with wide legs. These passed from fashion in 1978. Bras and slips merged into one garment for those in pursuit of minimal bulk under close-fitting dresses. Occasionally, a romantic alternative was offered by way of a lacy camisole and long, ruffled petticoat. Camisoles were offered as outerwear during the last half of the decade.

Sleepwear included minishifts combined with bikini panties or transparent long gowns for mild weather. Chilly temperatures brought out full-length nightgowns of brushed nylon or cotton. Floral patterns were pervasive in everything from electric hues to pastels. Cuddly bathrobes came in fleece, quilted materials, and terry cloth. Loungewear continued to advance as a category, including floaty caftans and jumpsuits suitable for wear outdoors. Stretch terry cloth had particular appeal.

Accessories

The first half of the 1970s was the time of platform shoes, inspired by a combination of 1930s and 1940s influences and a popularity of Eastern cultures, seen in Japanese-style platforms. Platform shoes ranged from a half inch in front with large, chunky heels, to extremes of height, more popular with the young (see Figure 8.3). In addition to platforms, there was a vogue for wedges on both shoes and boots. The platform faded in the mid-1970s, replaced by a variety of slimmer and more graceful shoes. Boots (see

Figure 8.20) and clogs remained popular throughout the period.

Hats declined in popularity, except for practical knitted caps in the winter (Figure 8.20). However, a number of 1930s-inspired styles appeared frequently in fashion magazines, especially the men's-style fedora (Figure 8.19) and tight-fitted turbans.

A wide variety of accessories was available, with a focus on real jewelry and metals rather than on costume jewelry, for those who could afford it. Gold in particular was popular in hoop earrings and gold chains. Several designers made bold and geometric jewelry popular. **Elsa Peretti,** who designed jewelry for several U.S. designers, was best known for her work with Halston in the 1970s. Her large, horseshoe shaped belt buckle made a dramatic accent on the simply cut, draped dresses. She also created other bold and often-copied pieces (Figure 8.26). Women carried both shoulder bags and a variety of clutch-style purses, but the briefcase was the required accessory for the dress for success woman.

Men's Styles

The peacock revolution of the late 1960s peaked in the first half of the 1970s. Fashion offered men more variety than they had enjoyed in decades. Style tended to be divided by age, with older and more conservative men continuing to wear traditional styles while younger men opted for the more elaborate colors, patterns, and styling. The dress-for-success trend calmed down men's styles by the last half of the 1970s. The casual trend in women's fashion also applied to men's clothing, as did the popularity of knitwear for both casual dressing and for jackets and suits.

Suits and Outerwear

The safari suit for men and women was introduced in the late 1960s, and in 1971 Ralph Lauren highlighted a knit safari suit in his line. This suit style evolved into the style of dressing most associated (usually negatively) with men's clothing of this period—the leisure suit. Most were made of polyester or a polyester blend in pastel shades, sometimes with contrasting stitching. Some had pocket details and yokes that had more visual connection to the detailing on western jackets (Figure 8.27). By the end of the decade the leisure suit was already in decline, a style neither appropriate for the office nor fashionable enough for casual occasions.

Other more traditional men's suits had wide lapels and shaping through the waist (see Figures 8.19 and 8.28). Jackets retained a defined contour through the decade. Three-piece suits began to appear by the middle of the 1970s.

Trousers were usually flat front with a flared leg at the beginning of the period, narrowing by the end of the 1970s. Formal dress still existed, although the trend for casual wear also affected men's clothing. Tuxedo shirts came in colors and had ruffled shirt fronts and cuffs.

There was a return to more conservative dressing by the mid- to late 1970s, helped in part by John Molloy's book. Narrower lapels appeared, as did straight-legged, uncuffed trousers. A layered look, and what was called the preppy look, a style with roots in the 1950s, was characterized by tweed jackets, sometimes with leather elbow patches, and vests. Also in the mid-1970s Giorgio Armani introduced his first men's collection, featuring unconstructed jackets and soft tailoring, a look that continued into the 1980s.

The popularity of the white polyester suit, as shown off by John Travolta in *Saturday Night Fever,* continued until the end of the decade. The suit was worn with wide collared shirts unbuttoned to reveal chest hair and gold jewelry and soon became the fashion to parody from the disco years.

Figure 8.27 A variation on a man's leisure suit, July 23, 1975. Fairchild archives.

Figure 8.28 Three 1974 suit variations from Yves Saint Laurent still with wider lapels and flared trousers. ©Hulton-Deutsch Collection/Corbis.

Figure 8.29 Combining elements of men's fashion in the early 1970s: plaid flared trousers, a patterned shirt, and platform shoes. © Owen Franken/Corbis.

Casual Dress

Men's entire wardrobe began to shift to a more casual appearance with knit shirts, jackets, and sweaters and casual and patterned trousers. For a few years in the early 1970s it seemed that shirts came in every color except white. Fitted knit shirts, usually in polyester or triacetate, had a wide collar and came in a variety of prints and patterns (Figure 8.29). Men's knitwear sold briskly in the early 1970s. Some men opted for turtlenecks instead of shirts or for the **dashiki**, inspired by African dress that evolved as part of the civil rights movement.

Jeans were a staple of men's wardrobes and followed trends similar to women's jeans. Hip-hugger, flared styles dominated the first years of the 1970s, with straighter legged designer styles prevalent by 1979. The trend in athletic clothing also inspired men's casual clothing, including jogging suits, T-shirts, and sweatshirts (Figure 8.30).

Men's snug-fitting business shirts—and the hairy-chest fad—helped increase the popularity of lean, tank-style undershirts or no undershirt at all, although T-shirt styles were also offered. Hip-slung briefs came in bright colors and geometric prints to coordinate with the tank tops. Boxer shorts complemented T-style undershirts. Support underwear of nylon and spandex claimed to mask a paunch. Pajamas included shirt styles in woven cottons and blends and cuffed ski styles in cotton or blended jersey. Robes were terry or fleece in dark colors. Loungewear in the early 1970s included caftans.

Shoes and Accessories

Men's ties widened by 1969 to at least 4 inches and often were covered with bold patterns, although a few men also sported scarves. By the late 1970s the return to conservative dressing brought narrower ties with small patterns.

Figure 8.30 Tennis star Arthur Ashe in a running suit, June 19, 1979. ©AP Wide World Photos.

Platform shoes were also popular for younger men in the early 1970s, with variation in height of platform and heel (see Figure 8.29). Chunky, square-toed shoes and boots, particularly Frye brand, were worn. Shoes tended to get slimmer by the end of the decade.

Children's Styles

Children's clothing and even teen styles closely followed the trends in adult clothing, as the baby boomers remained the largest segment of the population. Casual clothing was the standard for children, and decorated T-shirts with names and images on the front appeared for the first time. Skirt lengths for girls also followed those of adult women, with longer lengths appearing early in the 1970s (see Figure 8.31a).

Some styles mimicked the ethnic looks seen in women's

Figure 8.31a (TOP) Young girl modeling classic styles of the period: flared gored skirt and top; and figure 8.31b (BOTTOM) tailored pants and blouse July 31, 1973. ©Photographs by Peter Simins, courtesy of Fairchild archives.

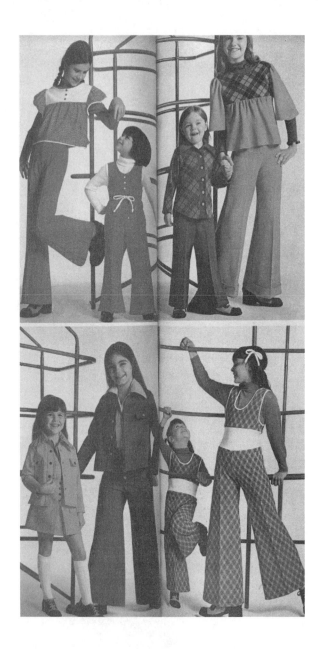

Figure 8.32 (LEFT) Girls knitted separates, including flared-leg pants and jumpsuit. Spiegel catalog, fall/winter 1973.

Figure 8.33 (BELOW) Young boys in leisure suits. *Spiegel Catalog*, fall/winter 1976.

clothing, with long ruffled skirts. Although girls had long been wearing pants for play, it now became acceptable to wear them to school (Figure 8.31b). Older girls also dressed in styles similar to adults. Part of the look included tunics worn over pants and a variety of knit styles (Figure 8.32).

Boys had many of the same fashion options as did men, including leisure and western styled jackets and suits (Figure 8.33). The popularity of jeans extended to all ages, with flared legs in the early part of the period.

Little girls' undergarments seemed to take the cue from older ones, with bright printed panties in a low-hipped line. Both nightgowns and pajamas were shown in materials that met the recently enacted rules about flame retardancy. Styles of sleepwear and even a child's hostess gown mimic-

ked what teens and adult women wore. Boys' sleepwear and underwear paralleled men's styles, although sports team logos or generalized athletic themes showed up on young boys' pajamas. Short-sleeved tops and jumpsuits were offered for summer.

Hair and Grooming

Long hair remained popular with younger women and teens through the early 1970s, with a trend toward shorter cuts by 1975. Hairstyles were, however, quite diverse and reflected the trend to making a personal statement in both dress and grooming. The skater Dorothy Hamill popularized a short, wedge cut hairstyle in 1977, and Farrah Fawcett-Majors made her full, layered style all the rage (see Figure 8.5).

In makeup, a natural look prevailed, although to give the impression of not wearing cosmetics required significant time and effort with neutral colors and lip gloss (introduced in 1971). By the end of the 1970s, the natural look was gradually being replaced by a more obvious use of color in makeup, a trend that lasted into the 1980s.

Long hair for younger men continued into the early 1970s, although a variety of lengths was worn by all men, as medium lengths became more acceptable for all ages. Beards, mustaches, and sideburns were also acceptable by the beginning of the 1970s. Although some men continued to wear long hair, shorter, fuller, and more styled hair appeared, aided by the beginning tendency for men to visit styling salons rather than the traditional barber (see Figure 8.28).

Summary

From hippie to dress-for-success styles, the period from 1969 to 1978 is a time of diversity in fashion, but also a time when individual choice took precedence over dictates from fashion designers. For the first time, fashion borrowed and mixed many inspirations from the past, a trend that continues. By the end of the period, shapes began to get looser and less body conscious, inspired by a new group of Japanese designers working in Paris who would influence styles at the beginning of the 1980s. American designers, who truly set the tone for ready-to-wear fashion in the 1970s, would continue to do so.

Suggested Readings

Bailey, Beth, and David Farber(eds). *America in the Seventies.* Lawrence, KS: University of Kansas Press, 2004.

Bryant, Michele Wesen. *WWD Illustrated: 1960s–1990s.* New York: Fairchild, 2004.

Edelstein, Andrew J., and Kevin McDonough. *The Seventies: From Hot Pants to Hot Tubs.* New York: Dutton, 1990.

Fraser, Kennedy. *The Fashionable Mind: Reflections on Fashion, 1970–1981.* New York: Alfred A. Knopf, 1981.

Gross, Elaine, and Fred Rottman. *Halston: An American Original.* New York: Harper Collins Publishers, 1999.

Herald, Jacqueline. *Fashions of a Decade: The 1970s.* London: S.T. Batsford Ltd., 1992.

Kennedy, Pagan. *Platforms: A Microwaved Cultural Chronicle of the 1970s.* New York: St. Martin's Press, 1994.

Lucie-Smith, Edward. *Art in the Seventies.* Oxford: Phaidon Press Limited, 1980.

Schulman, Bruce J. *The Seventies: The Great Shift in American Culture, Society, and Politics.* New York: The Free Press, 2001.

Slocum-Schaffer, Stephanie A. *America in the Seventies.* Syracuse, NY: Syracuse University Press, 2003.

CHAPTER 9

1979-

U.S. Events and Trends	Iran hostage crisis	Ronald Reagan elected John Lennon assassinated	Iran releases hostages Assassination attempt on President Reagan	*Time* magazine names the computer the Man of the Year	Terrorists bomb U.S. embassy in Beirut

	1979	**1980**	**1981**	**1982**	**1983**
U.S. Fashions	Dress for success look widely worn	Ralph Lauren shows an American West–inspired collection Designer jeans gain popularity	Nancy Reagan and Lady Diana help to inspire a return to glamorous dress MTV begins broadcasting, influencing fashions	Long skirts shown; shoulders become broader	*Flashdance* inspires copies of dance fashions, off-the-shoulder styles Japanese designers create waves in Paris

1988

Democrats nominate Walter Mondale and Geraldine Ferraro, first woman to run for vice president

President vetoes shoe and textile import quotas

Shuttle Challenger explodes after liftoff

Stock market crash in October

George H. Bush wins presidency

 **1984**

 **1985**

 **1986**

 **1987**

 **1988**

Popularity of androgynous fashions

Donna Karan founds own company

Oversize tops worn with stirrup pants

Bright colors and geometric shapes in accessories and surface designs

Lacroix shows pouf skirts

Much variety in fashion: both long and short skirts, close fit, and oversize silhouettes

Glitz to the Max

The decade from 1979 to 1988 was a time when the United States began to make the transition to the fast-paced and technology-driven world that we know today. It was also a time of reaction to the economic woes of the previous decade, as conservatism in politics went from a position on the sidelines to center stage by the mid-1980s. Significant social changes in the approach to work and lifestyle occurred as baby boomers moved from roles as the social reformers of the previous decades to a search for material comforts and the purchase of status symbols in everything from food to fashion. In the business world, hostile takeovers, leveraged buyouts, and mergers created a new and ostentatious billionaire class. Although there was a continuation of the importance of individualism, the search was less on finding oneself than on finding business success.

Domestic and International Politics and Economics

This decade began discouragingly, with a continuation of the economic problems of the previous period. When Jimmy Carter took the oath of office in 1977, the economy had begun to recover, but inflation soon climbed again, reaching 13 percent by 1980. Interest rates also rose dramatically, and unemployment reached its highest point since the Great Depression of the 1930s. All this meant a continuation of the stagflation of the 1970s and a serious recession. The unrelenting energy crisis contributed to the problems, as the United States imported more than half of all the oil it consumed. American vulnerability came to a head in 1979, when a revolution in Iran forced out the country's shah, Mohammad Reza Pahlavi. Oil supplies immediately dwindled, and a repeat of the 1973 gas shortages occurred. Prices soared, and often angry drivers waited in line for hours to fill their tanks. Then, in November 1979, a group of Iranian students seized the American embassy in Tehran and took 66 American hostages. Some hostages were soon released, but 52 were held for 444 days. Americans were shocked at the anti-American sentiment and at Carter's and the military's inability to rescue the hostages.

When Carter faced the Republican candidate Ronald Reagan in the 1980 presidential election, his approval rating was at an all-time low for any president. Reagan, a former film star and governor of California from 1966 to 1974, campaigned on a platform of smaller government, a return to traditional morality, and a more forceful foreign policy. On Election Day, he won by the largest margin ever against a sitting president. Between the election and his inauguration, serious negotiations with a new Iranian government

began, and, on January 20, 1981, just hours after Reagan took the oath of office, the hostages were released.

The rest of the decade was dominated by the economic and foreign policies of Reagan and his advisers. The Reagan inaugural ceremonies gave a hint of the style of the new administration, with lavish balls, high-fashion furs, and limousines everywhere, a direct contrast to the quieter tone and style of the Carter years (Figure 9.1). Nancy Reagan made news for the $25,000 spent on her 1981 inaugural wardrobe, but many seemed ready for a First Lady who could bring an aura of glamour back to the White House.

However, the economic woes of the country continued for the next two years as Reagan applied what he called supply side economics. This economic theory held that a decrease in taxes would allow business owners to invest their money, thus expanding their businesses and the economy. The resulting trickle-down effect would eventually reach the average American. The administration proposed and Congress endorsed a series of budget cuts and a large tax reduction. The changes did not bring immediate relief, however, and the economy worsened into a deep recession from 1981 to 1983. Interest rates finally started to drop in 1983, and employment rose, marking the beginning of a period of economic prosperity. Economic changes also occurred elsewhere in the world. Margaret Thatcher, the first female prime minister of Great Britain, attacked inflation and stagnation through tax reform, reduced government spending, and privatized state-owned industries. With return to a stronger economy, the middle and upper classes began to feel more secure and upbeat, had more disposable income, and responded by spending significantly more money on nonessential goods, including clothing.

In addition to a faltering economy, Reagan inherited an ongoing diplomatic crisis with the Soviet Union. Relationships with the Soviets had been deteriorating since the mid-1970s, despite continued talks aimed at limiting nuclear missiles. In December 1979, Soviet troops invaded Afghanistan to prop up a declining communist regime. Carter did not respond with military action but ordered a boycott of the Olympic Games scheduled to be held in Moscow and imposed trade sanctions, stopping the exportation of grain and high-technology equipment to the Soviets.

A staunch anti-Communist, Reagan expressed his hostility toward Communism in strong language, predicting the Soviet Union's downfall early in his first term and describing it as an evil empire. When Solidarity, a reform movement in Poland, was suppressed by the Communists in 1981–1982, it added further incentive to his anti-Communist convictions. As Reagan pumped substantial amounts of money into a buildup of the military, there were increased fears that his language and actions would lead to proliferation of nuclear

Figure 9.1 Ronald and Nancy Reagan at 1981 Inaugural ball. Mrs. Reagan's dress is designed by Galanos. ©Bettmann/Corbis.

for elimination of a class of nuclear missiles despite Reagan's unwillingness to eliminate his SDI initiatives. When Reagan visited Moscow the next year, he was well received, making it clear that the Cold War was waning. By 1991 the Soviet Union collapsed.

Business Trends and Deregulation

One of the integral components of Reagan's policy was deregulation, including both social programs and the marketplace. These changes would eventually affect much of the population. Initially, staffs and activities of the Environmental Protection Agency, the Consumer Product Safety Commission, and the Occupational Health and Safety Commission, among others, were reduced. However, most of the agencies had strong support and returned to previous budget levels by the end of the decade.

The deregulation of the airlines actually began under Carter, when he passed a bill in 1978 to remove restrictions on the airline industry, overseen by the Civil Aeronautics Board (CAB). Most of the changes took effect in the early 1980s, however, with elimination of the CAB's authority to set fares and an easing of regulations related to the establishment of new airlines and new routes. Fares fell, the number of passengers rose, and airlines gained flexibility in matching plane size to demand on particular routes. Ultimately, some airlines suffered losses and eventual bankruptcy, but other low-cost, no-frills airlines entered the market. Deregulation of other transportation industries followed, including the trucking industry, railroads, and buses.

The regulatory change that perhaps affected the largest number of people was the breakup of American Telephone & Telegraph (AT&T), which had provided all long-distance and most local service in the United States. Technological advances allowed emergence of competitors, who in 1974 filed an antitrust suit. AT&T agreed to divest itself of all its local telephone companies and to compete only in the long-distance market. Initially, the cost of phone service rose, but, as competitors such as Sprint and MCI entered the market, rates began to fall. Technologically advanced fiber-optic cables began to be laid, making the dramatic telecommunications expansion of the next decade possible.

Another sweeping change was the deregulation of the market and relaxation of antitrust policies. Updated guidelines, created in 1982, allowed mergers within industries to occur. To finance such potentially large mergers, a scheme was devised by bond trader Michael Milken, who began to use what were called junk bonds to raise money to finance takeovers. Junk bonds had a high rate of return but were risky. The rate and size of mergers and takeovers escalated dramatically, with such deals as the purchase of R. J.

weapons and even to war. In 1983, Reagan ordered a U.S. invasion of the small Caribbean country of Grenada to oust the Communist government there. Despite some criticism, the effort was successful, and he received general support from the American public. More controversial was his Strategic Defense Initiative (SDI), a plan to construct a high-tech defensive shield that could intercept missiles while they were still in space. The media labeled the initiative Star Wars, as it called for technology that did not yet exist. The concept faded by the end of the 1980s.

The anti-Communist rhetoric began to soften in 1985 when Mikhail Gorbachev became the General Secretary of the Communist Party in the Soviet Union. He quickly began to restructure the economy and to allow more freedoms in his country. Internationally, his concern with the U.S. military buildup, the SDI initiatives, and anti-Communist efforts in Poland led to a series of talks with Reagan, beginning in 1985 and continuing through 1988. After his visit to Washington, DC, in 1987, he and Reagan worked out details

Reynolds and Nabisco by the law firm Kohlberg Kravis Roberts and the merger of Time, Inc. and Warner Corporation. In some cases the new owners sold off parts of the company, leaving many Americans without the jobs they had held for years. Particularly vulnerable were managers more than 50 years of age, who had a difficult time finding other positions. Eventually, Milken and others engaged in insider trading were sentenced to prison. In the long run, however, the deregulation proved successful in forcing companies to operate more efficiently, leading them to invest in new technologies to improve productivity and competitiveness.

The stock market continually hit new highs in the 1980s. Many middle-class investors began to enter the market through the new availability of discount brokerage services and mutual funds, offered through banks and even through Sears. With the increased use of computers to track changes in the market, speculators could move huge amounts of money quickly. Resulting instability in the market led to a crash on October 19, 1987, called Black Monday. The Federal Reserve Board stepped in quickly with millions of dollars to keep the system functioning and to prevent a slide into depression. The market stabilized, eventually ending the year slightly higher.

Social Life and Culture

The period from 1979 to 1988 was a time of social and cultural transformation and occasionally of conflict, the result of significant demographic shifts. The trends of the 1970s continued, with more unmarried couples living together and more women in the workplace. Although it would be imprudent to make generalizations about the increasingly diverse population in the United States, by and large approaches to work and to lifestyle changed as baby boomers aged and looked for more financial security.

Demographic Shifts and Immigration

The population of the United States grew from 226 million to 248 million between 1980 and 1990, with the largest growth percentages in the Asian and Hispanic populations. Immigration began to change the structure of the United States, with more than seven million legal immigrants, more than one million refugees, and uncountable millions who entered illegally. At least half were from Latin American countries and the Caribbean, while 40 percent were from Asia.[1] Some of this change led to racial conflict, particularly in urban areas and especially from those on the lowest socioeconomic rungs.

Although long-term job security in established industries no longer existed, many Americans were better off financially after the economy turned around. More women went to college and often chose a career over starting a family immediately after marriage. The result was smaller families begun at a later age. The two-income family became even more common, as families attempted to maintain a high standard of living. Women made strides in very visible areas, with the first woman on the U.S. Supreme Court, Sandra Day O'Connor, and the first woman vice presidential candidate in 1980, Geraldine Ferraro. However, they also took on a superwoman approach—they could work, have families, and maintain a home, juggling it all at one time (Figure 9.2).

Although the baby boom generation continued to shape society, the generation born from the mid-1960s to about 1980, usually called Generation X by demographers, exerted an influence on popular culture and on purchasing patterns. As teenagers in the 1980s and early 1990s, they had different expectations and outlooks from their parents. They rejected, by and large, the idealism of the 1960s and were cynical about their parents' quick abandonment of noble goals in exchange for the enticements of materialism. Generation X was also used as a marketing and advertising term to identify this particular target customer, one who was fashion-conscious and spent a larger percentage of income on clothing.

Lifestyle and Consumerism

America in effect went shopping in the 1980s, perhaps as a relief from the economic woes of the previous 10 years; for whatever reason, consumption was on the rise. Spending patterns began to change, particularly with the introduction in this decade of new and improved technology such as personal computers, videocassette recorders (VCRs), microwave ovens, and compact disc (CD) players. Although spending increased for most consumer groups, the media focused on young, upwardly mobile professionals—yuppies. Although most people probably would not have admitted to the label, the term characterized a group between college age and their 40s who were famous for a self-indulgent lifestyle focused on status consumer goods (Figure 9.3). The other acronym used to categorize a specific lifestyle was dinks—double income, no kids—who had enough discretionary income to indulge in expensive homes, luxury cars, gourmet foods, and high-tech toys.

The sexual revolution of the 1960s and 1970s continued briefly into the 1980s, despite calls from religious groups for a return to chastity before marriage. It was the AIDS epidemic, however, that changed people's sexual behavior, if not necessarily their morality. Acquired immune deficiency

Figure 9.2 Supermom could have it all: full-time motherhood and a full-time job. ©Roger Ressmeyer/Corbis.

Figure 9.3 Power suit dressing for the upwardly-mobile man, accessorized by one of the earliest laptop computers. ©Bettmann/Corbis.

(AIDS), the disease that results from the human immune virus (HIV) was first identified in 1981 after a number of homosexual men began to die of mysterious ailments in the late 1970s. Africa was established as the probable origin of the disease, which spread through exchange of bodily fluids during sex or from tainted blood from transfusions or the sharing of needles. The first celebrity to openly acknowledge that he had AIDS was Rock Hudson, who died of the disease in 1985. AIDS hit the apparel industry particularly hard, as it lost many creative talents to the disease.[2]

Technology and Communication

Science and technology dramatically altered many aspects of daily life in the 1980s. The personal computer, in its infancy in the 1970s, became an integral and indispensable machine in businesses, schools, and homes. Computer technology with the GUI (graphical user interface) transformed the ability to use the computer through the point and click approach. When Apple introduced the Macintosh in 1984, it provided users with an alternative to typing in the dozens of commands required on IBM-based machines. In 1985, Microsoft introduced the first version of Windows, making the personal computer (PC) and Microsoft the standard, with more than 22 million computers sold in 1988.[3]

Space exploration, both manned and unmanned, expanded knowledge of the universe in the 1980s. Viking 1 sent back pictures of Jupiter, Pioneer 11 identified the content of Saturn's rings as ice-covered rocks, and Voyager 1 and 2 explored Saturn's moons. The first successful space shuttle, Columbia, was launched in 1981. After a series of successful missions that included untethered space walks, the accomplishments of the shuttle created a sense that it was safe enough for the average American. Tragically, on

January 28, 1986, the space shuttle Challenger exploded shortly after liftoff, killing all seven astronauts, including schoolteacher Christa McAuliffe.

The period started out with the failure of technology of another type, as several potentially catastrophic nuclear accidents occurred. The first was at Three Mile Island in Pennsylvania in 1979 and the second in 1986 at the Soviet Union's Chernobyl nuclear plant. There were, on the other hand, major advances in treatments for heart, cancer, and other diseases. Genetic research also continued, leading to the 1988 funding of the Human Genome Project.

Sports and Leisure

The exercise and fitness obsessions of the 1970s continued, extending beyond jogging to include a variety of forms of aerobic and dance-based exercises. There was a flood of exercise and dance classes and aerobics videotapes. Actress Jane Fonda led in developing aerobics-related books and other products, but many others followed, including diet and fitness guru Richard Simmons. The popularity of dance exercise and aerobics was a boon for marketers, as a seemingly endless line of product tie-ins became available, including shoes, clothing, books, and magazines. Consumers created a demand for spandex exercise clothing such as bright-colored tights, leotards, wrap skirts, and leg warmers, often worn in a multitude of layers and combinations. Shoe manufacturers recognized the marketing potential and began to produce shoes designed specifically for aerobic exercise. Reebok captured the market early on but was soon joined by many others.

If television had made professional and collegiate sports available to a wide audience earlier, now cable television stations broadcast sporting events every hour of the day and night. The most popular sports broadcaster, ESPN, aired even previously obscure sports. The major sports of football and baseball remained popular, the Super Bowl continuing to attract one of the largest audiences for any event. The popularity of professional basketball increased significantly with superstars Magic Johnson, Larry Byrd, and Michael Jordan, the last of whom led the Chicago Bulls to two championships during the decade. Jordan's reputation led to endorsement of numerous clothing products, particularly Nike athletic shoes, which became the sought-after footwear despite high prices. In a highly lucrative sports-endorsement contract, Nike introduced the Air Jordan in 1985.

The 1984 Olympic Games in Los Angeles reflected the new mood of both prosperity and patriotism in the country. The Soviet Union and Eastern European countries boycotted the games in retaliation for the 1980 boycott of the Moscow games, leaving many sporting events open to American athletes. The United States won by far the most medals, and the games made celebrities of Carl Lewis in track, Mary Lou Retton in gymnastics, and Greg Louganis in diving.

The connection between athletes and fashion appeared in other arenas. Olympic champion Florence Griffith-Joyner, Flo Jo, created a sensation with both her running and her off-beat attire, appearing at the 1988 Olympic trials in a series of unique body suit and legging styles (Figure 9.4)

Literature and Magazines

Books had to compete with VCRs and a variety of new lifestyle magazines for people's leisure time. However, there were numerous best-sellers, including romance novels, spy thrillers, and horror novels. These included novels by Danielle Steele, Tom Clancy, Robert Ludlum, and Stephen King. Raymond Carver wrote widely acclaimed short stories about real life. Alice Walker and Toni Morrison both wrote fiction that focused on the country's continuing racial problems. Readers attempted to understand how the cosmos came into being with *A Brief History of Time* by Stephen Hawking. Larry McMurtry, James Michener, and John Irving were also among the popular writers of the decade.

Business books, of course, gained a wide readership in a period of increased interest in the economy and in stock market investment. These included *The Art of the Deal* by Donald Trump and Tony Schwartz and *Day of Reckoning* by Benjamin Friedman. Tom Wolfe's novel *The Bonfire of the Vanities* captured both the fever for wealth and the use of clothing to describe attitude and approach. Television shows, such as Louis Rukeyser's *Wall Street Week* and Na-

Figure 9.4 Florence Griffith-Joyner competing in the 1988 Olympic trials. Note the lace bodysuit and the jogging bra. ©Duomo/Corbis.

tional Public Radio's *Sound Money*, gave guidance to novice investors.

Art, Music, Television, and the Movies

In the 1980s, the art world in part reflected the consumerism of the Reagan era. Art got bigger and more public in scope, and toward the end of the decade what were termed the culture wars arose. This pitted conservative politicians against organizations such as the National Endowment for the Arts that funded artists who produced art that was considered antireligious or morally questionable. The blending of fashion, architecture, interior design, furnishings, and even music created a fertilization of design ideas that crossed all fields.

Art and Architecture

The postmodern trend in architecture and interior design

continued into the 1980s and produced some of the more original designs of the period. With an appropriation and melding of elements of the past along with various other styles, postmodernism appeared in everything from restaurants to boutiques to housing. There was noteworthy construction of offices, apartments, and public buildings by architects such as Philip Johnson and Michael Graves. The latter was named Designer of the Year in 1981 by *Interiors Magazine.*[4] An important monument of the decade was the Vietnam Memorial, dedicated in 1982 and designed by Maya Lin. Lin, a Yale college student, was selected from more than 1,000 entrants in a nationwide competition.

There was considerable synergism between postmodern architecture and interior design throughout the 1980s. The Swid Powell collection, launched in 1985, brought together a prestigious group of architects that included Richard Meier and Robert Venturi to create designs for the tabletop. It also appeared in a new style called Memphis, produced by a Milan-based collective of designers led by architect and industrial designer Ettore Sottsass. The Memphis style, with its postmodernist use of unconventional materials, borrowing of historic forms, and gaudy color, dominated early 1980s design for interiors and household objects (Plate 9.1a). Elements of the style also appeared in fashion and accessories (Plate 9.1b). The practitioners blurred the boundaries between fine art and mass-produced goods and influenced designers of many products during the period.

While the prominence of abstract art continued, a new art movement called neo-expressionism dominated the art market until about the mid-1980s. A group of young artists, reacting to the intellectual abstract style of the 1970s, began to portray the human body and other objects more realistically. The artists included Julian Schnabel, David Salle, Sandro Chia, and Georg Baselitz, among others. Although they produced a diverse body of work, in general they rejected traditional standards of composition and attempted to reflect the tension and alienation of contemporary urban life. Viewed as a highly commercial movement, it generated controversy through use of aggressive media promotion and marketing by dealers and galleries.

Federal funding of the arts decreased during the Reagan years, at least in part a reaction against government backing in general and the reduction in tax dollars available. An exhibit of sexually explicit photographs by Robert Mapplethorpe initiated a huge controversy that caused The Corcoran Gallery in Washington to cancel his show in 1989 despite the fact that it had been exhibited for years without any debate. Another confrontation involved removal of Richard Serra's sculptural installation *Tilted Arc* from a federal plaza in New York City in 1989 after several years of

controversy led by employees who objected to the large, rusted metal sculpture.

Although graffiti, defined as unsolicited marking, painting, or writing on public or private property without permission, has always existed, graffiti as art began to appear in the late 1960s. With the popularity of hip-hop music, the style slowly gained respect as an art form in the 1980s. Two artists in particular, Jean-Michel Basquiat and Keith Haring, started out by tagging (a stylized way to write a name) subway cars and later entered the mainstream art world.

Money defined the world of art as it did many other aspects of the free-spending 1980s. Art auctions in New York and London sold paintings of both long-established and contemporary artists for enormous sums. Vincent van Gogh's *Irises,* for example, sold for a record $53.9 million dollars, and a contemporary painting by Jasper Johns went for $17 million. Many of the purchasers were corporations, rather than individuals, but the escalation of prices made it impossible for most museums to purchase new art works. In fact, the prices for other collectibles and antiques also soared.

Television

Both cable television and home VCRs transformed television viewing in the 1980s. There was an explosion of programming on cable, while at the same time viewers could record and replay programs or rent and watch movies whenever they chose. Video games provided another use for the television, particularly for young boys.

Numerous television shows debuted in the 1980s, many of which both reflected and influenced fashion. The prime-time soap operas, in particular, promoted a world of glamour and ostentatious lifestyles. *Dallas, Dynasty, Falcon Crest,* and *Knots Landing* portrayed wealthy, usually greedy, and scheming characters and became the shows discussed the next day at work. *Dynasty,* with costumes by Nolan Miller, promoted the fashion of the broad, padded shoulder (Figure 9.5). Many viewers watched because of the often exaggerated fashions. Product tie-ins included fashion dolls dressed like the main characters. In another example of the high-flying 1980s approach, *Lifestyles of the Rich and Famous* showed the real-life, ostentatious standard of living of the very wealthiest Americans.

Miami Vice, a police detective show set in Miami, Florida, got the nickname MTV cops because of the use of popular rock songs. The show also influenced men's fashions, particularly the unstructured jackets worn over T-shirts, soft pastel shades, and shoes worn without socks (Figure 9.6). Other dramas of the era included *St. Elsewhere, Hill Street Blues,* and *L.A. Law.* Three shows usually in the top 10 were *The*

Figure 9.5 The cast of *Dynasty*, with costumes by Nolan Miller, promoted the broad, padded shoulder. ©Bettmann/Corbis.

Figure 9.6 *Miami Vice* stars Philip Michael Thomas and Don Johnson in the casual style that set a trend. ©Sunset Boulevard/Corbis Sygma.

Cosby Show, Family Ties, and *Murder, She Wrote. The Cosby Show,* starring Bill Cosby as a physician, portrayed a professional, loving, and nuclear black family as it faced a variety of family issues with humor and intelligence. *Family Ties* reflected the changing values of the 1980s, as a couple who still championed 1960s liberal values raised children in the 1980s. Their conservative and business-oriented oldest son supported supply-side economics and aspired to work on Wall Street.

By the 1980s, more than half the population had grown up to the sounds of rock and roll, and in 1981, the way rock music was broadcast changed forever with the introduction of MTV (the Music Television channel) on cable, broadcasting music videos 24 hours a day. Fittingly, MTV began its first broadcast with "Video Killed the Radio Star" by the Buggles. It now became possible to both hear and see artists. Music videos became an essential component of producing a record, jump-starting the careers of several film directors and coining a new term, VJ (video jockey, the video version of the radio disk jockey). The images and clothing worn by rock and roll performers became even more influential, setting numerous teen fashion trends. Madonna and Cyndi Lauper both wore an eclectic mix of vintage and new clothing, large amounts of bold jewelry, and often either head bands or other fabric head wraps (Figure 9.7).

Movies

Films of the decade ranged from high-tech futurism to teen angst, from big-budget blockbusters to low-budget independents. The success of the VCR augmented the popularity of films, and the financial success of a film included money made through licensing a wide range of products, including toys, video games, dolls, and T-shirts. A significant number of filmmakers worked with new technologies for creating illusions, generating a wave of science fiction and futuristic movies. These included one of the most widely watched films of the decade, *E.T., The Extra-Terrestrial,* and the next two installments of the Star Wars series, *The Empire Strikes Back* (1980) and *Return of the Jedi* (1983). The Indiana Jones films *Raiders of the Lost Ark* (1981) and *Indiana Jones and the Last Crusade* (1988/89) were also enormously popular. Other futuristic hits included *Alien* (1979), *Aliens* (1986), and *Back to the Future* (1985).

Numerous films provided commentaries on social issues or on solving the inner struggle to finding oneself. *Wall Street* (1987), with the frequently quoted line "Greed is good," delved into the world of stock market traders who sacrificed all for profit, perhaps a fitting commentary on the

Figure 9.7 Madonna (right) and Rosanna Arquette in *Desperately Seeking Susan*. Madonna's costumes in the movie pretty much matched the clothes she wore in concert. ©Orion/Everett Collection.

Figure 9.8 *Flashdance* star Jennifer Beals, in the style that became widely mimicked. ©Everett Collection.

conspicuous consumption of many in the 1980s. In *Tootsie*, on the contrary, an actor only achieves his potential by impersonating a woman, and the main character in *Desperately Seeking Susan* (1984) loses her memory and discovers a world beyond her quiet suburban life, one where clothing is a critical element. This film also starred Madonna, adding to her fame and to her fashion influence, including the lace gloves and head wrap she wore in the film (Figure 9.7). Films of the 1980s also included a series of teen films such as *The Breakfast Club* (1984) and *Pretty in Pink* (1986), starring a new group of young actors labeled the Brat Pack.[5]

Dance and theater films had noteworthy influence on fashion in the 1980s. In particular, *Fame* (1980), about a group of students at the New York City High School of Performing Arts, and *Flashdance* (1983), the story of an aspiring dancer who works in a steel mill by day, inspired young women to adopt myriad dance-related styles, from off-the-shoulder, loose tops to leggings and legwarmers (Figure 9.8). Other dance films followed, including *Footloose* (1985) and *Dirty Dancing* (1987).

Music

The music world was dominated by rock and roll in a variety of styles that included new wave, punk, and rap, with rock stars who became style and trendsetters. The punk music of the late 1970s had begun to diminish in impact, while a new wave of progressive artists such as Talking Heads, the Police, and Elvis Costello gained popularity (and gave the term new wave to the style of music). Bruce Springsteen became an outspoken voice of rock as he questioned the nature of the American Dream through his songs. Synthesized pop music of the early 1980s gave way to the music of bands such as U2 and R.E.M. However, it was Madonna who best embodied the image and voice of the decade with a postmodern style that included the borrowing of both personas and fashions from previous decades, particularly fitted corsets and other lingerie styles. Her song *Material Girl* seemed to resonate with the conspicuous consumption of the period.

MTV made household names out of a large number of rock stars of the 1980s. Michael Jackson, a star with his brothers in the Jackson Five the previous decade, became a

Figure 9.9 The rap group Run-D.M.C. wearing athletic shoes and jackets, 1984. ©Michael Ochs Archives/Corbis.

major pop performer and MTV video staple. The introduction of Jackson's videos from his album *Thriller* made him one of the first black performers to be broadcast on MTV, but it was his performance on *Motown 25: Yesterday, Today, and Forever* (1983) that sent fans to the store for the album. His fashion for wearing one sequined glove was copied by many fans.

There was also considerable visual androgyny among some rock stars of the period, both men and women. Annie Lennox and Grace Jones both took on strong masculine images, while male performers such as Prince and Boy George adopted clothing traditionally considered feminine.

Hip-hop began in the 1970s in the South Bronx as a cross-cultural blending of Jamaican and black styles of music. It has become one of the most influential cultural movements of the last quarter of the twentieth century, spawning art and dance forms, clothing styles, and, of course, rap music. Early artists included Kool Herc and Grandmaster Flash, who used the record turntable as a musical instrument, cutting and blending back and forth between two records. Break dancing became part of this culture. By the late 1970s, DJs were using rhyming rap lyrics between songs, and rapping began to become an art form in and of itself. The first rap records were released in late 1979. These recordings, along with graffiti artist Fab-Five Freddy, inspired new wave band Blondie to record a rap-inspired record in 1981, which took the style to a wider audience. It was in 1984, however, when Russell Simmons and Rick Rubin founded Def Jam Records with performers like L.L. Cool J and Run-D.M.C., that rap was truly brought into the mainstream of rock music. Along with the music came fashion and art styles that would dominate youth culture for the rest of the century. For break dancers and hip-hop

artists, fashion was an important component of their identity. Many wore Adidas shoes with thick laces, and nylon jumpsuits that, in addition to being fashionable, allowed the dancer to more easily slide on the floor (Figure 9.9).

Manufacturing and Retailing

During this period, apparel manufacturers rose to the challenges of filling huge orders from special-line supermarkets (later called big-box retailers or category killers), discounters, and holding companies (owners of several department stores). Financially able to buy in large volume, major groups or chains controlled the design of many products. The 10 largest apparel makers did 20 percent of domestic business in 1984 and 1985. Some makers responded to pressures from demanding merchants by selling directly to consumers through outlet malls, which spread throughout the decade. Producers of apparel, especially shoes, suffered from competition from overseas; America's apparel trade deficit stood at $7.2 billion in 1982 and continued to grow.[6] Marketing gained ascendancy over design, as companies such as Polo-Ralph Lauren promoted lifestyle and image.

Technology became steadily more prominent in apparel firms. Computer programs tracked goods at the warehouse; could be used to design, produce, and store patterns; and automated some sewing operations. Laser beams could cut fabric accurately, although the majority of firms continued to use an electric knife. Fusion of seams and heat-set shape saved money for some manufacturers. Computer control even expedited dyeing and certain fabric printing operations. Large producers could better afford the latest technology, but the day of the personal computer was dawning in the 1980s and with it came affordable electronic systems for smaller companies. Electronic technology began to alter the supplier-to-retailer connection. Individual tagging of garments with bar codes allowed stores to reduce inventories because of their ability to monitor more carefully. The sales information could then be shared with suppliers.

The trend to relocating womenswear manufacturing away from New York City continued in this decade, as plants were built in upstate New York, New Jersey, Pennsylvania, and Alabama. Menswear shifted from the mid-Atlantic to the southern states and to the Caribbean basin. Population growth centered in the Sunbelt states, adding to the appeal of locating companies there. Manufacturers moved the labor-intensive sewing of cut patterns offshore to countries such as Taiwan and South Korea, where wages remained substantially below U.S. levels. Reagan's Caribbean Basin Initiative led to an increase in apparel coming from Caribbean countries.

In an attempt to fight the steady rise of imported clothing, the apparel industry formed the Crafted with Pride in U.S.A. Council and began a national campaign to raise public awareness and gain support for products made domestically. The "Made in U.S.A." labeling legislation was passed in the mid-1980s. Nonetheless, free-trade agreements continued to stimulate growth of off-shore production of apparel.

Consumer spending power suffered between 1979 and 1983 because of rising taxes and steep inflation, forcing retailers to compete ferociously for market share. Department store chains including Sears and JC Penney held their own, while special-line supermarkets like Pier 1 Imports and Toys "R" Us thrived. Discounters such as nationwide Kmart and the regional company Caldor did well, but even they were challenged by cost-cutting in conventional department stores. Target and Wal-Mart grew and entered the apparel fray. Wal-Mart went from more than $1 billion in sales in 1980 to more than $20 billion in 1988.[7] Many independent department stores fell victim to the merger and leveraged buyout mania of the decade, including Dayton-Hudson, Allied Department Stores, and Federated, which owned national strings of stores. Most retained their regional or local names but surrendered control to a central office.[8] Department store sales stood at $89.1 billion in 1979, so serious money was at stake.

On a local scale, consignment shops and thrift shops proliferated, as Americans struggled to stretch their inflation-ridden dollars at the beginning of the period. Thrift-shop dressing also became fashionable, as it permitted a postmodern blending of period and contemporary styles. The biggest winners in the retail sector, however, were catalogs from both conventional retailers and catalog-only operations. Together these numbered 5,000 in 1981 and enjoyed annual growth rates of 15 percent, which few stores could match. Telephone ordering and use of credit cards enhanced the convenience of catalog shopping. Indeed, utilitarian clothes from companies such as L. L. Bean and Lands' End gained a new chic as weekend wear for businessmen and businesswomen tired of suits. Victoria's Secret prospered by offering alluring lingerie by mail.

Specialty chains such as Jeans West, Susie's Casuals, The Gap, The Limited, and Kinney's, all located in malls, also thrived. Other specialty shops were geared to the new customer groups gaining prominence in the eyes of retailers. In an era when half of all married women worked outside their homes, retailers and manufacturers who offered affordable career wear prospered. Among the thriving chains were Talbots for career clothing and Mothers Work, which sold professional maternity apparel for working women. Liz Claiborne, who designed affordable work wear, briefly became Wall Street's favorite when her firm went public. Retailers who catered to special sizes garnered strong sales: plus sizes and petites were getting attention. Athletes and fitness enthusiasts helped make Early Winters catalog and active wear shops a success story. Black and Hispanic populations enjoyed rising incomes and consequent power in the marketplace. Even the long-neglected over-65 population drew notice, as they increased in numbers, improved in health, and adopted leisure lifestyles.

Competition within and among categories of retailers drove several changes in the apparel retailing business. Sales staff were downgraded in skills and generally limited to part-timers among most retailers; national advertising, not skilled clerks, sold the goods. One exception was personal shoppers or wardrobe consultants employed by stores such as Nordstrom's to assist time-starved working women in selecting appropriate clothing. Conversely, retail management became better trained and paid, but there was a chasm between managerial and sales personnel that could not easily be bridged. Sales jobs no longer constituted an entree to a career with the potential for rising responsibilities and remuneration. Store hours became longer, as blue laws that restricted Sunday opening were overturned in many locales. Private-label goods, which had been replaced by brand names since the 1910s, made a comeback in the 1980s because they offered merchants higher margins and a means to overcome the sameness of widely available brands. Private labeling began to blur lines as retailers now competed with manufacturers.

Fashion Influences

As in the previous decade, fashion influences came from a wide variety of sources, including music, a new wave of fashion designers, and continued resurrection of styles from the past. Much fashion seemed in direct opposition to the trends of the previous period. People aspired to exhibit a toned body and at the same time to flaunt their importance through status symbol dressing and logos that were prominently displayed. The fashion magazines now photographed the stars of music or film as fashion trendsetters, along with models.

The Fashion Trendsetters

Although many rock and roll stars were fashion icons of the period, it was Princess Diana of Great Britain who was the most photographed and watched celebrity. From her wedding to Prince Charles in 1981, with a wedding dress copied by the thousands, until her death in 1997, she was a style leader, the press following her every move and fashion (Figure 9.10).

First Lady Nancy Reagan was one of the style leaders in the United States, with her slim figure and sophisticated style. Although she drew criticism early in the 1980s for accepting donations of expensive designer fashions and jewelry that were never returned, she soon toned down her approach and continued to exude the sense of wealth and privilege that embodied the era.

Donald Trump and his wife Ivana perhaps best symbolized the financial excesses and greed of the consumer 1980s. Trump built huge buildings in Manhattan, including Trump Tower, while Ivana appeared frequently on the fashion pages of W and Women's Wear Daily. A new and prominent New York jet set also dominated the gossip and style columns.

A succession of historic costume films and museum shows throughout the period fueled many designers' creations. Amadeus (1984) inspired designers to borrow from earlier centuries, while Diana Vreeland's elaborate costume exhibits at the Metropolitan Museum in New York in the 1970s and early 1980s brought designers the opportunity to see and be inspired by actual period clothing.[9]

Figure 9.10 Prince Charles and Princess Diana on their wedding day, July 29, 1981. ©Corbis Sygma.

Photography and Illustration

Photography continued to dominate the pages of the fashion press, although fashion illustration was more visible than it had been in the previous two decades. Innovative fashion photography, which relied less on showing the clothing and more on creating a mood, continued to be seen in the mainstream fashion publications, although there was a somewhat more conservative approach. Many of the important photographers of the previous decade—including Richard Avedon, Helmut Newton, Irving Penn, Deborah Turbeville, and Guy Bourdin—continued to appear and exert an influence. A new and highly influential photographer of the 1980s was Bruce Weber, who did fashion photographs for GQ in the 1970s, and his first fashion spread for British Vogue in 1980. He was best known, however, for his advertising campaigns for Ralph Lauren and Calvin Klein, which changed the way men were portrayed in fashion ads, as he created more openly sexual and physical images (Figure 9.11).

Nan Goldin and Steven Meisel created sophisticated photographs that always focused on the fashion being shown. Patrick Demarchelier, who worked for many magazines, including Vogue, GQ, and Rolling Stone was also an important creator of fashion images. A different photographic style is that of Bill Cunningham, who candidly recorded fashion on the street for the "On the Street" column for The New York Times. He also photographed and wrote about women's fashion for Details magazine, an alternative women's fashion publication in the 1980s.[10]

Mats Gustafson, who grew up in Sweden, launched his career when the number of fashion illustrations was dwin-

Figure 9.11 (RIGHT) Bruce Weber photograph for Calvin Klein men's underwear, displayed on a 40-foot billboard above Times Square, New York. ©Bettmann/Corbis.

Figure 9.12 (BELOW) Antonio illustration of Norma Kamali swimwear. *Vogue,* November 1984, 432, courtesy of Paul Caranicas.

dling. His work was often featured in leading fashion magazines around the world, and he is especially known for his illustrations of haute couture designs. He illustrated ads for numerous designers, including Chanel, Calvin Klein, Romeo Gigli, and Yohji Yamamoto. Illustrators Kenneth (Kenneth Paul Block) and Steven Stipelman drew the latest styles for *Women's Wear Daily* and *W,* and Antonio illustrations appeared frequently in the 1980s, for both the fashion press and for the retail and design customers (Figure 9.12).

As the 1980s progressed, the ideal image for models was that they be broad shouldered, muscular, and more full breasted. These models were sometimes referred to as the Glamazons, a group that continued into the next period. Prominent models of the decade included Brooke Shields, Christie Brinkley, and Iman.

The Designers

United States fashion designers continued to be influential throughout the 1980s, but the extravagant mood of the decade led to a resurgence of Paris couture. After predic-

tions only a few years previous that it was no longer viable, the French couture designers made a dramatic comeback in the 1980s. Although certainly only a few women could afford couture, the European designers influenced many of the styles of the decade.

Europe

Glamour and luxury emanated from the pages of fashion magazines, particularly from the French design houses. Some created elaborate and elegant styles, others provided sharp, modern fashion with an edge of exaggerated fantasy, while a group of avant-garde Japanese designers attracted a new and international audience.

German born **Karl Lagerfeld** was the well-respected head designer for the house of Chloe when he was invited to become the head designer for the house of Chanel in 1982. Lagerfeld began designing in the 1950s for Pierre Balmain and then the house of Patou. A prolific and talented designer, he also freelanced for the houses of Krizia and Fendi, founding his own line, Karl Lagerfeld Impression, in 1974. He continued to design for Chloe until 1984, when he resigned to design two lines under his own name in addi-

Figure 9.13 Chanel suit and accessories, 1985. ©Hulton Archive/Getty Images.

Figure 9.14 Side-laced, stretch dress, modeled by Grace Jones at the 1986 Azzedine Alaia fashion show. ©Pierre Vauthey/Corbis Sygma.

tion to continuing as designer for Chanel. The Chanel house had been mired in tradition since the 1971 death of Mademoiselle Chanel. Willing to play with the classic image of Chanel clothing, Lagerfeld took the recognized elements of her style, from the boxy jacket and knee-length skirts to the classic accessories of pearls and chain-handled purses, and rejuvenated them. By exaggerating and sharpening the proportions and silhouette of the suit, and using fabrics such as leather and denim, he attracted a new and younger customer to the house. Rather than knee-length skirts, he showed either long or very short hem lengths. Accessories became oversized and added a sense of fantasy (Figure 9.13).[11] Lagerfeld created a significant trend in the 1980s with the modernized Chanel look, copied at a multiplicity of price points.

Azzedine Alaïa was also a noteworthy designer of the 1980s, creating styles that were skintight, with spiraling seams and other design devices to emphasize a woman's curves. In this period of attention to a toned and fit body,

Alaïa represented a trend toward figure-conscious dressing. Born in Tunisia, he catered primarily to show business clients through the 1970s. His 1985 side-laced dress for singer Grace Jones made a significant impression on viewers (Figure 9.14). Alaïa's experimentation with stretch fabrics and sensual shaping set the stage for increasingly body-conscious clothing.

Jean Paul Gaultier designed some of the more notorious styles of the 1980s, from his conical bras and corset-inspired dresses to skirts for men. Creating what some saw as fetishist clothing, his often provocative designs had a sense of humor that allowed women to play with clothing as costume. He often created collections that explored the concepts of gender dressing. Using androgyny as a theme, he designed corsets and well-defined tailored jackets for both men and women. A designer with often unconventional ideas, he also designed for film and for performers such as Madonna.

Christian Lacroix created new excitement in the world of couture in the 1980s, first as head designer for the house

Figure 9.15 A Rei Kawakubo design for her company Comme de Garçons. Fairchild Archives.

founded his own company in 1980 while continuing to design for the house of Lanvin.

In the early 1980s, the fashion press become particularly enamored of the work of Japanese designers. **Kenzo Takada** (Kenzo) and **Issey Miyake** both began showing their collections in Paris during the 1970s. Kenzo opened his boutique Jungle Jap in 1970, creating brightly colored and patterned clothing that blended eastern and western influences. His first Kenzo boutique opened in New York in 1983, the same year he began creating menswear in the same colorful vein as his womenswear. Issey Miyake, one of the most innovative and experimental of designers, worked regularly with new technologies to create both textiles and garments. Miyake presented for the first time in Paris in 1973, always integrating new elements into designs that allow the wearer multiple options. He used new and experimental materials such as paper and plastics, and in 1982 he created a collection called Bodyworks of laminated polyester. His designs are often folded, twisted, pleated, or created in layers. Although always experimental, his clothing is also wearable and comfortable.

In addition to these Japanese designers already working in Paris, a new group began to show collections in the early 1980s. These included **Rei Kawakubo** and **Yohji Yamamoto**. They, along with Miyake, were the first to present a new avant-garde[12] style of fashion that was characterized by oversized proportions, asymmetry, and a frequent use of black or dark, somber colors. Their designs initially took inspiration from the textile processes and clothing styles of ancient Japanese history. Although all these designers had been working in Japan and/or Paris before this point, it was in 1982 and 1983 that they emerged into the international fashion spotlight.

Rei Kawakubo opened her business, Comme des Garçons (like the boys), in 1981. It was her 1983 line, with her intentional incorporation of holes or tears, oversized proportions, and nearly exclusive use of black, that created a sensation and that some described as post-holocaust. These clothes were entirely different in form from those of western designers, rejecting traditional definitions of femininity (Figure 9.15). Kawakubo continued to design with an aesthetic that challenged both viewer and wearer as she explored other forms for clothing, including abstract shapes. She also experimented with textile technologies to create unique fabrics. Yohji Yamamoto also established his first Paris boutique in 1981. His signature designs in the 1980s included asymmetrical closures and collars, oversized proportions, and unique use of standard clothing elements, such as lapels or pockets. He also used black as a principal color, and together he and Kawakubo are credited with making black a signature fashion color for more than a decade.

of Patou and with his own couture house beginning in 1987. His collections were a riot of color, with bright and theatrical designs that appealed to the customer looking for something adventurous and unique (Plate 9.2). Recognizing that couture had to be both distinctive and extravagant in order to survive, he blended textile patterns and textures with a borrowing of historical forms both at Patou and on his own. His 1987 **pouf** skirt, a full, gathered skirt pulled in at the bottom, was widely copied.

Claude Montana and **Thierry Mugler,** two proponents of the broad-shouldered silhouette of the 1980s, created streamlined, bold, tailored silhouettes. Mugler designed a line that emphasized the shoulders as early as 1979 and created cinched-waist suits and dresses. Best known for his combination of historic and futuristic inspirations, by the mid-1980s, he began to design the asymmetrical and angular suits that became his trademark. Montana helped to make leather fashionable, creating broad oversized jackets with padded shoulders. He

Figure 9.16 Softly draped linen Armani suit. *W,* September 23, 1983, 64, photograph by Guy Marineau, courtesy of Fairchild Archives.

Figure 9.17 Donna Karan's softer version of professional clothing for 1986, including body suit, sarong style skirt, and jacket. ©Bettmann/Corbis.

Italian designers continued to influence fashion in the 1980s, with **Giorgio Armani, Gianni Versace,** and **Franco Moschino** leading the way. Armani was known initially for his menswear, entering the womenswear field in 1975 with tailored clothing inspired by his men's collections. His signature and influential designs for both women and men in the 1980s involved use of neutral tones and drapable fabrics that did not rely on heavy and structural tailoring for their shape. His deconstructed suits created a modern and seasonless style of dressing (Figure 9.16). Versace presented his first collection under his own name in 1979. His clean-lined and sensual designs became his trademark, along with strong colors and fluid silk prints. Moschino was known for his intentional send-ups of the fashion world. He added a line called Cheap and Chic, in addition to creating men's and childrenswear.

A group of London designers also created fashion waves. **Vivienne Westwood** moved away from her early punk roots and began a career independent of partner Malcolm McLaren. She created a splash with her 1981 Pirates line and continued to create collections frequently inspired by historic research. She was one of the first to present bras worn over rather than under shirts in 1982. **Katherine**

Hamnett founded her company in 1979, creating clothing often inspired by working wear from other countries. A peace activist and feminist, she was best known in the mid-1980s for her oversized message T-shirts, with slogans such as Worldwide Nuclear Ban Now.

United States

American designers continued in their ready-to-wear tradition, making clothing that was wearable and modern, but in addition they began to focus on creating and selling an image. This became a considerable component of the ready-to-wear fashion business. American designers generally avoided the excesses and outrageous design statements that seemed to emanate from European designers. The group of designers who gained prominence in the 1970s continued to be important. These included Ralph Lauren, Calvin Klein, Geoffrey Beene, and Louis Dell'Olio and Donna Karan for Anne Klein. A few designers closed their companies. Halston was the most prominent of these. When he began to design lower-priced clothing for JCPenney some of his high-end clients ceased to carry his line, an example of the importance of image.

Figure 9.18 Menswear inspired separates from Perry Ellis. Photograph by Dustin Pittman, March 31, 1983, courtesy of Fairchild Archives.

Although space does not permit a discussion of all the American designers of the 1980s, a few new names were particularly influential. **Donna Karan** left Anne Klein in 1984 to open her own company. With her first collection, she immediately established herself as one of the most influential designers for the modern woman. She used a knitted body suit as the foundation for sophisticated clothing that was also comfortable. Her designs appealed to the professional woman who was tired of the overly masculine or homogeneous look of business suits (Figure 9.17). **Liz Claiborne** also designed for the busy working woman, offering affordable, relaxed separates. She opened her business in 1976, expanding in the 1980s to add leisure clothing, but she focused on transforming fashion trends into wearable and stylish clothing for working women with a variety of body types.

Norma Kamali, along with her husband Eddie Kamali, started in the 1970s by selling European imported clothing along with some of Norma's designs. After she was divorced, she opened her own boutique and wholesale company called OMO (On My Own) in 1978. She became known in the 1980s for her adventurous clothing, inspired by the exercise trend and often made of sweatshirt fabric

or other knits supported with large shoulder pads. Many of her designs had 1940s inspiration, and she was also recognized for her bathing suits and jumpsuits (see Figure 9.12). **Perry Ellis** began designing in his own business in 1978 under the name Portfolio. Previously he had designed for John Meyer of Norwich and Vera. Successful from the start, he focused on separates made from natural fiber fabrics. He had an always youthful approach but with a sophisticated sense of proportion, as he mixed textures of woven pieces with hand knit sweaters. Many of his designs incorporated menswear elements, modified for a woman's figure (Figure 9.18).

Fashion Trends

Images of fashion in the decade from 1979 to 1988 often exude a sense of wealth and extravagance, but it was a time of a multiplicity of styles and silhouettes that went from hugely oversized to tight and body conscious. With over half the baby boom generation past 30, professional clothing moved from the somewhat uniform dress for success look of the late 1970s to a more diverse power dressing style for the 1980s, usually with broad shoulders. While subcultural styles, such as those of the bohemians, beatniks, and hippies, had existed for years, this period witnessed an expansion and prominence of these style trends. Rock and roll continued to strongly influence fashion for the youth market, but it was less cohesive an influence, segmenting into hip-hop, pop, and a continuing of punk styles from the late 1970s. Retro dressing was particularly apparent, with borrowing from almost every historic period in evidence.[13]

Textiles and Technology

During the late 1970s there was a reaction against synthetic fibers, as many viewed them with distaste. Although there are undoubtedly numerous interconnected reasons, the stiffness of polyester double knit and the connection of synthetics with the increasingly out-of-favor disco style contributed to the loss of appeal. The return to natural fiber fabrics became part of a designer culture that promoted the luxury of natural fibers as a status symbol. By mid-decade, the Japanese avant-garde designers experimented with and encouraged development of a new wave of synthetics through Japanese fiber producers. These manufacturers worked in conjunction with the designers to experiment with existing fiber technology and to create new textiles with unique properties. One area of experimentation was with microfibers, fine fibers that opened up a range of new possibilities for synthetics. Other new fiber technology from U.S. producer DuPont included high-performance fibers,

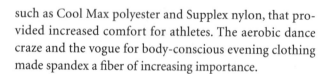

Figure 9.19 Wedge-shaped dress, with broad shoulders and narrow hem. *Women's Wear Daily,* October 4, 1982, courtesy of Fairchild Archives.

Figure 9.20 Dress inspired by the American southwest. Neiman Marcus Catalog, spring 1982.

such as Cool Max polyester and Supplex nylon, that provided increased comfort for athletes. The aerobic dance craze and the vogue for body-conscious evening clothing made spandex a fiber of increasing importance.

Women's Styles

The postmodernist trend affected fashion, with influences that came from a wide range of sources, including historical styles, and no single silhouette or hem length dominated the decade. For daytime and professional use, both suits and dresses generally had broad shoulders. Despite the prevalence of oversized tops with fitted bottoms, there was tremendous variety and a trend to more body consciousness. Clothing frequently crossed categories, as active wear styles were also worn as street attire, and a trend began for use of lingerie as outerwear. European designers often presented extreme fashion statements. Although not widely

adopted, elements filtered down to the mass market. An attempt by designers to dictate short skirt lengths in 1987 was a singular failure as women rejected the change. However, within a few seasons, skirt lengths had risen again.

Dresses

Day dresses came in a wide variety of styles, from oversized sweatshirt dresses to chemises to the **wedge**, an inverted triangle with broad, padded shoulders and narrow hem (Figure 9.19). In the first years of the decade, oversized silhouettes predominated, often with deep-cut **dolman** or **batwing** sleeves. Throughout the period, however, designers' inspirations included many historical periods, ethnic dress of various cultures, and the American southwest, the latter with elements of Mexican influence (Figure 9.20).

Shirtdresses continued their popularity from the previous decade, with a variety of silhouettes, usually with shoulder pads. A frequent style for business attire included the

Figure 9.21 Tailored coat dress by Donna Karan. *Vogue,*
April 1987, 327.

coat-style dress, which gave a tailored appearance (Figure
9.21). Some dresses had wide belts, particularly in the early
1980s, while others had a dropped waist for a look reminiscent of the 1920s except with broader shoulders in styles
with sleeves. The padded shoulder also inspired some designers to create 1940s-inspired silhouettes with a fuller,
long skirt.

Dresses were also sometimes worn as ensembles, with
matching jackets. More casual styles included knit and
sweatshirt dresses, sometimes worn off the shoulders, particularly in the first half of the decade. From the mid-1980s
until the end of the period there was an increasing attention
to the body, and stretch fabrics were used to a large extent
for both day and evening dresses.

For evening, elaborate and usually fitted looks were
prevalent, often with large flounces and gathered or pleated
sections (Figure 9.22). Much inspiration for evening and
formal dresses came from the French couture designers,

Figure 9.22 Flounced and gathered evening dress. *Women's Wear
Daily,* October 28, 1985, 48, courtesy of Fairchild Archives.

Figure 9.23 Romantic style dresses, with varied waist placement and much lace. ©Roger Ressmeyer/Corbis.

Figure 9.24 Broad shoulder jacket with long lapel over skirt. ©Ewing Galloway/Index Stock.

whose creations were widely copied at a variety of price points. The glamour of evening dresses included embroidery or sequin trims. What was termed the New Romantics in the early 1980s included period-inspired dresses, sometimes with lace or with full skirts (see Figure 9.22). Full-skirted, fitted-bodice dresses were popular for evening, and the pouf and crinoline-supported skirts shown by Lacroix in 1987 and 1988 inspired a wave of copies (Plate 9.2). Although the length of formal and evening dresses varied, there was a definite trend toward short skirts by the end of the decade.

Suits, Business Wear, and Coats

The term power dressing was used to describe the broad-shouldered suits and jackets of the 1980s. Professional apparel for the office became a huge business, as more women held positions of authority and often continued to work after having children. From the late 1970s into the early 1980s, suits tended to a uniform look, with trim blouses, just-below-the-knee skirts, and tailored jackets. As the decade progressed,

there was wide variation in jacket styles, from long to short, with or without collars. The revival of the Chanel-style suit by Lagerfeld, with all the accompanying accessories, was widely copied. Jackets were sometimes worn with matching skirts or pants, but there was also a trend for a mix-and-match style for business attire. By 1981–1982 the broad-shouldered look was well under way for jackets, and almost all had shoulder padding, although some jackets imitated those by Armani and tended to a softer silhouette. Longer jackets most often had a very deep lapel line, with the first button placement at or below the waist (Figure 9.24). How jackets were worn was also important. Collars were flipped up and sleeves pushed up the arm.

Skirts worn with jackets varied in length. In the early 1980s designers introduced very long skirt lengths, but in general hems ranged from just below the knee to mid-calf until the end of the decade, when they began to shorten. Designers showed very short skirts in 1987, but these were not widely accepted. Women, however, wore what they felt comfortable in rather than following exactly the designer

Figure 9.25 Oversized coats with broad shoulders by Aquascutum. Photograph by Tony Palmi, April 6, 1983, courtesy of Fairchild Archives.

Figure 9.26 Cowl-collar top over fitted stirrup pants. *Spiegel* spring/summer 1979 catalog.

offerings, and catalogs continued to offer them variety. Trouser styles varied, although pleated styles were shown more frequently in the first half of the period. Leather skirts also were worn with oversized jackets and sweaters.

Coats and outerwear also tended to the oversized and broad-shouldered silhouette (Figure 9.25). Down and other fiberfill coats were popular, as was fur, both real and imitation. **Swing**-style coats, with very full hems, a silhouette borrowed from the 1950s, also were worn.

Casual Sportswear, Separates, and Active Sports Clothing

Separates were important wardrobe staples, allowing women to mix and match to create their own versions of the fashion of the period. Even with casual clothing, the jacket, or an oversized shirt that could double as a jacket, was frequently worn to coordinate an outfit. Sweatshirts and other styles made with sweat shirting fabric became an important fashion trend. Fueled in part by dance films such as *Flashdance* and by the sweatshirt-inspired designs of

Norma Kamali, the trend included dresses, skirts, pants, and tunics. Some were worn to appear torn or off the shoulder in imitation of dancers. Others had enormous shoulder pads. Shirt styles ranged from a large and oversized version of traditional tailored shirts to soft blouses with full, puffed sleeves. The oversized shirt was often worn as a tunic or jacket over fitted pants, stirrup pants, or skirts (Figure 9.26 and Figure 9.27). Jumpsuits, sometimes in sweatshirt fabric, also appeared at the beginning of the 1980s.

Jeans and pants in a variety of styles continued to be a casual wear standard (Figure 9.27). Jean jackets were also widely adopted. At the end of the 1970s and beginning of the 1980s the promotion of designer jeans as a status item took off, inspiring articles on which fit the best and numerous advertisements to connect the brand with an image. The most notorious was the Calvin Klein ad with Brooke Shields claiming that nothing came between me and my Calvins. In general, jeans were very fitted throughout most of the decade. Acid-washed jeans also appeared for the first time in the 1980s, for a soft and worn appearance.

Figure 9.27 Casual separates, oversized shirt and jacket over relaxed pants. ©Roger Ressmeyer/Corbis.

Figure 9.28 Oversized sweater worn with knitted pants. Note the broad shoulder. *Spiegel* fall/winter 1989 catalog.

Knits continued to be a critical part of women's wardrobes and included the traditional sweater, as well as tunics worn over skirts, pants, leggings, or stirrup pants. Designs included not only a range of solid colors but also animal prints and bold-colored geometrics (Figure 9.28). Like jackets, many sweaters and tunics had broad shoulders supported with padding. T-shirts continued to be worn for casual dress, sometimes embroidered or otherwise decorated. The importance of aerobics, jogging, and other sports made athletic apparel a critical element of the wardrobe and sometimes doubled as streetwear. Fabrics blended with spandex aided both comfort and fit.

Foundations and Lingerie

Padded shoulders and loose tops eclipsed breasts during much of the period 1979–1988. In high fashion the underwear as outerwear trend appeared toward the end of the decade. Everyday bras remained soft and rounded, with most of the interest being provided by decorative materials. Underwires and front fastenings were frequent features. To sell lacy bras, camisoles, and panties in coordinated pastel colors, advertisers urged business-suited women to rebel against their tailored attire with ultrafeminine, sexy undergarments (Figure 9.29). Besides wielding more power in corporate offices, women of the 1980s flexed their muscles in the gym and on the jogging paths. Extensive marketing of sports bras began in 1979 and continued through the period. These were engineered in myriad ways to prevent the breasts from jiggling uncomfortably or embarrassingly during exercise (Figure 9.30 and 9.4). Racer-back styles typified even some daywear bras. Spandex with a Cool Max lining, which carried moisture away from the body, proved popular with fitness enthusiasts.

In the absence of body-molding outerwear, foundation garments dwindled almost to the vanishing point during this era. A few smoothers were shown, and catalogs of-

Figure 9.29 Lace-trimmed lingerie contrasts with man-tailored outerwear of the period. Photograph by Thomas Iannaccone, courtesy of Fairchild Archives.

Figure 9.30 Exercise bra and knee-length pants, November 23, 1988. Fairchild Archives.

fered control briefs—panty girdles—with natural or high waists. Erotic enticements came in the form of garter belts, for use with stockings. Of course the major type of leg covering remained panty hose and body stockings (see Figure 9.4); stockings, some with seams, were generally just a fashion accessory for dressy occasions. Panty hose also appeared in a variety of patterns and colors. Control tops on panty hose served to flatten the tummy or tame the derrière and hips.

Panty styles included bikinis, hip huggers, and waist level briefs. Loose-cut tap pants, worn with camisoles, enjoyed another fashion moment. At the opposite end of the fashion–function continuum, silk tricot or cotton knit **long johns** (long drawers, fitted to the body) and tops offered warmth for winter sports and bitter cold days. Slips normally consisted of petticoats, worn with or without a matching camisole.

Nightwear included both gowns and pajamas, in brushed cotton flannelette, brushed nylon tricot, or thin cottons for warm weather. Kimono-style bathrobes echoed menswear, in terry cloth, fleece, or down-filled quilted materials. Hostess robes featured a front-zippered closure for a dressy look and often were made of velvety washable velour.

Accessories

Both flat and high-heeled shoes were worn throughout the decade, heels tending to be tapered. Some came in bright colors or geometric patterns. With the longer skirts in the early to mid-1980s, boots were the footwear of choice in winter months. During the summer, shoe options included espadrilles and sandals.

Belts were important additions to many styles, often used to cinch in oversized tops or dresses. Some were in dramatic widths. Many belts were brightly colored leathers or fabric in the early 1980s (see Plate 9.1b). Gold leather accessories and gold trims on clothing also appeared. In ad-

Figure 9.31 (RIGHT) An example of men's casual wear. *Spiegel* spring/summer 1980 catalog.

Figure 9.32 (OPPOSITE, LEFT) Casual oversized jacket worn with jeans and exercise shoes. ©Deborah Feingold/Corbis.

Figure 9.33 (OPPOSITE, RIGHT) Licensed cartoon characters were popular on T-shirts of the late 1970s and 1980s. Courtesy of Andrew Weber, c. 1979.

dition to a briefcase and handbag, an essential accessory for businesswomen was a personal organizer.

Bold colors in jewelry included substantial plastic bracelets, earrings and necklaces. Swatch introduced brightly colored and patterned watches, helping to make the once standard wristwatch another accessory that could be matched to an outfit. There was also a fashion for bold-colored and patterned gloves, often with the gauntlet style cuffs reminiscent of the 1950s. For those less inclined to such a bold jewelry statement, the popularity of the Chanel style made chain belts and faux pearl necklaces widely accepted (see Figure 9.13).

Men's Styles

The decade from 1979 to 1988 was one of significant change in the presentation and marketing of men's fashion. Although men had become more fashion conscious during the late 1960s and 1970s, by the 1980s they had more options and more designers who focused on creating styles for them. Like women, men spent money on clothing and used fashion to define lifestyle and to display wealth. Designers who catered to men included Gianni Versace, Giorgio Armani, Calvin Klein, and Ralph Lauren. The avant-garde European designers created men's collections that pushed the envelope in terms of definitions of masculinity, experimenting with the idea of skirts for men and other nontraditional approaches. Although not adopted by most men, it indicated a new awareness of men as fashion customers.

Suits and Outerwear

A variety of suit shapes was available, choice depending on a man's connection with the fashion world. The three-piece suit had returned to popularity in the late 1970s, and jackets were cut with a deep, long lapel, much like women's (see Figure 9.6). For some, the broad-shouldered look was important, but men could also purchase a traditional cut. The biggest change in men's suits and jackets was the lighter and less fitted jackets introduced by Armani (Figure 9.6). His jackets had a rounded and more natural shoulder line and were tailored without the layers of inner linings and support, producing a softer drape. Power dressing also existed for men, as exemplified by the carefully chosen suits, shirts, and suspenders worn in the film *Wall Street* (see Figure 9.3 for an example of this style). Trousers were often pleated, and shirts were in white or pastels.

Coats and other outer garments for men followed a pattern similar to women's, with broad shoulders in many styles. Although the cut was more generous, the basic types of coats continued to be the trench coat and wool topcoat for more formal wear. For casual outerwear, a variety of jacket styles was worn. Leather was also a fashionable alternative both for dress and casual coats.

Casual Dress

Sportswear for men also underwent change. Casual jackets with broad shoulders and short, waist-length jackets were sometimes worn. Men might mix and match different garments to achieve more flexibility, including sweater vests, ca-

sual and/or sport jackets over trousers (Figures 9.31 and 9.32). For warm weather, informal shirt jackets in linens might be worn with loose pleated pants, sometimes tapered at the ankle. Even a more traditionally cut jacket could be worn in a more casual way, with sleeves rolled or pushed up or collar turned up (see Figure 9.6). Designer jeans for men were just as popular as those for women in the first half of the period. They were generally close fitted and, by the mid-1980s began to appear in bleached and other distressed fabrics (Figure 9.32). Designer labels became important in other types of men's casual wear as well. The jeans and shirts of Marithé and François Girbaud, low cut and often with snaps or other closures to ensure a fitted cuff, were popular with younger men. Designer logos were seen everywhere on sport and polo shirts, from Ralph Lauren Polo to the traditional Lacoste alligator.

Athletic clothing and the fitness craze affected men's casual clothing by providing more stretch in both tops and leggings or shorts. The athletic style might also extend to street wear. The hip-hop fashion of bands such as Run-D.M.C. influenced casual wear for younger men, with oversized gold chains and leather vests and pants. It was style that came from the street rather than designers, although it was only a short time before designers picked up on the trends and provided their own interpretation.

Shoes and Accessories
Numerous shoe styles were available for men. The traditional dress oxford continued to be standard for more for-

mal business wear, and loafers were popular for casual wear with sport jackets. Athletic shoes came in a wide range of styles and types, depending on the activity for which they were worn. Jogging, tennis, and basketball all had special shoe designs, although many were worn only for reasons of style and not for sporting activity, as seen in Figure 9.32. Ties, along with lapels, were narrower than in the previous decade. Suspenders were briefly popular, sometimes in bright colors or patterns. Men continued to reject jewelry for the most part.

Underwear and Sleepwear
During this decade men wore both briefs and boxer shorts, made of cotton broadcloth, knitted cotton, or synthetics. Even such conservative merchants as the venerable Brooks Brothers offered plaids, stripes, and random patterns in boxers. Silk or cotton knit long-johns and shirts functioned much as women's versions did, for cold weather and sport uses. The most significant change in men's underwear was in how it was advertised. No longer was comfort or function the main objective; instead, men were photographed in sexually charged and often provocative poses (see Figure 9.11). The focus was on selling an image as much as a product.

Sleepwear consisted mostly of cotton broadcloth pajamas of tailored cut, but a few nightshirts were marketed by catalog merchants, including L. L. Bean and Brooks Brothers. Kimono-cut robes ran the gamut of materials, including broadcloth for warm weather and wool, terry cloth, or a wool–cotton blend (Viyella) for chilly evenings.

Figure 9.34 Children's casual clothing, including sweat shirt tops, jeans, and athletic shoes. Note the continued presence of classic style dress for young girls. Author's collection, c. 1989.

Children's Styles

Fashion and designer names began to be more prominent in the children's department by the end of the 1980s. Young children continued to wear rompers and one-piece outfits that accommodated diapers. However, in addition to the usual pastels, bright colors were popular in solids and a variety of patterns. While there was a selection of unisex clothing for children, there also was a significant amount of licensing of cartoon and other characters from film and television (Figure 9.33) and design inspiration from costumes. Many of these tended to be gender specific, with boys more inclined to wear action figures from the science fiction films. Girls chose to wear Cabbage Patch doll figures or the cartoon character Strawberry Shortcake.

Girls' clothing, especially for preteens, was influenced by the dance fad and exercise apparel, with loose sweatshirts, leggings, and tights. Other styles that filtered down from the teen and adult market were sweatshirt dresses and separates, jeans dressing, and all manner of athletic clothing. Early in the period girls wore dresses inspired by the romantic trend in women's clothing, which seemed a perfect match. Boys' clothing also took inspiration from popular adult and teen clothing, and they could be seen in loose jackets and pleated trousers tapered or snapped to fit at the ankle.

The importance of knits for adults extended to children, with T-shirts and brightly colored stretch knits in geometric patterns. Both boys and girls wore pants, and jeans (or jean skirts for girls) were popular. The footwear of choice for most children was sneakers or athletic shoes in increasing variety, much of it patterned after adult athletic shoes.

Girls also wore jelly shoes, flexible bright-colored plastic shoes that could be worn with or without socks, a fad also with teens (see Figure 9.34 for an example of the variety in children's clothing).

Cartoon and movie characters often enlivened undershirts and briefs for both boys and girls, although white, pastels, and nonlicensed prints were also shown. Short-sleeved shirts came in crewneck and lapped shoulder designs. Briefs usually reached to waist level, but older girls also wore hip-level and bikini styles.

For the most part, children's sleepwear followed adult styles. For boys there were tailored or knitted pajamas, in solids with characters or team logos for trim. Girls also had tailored pajamas, as well as granny-style gowns. Winter brought out fleece jumpsuits, often with feet for babies and preschool children.

Hair and Grooming

Glamour defined makeup during the 1980s, with a more sophisticated and mature appearance. Red lips outlined with lip liner were combined with dark-lined eyes. No single hairstyle or cut dominated the period, and, like much of fashion, hair was increasingly becoming personal choice. Styles in general ranged from very short and androgynous to shoulder length and trim to long and full. For the full, "big" hairstyles (see Figure 9.5 and Figures 9.17 and 9.25 show some alternate styles.) Hair was held in place with gels and mousses. Instead of hats, women wore a variety of hair ornaments. The sweat band or head band appeared early in the period as part of the exercise trend and continued off and on for several years. Long hair was also pulled back with bows or other trims, including a piece of mesh tied in the hair in imitation of Madonna (see Figure 9.7).

Summary

Fashion in the decade from 1979 to 1988 is characterized by glamour and extravagance. It is, however, a period with a multiplicity of often opposing silhouettes, from broad-shouldered business suits to elaborate and fitted dresses for evening. As the baby boomers matured and Generation X established a fashion presence, there was increasing division into lifestyle dressing. Fashion influences came from a profusion of sources, including most notably the music world and the past. Although the silhouettes of fashion would evolve in the next decade, it was these influences that continued to inspire the change.

Suggested Readings

Callaway, Nicholas (ed). *Issey Miyake Photographs by Irving Penn.* New York: Little, Brown and Co., 1988.

Coleridge, Nicholas. *The Fashion Conspiracy: A Remarkable Journey Through the Empires of Fashion.* New York: Harper & Row, Publishers, 1988.

Ehrman, John. *America in the Age of Reagan.* New Haven: Yale University Press, 2005.

Hill, Daniel Delis. *As Seen in Vogue: A Century of American Fashion in Advertising.* Lubbock: Texas Tech University Press, 2004.

Kawamura, Yuniya. *The Japanese Revolution in Paris Fashion.* Oxford: Berg Publishers, 2004.

Martin, Richard, and Harold Koda. *The Historical Mode: Fashion and Art in the 1980s.* New York: Rizzoli, 1989.

Ogg, Alex, and David Upshal. *The Hip Hop Years: A History of Rap.* New York: Fromm International, 1999.

Radice, Barbara. *Ettore Sottsass: A Critical Biography.* Great Britain: Thames and Hudson, 1993.

Rosen, Ellen Israel. *Making Sweatshops: The Globalization of the U.S. Apparel Industry.* Berkeley: University of California Press, 2002.

Russell, Beverly. *Architecture and Design 1970–1990: New Ideas in America.* New York: Harry N. Abrams, Inc., 1989.

Steele, Valerie. *Fifty Years of Fashion: New Look to Now.* New Haven: Yale University Press, 1997.

Wright, David. *America in the 20th Century: 1980–1989.* New York: Marshall Cavendish, 1995.

CHAPTER 10
1989

U.S. Events and Trends	Fall of the Berlin Wall signals end of Cold War	Iraq invades Kuwait, U.S. troops sent to Gulf area Federated and Allied stores file for bankruptcy	Persian Gulf War begins The Soviet regime collapses	Bill Clinton elected president	Ratification of the North American Free Trade Agreement World Trade Center bombing
	**1989**	**1990**	**1991**	**1992**	**1993**
U.S. Fashions	Long jackets over short skirts	Revival of 1960s fashions, with miniskirts, bright colors	Recession causes designers to reduce prices Gulf War brings patriotic-themed clothing	Animal prints are popular. Revivals of 1940s. Mall of America opens (America's largest) 1950s, and 1970s styles create eclectic look	The grunge look is shown in designer lines Models are thin, termed the waif look by some

1999

O. J. Simpson arrested for murder of his wife and her friend

1994

Fashions begin to become slimmer

Tom Ford hired by Gucci

The Oklahoma City bombing

Amazon.com begins operation

1995

Casual look reigns; T-shirts, chinos

Bill Clinton reelected

1996

Classic looks in fashion; high heels revived

Dolly the sheep is cloned

Princess Diana dies in Paris

1997

Designer Gianni Versace is murdered in Florida

Bill Clinton is impeached (acquitted in 1999)

1998

More glamorous looks begin to return to fashion

Massacre/suicides at Columbine High School in Colorado

Y2K frenzy

1999

At the end of the millennium, designers continue to recycle the past with additions of high-tech materials

Party
Like It's the '90s

The rapid expansion of computer technology and the arrival of the World Wide Web on the Internet defined many of the changes that occurred in the decade from 1989 to 1999. The Internet forever transformed daily life, revolutionizing both personal and business interactions in what was sometimes called the Information Age. A computer-driven culture changed routines as e-mail, cell phones, and other technologies pervaded everyday life. The technology boom also helped to convert a decade that began with a recession into one of economic boom and was instrumental in development of a global culture. The first years of the decade were also marked by the end of the long Cold War, something that had affected U.S. politics for decades. The excesses of the 1980s seemed to recede as people sought a quieter and less flamboyant lifestyle. Fashion conveyed an initial sense of anything goes, but, by allowing people seemingly infinite options, it became an even more complex means to express personal identity.

Domestic and International Politics and Economics

The decade began with the inauguration of a new president, George Herbert Walker Bush, in 1989. Bush promised to continue the prosperity of the 1980s, and not to increase taxes— a promise that could not be kept. The supply-side economic policies of the Reagan administration created a number of economic problems, including growing deficits in the federal government and shrinking middle-class income. This in turn affected business profits, and many workers began to be laid off. By the time Bush took office, the economy had entered a period of recession. The recession did not last long, but, even as the economy improved in 1991, the number of jobs did not increase. At the same time, there was a general shift away from manufacturing and an increased demand for workers trained in technology. With the recession of the early 1990s, more Americans lived below the poverty level, and homelessness increased. Disillusioned, many Americans looked for change. The economy dominated the 1992 elections, won by Democrat William (Bill) Clinton. President Clinton was the first member of the baby boom generation to be elected president, taking office in 1993.

The economic recovery began slowly, as many companies sought to hire both managers and white-collar workers again in 1993. By the end of the year, inflation had dropped, and unemployment was generally down. By the mid-1990s, the economy began to boom, led in large part by the rapid growth of technology-based businesses. Many people made huge fortunes in the technology sector as hundreds of new companies went public. The first company to set the pace for the dramatic rise of a new dot-com world on the stock market was Netscape, which went public in 1995. In 1 hour the stock rose from an initial offering of $13 to $78 a share.[1] By the late 1990s, there were as many as 10,000 new Web sites every day, as Internet companies proliferated. Many never produced a profit, but the enthusiasm for technology stocks helped the stock market to reach all-time highs. In addition, individual investors soon learned to buy and trade stock via the Internet.

After the brief slump at the beginning of the 1990s, the economy remained very strong through the rest of this period, with low interest rates, a booming stock market, and soaring construction rates, with a resulting government surplus rather than deficit. The strong economy was in large part the reason for Clinton's reelection in 1996.

International Relations

When the Berlin Wall was built in 1961, it came to embody the political divisions and tensions of the decades-long Cold War. By the summer of 1989, however, there were signs that it was at least symbolically beginning to crumble when Hungary allowed East Germans to pass through the country to Austria and West Germany. On November 9, 1989, with the announcement that travel across the wall would not be restricted, German citizens began to tear down whole sections, and the Soviet-controlled East German guards did nothing to stop them. By 1990, East and West Germany were united. Soviet troops also pulled out of Poland, Hungary, Romania, and Czechoslovakia, and at the same time many of the Soviet republics declared their independence. In 1988, Mikhail Gorbachev, president of the Union of Soviet Socialist Republics (USSR), had announced a decision to reduce troops in Eastern Europe as part of his policy of openness, with the result that the Communist Party began to lose authority. When he resigned as president of the USSR in December 1991 and turned his office over to Boris Yeltsin, the Soviet Union was officially dissolved. The Cold War, which had for more than 40 years affected politics, American attitudes, and even technological advances, was finally ended.

Despite the sudden, and to some degree unexpected, end to communism in Russia and other central European countries, China continued to embrace a Communist government. The U.S. relationship with China had improved by small steps over the previous two decades, with more travel between the two countries and increasing trade. However, Chinese troops crushed a demonstration by pro-democracy groups in Tiananmen Square in 1989, killing as many as 2,000. Although Bush responded by ending sale of military equipment to China and allowing Chinese students to extend their visas, he continued to attempt to maintain a relationship with a country that represented a significant trade force.

The United States took on roles as both peace keeper and enforcer in international conflicts throughout the decade of the 1990s, sometimes alone but often in alliances with other nations. Lessons from Vietnam led to a preference for negotiation over military action, although U.S. troops increasingly were deployed to trouble spots all over the globe. The first conflict began early in the decade when Iraq, led by Saddam Hussein, invaded Kuwait in August 1990. Iraq's actions were condemned by the United States, the United Nations, and the Soviet Union, and the United States began a troop build up in the area almost immediately. As tensions mounted and Hussein refused to withdraw his troops by a January 15 deadline, Desert Storm began. It was a war played out on television, making CNN a major news provider with round-the-clock coverage. Within six weeks, superior U.S. air power prevailed, and Hussein signed agreements to withdraw, although he remained in power in Iraq until 2003 (Figure 10.1).

Other international conflicts included the overthrow of

Figure 10.1 Families welcome troops home from Operation Desert Storm. ©Patrick Bennett/Corbis.

a military dictatorship in Haiti in 1994, led by U.S. troops as part of a multinational force. More than 15,000 American troops were also initially deployed to Bosnia in 1996 as part of a NATO peace-keeping force. By the end of the decade, there were still at least 25,000 troops there.

Rise of Terrorism and Violence

Violence, exacted by both foreign and domestic terrorists, seemed to occur with increased frequency, making Americans question their safety at home, work, and school. The conflicts in the Middle East led to an increase in violence in many countries there. In February 1993, Muslim terrorists detonated a car bomb in the basement of the World Trade Center, killing six and injuring many more.

On April 19, 1995, Americans were stunned by the bombing of the Alfred P. Murrah Federal Building in Oklahoma City. The explosion killed 168 people, including children from an on-site daycare center. Americans, feeling more vulnerable to terrorism, were surprised to find that the bomber was not a foreign terrorist, but U.S. Army veteran Timothy McVeigh. The 1992 videotaped beating of Rodney King, a black man who was being pursued by police in South-Central Los Angeles, caused severe riots after four white policemen were acquitted of assault charges. School violence also shocked the country. Between 1996 and 1999 there were over a dozen incidents of school shootings. The most deadly occurred on April 20, 1999, when 14 students and 1 teacher were killed at Columbine High School in Littleton, Colorado.

Globalization

The combination of computer and Internet technology and the redefining of trade relationships over the course of more than a decade led to a sense that the world was figuratively getting smaller. The trend toward globalization particularly affected the apparel industry. Negotiation of the North American Free Trade Agreement (NAFTA) with Mexico and Canada, a proposal that would allow free trade with few tariff restrictions, began during the Bush administration. Debates over ratification intensified during the early years of the Clinton administration, with final approval in late 1993. One argument in favor of the agreement was that it would increase productivity through an increase in exports to both Canada and Mexico (Figure 10.2). Labor unions objected that U.S. jobs would be lost. During the first years immediately after ratification exports to Mexico did rise, but the apparel industry experienced significant job loss. With the possibility of low-wage production, there was a rapid growth of apparel firms in Mexico. The South was hardest hit, losing 35 percent of its apparel production jobs.[2] In 1994, a new version of the General Agreement on Tariffs and Trade was approved by Clinton and Congress, another step in the globalization of the marketplace.

Social Life and Culture

The last decade of the twentieth century was essentially a prosperous one, with longer life spans and generally good health. As the baby boomers aged, they continued to exert an effect on lifestyles and spending patterns, although the new Generations X, those born between 1964 and 1980, and Y, those born in the 1980s and 1990s, began to make their presence known.

Figure 10.2 NAFTA supporters at a rally in Louisiana, 1992. ©Wally McNamee/Corbis.

Demographics

The population of the United States continued to grow, and, while there were more children born, they were a smaller proportion overall, as immigrants continued to constitute an increasing percentage of the population. By the end of the decade, more than 12 percent were from Latin American countries. The aging of the population generated considerable debate, with an estimated 20 percent over the age of 65 years by the year 2000, a trend that would continue as the baby boom generation aged.[3] As the cost of health care increased, there were widespread worries about the ability of medical and other support services to keep up with changing demographics. With record numbers of retirees predicted over the next decades, debates about the availability of Social Security in the future began in earnest.

The decline of the traditional family unit that had occurred over the past two decades slowed somewhat, and the divorce rate dropped slightly, but there was little indication that this meant a return to the demographic structures of the 1950s. While the baby boomers continued to be a focus of concern relative to the aging of the population, the generations born after 1965 were widely studied by marketers and targeted by advertisers. Generation X, the first generation to come of age in the postmodern era, was courted by the music and fashion industries. The next generation, just entering its teens in the 1990s, were sometimes called Generation Y or the echo boomers because they represented the mini baby boom of the 1980s. Generation Y is a large and ethnically diverse generation that is estimated at 70 million; there is still disagreement over how to define them as a group. The first generation to grow up with computers and with the Internet, they have been characterized as both education oriented and pampered. Because of their numbers they were targeted by advertisers, and they affected the sales

of everything from technology to clothing.

There was a continuation of the population shift away from rural America, as small farming gave way to corporate farms. Many of those still living in rural areas no longer worked in the farming industry at all and often commuted to jobs in the nearest town. The 1990s were a growth time for the travel industry, as many Americans enjoyed the country's affluence by traveling more. The United States also was a tourist destination, as international arrivals increased. The growth of the Internet aided tourism, as customers could increasingly compare prices and amenities and make air, hotel, and other reservations online.

Health and Education

The disease AIDS became an epidemic and no longer could be viewed as a something that affected only fringe groups of the population. It became one of the leading causes of death for people between the ages of 35 and 44 years, and worldwide the number of people infected with the human immunodeficiency virus (HIV) reached overwhelming figures, especially in Africa.[4]

The educational system in the United States caused concerns throughout the decade. Declining scores on national tests brought fears that U.S. young people were falling behind and would not be able to compete in the increasingly global economy. The truth was less clear-cut. The high school dropout rate was less than it had been a decade earlier, and more students were taking advanced placement classes for college. Rising numbers of high school graduates were going to college, but more had to take remedial courses in their freshman year. There also was a trend away from placing value on the gaining of knowledge and toward viewing education primarily as a way to achieve a comfort-

Figure 10.3 Young girls in school uniforms in California, 1995. Note the subtle variations in style. ©David Butow/Corbis Saba.

Figure 10.4 Computer professionals in casual office dress. ©Catherine Karnow/Corbis.

able lifestyle. The wave of violence in high schools at the end of the 1980s also fueled anxieties about the state of education. One response was an increase in the number of schools that instituted dress codes or required uniforms (Figure 10.3). Educators and the public believed that because gangs used various articles of clothing worn in specific ways as identifiers, the implementation of dress codes would decrease violent exchanges.

Technology and Communication

The rapid expansion of computer technology was certainly the most important advance of the 1990s. Although the Internet had existed since the 1960s, mostly in federal government facilities, it expanded rapidly in the late 1980s. Development and expansion of the World Wide Web at the beginning of the 1990s, opened up a vast range of possibilities for both personal and business users. Initially, access to the Web was through phone lines. When commercial Internet providers such as America Online created user-friendly sites and provided assistance in guiding members through the maze of possibilities, use expanded dramatically. As more and more people had access to the Web, the use of electronic mail (e-mail) for communication began to outpace telephone and traditional mail (now sometimes called snail mail). The Internet and e-mail also led to coining of new terms, such as cyberspace, chat room, spam, and emoticons—symbols used to represent emotions such as a smiley face :-). Another consequence of the computer culture was the growth of casual dressing, as the mostly young, male techies preferred jeans, chinos, and T-shirts over the traditional suit (Figure 10.4). Computer technology also was responsible for an end-of-millennium frenzy nicknamed Y2K or the millennium bug. There was concern

that, because the year in a computer program is represented by its last two digits, at the turn of the century computers would not recognize the difference between 1900 and 2000. Governments and businesses worldwide spent billions fixing Y2K bugs, and in the end the new year arrived uneventfully.

Along with computer technology, cellular telephone use proliferated in the 1990s. As their size became more compact, cell phones also began to become a fashion statement, offered in different styles and colors, and, with the possibility of creating individualized ring tones by the end of the decade, another means of self-expression. This diverted money that might otherwise have gone into apparel.

Computer technology linked with genetic research created an explosion of scientific discovery. Cloning was a technology that both fascinated and frightened many, unleashing a worldwide debate on the ethics of the process. In 1997, a sheep named Dolly became the first mammal cloned using DNA from another adult animal. Created by Scottish scientists at the Roslyn Institute near Edinburgh, Dolly was later discovered to have cells the same age as the 6-year-old sheep from whom scientists got the DNA; that meant she would eventually die prematurely. In 1998, the Human Genome Project, a plan to map the entire human genetic code, was announced. This also gave rise to ethical as well as political concerns, at least in part because of the issue of determining who would own the rights to these discoveries.

Literature and Magazines

Computers and the Internet fueled the biggest trends in the book world: selling through online bookstores such as Amazon.com and the early stages of desktop and online publishing. The other major change in the marketing of books was the rapid growth of superstores such as Borders and Barnes & Noble. These stores often drove the smaller stores out of business. They gained popularity not only through book sales but also by adding departments for music, videos, and DVDs and by creating cafés, making the store a social gathering place.

Oprah Winfrey encouraged people to read via a book club created as a segment of her talk show. Many of the books she recommended, frequently by first time authors, ended up on the best-seller list. In addition to Winfrey's book selections, many well-known authors had best sellers, including Anne Rice, Stephen King, and Tom Clancy. Romance novels continued to find a steady audience, and some began to become more mainstream. Robert James Waller's *The Bridges of Madison County* (1992), a variation of the romance genre, found a wide audience with characters who were not the stereotypical young couple. The legal thriller became a relatively new genre in the 1990s, led by authors Scott Turow and John Grisham. Self-help books also continued to be popular nonfiction reading, with *Simple Abundance,* an Oprah Winfrey recommendation, John Gray's *Men Are From Mars*, and *Chicken Soup for the Soul,* which generated a series of follow-up titles. Children's literature sprang to vigorous life with the publication of *Harry Potter and the Sorcerer's Stone* in 1997, attracting adult readers as well.

The number of magazines published increased rapidly in the 1990s, with some publishing in cyberspace rather than on paper. This included an uncounted number of zines, small-circulation, specialty magazines. New fashion and design magazines included *Allure, Mirabella, Marie Claire*, and *InStyle*.

Sports and Leisure

Although more Americans than ever were overweight, sports participation in the 1990s increased. New sporting goods retailers made sports gear fashionable, and each new sport developed its own clothing style. In-line skating became remarkably popular, quickly taking over from traditional skating.[5] Also popular with Generations X and Y were extreme sports, sports done to enhance a sense of excitement or challenge that used the equipment in a unique manner. Both skateboarding and snowboarding grew in popularity and generated a new group of sports celebrities such as skateboarder Tony Hawk. There also arose a whole subculture of fashion style associated with these sports, frequently baggy clothing and/or body piercing (Figure 10.5).

Professional sports were big business in the 1990s as stars gained celebrity status and were often sought after for product endorsements, frequently clothing. Women's professional athletics gained significant visibility in areas other than the traditionally watched gymnastics, swimming, or figure skating. Basketball and soccer developed a following, particularly after the U.S. women's soccer team took home the World Cup in 1991 and 1999. It also gave celebrity status to players such as Mia Hamm and Brandi Chastain. When Chastain pulled off her jersey after winning the final game of the 1999 World Cup to reveal her Nike sports bra, she unintentionally provided considerable publicity for the industry.

Men's basketball also grew in popularity, with players such as Michael Jordan, Dennis Rodman, and Shaquille O'Neal becoming major celebrities, a status that led to numerous product endorsements. Many of the ads were for athletic clothing, but Jordan also did commercials for Hanes underwear. In golf, Tiger Woods became the youngest player to win the Master's Tournament in 1997. He also endorsed a variety of products, including clothing

Figure 10.5 Skateboarders in oversized pants. ©Getty Images/Photograph by Lara Jo Regan/Liaison.

and Rolex watches. Computers entered the world of game events through the much discussed chess match between an IBM computer nicknamed Deep Blue and chess grand master Garry Kasparov; the final match was won by the computer.

Architecture and Art, Television, Movies, and Music

Almost all of the arts were affected by the world of computer technology. Digital design processes began to enter production. Computers became an essential component in the design process for architects, interior designers, and graphic designers. The proliferation of computers also required architects and designers to rethink the configuration of workspaces to accommodate technology either in addition to or instead of traditional paper filing systems.

Architecture and Art

One of the most dramatic visual changes in the 1990s in terms of architecture was not in the dramatic building of experimental buildings or in new styles but rather in the proliferation of the more utilitarian buildings that altered urban, suburban, and rural landscapes. Along shopping strips in communities of almost every size, there emerged shopping areas dominated by big-box stores such as Wal-Mart, Target, and Best Buy, which created a sense of standardization across the United States. The housing market also succumbed to the pattern of homogeneous construction, as large and often uniform-appearing suburban homes were built in developments that, at the most extreme, controlled who entered. The sameness of these often large houses led to the coining of the term McMansions as a way to describe both their size and their uniformity, a reference to the uniformity of food served at fast food restaurants such as McDonald's.

Despite the monotony of stores and houses, a number of architects also designed creative and experimental structures. Frank Gehry received accolades for his design for the Guggenheim Museum in Bilbao, Spain. Another museum project, designed by Richard Meier, the Getty Center in Los Angeles, opened in 1997 and was an art complex of six buildings created in a modern style. The San Francisco Museum of Modern Art (1994), with its geometric design and massive skylight, was designed by Mario Botta.

There was also a mushrooming of casinos and theme restaurants such as Planet Hollywood and the Hard Rock Cafe. As more and more Americans turned to gambling for entertainment, casinos proliferated along the Gulf Coast as well as inland along rivers and of course in Las Vegas.

Figure 10.6 Clarke's shoes advertisement designed with CAD program. ©Jerry Mason/New Scientist/Photo Researchers, Inc.

The art world reflected the influence of the computer and Internet boom and the end of the Cold War. The lines became increasingly blurred between the real and the virtual. Many exhibits were installations that included interactive works of art. The decade began with the art controversies of the late 1980s spilling over into the 1990s, leaving many avant-garde artists without one of the few funding sources. Government agencies such as the National Endowment of the Arts chose to support fewer new or experimental artists. The decade also ended with controversy, with the show titled "Sensations: Young British Artists From the Saatchi Collection." The show was considered macabre and tasteless by many and generated a number of lawsuits.

A considerable amount of art was politically motivated, as artists set out to advance certain agendas. The AIDS epidemic in particular became a focus of numerous works of art, especially as the art world lost many to the disease. The most famous was certainly the NAMES Project Quilt, begun in 1987. The quilt was made of individual panels, each commemorating someone who had died of AIDS. By the mid-1990s, the quilt had over 44,000 panels, a small percentage of those who had died. It soon grew too large to exhibit in full.

Computer-related art, both art that reflected the new age of technology in its content and art that was computer generated, became more widespread in the 1990s (Figure 10.6). The ability to manipulate an image raised ethical issues in journalistic photography in the 1980s and 1990s, when several photographers altered their images.[6] Development of the Adobe Photoshop program in 1989 expanded exponentially the ability to manipulate images and created unique artistic approaches, often with a surrealist approach.

Television

By the end of the 1990s, 98 percent of Americans owned at least one television, but television viewing actually declined slightly over the course of the decade, replaced by a combination of new entertainment options, including the Internet and movie rentals. Americans continued to get most of their news information from television, and many became couch potatoes, a term coined to describe a sedentary lifestyle spent in front of the television. This seemed to transpire despite the fitness craze of the 1980s, as remote controls allowed endless changing of channels, and a wealth of new cable channels provided more viewing options. Video game technology became more advanced, with game systems such as Super Nintendo Entertainment System, Sony Playstation, and Sega Dreamcast.

In 1996, the television industry announced a television Parental Guideline rating system. It may, however, have created an increase in sexuality and violence in many shows because viewers could now be warned in advance of the content and choose not to watch.

The most significant change in television in the 1990s was the rise of reality TV, programming that blurred the distinction between news and entertainment. Many news magazine shows, such as *Hard Copy* (1989–1999), provided dramatized and frequently sensationalized accounts of stories that showed only their most spectacular or titillating moments. Other examples of these programs include *Cops*, which showed police officers responding to calls, or *America's Most Wanted*, which presented dramatizations of crimes in an attempt to apprehend the fugitives. Another type of reality show that began in the 1990s and set a precedent for a wave of similar programming was MTV's *Real World*, which documented the interactions of a group of strangers living together.

Television dramas seemed to take center stage in the 1990s, with critically acclaimed shows such as *Homicide: Life on the Streets*, *Law and Order*, and *NYPD Blue*. The last of these garnered unfavorable attention for the level of violence and nudity portrayed. Medical dramas also proved popular (*ER* and *Chicago Hope*) as did science fiction (*The X-Files* and *Star Trek: The Next Generation*). *Ally McBeal*, a blend of drama and comedy, starred Calista Flockhart as a young attorney in a new firm. Although Flockhart's performance was well reviewed, she was plagued by rumors of anorexia, a problem recently in the news because of the current ideal of over-thin fashion models.

Youth dramas such as *Beverly Hills 90210*, *Dawson's Creek*, and *Party of Five* also gained substantial audiences. By the end of the decade, cable television networks were be-

ginning to produce series dramas. The two most successful initially were *The Sopranos* and *Sex and the City*, both on HBO. *Sex and the City* debuted in 1998 and portrayed the lives of four young professional women in New York City. The show ultimately created trends for many of the fashions worn by the actresses, including Manolo Blahnik shoes (Figure 10.7).

Two comedies dominated television in the 1990s—*Seinfeld* (1990–1998) and *Friends* (1994–2004). *Seinfeld*, a show supposedly about nothing, focused on the minutia of daily life while satirizing the clichés of modern urban existence. *Friends* followed the interactions of six 20ish to 30ish friends as they negotiated life in the city, both working and playing. It also created style trends, particularly the hairstyles of the women stars. Television comedy in the 1990s also gave rise to cartoon shows aimed at both adults and teens. Among the most successful were *The Simpsons* (1989–), *Ren & Stimpy* (1991–1995), *Beavis and Butthead* (1993–1997), and *South Park* (1997–). All generated substantial sales of tie-in merchandise.

Figure 10.7 The four stars of *Sex and the City* in clothing by costume and fashion designer Patricia Field. Everett Collection.

Movies

As with other areas of the media arts, movies were influenced by digital and computer technologies, especially in the area of special effects. Steven Spielberg's *Jurassic Park* (1993), with its realistic dinosaurs, became the most viewed film of the decade. The end of the period, the fourth film in the *Star Wars* series, *Episode I: The Phantom Menace*, brought spectacular visual effects, although it received mixed reviews. Computer technology also was used in animated films such as *Toy Story* and in a unique manner in *Forrest Gump*. In the latter, the main character was digitally inserted into historic events, blurring the lines of historic reality. This technique would also be used in television commercials. The futuristic film *The Matrix* (1999) relied on a variety of new technical filming techniques and set a number of fashion trends, especially for the sunglasses and black trenchcoats worn in the film (Figure 10.8).

Established directors created numerous acclaimed films during the 1990s. In addition to *Jurassic Park*, Spielberg directed two much-admired films, both historically based, *Schindler's List* (1994) and *Saving Private Ryan* (1998). Robert Altman directed a film about the fashion industry, *Ready to Wear* (1994). The other film about fashion, the documentary *Unzipped* (1995), portrayed the creative process of designer Isaac Mizrahi as he developed his fall 1994 collection.

New directors also had hits in the 1990s. The films of Quentin Tarantino in particular attracted an audience and commentary, both for their hipness and the amount of graphic violence. The black suits worn with narrow ties sported by fast-talking gangsters in *Reservoir Dogs* became a popular style in an age when casual clothing was the norm. Uma Thurman's character in *Pulp Fiction* also set a style trend with her black pants, white shirt, and blunt-cut, banged black hair.

Music

Rock and roll fragmented into a variety of styles including rap, pop, indie rock, techno, and even contemporary Christian rock. Country music also enjoyed a revival, especially as some of the musicians moved to a more pop rock sound. These included Garth Brooks, LeAnne Rimes, Faith Hill, and the Dixie Chicks, who flaunted both their looks and their fashion style. One of the significant alternative rock styles was grunge, a term used to describe the bands that came to prominence in the early 1990s, particularly in the Seattle area. The most prominent of these were Nirvana and Pearl Jam, whose music appealed to the adolescent sense of alienation and contempt for contemporary pop music. The success of Nirvana opened the door for other bands and

Figure 10.8 Laurence Fishburne in *The Matrix* wearing a long coat and sunglasses without earpieces, a style many found difficult to wear, 1999. © Corbis Sygma.

created a fashion trend for their clothing style, worn plaid flannel shirts and stone washed jeans.

Mainstream pop music had a resurgence in the 1990s and was particularly popular with young teens and preteens. Both boy bands and young girl singers were promoted at least as much for their image as for their music. The boy bands the Backstreet Boys and 'N Sync presented a relatively clean-cut image, while girl groups and singers were marketed in a more sexualized manner. The Spice Girls became popular in the early 1990s, while at the very end of the decade singers like Britney Spears pushed the envelope with scanty attire—low-cut pants and bare midriff. Although cropped tops that exposed the midsection had been a minor fashion trend for a number of years, Spears created a wave of fashion mimicry by young girls that extended well into the next decade (Figure 10.9).

Rap and hip-hop, initially ignored to a large degree by commercial radio and by MTV, gained popularity rapidly in the 1990s. Rap largely replaced traditional rock and roll in appeal with youth. The hip-hop and rap sound of the 1980s began to segue into gangsta rap, a style that created controversy for its violent, and what many considered obscene, lyrics. It came to the attention of a wider audience when the 1989 album of the group 2 Live Crew was ruled obscene. Although they were eventually acquitted of obscenity charges, the controversy over gangsta rap continued, especially touching the groups that recorded for Death Row Records, including Snoop Doggy Dogg and Tupac 2Pac Shakur, arguably one of the most recognized rap musicians of the decade. His 1996 murder did nothing to still the controversies. These black rappers were soon joined by a barrage of others, including girl groups (Figure 10.10) and white rappers such as Eminem, one of the most successful.

Retailing and Manufacturing

Between 1989 and 1999, department stores faced well-established rivals such as direct-mail (catalog) merchants,

Figure 10.9 Britney Spears performing at the 1999 MTV Video Music Awards. ©Reuters/Corbis.

plus challenges from home shopping television stations, including QVC and HSN (Home Shopping Network). This source of purchasing burgeoned but so did the more formidable rival of Internet shopping, which was experiencing its first boom. Many highly successful Internet companies were set up, including current giants Amazon and EBay. Among apparel firms, Lands' End took the plunge into e-tailing in the mid-1990s, and by 1997 it offered 500 products on its Web site.

Discounters and Department Stores

Discounters blossomed, growing from 27 percent of all retail sales in 1987 to 41 percent in 1996.[7] Department stores' share sank from 20 percent to 14 percent during the same 10-year span. Wal-Mart had almost 3,000 stores by 1996. Chains such as Gap prospered strongly, too, selling apparel with simple chic that fit the mood of the era and the demands of global production.

Faced with the problem of clicks (Internet) and bricks (physical store) competition, department stores continued to merge. Dayton Hudson (Target) acquired Marshall Field. Stores that began as multiproduct emporia dropped such lines as furniture, housewares, toys, and electronics, all of which were purveyed more successfully by category killers such as Toys "R" Us, Best Buy, RadioShack, and Bed, Bath, and Beyond. Apparel, jewelry, and cosmetics became mainstays of surviving department stores. A few independent stores survived, including Nordstrom, with its high emphasis on customer service and depth of assortment, especially in footwear. Conglomerates Federated and May, plus single entities Dillard's and Nordstrom, collectively controlled more than half of all department store sales in the late 1990s.[8] High-end retailing was concentrated in Saks, Neiman-Marcus, and Barney's, plus the boutiques of various European and American designers.

Advances in computer technology assisted department stores by allowing the store's computer to connect directly to the computers of the major brands carried by that store, two examples being Tommy Hilfiger for men and Eileen Fisher for women. This made it easier to replenish merchandise during the selling season. However, matrix[9] buying reduced choice for retailers and, conversely, limited the number of retail accounts served by a vendor. Retailers also increased the design and production of profitable private-label merchandise, bringing more of the processes in-house and contracting with vendors whose own name never appeared on the merchandise.

Increasingly, department stores resembled a collection of designer boutiques, including units of Tommy Hilfiger and Ralph Lauren for men. Women's brands included Donna

Figure 10.10 The Atlanta band TLC in oversize clothing usually worn by male rap stars, 1992. ©Getty Images Entertainment.

Karan, Bill Blass, and Giorgio Armani at the top end; Ellen Tracy and Emanuel (a secondary line of Emanuel Ungaro) at the bridge level; and Liz Claiborne and Jones New York at the better level. Bridge, a concept that started in menswear, grew strongly in womenswear during this decade to include DKNY, Ann Klein II, and Adrienne Vittadini as well as Tracy and Emanuel (Figure 10.11). With prices approximately 30 percent lower than the designer level, bridge lines appealed to executive women who wanted chic, wearable clothes that suited their demanding schedules.

Casualization of the Workplace

Many societal changes weighed on retailers during this decade, not least of them being the casualization of the workplace. Beginning with high-tech firms in Silicon Valley, companies around the country offered dress-down Fridays as a perquisite for employees, believed to improve morale, productivity, and creativity. Soon, there were summertime relaxations of the usual suited dress code, succeeded by everyday business casual. In 1998, 60 percent of U.S. companies had some degree of casual dress.[10] Sales of suits for men and women, and even of dressy jackets for men, took a sharp downturn. Manufacturers and specialty retailers went out of business. What boomed instead were sweater makers and firms such as Levi Strauss, sales of whose Dockers brand of casual pants skyrocketed. A small industry sprang up to work with employers on developing and communicating guidelines for business-appropriate casual

dress. Inevitably, however, serious abuses occurred, with downright sloppy or overly revealing apparel invading the office. Reaction set in only with the evaporation of dot-com companies and the general business recession at the start of 2000. Apparel makers and sellers faced a long-term crunch because the average household spent only 5.5 percent of its budget for apparel and its upkeep; electronic gadgets and other entertainments absorbed a growing share of Americans' discretionary dollars.

Competition

Competition beset U.S. apparel manufacturing, too, specifically in the fast-growing volume of clothing imported from Asia and from Latin America. In 1990, only half of apparel purchased in the United States was made domestically. Large American manufacturers, such as Liz Claiborne, manufactured goods in as many as 40 countries at any one time.[11] Minimalism, classic styles, and simple chic were promoted, because these were easier to manage in offshore production. Arrangements varied concerning the relative responsibilities and ownership of materials between the offshore contractor and the contracting U.S. firm. Some domestic companies designed and cut apparel in the United States for assembly elsewhere, usually in Latin America and the Caribbean area, under Section 807 of the U.S. Tariff Code. This provision taxed the returning apparel only on the added value from assembly. Trousers, slacks, shorts, bras, shirts, blouses,

Figure 10.11 Jacket, silk shirt, and twill pants by Ellen Tracy. ©Timothy Clary/AFP/Getty Images.

Worldwide, consolidation of manufacturers occurred throughout the decade. Luxury brands, including apparel, fragrances, and deluxe food and beverages, were increasingly under the control of huge international conglomerates, such as LVMH (Möet Hennessey-Louis Vuitton) and the Gucci Group. In late 1999, Gucci allied with PPR (Pinault-Printemps-Redoute), one of Europe's most effective luxury products distributors. This alliance also brought the Yves Saint Laurent brand under Gucci's ownership and control.

Quick-Response Manufacturing

Of longer-lasting significance was an outgrowth of the Crafted with Pride initiative: **Quick-response manufacturing** (QR). This process gained importance in the late 1980s and really flourished in the 1990s. The goal was to shorten the cycle of production, placing both initial orders and re-orders into stores more quickly. Early advances shortened the fabric-to-store cycle from 66 to 40 weeks, and further acceleration occurred thereafter. Although the system used computer technology, including **Universal Product Codes** (bar codes) to track merchandise, QR's main feature was full integration of producers and retailers.

Advantages for both manufacturers and retailers were the increased turnover of merchandise and the reduction of investments tied up in inventory.[13] Goods were in the store when consumers wanted them and were replenished during the selling season, sometimes several times. By 1998, QR made it possible to refill the retailer's stock of popular garments in about 1 week.[14] Levi's and V-F Corporation were among the leaders in implementing QR.

Mass Customization

Another strategy to help U.S. manufacturers to survive was the move to mass customization, embodying a variety of methods to give ready-made apparel some of the individualized style and fit of more costly custom-made clothes. Computer programs, both proprietary and publicly available, processed a few critical measurements to adjust the basic pattern for a pair of jeans, for example, to the size of one customer. The resized pieces were cut and kept together for assembly by a team instead of being processed one sewing step at a time in the factory's usual bundle method of sewing, a method more akin to the assembly line manner of manufacturing from the beginning of the twentieth century. By the end of the decade, optical scans from [TC]² were able to gather more complete body measurements, although the follow-through process for fitting garments more precisely was only in the beginning stages.

coats, and jackets were all made under this tariff system during the early 1990s.

In 1984, the American Fiber, Fabric and Apparel Coalition launched a Crafted with Pride in the USA campaign, but it was doomed by the low priority American consumers assigned to country of origin compared with fit, price, and style.[12] Although many acknowledged the poor working conditions in Third World countries, the problems in apparel manufacturing were brought home when a scandal erupted in the United States in 1995. A group of seamstresses was discovered in a raid on a sweatshop in El Monte, California (outside Los Angeles), where garment workers were found working in the equivalent of prison-like conditions for as little as 70 cents per hour. The incident raised awareness of the problem, and both government and industry initiated programs to regulate the working conditions in apparel factories both in the United States and around the world.

Fashion Influences

Fashion trends came from a wide variety of sources, providing infinite options and opportunities for creating a personalized look. European fashion established luxury global brands such as Gucci, Prada, and Louis Vuitton, while U.S. designers focused on modern and more minimalist ready-to-wear. Fashionable designers presented a range of elaborate runway creations, some intended more as concept or art wear. These elaborate shows tended not to resonate with the mass apparel consumer. In general, offerings in department stores became more uniform. With an eclectic mix of designer and classic styles, accessories became ascendant, offering an element of individuality and of prestige that could set apart a basic wardrobe. Movies, music, and film continued to influence fashion particularly in the creation of subcultural looks for young people. Fashion models were stars throughout the decade, although the ideal image changed from one of strong and more toned bodies in the first few years to an extremely thin appearance in the last half of the period.

Photography and Illustration

In the last years of the 1980s, fashion photography, much in keeping with the trend to individualism, moved away from presenting ideal images to construction of lifestyles. The growth of the Internet, cable television shows that focused on fashion, and new fashion magazines made fashion imagery widely accessible. There was also an overlapping of techniques between traditional fashion photography and art, as a number of art photographers began to photograph fashion. Many of the photographers of the previous decades continued to contribute work to the major fashion publications, and a few new names emerged. Steven Meisel was one of the most influential. Meisel's specialty was in combining both the reality of the clothing with the pretenses of fashion as lifestyle (Figure 10.12). After a brief resurgence in the 1980s, illustration was largely absent from fashion publications, although there were a few exceptions. The illustrations of designers appeared on occasion, as did the works of Ruben Alterio and Gladys Perint Palmer (Figure 10.13).

The models of the late 1980s and early 1990s altered the image of the fashion model from one of straightforward clothing mannequin into power woman. A group of six became the super models of the early part of the period: Naomi Campbell, Cindy Crawford, Linda Evangelista, Elle MacPherson, Claudia Schiffer, and Christy Turlington. Evangelista in particular seemed to capture the attention of the press and public as she morphed her appearances into seemingly endless variations inspired by both the stars and the fashions of the past.

By 1993, however, a new model image began to appear, one that was young, rail thin, and underfed. It sparked controversy when Calvin Klein cast Kate Moss in his ad campaign. Described as the waif look or gamine look, it raised concern that it sent a potentially dangerous message to weight-obsessed teens (Figure 10.14). This extremely thin and verging on unhealthy look characterized the appearance of models for the next several years. Others who initially personified the grunge, waif, or heroin chic appearance were Kristen McMenamy and Stella Tenant.

The Designers

Numerous young and talented designers joined the ranks of already established names in the 1990s, many at the helm of venerable fashion houses. It was a critical time for many older, established ateliers, as they went looking for new designers. Two Englishmen, John Galliano and Alexander McQueen, became heads of the Paris design houses Dior and Givenchy, while American Tom Ford became creative director of Gucci. The influential designers will be discussed by

Figure 10.12 Steven Meisel photograph of a Jil Sander sweater and skirt. *Vogue*, October 1997, 352, Art and Commerce.

Figure 10.13 Gladys Perint Palmer illustration of Barbara Cirkva in a sheer lace dress by Karl Lagerfeld for Chanel. The *New York Times: Fashions of the Times*, spring 1993, 53. Reproduced by permission of *Gladys Perint Palmer*.

Figure 10.14 Kate Moss at a fashion show, 1993. ©Lilly Lane/Corbis.

location of the company and not nationality of the designer, although many continued to present lines independently in their own countries.

Europe

Two Italian leather companies became not only important ready-to-wear trendsetters in the 1990s, but also major super brands, creating ultimate desirability for their clothing and especially for their accessories. When venerable leather goods company Gucci hired **Tom Ford** as creative director in 1994, he created a modern and sensual look for the company that almost immediately propelled it into a major brand name. Inspired in part by the sleek Halston style of the 1970s, Ford's overtly sexy dresses and separates were enthusiastically acclaimed. He was extremely successful with a mod look, inspired by many of the modernist American designers of the past. Tom Ford was also instrumental in the

evolution of the Gucci Group into a luxury goods giant in the late 1990s, with his discerning sense of which styles were right for the time (Figure 10.15).

Miuccia Prada, granddaughter of founder Mario Prada, took over as director of Prada in 1978, making early successes with black nylon handbags and the baguette, which became an essential for fashion insiders. The first Prada womenswear line was presented in 1989. This was followed in 1993 by a more affordably priced line called Miu Miu, aimed at a younger market, and a menswear line in 1994. Prada introduced a unique style that could be described as eccentrically classic, using classic styles but with a twist that altered proportion or fit, and was made up in fabrics and colors that Miuccia Prada described as having a bit of bad taste.[15] Her combinations seemed to strike a fashion chord, however, and her mixing of diverse elements found a devoted clientele (Figure 10.16).

Other European luxury brands hired young and innova-

Figure 10.15 Tom Ford dress for Gucci, inspired by the 1970s, for Fall 1996. Firstview.com.

Figure 10.16 Miuccia Prada suit from Spring 1996, mixing textile textures and patterns. Firstview.com.

tive designers during the 1990s to recharge their images. These included American **Michael Kors** at Céline, owned by LVMH, and **Martin Margiela** at Hermès. Margiela was one of a group of Belgian avant-garde designers who influenced fashion in the 1990s with a deconstructed and unconventional aesthetic.[16] Although deconstruction was first introduced by the Japanese designers in the 1980s, the main proponents in the 1990s were from Belgium. Others in this group included **Ann Demeulemeester** and **Dries Van Noten.** Demeulemeester often paired unexpected fabrics or an assembly of garments or garment components that was deliberately askew or seemingly unfinished. Van Noten is known for his color sense and for creating looks that are often layered and antique in aesthetic rather than deconstructionist. German-born **Jil Sander** represented the antithesis of the design houses that expanded into multiple areas of fashion products and licensing. A minimalist designer who worked in luxury fabrics, she offered clothing that was clean lined and

modern. She also designed a men's collection that was equally modern. Her company was acquired by the Prada Group in 1999, and she left the company as head designer in 2000.

The viability of haute couture was again questioned in the early 1990s, after its resurgence in the 1980s. Some of the couture houses continued to be active, but all relied on their prêt-à-porter collections and other branded merchandise for financial survival. Although the Japanese designers made a name for themselves in Paris in the 1980s, in the 1990s it was two English designers who reigned. **John Galliano,** born in Gibraltar, grew up in London and graduated from Central St. Martin's College of Art, where he immediately gained fame with colorful and unconventional creations. He began to show his often historically inspired lines in Paris in the early 1990s. In 1995, he was named head designer for the house of Givenchy after Hubert de Givenchy's retirement. After two years he left to become creative director at the house of Dior, showing his first collection in spring 1997.

Figure 10.17 Oversized, hip-hop inspired clothing from Tommy Hilfiger for spring 1997. Firstview.com.

At Dior, he was able to let loose his often eclectic imagination, revitalizing both Dior and couture and making Dior another one of the super luxury brands of LVMH (Plate 10.1). Galliano created elaborate and theatrical fashion presentations both for Dior and under his own name.

Alexander McQueen, another Londoner and graduate of Central St. Martin's, was named designer of Givenchy at the age of 26 after Galliano left. McQueen also recognized and embraced the theatrical aspects of fashion early in his career. Sometimes dubbed the enfant terrible of fashion, he gained recognition early in his career for the use of style elements that were sometimes considered shocking. He left Givenchy shortly after the Gucci Group purchased a controlling interest in his own company in 2000.

United States

In the United States, ready-to-wear designers created identifiable brands that offered lifestyle dressing. **Tommy Hil-**

figer was very much representative of the designer success story of the 1990s and of the direction in which fashion appeared to be headed. Starting in 1985, he was sponsored by Murjani International to design men's casual clothing styled like that of Ralph Lauren but at a lower price point. When Murjani encountered financial difficulties, Hilfiger formed a partnership with a private-label contractor, founding the Tommy Hilfiger Corporation in 1992. Hilfiger, a blatant marketer of his brand and image, interpreted an American ready-to-wear style, often in red, white, and blue. In 1994, he gained a significant boost and new direction for the company when Snoop Doggy Dogg wore a rugby shirt—emblazoned with Tommy on the front and Hilfiger on the back—on *Saturday Night Live*. Sales skyrocketed, and he immediately recognized the potential of tapping into the black urban subculture. Altering the portions for the oversized look that was in style, he enlisted various rappers to wear his designs (Figure 10.17). He also continued to create more conservative clothing for men, and added a women's collection in the mid-1990s.

Isaac Mizrahi was one of the most publicized New York designers of the decade, creating classic American sportswear with a contemporary twist. A 1995 movie, *Unzipped,* documented his creative process and provided insight into the fashion world. Mizrahi opened his company in the late 1980s, after six years of working in the fashion industry. Inspired by the classic styles of American ready-to-wear designers such as Geoffrey Beene, Norman Norell, and Claire McCardell, his sophisticated design style and exuberant personality made him a favorite with the fashion industry. Unfortunately, he failed to find a consistent customer following and was forced to temporarily close his business in 1998.

Marc Jacobs began to build a reputation as a creative and innovative designer even while in college. After graduating from Parsons School of Design in 1984, he initially started his own business but was named designer for the Perry Ellis womenswear collection in 1988. He was successful at creating a sophisticated and young sportswear collection for the company. He infamously promoted the grunge trend at the designer level in the early 1990s (Figure 10.18). Few people were willing to pay high prices for clothing that had the appearance of originating in a thrift store, and he was released from his contract. He returned to successfully designing his own line in 1994, soon catching the eye of directors at LVMH. They provided him with financial backing and hired him to create a ready-to-wear collection for Louis Vuitton.

Anna Sui presented her first solo collection in 1991, blending high-fashion touches with both street styles and retro 1960s hippie elements. Sui targeted a young customer with her eclectic mixtures of design elements, and by the mid-1990s she was moving away from the 1960s influence toward 1920s inspirations.

In the late 1990s, a number of designers and companies appeared that targeted African American customers. With a particular orientation to young customers with a sense of urban street style, all these companies enjoyed commercial success. One of the first was **FUBU** (For Us, By Us), founded by friends Daymond John, Carl Brown, J. Alexander Martin, and Keith Perrin. The company specialized in clothing that defined an urban style for young blacks and gained a following when it enlisted rappers such as L.L. Cool J and Busta Rhymes to wear the label. Their intended target market was the young black customer who had been ignored by most apparel companies, but the look was quickly copied by suburban white teens. Also in 1992, Russell Simmons, founder of Def Jam Recordings in the 1980s, introduced a fashion line called Phat Fashions. The style was developed to bring hip-hop culture of the streets to the fashion world. His company grew rapidly and he added a womenswear line—Baby Phat—in 2000. In 1998, rapper Sean Combs launched a collection of sportswear under the name **Sean John**.[17] His aim was to create clothing with an urban sensibility that was both well made and fashion forward.

Fashion Trends

Definitions of fashion changed in the 1990s, with image and branding more important than seasonal style changes. The trend toward informality, led initially by casual Friday dressing, represented a significant change in how both men and women dressed for work, as corporate America went casual. It also meant a new approach to clothing purchases. The end of the millennium continued the postmodern trend, with many elaborate designer styles that reflected globalization and a mixing of unexpected combinations of historic and multicultural elements into one design. The viable alternative was minimalism, with clean lines and often neutral colors. There was an eclectic mix of style trends, some lasting only a year or two as many people began to view the fashions presented on runways as irrelevant to their lives. Some looks, such as hip-hop styles in the youth market, continued through the decade and beyond, but others, including grunge, the waif look, and the monastic look (a minimalist style, usually black, and sometimes worn with religiously based accessories), were very brief.

Textiles and Technology

One new fiber was introduced in the 1990s. The fiber lyocell, produced under the brand name Tencel, was devel-

oped to be a more environmentally safe fiber. Chemically similar to rayon fiber, lyocell uses production methods that allow recycling of the chemicals involved.

Advances began to appear in textiles and fashion, as many designers became fascinated with the creative possibilities of laser, chemical, and computer technologies. Textile innovation began to drive the creative processes, as apparel designers hired textile designers to work with new ideas. Some of the experimentation was reminiscent of the 1960s interest in space-age ideas and materials, and a few of the design names from the 1960s, such as Courrèges and Rabanne, resurfaced in the fashion press. The more experimental designers used latex rubber, neoprene, or other synthetic materials, often in combination with more traditional textiles. Others incorporated holographic processes,[18] inflatable garment structures, or fabrics that could be molded to the shape of a body, eliminating traditional complex tailoring. Issey Miyake, always experimental with textiles, patented a pleating process for a line he called Pleats Please.

Figure 10.18 The grunge look as envisioned by Marc Jacobs. *WWD*: 90th Anniversary, 2001.

The heat-set garments are pleated after they are cut and sewn (Figure 10.19).[19]

Computer technology was used more frequently to control both knitting and weaving processes, making it possible to create complex imagery or multilayered cloth with jacquard looms. The other direction in which designers began to turn was the development of smart textiles. A group of researchers at the Massachusetts Institute of Technology initiated a project to work with computer technology for creation of garments that could act as an aid to the wearer, incorporating wireless communications or solar power, for example.[20] Some Japanese companies began work with ceramic fibers designed to protect the wearer from ultraviolet rays. Many of these were still in the experimental stage at the end of the decade.

Women's Styles

From the late 1980s on, fashion became increasingly pluralistic and, despite proclamations from the fashion press

Figure 10.19 Pleated dress by Issey Miyake, 1994. ©Orban Thierry/Corbis Sygma.

about the look of a season, no single silhouette or hem length dominated. Women continued to create individual looks that may have contained elements of runway trends, but they placed their own interpretations on style. In the first years of the 1990s, the fashion pendulum seemed to swing continuously, moving from short to long skirts and back, from grunge to hip-hop to the monastic look, all of it injected with borrowings from the past and from other cultures. Designers seemed in search of their own individual styles and wanted to attract a loyal customer with a similar style sense.

The focus on individual construction of image therefore makes it more difficult to describe a range of widely adopted or representative styles for this period. General trends include the shift away from the broad-shouldered silhouette, a more casual approach to dressing, and a general loss of occasion-specific dressing, as casual clothing became acceptable for almost any event.

After all the garish color combinations of the 1980s, black and other neutrals became the most dominant colors of the late 1990s, although there was a brief trend for color blocking (Figure 10.20). Spandex began to be woven and knitted into many fabrications and was no longer limited to active sportswear or undergarments. As manufacturers and retailers kept one eye on global profits, the options available at retail often appeared homogeneous or as diluted versions of one or two trends, creating a similarity from one store to another that customers began to find uninspiring, and clothing sales in general sagged. The plus-size market gained in importance, as the population not only aged but got larger.

Dresses

Dresses came in a wide variety of styles, from short and boxy 1960s-inspired silhouettes to longer, 1920s influences. Although the gold and other decorative touches prominent in the 1980s continued for the first few years of the period, they began to give way to a simpler and more minimalist style. The wide-shouldered wedge dress also was shown briefly into the early 1990s, and, although shoulder pads for the most part disappeared, it was possible to purchase both broad-shouldered and decorative styles through catalogs well into the decade. There was a trend for close-fitting slip dresses in the mid-1990s that evolved into more structured sheath dresses, worn for all occasions and seasons (Figure 10.21). Longer dresses were also available, in shirtdress styles, and more draped shapes in soft floral patterns. The monastic look generated copies in simple shapes, most often in black. Although hem length varied throughout the decade, shapes generally became slimmer.

Evening and more formal dressing continued to exist,

despite the trend toward casual wear for all occasions. Evening dresses tended to more embellishment, with gathers and flounces in the late 1980s and early 1990s, getting slimmer and more sinuous by the end of the 1990s. Soft, drapable velvets became popular, particularly **devoré** or voided velvets, in which a design is etched into the fabric with chemicals that remove the pile (Figure 10.22).

Suits, Business Sportswear, and Coats

Separates allowed women more options for creating that sense of individual style. Although the trend to casual office wear lessened the emphasis on suits, these continued to be essential elements in most wardrobes, more often as mix-and-match components rather that matched jacket, skirt, or pant. The revival in popularity of the Chanel-style suit continued and was interpreted by numerous designers at many price points and in various fabrications (Figure 10.23). Like those of dresses, skirt lengths and widths varied. For jackets, the oversized silhouette with broad shoulders disappeared, although many jackets were relaxed in fit and made in soft fabrics, particularly in the first half of the decade (Figure 10.24). Designers also played with proportions, putting short tops over long shirts or long shirts with jackets.

Borrowing from various historical inspirations, some designers presented dart- or seam-fitted jackets reminiscent of the late 1940s. There was also a vogue for jackets that zipped up the front (Figure 10.25). Sweater twin sets borrowed from the 1950s were also worn with both pants and skirts and were sometimes beaded (Figure 10.26). Pants were either full and pleated or slim, with a flat front. In general, the trend was toward a narrower silhouette as the decade progressed. Skirts were very long for only a few seasons in 1992–1993 before becoming short, although for most women length was a matter of personal choice. In the mid-1990s, soft sarong wrapped style skirts were also popular.

Coats also came in a variety of styles, including long and full cut, long and closer to the body and an array of short styles. Fake fur became a fashion in the mid-1990s, shown in jackets, coats, and wraps or as trim on jackets and sweaters. The fur might present the appearance of real pelts or be dyed or designed to give a clearly faux appearance. Fluffy fiberfill or down jackets also were sold, both for sports and for daily wear.

Casual Sportswear, Separates, and Active Sport Clothing

The casual trend encompassed a vast range of leisure and sport clothing. Many of the casual pieces became wardrobe basics, changing slightly in style or fabrication from year to year. In the early 1990s, leggings continued to sell, shown with heavy boots as part of the grunge style. Oversized sweaters also continued to be worn over both skirts and pants. Jeans and T-shirts were typical in any wardrobe, while chinos were the casual pant of choice for many, including for dress-down days at the office. Capri pants also entered many wardrobes,

Figure 10.21 Sheath dress and coordinating jacket, 1995. ©Timothy Clary/AFP/Getty Images.

Figure 10.22 Long slender evening ensemble of devoré velvet. ©Jon Levy/AFP/Getty Images.

some in a fitted silhouette, others looser and more relaxed. There was a brief trend for what were called **city shorts**, a knee-grazing tailored short, sometimes with cuffs, and worn with a jacket, blazer, and/or blouse (Figure 10.27).

With sustained interest in exercise and other sports activities, athletic and active sport clothing enjoyed a significant market. Spandex blends, often in shiny fabrications, were used for leggings and bicycle shorts, a shorter version of leggings intended for cycling. A short, stretch tank top, styled like a sports bra, was also made for outerwear (Figure 10.28). Bathing suits were offered in tanks, two-piece bikini styles, thongs, and the **tankini**, a two-piece with tank top and separate bottom. There were also some historically inspired styles, with the draped and more structured shapes reminiscent of the 1950s.

Foundations and Lingerie

As the broad shoulders and loose cuts of the 1980s gradually gave way to natural shoulders and body-hugging cuts,

brassieres and foundations garments regained some of their role in shaping womanly curves. Some women continued to wear full-cup bras, whereas others adopted demi-cups. Straps padded to widen the wearer's shoulders constituted a minor fashion during the first half of the decade. Suits and dresses cut close to the body called for structured bras, and several push-up styles complemented décolleté necklines. In fact, major companies competed vigorously to use new technology, including polypropylene keels—rigid sections at the bottom of the cup—and gel inserts, to achieve maximum enlargement of smaller breasts. Sara Lee Corporation bought the Wonderbra brand in 1993 and in 1994 vigorously promoted its Wonderbra push up; brisk sales brought shortages of supply, contributing to the bra's mystique as a desirable garment (Figure 10.29). Strapless bras with smooth cups were offered in both short and more elongated bustier styles. In contrast to such figure maximizers, spandex lace camisoles, short and long, substituted for bras for women with firm breasts and high-fashion

Figure 10.23 Chanel inspired suit by Bill Blass. ©Jon Levy/AFP/Getty Images.

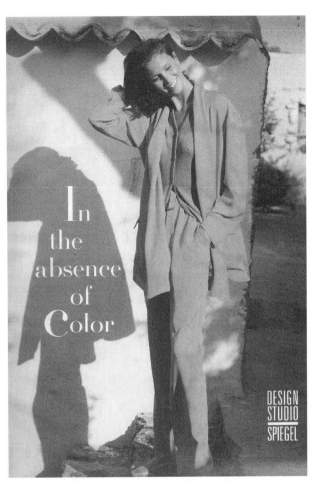

Figure 10.24 Soft and relaxed separates. Spiegel spring/summer 1994 catalog, 21.

tastes. At the other end of the fashion–function continuum, sports bras of myriad types, with and without underwires, helped joggers, runners, tennis players, and other athletes. Some sports bras could function as outerwear, such as the Nike style revealed by Brandi Chastain at the Olympics.

Lightweight spandex gave a new appeal to what were earlier called girdles but now bore the names body-briefers, panty smoothers, and thigh slimmers. Some control garments had high waists, whereas others stopped at or slightly below the natural waistline. Waist cinchers nipped in just that part of the anatomy. A few smoothers did for the derrière what the push-up bra did for the breasts: augment and accentuate what nature provided. All-in-one garments, with and without straps, shaped the entire torso. The conversion of traditional undergarments worn as outerwear continued, with a variety of boned corsets and bustiers for both day and evening. Among those clearly intended for public view was the sequined bustier offered by Badgley Mischka for $2,980.[21]

Colors in bras and other foundations adhered to the white–beige–black range, with occasional flashes of intense turquoise or purple or of pastel pinks and blues. Luxury was more a matter of lace and silky textiles than of the riotous prints and colors of the 1960s and 1970s. Such subtlety harmonized with the penchant for black, gray, and beige outerwear that typified the 1990s in urban areas of the northeast.

Panties ranged from natural waistline, to hipsters, to bikinis and thongs, but most had legs cut high on the thigh. Spaghetti-strap slips, tap pants (loosely cut legs, fitted waist), and minilength petticoats completed daytime lingerie. A lacy camisole, or a bra trimmed with a lace top to simulate a camisole, was sometimes chosen to fill the neckline of a tailored suit. The underwear-as-outerwear assortment included lacy leggings and even a complete dress of elastic lace to wear as an underlayer.

For nightwear, pajamas and gowns came in long and short versions, with straps, short sleeves, or long sleeves.

Figure 10.25 Slim fit, zip-front jacket and trousers from DKNY. First view.com.

Figure 10.26 Beaded twin set with skirt, 1999. ©Stan Honda/AFP/ Getty Images.

Some were utilitarian cotton flannelettes; others, satin with abundant lace trim. Wrap-and-tie robes, plus zippered styles, came in fluffy pile fabrics and silk charmeuse; colors spanned neutrals through pastels to jewel tones. Lounge-wear included styles similar to sweatsuits and elegant, draped gowns suitable for at-home entertaining.

Accessories

The predominance of wardrobe basics, with little dramatic change from season to season, created a desire for accessories as status items, especially the logo bags, scarves, and watches of luxury brands like Gucci, Louis Vuitton, and Prada. In the United States, Kate Spade created a revolution in handbags, with her colorful designs, often in

brightly colored fabrics but relatively simple shapes. Spade won the Council of Fashion Designers Award in 1996 for New Fashion Talent in Accessories. The popularity of designer handbags, including Spade's, also led to a wave of illegal copies. Many women and some men also wore a bag attached to a belt worn around the upper hip sometimes called a "fanny pack."

The wedge shoe style was popular in the mid-1990s, and, by the end of the decade, stiletto heels with pointed toes were standard for dress. The platform shoe reappeared, the more extreme versions most popular with the junior market, but platform sneakers and espadrilles also were worn. Square, blunt toes were common in these designs. However, women could choose from a wide variety of styles, from

Figure 10.27 City shorts and coordinated jacket. Spiegel spring/summer 1993 catalog, 46.

Figure 10.28 Active wear with sport bra style top and leggings. ©Cathrine Wessel/Corbis.

low-heeled walking shoes, menswear–inspired oxfords, slides, and mules. Boots in a variety of styles were also worn throughout the decade.

Jewelry was also subject to the individualism of the period. Some wore bold and geometric styles, whereas others chose classic and quieter styles. First Lady Barbara Bush created a style trend with her three-strand pearl necklaces.

Men's Styles

As more and more designers entered the business of men's fashion, choices expanded and styles became more varied, sometimes to the dismay of male shoppers. Like women's fashion, the choices seemed to split between the avant-garde, often experimental, styles shown on the runway and the traditional, classic options that many men favored. Most men kept to a relatively conservative appearance. The decade began with bold-shouldered power suits, but the suit quickly lost ground to the supremacy of separates, with less formal jackets paired with pants, vests, and sweaters in mix-and-match combinations (Figure 10.30). The most pervasive change of the decade was casual wear. American designers, in particular, excelled at responding to the demand for less formal apparel for the office.

Suits and Outerwear

Despite the predominance of casual clothing, the suit was still a standard wardrobe item for many men. Both Italian

Figure 10.29 Wonderbra® by Sara Lee. ©Julian Wasser/Getty Images.

Figure 10.30 Men's separates modeled by designers Larry Harshbarger (right) and Ray Willis. ©Roger Ressmeyer/Corbis.

and English tailoring were fashionable, with U.S. menswear companies suffering from both the imports and the casual trend. The broad-shouldered silhouette of the beginning of the decade gave way to a slimmer silhouette that included one-, two-, three-, and even four-button styles (Figure 10.31). Both single and double-breasted options were available. By the end of the decade styles were very streamlined, and suits began to return as office wear, as the casual dress trend receded slightly. Trousers were available in a variety of cuts, from slim and flat front to pleated, although pleated pants were less popular at the end of the decade.

Shirts were still in basic colors, usually white, pastels, or narrow stripes, but darker colors became a trend late in the decade. French blue shirts and colored shirts with white collars were also popular. Men's fashion continued to be defined by details. Collars, for example, were offered in many variations. The casual wear trend led to other

shirt choices with a suit, including polo shirts, knit tops, and sweaters.

Men's coat styles included the traditional range of top-coats, trench styles, and parkas. As suits became slimmer, so did overcoats. Leather jackets and western-inspired styles were also worn, as were variations of the traditional navy **pea coat**.

Casual Dressing

Khakis or chinos and cargo pants were the dominant style for pants, influenced in part by the dynamic advertisements of The Gap. Even fashion critic Carrie Donovan appeared in advertisements for the casual style of Old Navy, the lower-price store owned by The Gap. Chinos were combined with a variety of casual shirt styles, including the traditional polo shirt; sport shirts in solids, stripes, and especially plaids; and rugby shirts (Figure 10.32). The T-shirt, of course, remained a wardrobe staple. As in the

previous decade, how clothing was worn was important. For example, as part of the grunge style plaid shirts were worn tied around the waist, whereas the more preppy approach was to wear a sweater tied around the shoulders.

For athletic wear, warm-up suits continued to sell, as did sweatpants and sweatshirts. Like women's styles, men's active wear included bicycle shorts and tank-style tops with significant amounts of spandex.

Shoes and Accessories

Shoe styles became less occasion-specific with the trend to casual styles. Oxfords and wingtips continued to be worn with suits, but, as business separates became more relaxed, loafers, deck shoes, and even athletic shoes might be worn. Doc Martens and other boot styles were popular, as were athletic shoes that came in a wide range of colors and styles. Although athletic shoes were designed for specific activities—running, tennis, basketball—many people simply wore them as a fashion statement (Figure 10.32).

Underwear and Sleepwear

Men's underwear diversified in patterns and colors, with boxer shorts offered in various dark solid colors, plaids, stripes, paisley, and sports motifs. Briefs, both waist-length and bikini styles, were typically white, gray, or dark solids. Long-legged briefs were offered, and a nylon-span-

Figure 10.31 (ABOVE) Men's four-button suit by Kenneth Cole. ©AP Photo/Louis Lanzano/AP Wide World.

Figure 10.32 (RIGHT) Men's casual wear separates by Paco Rabanne for fall/winter 1997/98. ©Cardinale Stephane/Corbis Sygma.

dex body trimmer claimed to spiff up the wearer on days he was feeling less than fit. Undershirts could be acquired in short-sleeved crew and V-necks or in tank style (Figure 10.33).

Nightwear had considerable variety. Nightshirts of flannel, jersey, or lightweight woven cotton came in stripes, novelty prints, and holiday-themed styles. Standard kimono bathrobes varied little in cut but diversified in colors—jewel tones, dark stripes, geometrics—and materials—velour, terry cloth, twill paisley, or seersucker for summer. Short or long robes were worn, and there were even some hooded maxi styles. One menswear catalog showed a short velour robe over shirt and trousers, explaining that it was for after work relaxation and admitting sheepishly it once was called a smoking jacket.

Teen Styles

Fashion in the teen world was more segmented into styles that were identified with specific street or subcultural looks. The fashion for those in their teens and early twen-

Figure 10.33 Calvin Klein ribbed tank undershirt and Fruit of the Loom boxer briefs. *DNR* May 7, 1999, 18, photograph by George Chinsee, courtesy of Fairchild Archives.

ties continued as it had in the past to be mostly antifashion, although some trends were widely adopted and crossed over from one group to another. The adolescent market was influenced by MTV, as well as by some of the trends from the past, but the dominant look for young men was inspired by rap and hip-hop. Although this style started out primarily in the urban black music culture, in the 1990s it was widely adopted by suburban white youth. The clothing was extremely oversized, with loose jeans, bagged at the ankle, oversized shirt and sweatshirts, and either heavy boots or athletic shoes. For adolescent girls, fashion included hip-hop looks but more often a combination of styles from the 1960s and inspirations from female rock performers. Girls and young women's clothing was generally more fitted than that of boys, but frequently included layers, with vests over blouses or dresses over leggings (Figure 10.34). Brand names were just as important for both teen and children's clothing as for adults and became status symbols in the same way. By the end of the decade, most of the major brands, such as FUBU, DKNYKids, Tommy Hilfiger, and Ralph Lauren, were available in clothing for teens and even children.

Children's Styles

Children, like adults, enjoyed a wide range of clothing choices in the 1990s, shaped by many of the same influences. The entertainment industry, musicians, fashions from the past—all could be seen in the eclectic mix. For young girls, skirt lengths could be midthigh or down to the ankle (Figure 10.35). Mod and other sixties influences were seen, as well as some of the urban, streetwear styles. Television cartoon characters from shows such as *The Simpsons* or, for younger children, *Sesame Street* and *Barney,* were licensed for apparel.

A major shift in clothing trends for young children was the expanded color range that now included pastels, saturated brights, and, by the end of the decade, even some of the dark neutrals so popular in adult clothing. Casual clothing was the standard for both boys and girls and included jeans, cargo pants, and khakis, and, although much casual children's clothing could be considered unisex, there were some distinct differences (Figure 10.36). For girls, the same cargo pant styling, with numerous pockets, could also be found in skirts. For the most part, fashions for boys and girls followed that of teenagers, if slightly modified for age appropriateness. Girls, like teens, wore bell-bottom pants inspired by the 1960s and even cropped tops that exposed bare midriffs. Young boys were more inclined to wear the oversized pant style. T-shirts, polo shirts, and rugby shirts were standard for boys and were also worn by girls. Despite the predominance of casual attire, there con-

Figure 10.34 Dresses worn with leggings and military style boots were popular with teens and young adults, 1993. Fairchild archives.

Figure 10.35 Girls' long floral skirt and polo top. *Talbot's kids catalog,* fall 1998, 13, courtesy of Talbot's kids.

tinued to be a market for special-occasion dress clothing for both boys and girls.

The footwear of choice for children was athletic shoes in a seemingly infinite variety of styles, often with special features such as flashing lights in the soles. The trend for hiking-style boots for adults filtered down to children's markets. Backpacks were the essential accessory for school-age children, although concern began to arise about the amount of weight they were carrying to and from school on a daily basis (Figure 10.37).

In underwear, briefs and tank shirts for little girls came in white, delicate prints and pastel solids. One undershirt style was billed as a camisole, relating it to adult womenswear. Frilly nightgowns were typical, some with a drop waist in what was called ballerina style. Robes and sleepwear were often coordinated in color or pattern. Flannelette and terry cloth were used, as was some synthetic velour.

Boys' briefs were white, dark solids, bright stripes, or small (often themed) prints. Tank shirts were shown. Like girls sleepwear, boys' robes and pajamas matched up. Terry cloth robes were popular for summerwear, ski pajamas for winter use.

Hair and Grooming

Hairstyles for women reflected the fashion diversity of the decade, as both hair and makeup were viewed as a mark of individuality. Many younger women experimented with hairstyle and color, but both short and long styles were worn. The revival of 1960s styles created a fashion for long straight hair with young girls (see Figure 10.35). Makeup was more natural in color and application than in the previous decade. Hats for women were not worn much except for protection from inclement weather, and for some groups they remained a fashion item for church and special occasions.

Figure 10.36 Children's characteristic casual clothing—jeans, T-shirts, and athletic shoes. ©Photograph by Ariel Skelley/The Image Bank/Getty Images.

Figure 10.37 Young boy wearing baggy jeans and sweater and carrying a backpack. ©Photograph by Jose Luis Pelaez, Inc./Blend Images/Getty Images.

Tattooing and body piercing, associated with punk and other subcultures in earlier decades, became a more widespread fad during the 1990s. Many young women no longer pierced their ears just once but did multiple piercings, which also might include the navel, eyebrows, and tongue. Young men also began to sport jewelry worn in pierced body parts.

Men wore their hair in various styles and lengths, again a symbol of individualism, although for the most part styles were short. Other than for cold weather protection, hats were not much worn. Baseball caps, however, were popular with young boys and adolescents, the way they were worn sometimes a symbol of group identification.

Summary

It would seem easy to define the 1990s as a time of anything goes in fashion, when dress codes seemed to dramatically diminish. The trend for casual dressing occurred not only in the office but also for more formal social occasions. This plurality of dress in fact meant a more complex approach to style involving choices that were intended to express a person's individuality. Few people unquestioningly obeyed the fashion press or fashion designers when they made statements about the latest trends. In the youth culture, however, there continued to be interest in fashion and group identity. Some designers attempted to use street and subcultural fashions as inspirations, but it did not translate well to a more commercial market. An eclectic mix of ethnic and retro became the major source of inspiration for designers throughout the 1990s and into the new millennium, although most people continued to follow an individual approach to dressing, a true example of the postmodern to fashion.

Suggested Readings

Agins, Teri. *The End of Fashion: The Mass Marketing of the Clothing Business.* New York: William Morrow and Company, 1999.

Braddock, Sarah E., and Marie O'Mahony. *Techno Textiles: Revolutionary Fabrics for Fashion Design.* New York: Thames and Hudson, 1998.

Gershenfeld, Neil. "Digital Dressing, or Software to Wear." *The New York Times Magazine: Men's Fashion of the Times*, March 24, 1996, 14.

Johnson, Haynes. *The Best of Times: America in the Clinton Years.* New York: Harcourt Inc., 2001.

Jones, Terry, and Avril Mair, eds. *Fashion Now: I-D selects the World's 150 Most Important Designers.* London: Taschen, n.d.

Oxoby, Mark. *The 1990s.* Westport, CT: Greenwood Press, 2003.

Rosen, Ellen Israel. *Making Sweatshops: The Globalization of the U.S. Apparel Industry.* Berkeley: University of California Press, 2002.

Steele, Valerie. *Fashion, Italian Style.* New Haven: Yale University Press, 2003.

CHAPTER 11

2000-

Stocks Down,

2004

U.S. Events and Trends	Federal election: G. W. Bush vs. A. Gore Stock market downturn begins	September 11 terrorist attacks	War in Afghanistan; Taliban toppled Business scandals erupt	Invasion of Iraq; Saddam Hussein deposed, captured Economic rebound begins	Federal election: G. W. Bush again vs. J. Kerry Apparel industry prepares for the end of quotas on imports

2000 **2001** **2002** **2003** **2004**

U.S. Fashions		New York fashion regroups Red-white-blue fashions Textured hair	Yves Saint Laurent retires Pronounced eclecticism in fashion	[TC]^2 sizing census Tweeds become big fashion	Women's jackets popular Men's suit sales rebound Preppy styles revived Fad for striped shirts Tapered-leg jeans return

Dressing Up

O<!---->**ceans** of champagne and tons of confetti welcomed the year 2000, along with sighs of relief that the dreaded millennium bug had not brought the world's computers to a halt. Depending on point of view, people's moods were ebullient or reflective, optimistic or pessimistic, but few guessed at the drastic changes that loomed in the new era. Arguments raged over whether 2000 or 2001 constituted the new century or the new millenium. For convenience, we will use the term early 2000s.

Politics and War

American life in 2000 was dominated by a fiercely fought election, which was decided only after recounts—complicated by confusion in voting procedures—and a Florida Supreme Court decision to end Al Gore's challenge and pave the way for George W. Bush's victory. The closeness of the contest demonstrated how nearly balanced the American electorate was between Republicans and Democrats. New jargon entered the U.S. vocabulary, when states that voted for Mr. Gore were labeled blue states and those that selected Mr. Bush were termed red states. Although politicians debated their classic political positions over the size of government, its role in American life, and the management of the economy, the hottest disputes involved cultural matters, including gun control, abortion, gay rights, and the permissible levels of sexuality and violence in media, arts, and entertainment.

Violence at a devastating level struck on September 11, 2001, producing nearly 3,000 deaths and briefly fusing red and blue into a red-white-and-blue whole. Americans of all regions and persuasions burst out in tricolor and flag motifs, on jackets, sweaters, caps, neckties, pins, T-shirts, and other apparel (Figure 11.1).[1]

Stunned Americans realized they were vulnerable to attack by terrorists, as 19 al-Qaeda[2] members flew planes into New York City's World Trade Center twin towers and the Pentagon in Washington, DC. A fourth plane crashed in a Pennsylvania field instead of into a government building in Washington, where it was presumably aimed, thanks to the heroic intervention of the passengers on United Airlines Flight 93. Politics were temporarily set aside as unified leaders strove to cope with the physical destruction and loss of life. Americans from every state and sympathetic citizens of many nations gave emotional, material, and personal support to assist the bereaved and traumatized New Yorkers, Washingtonians, and Pennsylvanians. New York suffered the worst of the attack, losing an estimated 100,000 jobs as a direct result.

Congress quickly enacted security measures to try to prevent recurrence of such a tragedy. Airports and public

Figure 11.1 An American flag inspired design (2001) by Catherine Malandrino. Fairchild archives.

buildings bristled with new equipment for screening, and long lines typified airports, where passengers had to shed outer clothing and shoes and have bags searched for dangerous materials. Scares about deadly anthrax spores sent through the mail broke out in late 2001 and 2002. Americans were decidedly edgy, as a new Department of Homeland Security enacted a color-coded threat designation to communicate the level of safety measures required.

Determined to take the fight to the terrorists, the United States in early 2002 attacked the Taliban regime in Afghanistan, which had harbored al-Qaeda, inflicting serious damage on the terrorist infrastructure and bringing an end to Taliban rule. This operation had broad support internationally. More controversial was the spring 2003 preparation for war against the dictator Saddam Hussein in Iraq, who was believed at the time to have weapons of mass destruction or be in the process of obtaining such weapons. The United Nations withheld sanction for the war, for reasons that are still debated. Europeans were divided, with

France and Germany opposed and Italy, Spain, and—most prominently—England in favor. Hussein was toppled on April 10 and captured December 15. War continued, but control was ceded to an interim Iraqi government, and efforts at reestablishing a new, broadly acceptable permanent government proceeded, despite difficulties, through 2004. American troops, although suffering casualties, remained in Iraq in significant numbers while working to train Iraqi troops to thwart dissidents.

Controversy about the Iraqi conflict featured prominently in America's 2004 presidential campaign, but economic policies and cultural issues similar to those that characterized the 2000 election were debated intensely. Massachusetts Senator John Kerry challenged George W. Bush, without electoral success. The campaign used electronic communications to an unprecedented degree. Both Kerry's and Bush's supporters raised money via the Web and argued political topics on their respective Web logs (blogs).

Economic Conditions

By the end of 1999, the so-called dot-com boom was petering out. Companies operating without profits or prospects of becoming profitable began to fail. Early 2000 brought a downturn in the U.S. stock market. Stock brokerages, advertising agencies, airlines, media companies, and computer technology companies experienced serious erosion of business.

Then came the September 11, 2001, terrorist attacks, creating further economic turmoil. Everyone had to operate under new conditions, including the fashion industry, which sustained a heavy blow, because the attacks occurred when New York designers were beginning to show Spring 2002 lines.[3] Marc Jacobs had hosted a gala bash to launch a new fragrance and his apparel collection on September 10; Diane von Furstenberg, Catherine Malandrino, and the Badgley–Mischka team also had shown their designs. Many others were less fortunate. Oscar de la Renta, who was scheduled to show in Bryant Park, and Donna Karan, who had booked the New York State Armory building, had to change their plans. The Armory became a center for emergency services instead of a fashion venue. Many apparel firms had all they could do to help stranded employees find temporary lodging and get in touch with family members in the immediate aftermath of the calamity. Later in September, some designers presented collections by private appointment or put on small showings. *Vogue* and Style.com sponsored a group show for 10 smaller design firms, in Carolina Herrera's showroom, generously lent for the occasion. Overall, the fashion industry overcame its usual competitive tone to emphasize camaraderie and determination to help New York City and its industry weather the crisis.

The president and Congress struggled to formulate relief packages and tax cuts to help beleaguered companies (and consumers) and to give them a chance to recover profitability. By 2003, a rebound was occurring, although it was unevenly spread through economic sectors. Whereas business outlays flagged, consumer spending picked up the slack. In part, low interest rates had enabled consumers to incur large mortgages and to take second mortgages. Housing boomed, and prices rose through 2004.

Other factors in America's turbulent economy were the business scandals that undermined confidence. Company accounts were falsified to make balance sheets look strong for firms that were deeply in debt or losing money. Entities such as Enron (an energy trader), World Com (telecommunications), and Arthur Andersen (accounting) went out of business, harming many innocent employees, shareowners, and pension holders. Congress quickly enacted the Sarbannes-Oxley law to force companies of all sizes to overhaul their accounting and reporting practices. Gradually, many guilty parties were tried and sentenced, some messes were cleaned up, and many companies' balance sheets returned to positive territory. However, a number of those who lost jobs and pensions did not recover financially.

Europe struggled with its own set of challenges in the early 2000s. First, the unified European currency, the euro, debuted as the everyday medium of exchange in 12 countries. This was successful in some respects, easing cross-border trade, but use of the euro imposed conditions on governments with different economic circumstances that invited violation of a stability-and-growth pact that was supposed to cap government debt and curb inflation. For various reasons, Euro-area economies lagged behind activity in the United States during much of the period of 2000–2004. However, European prospects began to improve in 2004, and the euro strengthened against the dollar. In that year Europe also confronted the tricky matter of admitting to the European Union (EU) 10 more countries, many from the former Soviet bloc. New strains were placed on EU budgets by assistance to the poorer new members; western countries also faced the prospect of lower-cost labor drawing jobs away from their higher-waged economies.

Outsourcing of jobs to developing nations, notably China and India, created problems for both Europe and the United States.[4] Chinese businesses manufactured a huge array of products, including apparel and textiles. Office work, such as phone centers and computer programming, migrated to India, with its educated, English-speaking middle class. Trade, too, became a complex matter. No country wanted to expose itself to too much competition; bilateral (two-country or two-bloc) trade deals were signed, to the detriment of multilateral world trade. Nonetheless, manufacturing continued to dwindle in the developed world, where economies depended increasingly on service professions. Even those were vulnerable to developing world incursions. Optimism jostled with apprehension among American working people. Antiglobalization agitators frequently assailed trade meetings and conclaves of international bankers.

Demographics

American demographics offered a mixture of benefits and problems. Unlike most of Europe, where fertility stood below replacement levels (1.4 children per childbearing-age woman), America had a fertility rate close to replacement level (which is 2.1).[5] Even China, which strictly enforced a policy of one child per couple, had a 1.8 level in 2003. However, U.S. immigration, both legal and illegal, remained active. More people were admitted to the United States in the 1990s than in any previous decade: in 2002, 33 million U.S. residents had been born elsewhere. America's median age of 36 years was below Europe's (38 years) and was projected to stabilize as Europe aged further.

Among immigrants, Hispanics were most numerous, but much diversity characterized the newcomers. Population continued to shift southward and westward. A growing number of cities of large and medium size had majority–minority populations, meaning that those cities, non-Hispanic whites constituted a minority of the population. Both political and purchasing power grew among all minorities. America's suburbs continued to evolve, too. About one-half of all Americans lived in suburbs, whereas fewer than one-third of Europeans lived outside of cities. Suburbs became more socioeconomically diverse, including poor, middle class, and wealthy people. Businesses flourished in suburbs, where 90 percent of new office buildings were sited.

Growing segments of the population included senior citizens (65–80 years old); the oldest-old (over 80 years); and college-agers, termed the echo boomers. Families with empty nests—children gone from home—multiplied, stimulating sales of recreational and hobby equipment and encouraging travel. Americans' physical characteristics changed, too: obesity and overweight typified an ever greater number of people. Average height was declining, partly a result of recent arrivals from Latin America and Asia, where heights are less on average than among northern and western Europeans and their American descendents.

These shifts affected clothing, as companies grappled with problems of realistic sizing for very large and very small customers. In 2003, [TC]^2, a Cary, North Carolina, group, coordinated a sizing census, using body scanning technology to take three-dimensional measurements of 10,000 men and women to replace old tables of measurements based on 1940s data (Figure 11.2). The goal was to make these statistics available to sponsors of the project and to manufacturers who paid a fee.[6] The highly successful women's specialty chain Chico's converted standard size designations to numbers 0 through 3, rather than 6 through14, in one example of vanity sizing.[7] The Gap planned to launch a new a division in 2005 to capture the over-35 age group with appealingly styled and sized apparel. Some department stores (such as Saks Fifth Avenue) established a plus-size salon, grouping up-market labels for sizes 16 to 24. Designers, on the whole, resisted doing apparel for sizes above 12, although 48.8 percent of American women wore size 12 or larger. Among minority populations, the number of overweight women exceeded 70 percent.[8]

Medicine and Technology

Old and new challenges confronted the medical profession in the years after 2000. Health professionals directed major efforts at controlling and treating AIDS, with some success. Frightening diseases erupted in Asia and threatened to spread around the world; these included the SARS (severe acute respiratory syndrome) epidemic and the outbreak of avian influenza. One prevailing fear was that animal-based diseases would mutate and begin to spread person to person, not just animal to person. Bioterrorism hovered threateningly in the background, leading to efforts to stockpile vaccines for smallpox, anthrax, and similar killer diseases.

Medicine improved its ability to diagnose and treat chronic diseases. Some cancers came to be regarded by physicians as chronic diseases, to be controlled by gradual measures, for better quality of life. Modest progress was made in mitigating the effects of Parkinson's and Alzheimer's diseases by medication and lifestyle changes. The mapping of the human genome yielded insights into the relationship of particular genes to specific diseases and their variants. The possibility of individually tailored treatments for disease and the use of gene modifications (gene therapy) for amelioration of some conditions held promise for the future. Other intriguing but controversial treatments required use of stem cells, multipotential cells that were generally derived from human embryos; this provoked an outcry from pro-life groups, which supported a search for other sources of stem cells that did not require the use of embryos as commodities.

Lifestyle medicine also became more complicated and pervasive. Physicians and nutritionists sought ways to stem the spread of severe obesity. Bariatric surgeons reduced the sizes of the stomach in dire cases. Nutrition specialists argued for balanced nutriments and smaller portions, but fad diets—notably the various low-carbohydrate regimens—enjoyed an avid following. These were fading in popularity by the end of 2004. Elective surgeries were performed increasingly on face or body for cosmetic purposes. In 2002, American women and men, including adolescents, had 6.9 million cosmetic procedures (surgical and injection), more than triple the number performed in 1997.[9] Face lifts, eyelid surgery, tummy tucks, liposuction, and breast augmentation ranked among the most popular procedures.[10]

For those leery of the knife, there was the needle, filled with botulinus toxin (Botox), which freezes facial muscles and reduces certain kinds of age lines. Expensive external techniques entailed application of special creams and lotions, some produced by physicians-turned-cosmeticians. Makers couched their claims for beauty creams in relatively vague terms to ward off lawsuits if significant benefits were not forthcoming.

Whereas biotechnology flourished, promising even industrial applications, such as microorganisms to clean up environmental pollutants, publicly funded space exploration suffered from the disintegration of the shuttle Columbia in 2003, killing its seven astronauts. Privately funded efforts succeeded where NASA bureaucracy had failed. Entrepreneurs managed to develop craft that could reach suborbital levels, feeding the hope for commercial space travel.

Fashion drew upon technology in a very visible way when Apple introduced its version of a digital audio player, the iPod. The stylish design and rapid introduction of fashionable covers made it the accessory *du jour* among hip young people, who wore them as status symbols. Macintosh's business fortunes revived dramatically with the popularity of iPods and from the company's embrace of the Unix operating system. Among personal digital accessories, Blackberries (nicknamed crack-berries for their supposed addictive power) offered instant access to e-mail along with cell-phone capability and computing in a size that could fit easily in the hand.

Sports

Fashionable athletes included tennis stars Serena and Venus Williams, soccer luminary David Beckham and his wife Victoria, a former member of The Spice Girls rock band. The 2004 Summer Olympics in Greece centered world attention on all things Greek, helping confirm a trend toward draped goddess gowns of sheer, flowing silk, and other close-to-the-body draped designs.

Figure 11.2 A body scanner producing an image with multiple points of measurement. Courtesy of [TC]², Cary, NC.

Arts and Entertainment

Like apparel, the world of the arts and entertainment showed considerable diversity during the years 2000–2004 and fragmentation of markets much like those for apparel.

Music

One prominent feature of popular music in the early 2000s was its ubiquity. Computer technology made it easy to share music files, arousing the ire of both recording companies and artists. Among genres, rap still reigned, with practitioners Sean "P. Diddy" Combs and Eminem continuing in popularity. Hard rock also had an audience, mostly young and male, with bands such as Linkin Park. Numerous new artists not only launched recording careers but also entered the fashion business, following in the footsteps of artists such as Sean Combs and Jennifer Lopez. Lopez's line, called J. Lo by Jennifer Lopez rapidly became one of the more successful. Kanye West, Jay-Z, and Gwen Stefani all introduced clothing lines. Stefani's line, L.A.M.B., mimicked the clothing she wore on stage, including bikini tops and low-slung pants (Figure 11.3). Celebrities largely replaced professional models on the covers of fashion magazines between the mid-1990s and the early 2000s.[11]

Country-and-western music gained new fans as it crossed over into a rock and roll–influenced mode; Alison Krauss, Faith Hill, and the Dixie Chicks had strong followings. Reality television also invaded the music world with *American Idol*, making household names out of some of the contestants, at least a few of whom are maintaining music careers.

Television, Movies, and Theater

Reality television persisted, with offerings including Donald Trump's *The Apprentice, Survivor,* and makeover formats, including *Queer Eye for the Straight Guy*, in which five gay men assist straight men to improve their fashion selections and home décor. Fashion also entered the reality scene with *Project Runway*, a competition among both designers and models for a final prize that included an opportunity to

Figure 11.3 Gwen Stefani showing L.A.M.B. styles. ©Photo by Mark Mainz/Getty Images.

show a collection at New York's seasonal fashion presentations in Bryant Park. Cable television drew larger audiences than networks with shows such as the *Sopranos*, although the networks also had some resounding hits, such as *West Wing* and various law and medical programs. The cable series *Sex and the City* ended in 2004, but Sarah Jessica Parker's celebrity continued. Of course a large number of teens and young adults preferred video games, notably online games, to any television programs.

Technology continued to raise audience expectations for special effects in films, particularly animated films. In fact, hand-drawn animation largely ended during this period, replaced by computer animation. Live-action movies often came in series, such as J. R. R. Tolkien's *Lord of the Rings* trilogy and the first *Harry Potter* films. *The Matrix* continued to have a large following and perhaps confirmed the popularity of black clothing. Period films with fashion impact included *Moulin Rouge, Chicago,* and *The Aviator.* More than film costume, stars' wardrobes helped to launch or reinforce fashions. Designers fell over themselves to dress celebrities for so-called red carpet events, when the cameras would be rolling for the viewing of millions and the stars revealed *who* they were wearing. Such events grew to include not only film and television award ceremonies but also music and fashion events (Figure 11.4). There were even films about the fashion industry itself, including the 2001 *Zoolander.* The Bridget Jones novels, the story of a year in the dating and work life of a 30-something single woman, were made into popular movies and added new words such as singleton to the vocabulary.

Product placement in the movies and on celebrities in general was hardly new. Reece's Pieces shot to fame as the lure that caught E.T. in the eponymous movie of the 1980s. However, the trend went much further in 2000–2004. Sarah Jessica Parker almost single-handedly launched fashions for name-plate necklaces, flower pins, and of course stiletto heels by Manolo Blahnik, Jimmy Choo, and other designers. Stores as well as designers sent sample goods to film and television personalities, hoping for publicity. By this technique Intuition, a small boutique in west Los Angeles, managed to promote Ugg boots, "Oy veh"–inscribed T-shirts, and Jelly Kelly handbags—brightly colored rubber imitations of the costly Hermès leather versions.[12]

Among theater offerings, *Rent* was highly popular, as was *The Producers*, although the music from Broadway did not generally become mainstream listening.

Retailing and Manufacturing

Rapid change in the apparel sector derived from a mix of expanded technology, globalization, and shifting relation-

Figure 11.4 Actress Charlize Theron arrives to the Academy Awards ceremony wearing a Gucci dress. *Women's Wear Daily,* March 2, 2004, 5.

Figure 11.5 Isaac Mizrahi promoting his alliance with Target, June 21, 2003. ©Photo by Frederick M. Brown/Getty Images.

ships among the parts of the retail chain. Department stores in the mid-price range (Macy's, Dillard's, and Bloomingdale's—the latter also a high-end retailer of designer clothing) continued to stay afloat but did not thrive in the early 2000s as much as luxury chains, such as Neiman-Marcus, and the livelier mass-market stores. Among the latter, Target flourished as a trendy purveyor of low-priced goods; the chain gained cachet from unique designer alliances, including Michael Graves in the home and garden area and Isaac Mizrahi and Liz Lange in apparel (Figure 11.5). JCPenney revived, helped by fashion brands such as nicole by Nicole Miller. *Louis Rukeyser's Wall Street* newsletter reported that private-label merchandise generated 40 percent of Penney's revenue; 80 percent of Target's clothing was private label.[13] Niche stores also grew steadily. Chico, a chain devoted to women aged 35–55 years, operated more than 400 stores by 2003. Christopher and Banks shunned fashion-forward merchandise and sold comfortable apparel to women in

their forties. Teen merchants, including Hot Topic and Abercrombie & Fitch, enjoyed remarkable growth, as did Victoria's Secret, which reached young customers while also offering selections for adults.

Mass merchandisers often had leverage over their suppliers. Levi Strauss, Inc., overhauled its manufacturing and distribution system in order to sell a new label called Signature to mighty Wal-Mart. The process, often painful, cut production of a new season's styles from 12 to 15 months to 7½ to 10 months. Merchandise passed through fewer steps in distribution, putting it in stores faster.[14] After a rocky start, Signatures began to do creditable business, but not all Wal-Mart ventures succeeded. Its George brand of apparel languished in the United States, although it was popular in Wal-Mart's Asda chain in Britain.[15] In 2000, Target became one of the founders of World Wide Retail Exchange, an Internet business-to-business (B2B) marketplace serving 60 members; this competed against the proprietary online trading system used by Wal-Mart and its suppliers.[16] Heavy retail competition drove mergers among purveyors of apparel and other consumer goods. Sears acquired Lands' End in 2002 but was itself scooped up by Kmart in 2004.

E-tailing prospered: eBay added sale of apparel to its existing auction house functions. Online sources for fashions grew in popularity, as did sites for other types of products. Merchants of all types faced laser shoppers, who were armed with precise knowledge of what they wanted and the best available price for each item.

Mass customization continued to grow. Lands' End sold shirts and pants in custom sizes via its Web site. Garment assembly became faster: from a typical six-week process it fell to as low as one week, so crucial in a market where customers demanded a steady flow of new stuff. Challenges from the Spanish company Zara and from H & M (Hennes & Mauritz, AB of Sweden), noted for fast fashion, forced other companies to expedite product cycles. H & M also forged alliances with well-known designers, including Karl Lagerfeld and Stella McCartney, to present one-time collections for the store. Despite a huge increase in apparel manufacturing in Asia and the Americas, in 2002 about 30 percent of American-consumed apparel was made domestically, notably in Los Angeles, New York City, and the environs of San Francisco. Analysts predicted that the volume of domestic product would continue to fall when restrictions on quantity from any one country (e.g., China) expired at the start of 2005.

Conglomerates of luxury brands continued their prominence among fashion sources but struggled to balance the need for creative design with the demands of keeping profits on an upward trajectory from quarter to quarter. Designers unhappy with overarching management, such as Tom Ford at Gucci Group,[17] decamped to other firms, often in different sectors of the luxury market. Privately held companies also suffered from the tension between financial stability and the inherent flux of fashion.

How fashion was made changed as rapidly as the places it was sold. Contractors who had once made the clothes designed by prominent names (Helmut Lang, Alexander McQueen) found themselves excluded by luxury conglomerates that increasingly used their own factories.[18] China began to offer to such mega brands as Liz Claiborne one-stop shopping for all of its sourcing and production needs. Designers could meet with production engineers on a campus that brought together the materials and the manufacturing capability. This greatly expedited development of a new line: from concept to shipping in 60 days, instead of the previous 90 days. Undoubtedly this type of service was encouraged by the impending (January 1, 2005) expiration of quotas on apparel. No longer would apparel companies need to source in 35 countries, among 250 suppliers, when integrated operations such as Luen Thai Holdings Ltd. could provide a full range of services.[19] Large makers expected to save significant money on production, but there was no guarantee these savings would be passed on to consumers.[20]

Fashion Influences

Celebrities of film and television—Nicole Kidman, Gwen Stefani, Jennifer Lopez, Beyoncé Knowles, 'Lil Kim, Queen Latifah, Keanu Reeves—exerted an influence on fashion. Actress Sarah Jessica Parker became spokesperson for Gap in 2004 because of her highly personal style that gave a new boost to Gap's classic sportswear. Socialite Paris Hilton's revealing apparel and uninhibited behavior set the style for some adolescents, despite parental objections. Equally controversial were entertainers Britney Spears, Christina Aguilera, and Janet Jackson, with their all-too-visible assets. Ms. Jackson revealed a nipple during an interlude in the Super Bowl of 2004, sparking vigorous controversy about standards of decency on television.

Stars in various media turned their hands to participate in the designing of signature clothing lines. Sean Combs carved out a second career in fashion, launching the Sean John line in 1998. By 2004, Combs's products included sportswear, outerwear, children's clothing, and accessories. Combs bought a major stake in the firm of Zac Posen, a hot new star of women's high fashion, helping to extend the reach of both men's designing. In fact, urban wear[21] had become so mainstream by the early 2000s that major businesses were investing in the makers, from Kellwood's participation in Phat Farm to Liz Claiborne's stake in Enyce. Roca Wear and FUBU were other major brands of urban apparel, which collectively boasted sales of $6 billion in 2003 (Figure 11.6).

Models

Although no longer emaciated as in the previous decade, models differed sharply from the portly, none-too-tall majority of the population. Many Russians and Central Europeans won prominence as models, including 17-year-old Dalia Dubrindyte and Eva Herzigova.

Media

Shopping magazines gained a large following, starting with *Lucky* (Condé Nast, 2000) and *Shuz* because they focused on style, price, and source of garments, with mini-

Figure 11.6 Argyle sweater and oversized pants from Sean John, fall 2000. Firstview.com.

Illustrators and Photographers

Fashion illustration continued to take a back seat to photography, although some retailers and design houses hired illustrators to create special advertising campaigns. Well-known artist and illustrator Ruben Toledo, for example, drew a series of ads for Nordstrom. Toledo had been creating illustrations, often as witty commentary on the fashion industry, in numerous fashion magazines, including *Harper's Bazaar, Details,* and *Paper* for at least 15 years (Figure 11.7). Illustration was more likely to appear in trade and fashion forecasting publications as was computer generation of fashion drawings, particularly for use in trend forecasting.

Fashion photography varied from straightforward depiction of clothing to staged scenes, such as a *Vogue* presentation of fashion in settings that mimicked a survivor reality show. Pivotal photographers of the previous decade continued to exert an influence. Juergen Teller had typified a shift toward more realism in the 1990s, and Bruce Weber continued to create sexually charged fashion photography. Arthur Elgort and Steven Meisel designed photo spreads for *Vogue*, while Patrick Demarchier worked for *Harper's Bazaar*. Designer Karl Lagerfeld also occasionally participated in photo spreads for *Harper's Bazaar*. Steven Klein devised new effects in photography with his photo spreads that sometimes emphasized gender ambiguity in the clothing or created a murky or sexually suggestive setting enhanced with exceptional lighting. Fashion photography was also recognized as an art form with an exhibit at the Museum of Modern Art in New York. "Fashioning Fiction in Photography Since 1990" spotlighted the work of 13 photographers who produced memorable fashion dramas.

Designers

More and more fashion designers became stars in the last decade of the twentieth century, celebrities who attracted media attention not only for their designs but also their lifestyles. New designers, too numerous to mention more than a few, entered the often tenuous and fickle fashion world. Even those fledgling designers who captured media attention and a celebrity following struggled to be profitable. Fewer retailers bought high-end womenswear, manufacturing costs—especially in the Italian factories preferred by designers—rose steeply as the euro appreciated, and money to launch profitable sidelines in accessories became difficult to obtain.[23] In the first few years of the 2000s, many well-known designers, particularly those who were at the head of companies owned by the luxury brand groups, left to start their own firms or to design for other

mal editorial commentary and no articles on extraneous topics. Often articles showed trends in various versions for different age groups and at diverse price levels. They were also practical for readers who did not live in fashion metropolises. Their photography was realistic, not arty or heavily fashionable, and showed ordinary people in the clothes, not exclusively models, socialites, or celebrities. Editors acted as readers' representatives rather than fashion arbiters and offered how-to advice instead of snobbish directives. Such periodicals gave publishers needed revenue from advertising, particularly in an era when traditional media struggled to attract advertisements. The shopping genre proliferated, with *Shop, Etc.* from Hearst, *Cargo* (menswear) from Condé Nast, and *Vitals* (menswear) from Fairchild.[22]

Live access to high-fashion events via the Internet gave consumers broader exposure to ideas and helped encourage highly personalized style among more venturesome women and men.

NORDSTROM

houses, and new and unfamiliar names took over the design positions they vacated, leaving open the question of how much a company image is tied to a designer name.

Tom Ford left Gucci and Yves Saint Laurent to begin a design enterprise under his own name. He was replaced by **Stefano Pilati** at Yves Saint Laurent and **Alessandra Facchinetti, Frida Giannini,** and **John Ray** in womenswear, accessories, and menswear, respectively, at Gucci. Gucci bought the YSL brand in 1999, with Tom Ford designing the ready-to-wear collection while Saint Laurent designed the haute couture collection. In 2002, Yves Saint Laurent retired,

and one of France's most prestigious haute couture fashion houses closed its doors, leaving only a handful of haute couture designers left in Paris. **Alexander McQueen** left the French fashion house Givenchy in 2001 to open his own salon and in late 2000 formed a partnership with the Gucci Group when it acquired controlling interest in his business. McQueen has since launched menswear and eyewear collections and his first fragrance, Kingdom.

Nicolas Ghesquière was one of the new stars in Paris as creative director and designer for the house of Balenciaga. He became designer of the venerable house in late 1997,

and, after a few slow seasons, his 2000 ready-to-wear collection established him as one of the influential designers of the early twenty-first century. His collections, including both strict tailoring and draped jersey dresses, were in such demand that the flagship Paris store could not keep them in stock. In 2001, Gucci Group N.V. acquired Balenciaga, retaining Ghesquière at the creative helm.

Many of the creative designers of the late 1990s and early 2000s created clothing that was conceptual or verged on art-to-wear. The design team of Viktor Horsting and Rolf Snoeren, who work together as **Viktor and Rolf**, became known for designs that exaggerate recognizable forms (oversized, multiple shirt collars, or huge bows) and also for their elaborate show presentations (Figure 11.8). Both born in the Netherlands, they teamed up the year after they graduated from the Academy of the Arts, Arnhem, to design haute couture. Recognized for their unconventional approach and elaborate presentations, they began to create ready-to-wear also. They later added a menswear collection and a fragrance.

Cyprus-born **Hussein Chalayan** is internationally regarded for his innovative use of materials and of new tech-

Figure 11.10 Hedi Slimane design for Dior Homme. *Women's Wear Daily*, September 20, 2004.

Figure 11.11 Zac Posen dress from his spring 2003 collection. Firstview.com.

nology. He is also a fashion designer known for both his conceptual fashion shows and his meticulous pattern cutting. A graduate of the Central St. Martin's College of Art and Design in London, Chalayan began designing professionally in 1994, and in 1997 he was appointed to design TSE's New York collection.

Although many designers moved to other houses, **John Galliano** continued his recreation and modernization of the Dior image, making it one of the most watched. **Christopher Bailey**, a relatively unknown name, received acclaim for his revival of Burberry as a high-fashion company.

Stella McCartney, daughter of former Beatle Sir Paul McCartney, became chief designer for French fashion house Chloe in 1997. Despite some initial comment that she was using her famous connections, her feminine, and often delicate, clothing was positively received by the fashion world and sold well. McCartney left Chloe in 2001 to develop her own label as part of the Gucci group (Figure 11.9).

Giorgio Armani remained influential, as did **Donatella Versace**, who took over the designing duties after her

brother Gianni's death. She had already been designing the young, ready-to-wear Versus line for the Versace company and continued to create a strong image for it. Her daughter Allegra Versace Beck inherited a controlling interest in the company on her eighteenth birthday, in 2004.

Menswear designers continued to flourish. **Hedi Slimane**, who designed the men's collection for Yves Saint Laurent before becoming creative director and designer for Dior Homme, had a faithful following and was best known for his sleek silhouettes with a contemporary edge. His goal is to revolutionize menswear, with meticulous cut and a somewhat androgynous appearance (Figure 11.10).

Michael Kors launched a line of better career clothing in 2004, which he dubbed carpool couture. This was directed toward working women in their 30s and 40s. Kors had the advantage of sizeable in-store shops and tightly controlled production, because it was not contracted out. Kors also gained substantial name recognition with his participation on the *Project Runway* reality show.[24]

Zac Posen, born in 1980, was one of the younger designers to begin showing in New York. He attended Parsons School of Design in New York, and Central St. Martins College in London, but left school to pursue his career. He won a spot in Gen Art's 2001 Fresh Faces in Fashion show, and with the quick success of his first shows, was awarded the Council of Fashion Designers of America's (CFDA) Swarovski–Perry Ellis Award for Ready-to-Wear in 2004. His designs were often historically influenced but also had a timeless quality to them. In 2004 Posen entered into a deal with Sean Combs to back Posen's business, with the possibility of adding both a menswear collection and a lower-priced bridge line (Figure 11.11).

The fashion company Proenza Schouler, headed by Lazaro Hernandez and Jack McCollough, created successful lines since its first presentation in 2002. The design team met in 1999, while in design school at Parsons, partnering for a thesis project and calling it by their mothers' maiden names, Proenza and Schouler. With a focus on a young and sporty look that includes color-blocked chiffon evening gowns with satin belts and sleek minimal silhouettes, the duo was presented with the CFDA's Perry Ellis Award for new talent in 2003.

Iranian-born Behnaz Sarafpour began her design career working for Anne Klein even before graduating from Parsons School of Design. She launched her own collection in 2001 and quickly made a name for herself creating streamlined separates, signature coats, and dresses.

As Four, a New York design collective, was made up of four designers who went only by their first names; Adi, Ange, Kai, and Gabi. The team made its runway debut in 2001 and was known for both its off-beat, sometimes strange, and sometimes beautiful designs as well as its quirky lifestyle, an experiment in communal living and working. They were perhaps best known for the circle bags seen on the HBO show *Sex and the City*, a shape that was quickly knocked off by other designers.

Ralph Rucci is the rare American designer who has done both couture and ready-to-wear. After graduating from the Fashion Institute of Technology in 1980, he began to show a signature collection through which he gained a small made-to-order clientele. In 1994, he renamed his company Chado Ralph Rucci. The word Chado designates a traditional Japanese tea ceremony.

Isaac Mizrahi did custom designs at the same time as he designed the popular-priced collections for Target. His 2004 plans included the launch of a mid-priced line. Mizrahi actually mixed custom pieces with Target items in his runway show, acknowledging a new reality: customers would combine costly apparel with discount-chic pieces.

Fashion Trends

In both women's and menswear, mixing colors, textures, patterns, and levels of formality supplanted the long-established aesthetics of matching pieces. Proportions changed, with short layers placed over longer ones. Asymmetry enjoyed a heyday in womenswear. A clean finish gave way to deliberately frayed or fringed edges, not just in jeans but also in couture tweeds.

Apparel designs for 2002 and onward showed eclectic mixes of texture: sheer with sturdy or opaque, rough and informal with fancy. Old, established names gained new cachet in fresh applications: Burberry's classic red, cream, and black plaid graced everything from scarves to bikinis.

Textiles and Technology

Emergent technology included heat transfer stamps for conveying garment information without tags. Gap was selling tagless, seamless T-shirts, and Sara Lee offered a tagless Barely There bra. Digitally printed clothing continued to grow, and digital applications began to be used to build three-dimensional structures, largely for medical purposes (such as blood vessels) but with promise for the future of apparel. Much more commonly used was the elastomer spandex, which gave some comfort to fashionably snug-fitting apparel. Spandex was blended with wool in men's and women's suits, with cotton in shirts and blouses, and with a full range of synthetics in many products. Improvements to the fiber made its presence less conspicuous, hastening consumer acceptance. The over-35 or sedentary crowd found that spandex helped them wear smaller sizes than would be feasible otherwise. Young, fit individuals appreciated the clinging properties of the fiber. Some companies even tried out a technology for producing blue jeans embedded with skin creams—anticellulite and moisturizers.

Cargill Dow LLC, a unit of private-trading giant Cargill, introduced a new fiber called Ingeo. Cargill initially teamed up with Dow to produce textile fibers from corn and other starches, using the carbon stored in plants as the basis for creating a resin known by the abbreviation PLA. It was advertised as a green fiber, because it uses less fossil fuel to produce and comes from corn, a renewable resource.

Fashionable textiles of 2000–2004 included tweeds in every fiber combination for fall, winter, and spring jackets, suits, and dresses (Figure 11.12). There were even tweed-like effects in linen-based fabrics for warm weather. Knitwear dominated fashion in everything from bulky to very thin structures. Colorful, pliable leathers were shaped into an array of outerwear and streetwear, including slim pencil skirts. Gold leather gave glitz to footwear. Designers

Figure 11.12 Tweed jacket by St. John worn with jewel-trimmed jeans. *Women's Wear Daily,* August 23, 2004, 7.

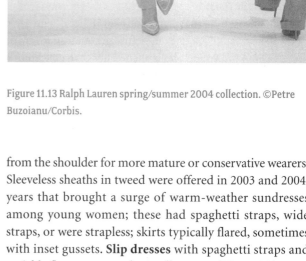

Figure 11.13 Ralph Lauren spring/summer 2004 collection. ©Petre Buzoianu/Corbis.

decorated textiles by employing laser technology in cut-work edges that would not ravel or used Third-World skills to create beaded and embroidered garments at different prices.

Women's Styles

One word describes women's apparel: revealing. Everything from tight, thin layered tank tops to sheath dresses to deep décolletages set off a woman's body, pressuring her to be slim and fit. Not everyone could attain this ideal, and some embraced fashion irrespective of its appearance on their particular bodies. Slim, lithe adult women even shopped in teen stores for lower-cost versions of high-fashion items. Young adults and adolescents often followed very similar styles.

Dresses and Suits

Dress styles were dichotomous: relatively short and fitted for younger, fashion-forward women and long and straight from the shoulder for more mature or conservative wearers. Sleeveless sheaths in tweed were offered in 2003 and 2004, years that brought a surge of warm-weather sundresses among young women; these had spaghetti straps, wide straps, or were strapless; skirts typically flared, sometimes with inset gussets. **Slip dresses** with spaghetti straps and variable flare were popular in all seasons (Plate 11.1).

Evening dresses showed back décolletage or off-the-shoulder (or off one shoulder) styling. Corseted looks with full skirts were partially influenced by films such as *Moulin Rouge*. Both long and short dresses were popular for parties.

Soft drapery typified the goddess style of evening gown, with fitted bodices and flowing skirts in thin materials, at least partially inspired by ancient Greek art.

Skirts of the period came in the knee-length, slightly tapered **pencil** style. Catalogs from retailers such as Talbots and Barrie Pace offered basic skirts in several lengths, from 21 to 35 inches depending on taste and use. Some skirts were flared, with bias inserts or flounces on the bottom. Full skirts

Figure 11.14 A poncho, reminiscent of the 1960s. Courtesy of Fairchild Publications.

young families favored slacks, twin sets, and loose jackets to facilitate changes from work wear to parent wear during hectic days.[26]

Coats and Other Wraps

Spring coats in fitted or straight silhouettes, often in bright or light colors, represented a 2004 revival of a traditional form last been seen in the 1960s. Coats varied from hip or knee length to long, flared styles. **Pea coats,** double-breasted, thigh-length jackets based on the design worn by sailors, satisfied informal purposes, and trench coats remained a rainy-day staple.

The early 2000s brought a widespread fashion for shawls, generously sized and made of wool, silk, or cashmere, also known by the Indian term *pashmina* (the most deluxe fibers). Less expensive blends of silk, cashmere, and lamb's wool appealed to the budget-minded fashion seekers. Shawls worked as evening wraps or as extra, warm layers over suits or coats. Sleeveless vests came in down-filled and suede varieties for wear over long-sleeved knit shirts. These were adopted first by students and then passed into adult fashion by 2004. A fad for ponchos, much like the knitted or crocheted styles of the 1970s hit in 2004 (Figure 11.14).

Casual Separates and Clothes for Active Sport

Pant styles included cargo pants, with multiple pockets on the legs and derrière and the nearly ubiquitous cropped pants, with hems several inches above the ankle. Women of all ages wore crops, often under the name **capris** (Figure 11.15). These were styled with a low rise for young women, for wear with abbreviated bustiers and camisoles or fitted out-blouses, or with traditional fit for mature women, accompanied by various knit shirts and blouses.

Jeans continued to diversify, with a revival of boot-cuts and wider bell-bottoms. Expensive styles from several makers had more trim—including embroidery or appliqué—fit that enhanced the derrière, and specially treated fabrics (see Figure 11.12). In 2004, a tapered leg appeared in jeans, sometimes so snug at the ankle that zippers were required at the bottom of the pant to get it over the foot. These were worn with everything from boots to heels to leg warmers, a revival from the 1980s. There was also a trend among the younger set for wearing a skirt over fitted capris.

Fitted shirts, designed to be worn over skirts or pants, had a strong following among many women. Three-quarter-length sleeves and French cuffs—worn open or closed—represented popular details. Bustier tops and baby-doll styles with floaty panels appealed to adolescents. For adult women, surplice-wrapped blouses continued in fashion from the end of the 1990s.

T-shirts became very snug and short, with different

with smooth, fitted **hip yokes**[25] flattered various figures in 2004. Asymmetry gained popularity and so did bohemian chic—in skirts that used recycled materials or were made to look as if they did. Also popular with young clientele were mini and micromini skirts. The latter were worn in cool weather with tights, boots, and sweater layers.

Zippered jackets, of many materials, had a considerable vogue (Figure 11.13). Some jackets had lightly padded shoulders and varied lengths, and fitted suit styles were intended to be worn without a blouse. After a plethora of sweater sets, by 2004 women were gravitating to jackets, but with softer cuts and feminine details, and in contrasting fabrics that avoid the matched look of formal business suits.

Pantsuits continued to be popular for corporate wear: pant legs were both narrow and, particularly starting in 2002, wide. Most were also lower medium rise. Women over a certain age found flattery in tunics over pants or long skirts, avoiding figure-cutting tucked-in looks. Women with

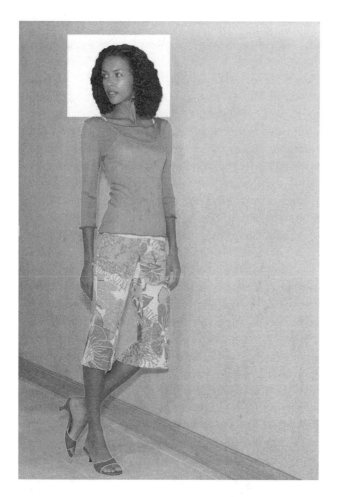

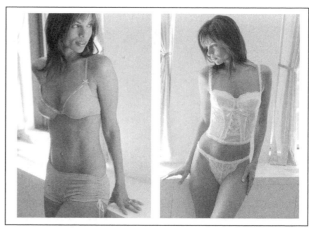

necklines each season. Halters and cropped tops displayed ample skin. Sweaters popular in the period included zippered **hoodies** (with integral hoods) and cardigans. Young wearers chose sleeves that reached over the hand. Sweater sets continued their popularity, tank plus cardigan being quite popular. As sweaters became briefer, they revealed the lower edge of the blouse or T-shirt they were worn over. There was a general fashion for layering two, three, or even four shirts or tops of different design. In 2004, a revival of the preppy look, last popular in the 1970s, brought cotton turtlenecks, **fair isle sweaters** with decorative yokes, and corduroy blazers into teens' wardrobes. Lily Pulitzer's vivid pink, lime, and blue prints became a teen fad, sparking the revival of a company closed 20 years earlier. A snug fit and cropped lengths made the new preppy look quite different from its earlier incarnation.[27] In contrast to preppy, Latina-flavored style comprised asymmetrical skirts, lacy tank tops, and stiletto sandals. The general tone was dressier.[28]

Underwear

Thongs became ever more prominent; even sanitary products were devised for use with thongs. Gel bras were popu-

lar, as were inserts containing water and oil mixes for augmentation, because low-cut, snug T-shirts and tops called for definite cleavage. Softer underwires promised less discomfort. VF Corp., Victoria's Secret, and Lily of France brands competed with one another to engineer desired features in bras. The underwear-as-outerwear trend continued from the 1990s, with camisoles and other traditional lingerie pieces worn alone or at least partially visible in a layered combination. Tank tops and camisoles had built-in bras. Panties and bras without seams were newly popular (Figure 11.16).[29]

Newsworthy lingerie made use of technical developments in textiles, such as microencapsulated moisture agents, odor inhibitors, and moisture-management materials. Colors were brilliant and often shiny.

Shoes and Hosiery

What hats had once been to the fashionable woman, shoes became in the early 2000s. Especially prized were stiletto heels by Manolo Blahnik (although his brand was beginning to have serious competition from Jimmy Choo). These came in all colors and various materials but gener-

Figure 11.15 (OPPOSITE, LEFT) Printed capri pants and cotton knit top from Bandolino. *Women's Wear Daily,* July 30, 2004, 13.

Figure 11.16a and b (OPPOSITE, TOP RIGHT) Intimate apparel: bra and briefs from JLo by Jennifer Lopez and corset by Lejaby Rose. *Women's Wear Daily,* July 12, 2004, 17, photos by Thomas Iannaccone.

Figure 11.17 (OPPOSITE, BOTTOM RIGHT) Handbags from Coach. *Women's Wear Daily,* March 1, 2004, 24.

ally featured toes as sharp as the heels. Sex appeal trumped comfort! **Kitten heels**, slim and pointed but lower than stilettos, were another variant, often backless. **Slides**, a broad category of backless shoes and sandals, came in many styles and materials. There were even moccasins and athletic shoes in slide variants. Clogs offered comfort to the sporty woman. For warm weather, flip-flop sandals and thongs—some with heels—drew a large following, whether they were discount-store versions or glittery trifles that fetched $600. Round-toed flats made an appearance in spring 2004 but did not become a major trend that season.

Chilly weather brought out boots of many types: stiletto-heeled high boots in leather and the flat, round-toed suede Uggs brand, the delight of teens and college women, worn as fashion and not just for cold-weather dressing. Calf-length boots, with blocky, medium heels and square or rounded toes were worn with pants for business.

Hosiery was often textured, including a revival of fishnet hose. Trouser and calf-length hose met the needs of pant wearers and women who favored long skirts.

Bags, Headwear, and Other Accessories

In earlier decades, women treated handbags as basic items, bought one or two a year, as needed. In the 1990s and early 2000s bags added personality and fashionable élan to simple apparel styles. Any design house worth its showroom had a group of signature bags; the more sought-after ones boasted waiting lists months long. Colors, patterns, and shapes ran riot, as did the types of embellishment. Prices reached five figures; some prices would make a substantial down payment on a luxury car. Even long-established leather companies took the lucrative plunge into fashion. Coach, founded in 1941 and known for classic, long-lasting leather bags, reinvented itself as a font of new categories of bag in leather, cloth, and combinations of the two. A woman could buy a weekend bag, evening bag, backpack, clutch, wristlet, tote, diaper bag, or briefcase from Coach, which in fiscal year 2003–2004 racked up $1.3 billion in sales (Figure 11.17).[30]

Headwear was not a major factor in fashion except for sporty baseball caps or other soft-crowned caps on very young women. Belts of 2003 were wide, with prominent hardware. Chain belts and multiple belts worn together constituted 2004 offerings. Fluffy mufflers in fur, crinkled fabrics, and marabou became indoor accessories as well as outdoor neck warmers.

Jewelry

Faceted gems and gold jewelry in profusion, constituting bling-bling and soon just known as bling, borrowed its name from rapsters' high-style and its aesthetic from earlier decades of glamour. Bold brooches, necklaces, and earrings came in diamonds and colored gems or were imitated in rhinestones, crystals, and just plain glass. Chunky jewelry was offered in 2002. Chandelier earrings had a vogue in 2003. After the glitter of the bling period, subtle materials, such as opaque gemstones and wood, began to make a comeback.

Men's Styles

A 2001 cartoon showed a boss telling his sloppily clad employee: "We're down 130 points . . . go out and buy a suit."[31] As the economy sank and stocks with it, makers and sellers of tailored suits began to see a gradual growth in business. Sales of menswear rose 19 percent from January to June 2004, after having dropped 11 percent in 2003.[32] Social commentators who had deplored the slide from casual to sloppy rejoiced. Customers were less gleeful. In the early 2000s, about 50 percent of men made their own apparel choices, instead of relying on wives or girlfriends, compared with 20 percent in the 1990s, so they were grappling with the problems of cost versus quality and coordination that routinely bedevil women shoppers.

Suits and Business Casual

That being said, suits of the early 2000s offered styling beyond the traditional cuts. Leanness was in, a trend helped by the inclusion of a hint of spandex or shine in some fabrics (Figure 11.18). Single- and double-breasted suits were offered, some with a matching vest. Pin-striped navy wool was shown in 2003–2004, as were variants of gray, blue, and black. Italian suits by such firms as Ermenegildo Zegna, Cavali, Brioni, and Ferragamo attracted a following among better-off businessmen.

All-black evening attire substituted a black shirt for the usual penguin-like arrangement, following a trend set by celebrities at media events. Young urban males hastened the acceptance of innovation in the once-invariant tuxedo. Even rental companies offered four- and five-button jackets, tails, brocade vests, and silk cravats to replace the traditional white or black bow-tie. High-fashion styles for less formal occasions included an olive green velvet suit or variously colored corduroy suits. Blazers, still acceptable for informal business wear, came in flecked tweed, herringbone, or moleskin, as well as smooth wools and blends; tapered cuts with high armholes typified 2004 styles. Pleated pants made a comeback, but flat-fronts remained on the scene.

Coats and Other Outerwear

Zippered sweaters continued to be popular, as was layering of many pieces, including T-shirt, shirt, pullover, and cardigan. Short winter coats were styled long enough to blend with a suit jacket, in down-filled materials or other warm fabrications. Vintage-looking jackets with team logos typified laid-back sport wear. Leather jackets remained perennial favorites.

Leisurewear and Active Sport

Cargos and, late in the period, cropped pants filled young men's closets (Figure 11.19). Knee-length **board shorts** drew on the styling favored by surfers and skateboarders. Jeans may best be described as low rise (to the point of revealing personal details) and high ticket. Prices of $150 to $225 typified the high-fashion brands. Even Levi Strauss did vintage styles priced at $150. Special washes, extra trim, and flattering fit supposedly justified the three-figure prices. Cargo pants continued to be ubiquitous (Figure 11.20), even paired with velvet jackets.

Shirts

One return to tradition hailed by some men was tucking in shirts, at least for wear with a business suit. Shirt colors

were numberless, and textures offered variety. Collars tended to be generous in width, not too long in the points, and usually not buttoned down. Striped shirts enjoyed a season of success in 2004, along with pink solids. Often the stripes were wider and more colorful than the classic seersucker sized, color-on-white stripes of the past. Untucked shirts still constituted acceptable wear in nontraditional businesses, academe, and the arts. Such shirts had border prints or asymmetrical patterning and loose styling.

Soft, knit shirts could be worn with suits, although men complained that the unconstructed shirt collar buckled under the pressure of the tailored suit jacket. Sleeveless T-shirts had a vogue, alongside the typical offerings of polo shirts, turtlenecks, and short-sleeved T-shirts.

Underwear, Accessories, and Jewelry

Underwear remained similar to the styles of the 1990s, but with the addition of pricey versions of the old staple, boxer shorts.

Part of the goal of casual dressing was to lose the necktie. Inevitably, return to suited looks meant ties were back, of-

Figure 11.18 (OPPOSITE) Kevin Bacon in a closely fitted pin-striped suit. ©Suzanne Plunkett/AP Wide World Photos.

Figure 11.19 (RIGHT) Casual young men's sportswear, including cropped pants. ©Stockbyte/Getty Images.

ten forming a monochromatic harmony with the shirt. Widths were medium, somewhere between the skinny ties of the 1980s and the ultrawide numbers from the 1970s. Scarves benefited from the shift to more careful accessorizing of basic clothing. Wool, cashmere, and silk prints were shown in 2004. For summer, flip-flops with patterned insoles adorned the fashionable male. Athletic footwear continued and diversified in a seemingly endless variety of shapes, colors, and trims.

Children's Styles

Childrenswear continued to borrow motifs from the 1960s, including bright colors and a preference for flared-leg pants. Fashionable little girls wore loosely cut dresses, often with raised waistlines. Warm weather brought out tank-top dresses. Jumpers accompanied by turtleneck or crewneck tops presented another option for dress-up in cool weather.

Much apparel imitated the casual side of adolescent attire. Boys and girls both wore bib overalls, jeans, and corduroy pants, embellished with appliqués, embroidery, or beading just like teen versions (Figure 11.21). Capri-length pants (for girls) and unisex cargo styles and beachcomber shorts aped teen fashions (Figure 11.22).

Outerwear encompassed **Henley sweaters** (pullovers with shawl collars), **barn jackets** (hip length, in cotton, with corduroy trim), and sweatshirts, some with hoods. Fleece pullovers and zip-front tops were also popular. Even young boys and girls enjoyed the sporty effect of duffle coats with toggle buttons (Figure 11.23). Dressy events for girls called for long coats, plain or with cape collars.

Classic children's footwear included canvas sneakers, flip-flops, suede ankle boots, and, for girls, Mary Janes. Underwear continued unchanged from the previous period, except for more diverse colors and patterns.

Hair, Cosmetics, and Grooming

By 2001, more textured hair was shown for women, although no one style predominated. Long hair had a vogue, in both straight and curly versions. Hair parted in a random or staggered line was popular with younger women. Varying hair colors was also a fashion choice for many.

Figure 11.20 (LEFT) Multipocket cargo style pants. Courtesy of Fairchild Publications.

Figure 11.21 (BOTTOM, LEFT) Sleeveless turtleneck top and embroidered jeans worn with wide belt. *Women's Wear Daily,* November 11, 2004, 10.

Figure 11.22 (BOTTOM, RIGHT) Skateboarder wearing loose shorts and a T-shirt. ©Jose Luis Pelaez, Inc./Corbis.

Figure 11.23 (OPPOSITE) Children's overalls worn with toggle-closure duffle coats. ©Photo by Clive Shalice/Iconica/Getty Images.

Makeup in 2002 tended to low-contrast effects in bronze and peach tones, but bright lipstick against pale skin made a comeback in 2003–2004.

For men, stubbly beards—creating the appearance of a few days' beard growth—signaled fashion-forward. Hair might be so close-cropped that it looked shaven. Tapered goatees had a following, as did more rounded chin beards. Hair bleaching and texturing were prominently shown in fashion spreads and appealed to high school or college students and young professionals.

Summary

Less and less did haute couture set the styles. Fragmented fashion came from a multitude of sources, including individual designers, celebrities, and do-it-yourself fashion enthusiasts. Fashion shifted faster than ever for its devotees, helped along by accelerated techniques of generating styles, taking new ideas from drawing board to sales floor in a matter of weeks. Some small-scale, niche producers flourished, but giant manufacturers and retailers controlled a large portion of ready-to-wear apparel offerings.

NOTES

Chapter 1

1. Nativists argued that immigration was destructive, siphoning money from native-born Americans to these new arrivals. "Too Generous by Half," *Vogue*, July 30, 1903, 102. Reformers countered that those up in arms were often immigrants themselves or descendants of immigrants.

2. See Jane Farrell-Beck and Colleen Gau, *Uplift: The Bra in America* (Philadelphia: University of Pennsylvania Press, 2002), 1–33, for discussion of the development of the bra between 1863 and 1917.

3. William Leach, *Land of Desire: Merchants, Power and the Rise of a New American Culture* (New York: Pantheon Books, 1993), 34.

4. Leach, *Land of Desire*, 328.

5. Bernard Smith, "Market Development, Industrial Development: The Case of the American Corset Trade, 1860–1920," *Business History Review* 65 (Spring 1991): 93, 103.

6. *Ladies' Home Journal*, November 1906.

7. Gustave Kobbé, "The Stage as a School of Costume," *Delineator*, January 1905, 63.

8. Kathy Peiss, *Cheap Amusements: Working Women and Leisure in Turn-of-the-Century New York* (Philadelphia: Temple University Press, 1986), 62–67.

9. Barbara Schreier, "Becoming American: Jewish Women Immigrants, 1880–1920," *History Today* 44 (March 1994): 25–31.

10. "Why Are We Women Not Happy?" *Ladies' Home Journal* 18 (December 1900), 22.

11. Laurel Wilson and Rick Newby, " 'Not Deficient in Beauty': Fashion in the Rockies," *Rocky Mountain Regional Culture* (New York: Greenwood Press, 2004), 27.

12. Self-propulsion of land vehicles had been investigated for centuries. Starting in the late eighteenth century English, French, and (later) American inventors devised steam, electric, and internal combustion engines for road vehicles. However, poor roads in England and the United States and railroad and shipping special interests held back the coming of the automobile. James T. Flink, *The Automobile Age* (Cambridge, MA: The MIT Press, 1988), 1–14.

13. See Maxine James Johns and Jane Farrell-Beck, " 'Cut Out the Sleeves': Nineteenth Century U.S. Women Swimmers and Their Attire," *Dress*, 2001, 53–63.

14. Lisle was made with fine, smooth cotton yarns; originally linen yarn had been used.

15. See Kathy Peiss, *Hope in a Jar: The Making of America's Beauty Culture* (New York: Henry Holt and Company, Metropolitan Books, 1998), chapters 1 and 2.

16. See Jane Farrell-Beck, Alyson Rhodes-Murphy, and Meredith I. Richardson, "Clothes Hangers: From Business Tool to Consumer Convenience, 1852–1936," *Clothing and Textiles Research Journal* 18 (2000): 9–18.

17. Mary Lou Andre, *Ready to Wear: An Expert's Guide to Choosing and Using Your Wardrobe* (New York: Berkley Publishing), 2004.

18. Colleen R. Gau, *Physical Performance and Comfort of Females Exercising on a Treadmill While Wearing Historic Tight-Laced Corsets* (M.S. thesis, Iowa State University, Ames, 1996); Gau, *Historic Medical Perspectives of Corseting and Two Physiological Studies with Reenactors* (Ph.D. dissertation, Iowa State University, Ames, 1998).

19. Tom Mahoney and Leonard Sloane, *The Great Merchants: America's Foremost Retail Institutions and the People Who Made Them Great* (New York: Harper & Row, Publishers, 1966), 246.

Chapter 2

1. Ford founded the company in 1903, after leaving the Detroit Auto Company.

2. "Tin lizzie" suggests the clankiness of the metal; "flivver" is said to have derived from the belief that the shaking one got while driving was good "for the liver." That's one explanation!

3. Nine hours per day had been the previous standard. To qualify for $5 per day, workers had to exemplify hard work, thrift, Americanism, and freedom from debilitating vices, especially alcohol and smoking. Ford's personnel staff actually monitored workers' families, which would be intolerably intrusive today but actually resulted in giving families some coaching in important life skills related to home hygiene, use of budgets, and other practical knowledge.

4. Although voting rights had been accorded with no limits by race in the late 1800s, in the South the Ku Klux Klan systematically terrorized black voters, and state governments instituted literacy laws and other stratagems to prevent minorities from voting.

5. Women had assisted with family farming for most of the nation's history, but independent farming was something new to them.

6. Wilson's Fourteen Points combined general principles—such as freedom of the seas and lower tariffs to encourage peaceful international relations—with specific solutions to territorial disputes among the warring nations.

7. William Leach, "Transformations in a Culture of Consumption: Women and Department Stores, 1890–1925," *Journal of American History* 71 (2) (1984): 319–342.

8. Leach, "Transformations," 328.

9. Jacqueline Field, "Dyes, Chemistry and Clothing: The Influence of World War I on Fabrics, Fashions, and Silk," *Dress, 28* (2001): 77–91.

10. Kathy Peiss, *Hope in a Jar: The Making of America's Beauty Culture* (New York: Henry Holt, Metropolitan Books, 1998), 101.

11. Deborah Saville, "Flappers and Bohemians: The Influence of Modern Psychological Thought and Social Ideology on Dress, 1910–1923," *Dress, 30* (2003): 63–79.

12. Poiret had worked briefly for Worth.

13. *La Gazette du Bon Ton*, quoted in Valerie Steele, *Paris Fashion: A Cultural History* (New York: Oxford University Press, 1988), 222.

14. Laura I. Baldt, *Clothing for Women* (Philadelphia: J. B. Lippincott, 1916), 12–13.

15. The original term was "spatterdashes," signifying that spats kept mud and other filth off the stockings and shoe tops.

16. Eleanor Chalmers, "Facts and Figures," *Delineator* (April 1914): 38.

17. The name derives from Kings Louis XV and XVI, who reigned in France in the mid to late eighteenth century, when aristocratic women's shoes featured curved heels.

Chapter 3

1. Nina Wilcox Putnam, "Ventures and Adventures in Dress Reform," *Saturday Evening Post*, October 7, 1922, 93–94.

2. Truck farmers supplied vegetables to a local area.

3. The name became *Women's Wear Daily* in 1927.

4. "Cake eater" has not been satisfactorily explained in 1920s literature, but "sheik" connoted a dashing young man and evoked the glamour of movie star Rudolph Valentino, one of whose films was "The Sheik."

5. The source of the word "flapper" is complicated. Young girls in England were called "flappers" in the late nineteenth century in reference to the flapping braids in which they wore their hair. Other sources comment on the loose-limbed, awkward movements of a growing girl as "flapping." Journalist H. L Mencken is alleged to have introduced the term to America in 1915. In any event, by the mid-1910s in America, the name was applied to early adolescent females.

6. In 1924, the J. Walter Thompson advertising agency interviewed many department store "foundations" buyers or department heads, who reported that the "chickens" or "flappers" wanted uplift, but the "stouts" wanted breasts flattened. JWT Archives, Special Collections, Duke University.

7. Amos St. Germain, "The Flowering of Mass Society," in *Dancing Fools and Weary Blues: The Great Escape of the Twenties*, eds. Lawrence R. Broer and John D. Walther (Bowling Green, OH: Bowling Green State University Popular Press, 1990), 26.

8. Ibid., 28.

9. Scottish inventor John Logie Baird made the first, brief television broadcast in England in 1925 and American Philo Farnsworth had a working electronic TV by 1927, but there was as yet no mechanism for network broadcasts.

10. " Satchmo" was said to be derived from "satchel-mouth," because Armstrong could open his mouth in an extremely wide grin.

11. The Exposition had actually been planned for before WW I, but the war put it on hold until 1925.

12. *Harper's Bazar*, September 1925, 79.

13. Robert S. Lynd and Helen Merrell Lynd, *Middletown: A Study in Modern American Culture* (San Diego: Harcourt Brace Jovanovich, 1929), 162–163.

14. Bruce Bliven, "Flapper Jane," *The New Republic* 44 (September 9, 1925): 65–67.

15. Susan Hannel, "Africana Textiles: Imitation, Adaptation, and Transformation during the Jazz Age," *Textile: The Journal of Cloth and Culture* 4 (1) (Spring 2006): 68–103.

16. This discussion derives from Robert Friedel, *Zipper: An Exploration in Novelty* (New York: Norton, 1993).

17. Marian Hall with Marjorie Carne and Sylvia Sheppard, *California Fashion: From Old West to New Hollywood* (New York: Harry N. Abrams, ca. 2002), 41, 43, 45.

18. The name was elided into Maidenform in 1949, at the time the ad campaign "I dreamed I . . . in my Maidenform bra" was launched.

19. A long tie, cut on the bias (diagonal grain) and worn with a knot at the throat.

20. Bliven, "Flapper Jane."

21. Kathy Peiss, *Hope in a Jar: The Making of America's Beauty Culture* (New York: Henry Holt, Metropolitan Books, 1998).

Chapter 4

1. The term "alphabet soup" was used to describe the many new federal agencies that were referred to by their acronyms.

2. Robert S. McElvaine, *The Great Depression: America,1929–1941* (New York: Times Books, 1961).

3. David M. Kennedy, *Freedom From Fear. The American People in Depression and War, 1929–1945* (Oxford: Oxford University Press, 1999).

4. For an overview of popular culture trends, see William H. Young and Nance K. Young, *The 1930s* (Westport, CT: Greenwood Press, 2002).

5. In the foundations industry, for example, 35 cents per hour—about $14 per week—became the "floor."

6. Sara Marketti and Jean Parsons, "Design Piracy and Self Regulation: The Fashion Originators' Guild of America, 1932 to 1941," *Clothing and Textiles Research Journal* (in press). In a landmark case, the FOGA was declared in restraint of trade in 1941 and disbanded.

7. The name came from "the screwball" pitch in baseball, a pitch intended to confuse the batter.

8. Alexander Liberman and Polly Devlin, *Vogue Book of Fashion Photography: 1919–1979* (New York: The Condé Nast Publications, Ltd., 1979).

9. For discussion of the connections between fashion and the surrealist movement, see Richard Martin, *Surrealism and Fashion* (New York: Rizzoli, 1990).

10. Caroline Rennolds Milbank, *New York Fashion: The Evolution of American Style* (New York: Harry N. Abrams, 1989).

11. Grace Darling Ely, *American Fashion Designers* (New York: National Retail Dry Goods Association, 1935).

12. David Chierichetti, *Hollywood Costume Design* (New York: Harmony Books, 1976).

13. A godet is a triangular-shaped inset used to create width at the hem.

14. A peplum is a short, often flared skirt attached at the waist of a dress or jacket.

15. November 11, 1932, 7.

16. Espadrilles were slip-on shoes that originated in Spain. They generally had a woven fabric (usually canvas) upper and a flexible, woven rope or hemp sole.

Chapter 5

1. Naval rebuilding had begun about 1935 because of the recognized threat of Japanese expansion in eastern Asia. Frank Friedel, *America in the Twentieth Century,* 4th ed. (New York: Knopf, 1976), 216.

2. Geoffrey Perrett, *Days of Sadness, Years of Triumph* (New York: Coward, McCann, 1973), 113. Land Grant schools had been established starting in 1862, partly to train Union officers during the Civil War, so military training was part of their tradition. In general, Land Grant schools specialized in agriculture, home economics, science, and engineering.

3. Ultimately, America spent $400 billion on the war.

4. Russians also fought the Germans bravely, but did not share in planning strategy; instead, they pursued their own agenda for the postwar world. Friedel, *America in the Twentieth Century*, 251.

5. David Kennedy, *Freedom from Fear. The American People in Depression and War, 1929–1945* (New York: Oxford University Press, 1999), 781.

6. Kennedy, *Freedom From Fear,* 748.

7. Stuart Cosgrove, "Zoot Suit and Style Warfare," in *Zoot Suits and Second-Hand Dresses: An Anthology of Fashion and Music,* ed. Angela McRobbie (Boston: Unwin Hymen, 1988), 3–22.

8. A cooked luncheon meat made from pork shoulder, ham, salt, water, and sugar; the name dates from the 1930s, but the source of the name has never been resolved.

9. The L stood for "Limitation Order." The specifics of these orders were formulated in consultation with the relevant industry but still proved painful to implement.

10. Utility apparel was made in a very limited range of styles, fabrics, and colors and was devoid of trim. To boost morale, a number of well-known designers, including Molyneux and Hardy Amies, also created Utility Clothing designs in 1942.

11. For an illustration of this, see Jane Farrell-Beck and Colleen Gau, *Uplift: The Bra in America* (Philadelphia: University of Pennsylvania Press, 2002), Figure 27.

12. French couture did not collapse completely. Chanel, Vionnet, and others closed their ateliers, but some couturiers, including Lelong and Schiaparelli, remained open, improvising with whatever materials they could obtain and serving the few French women who could still buy, plus the wives and mistresses of German officers. No French products reached the United States, because Germans controlled the Paris industry.

13. Rejecting Nazi enticements to return to Germany, Dietrich defiantly became a U.S. citizen in 1939 and ultimately received the American Medal of Freedom for her wartime work.

14. Quoted in Annette Tappert, *The Power of Glamour* (New York: Crown, 1998), 113.

15. *The Road to Morocco* (1942) and *The Road to Singapore* (1940). The three travelers got themselves into and out of interesting misadventures in each of these films.

16. Lou Taylor, "Paris Couture, 1940–1944," in *Chic Thrills: A Fashion Reader,* eds. Juliet Ash and Elizabeth Wilson (Berkeley, CA: University of California Press, 1993), 127–144.

17. Susan Train, ed., *Theatre de la Mode* (New York: Rizzoli International Publications, 1991), 79.

18. Civil Defense included air-raid wardens, plane watchers, and others prepared to give leadership in an attack or other emergency.

19. Kennedy Fraser, "On and Off the Avenue," *The New Yorker* (April, 1972), 97. As quoted in Valerie Steele, *Women of Fashion:*

Twentieth-Century Designers (New York: Rizzoli International Publications, 1991), 109.

20. *Vogue*, October 15, 1940.

21. *Vogue*, April 1, 1942.

22. *Vogue* April 15, 1942.

23. *Vogue*, September 1, 1946.

24. Barbara A. Schreier, *Fitting In: Four Generations of College Life* (Chicago: The Chicago Historical Society, 1991), 44–45.

25. *Vogue* editorial staff, p. 35.

26. Personal communication, Geitel Winakor, December 3, 2004.

27. G I was an abbreviation for "Government Issue" (referring to their uniforms and equipment) and became a synonym for "soldier."

28. There is some suggestion that supplies of vivid pigments ran short, as chemicals were diverted to military uses.

Chapter 6

1. Some who were accused were or had at one time been Communists, but most were innocent of plotting to overthrow the U.S. government.

2. William H. Young and Nancy K. Young, *The 1950s* (Westport, CT: Greenwood Press, 2004).

3. David Halberstam, *The Fifties* (New York: Villard Books, 1993), 173–179.

4. Watson and Crick won a Nobel Prize for their research in 1962.

5. Nixon had been accused of taking illegal funds and improper gifts, and the speech was named after Nixon's dog Checkers, given to him as a gift. In his speech he somewhat melodramatically challenged anyone who might attempt to take the dog from his daughters. Television would work to his disadvantage during the presidential debates in 1960, when he came across looking tired compared with John F. Kennedy.

6. Halberstam, *The Fifties,* 144–154.

7. Garter-belts were elasticized bands with garters or supporters that hung from the waist, used to hold up stockings.

8. Other influential fashion photographers of the period include Louise Dahl-Wolfe, William Clarke, and Henry Clarke.

9. Nigel Cawthorne, *The New Look: The Dior Revolution* (London: Reed International Books Limited, 1996), 100–101. There are numerous books about Dior and the New Look.

10. Alexandra Palmer, *Couture & Commerce: The Transatlantic Fashion Trade in the 1950s* (Vancouver: UBC Press, 2001), 17.

11. *New York Times Magazine,* December 16, 1956, 35.

12. For biographies of Norell and Trigère, see Sarah Tomerlin Lee (ed.), *American Fashion* (New York: Quadrangle/The New York Times Book Co., 1975).

13. Caroline Rennolds Milbank, *New York Fashion: The Evolution of American Style* (New York: Harry Abrams Inc., 1989).

14. Junior sizing was intended for a youthful figure, generally slightly shorter, slightly higher waisted, and slimmer than the misses size range.

15. Susannah Handley, *Nylon: The Story of a Fashion Revolution* (Baltimore: The Johns Hopkins University Press, 1999).

16. For a crew cut hair, is cut evenly short all over and conforms to the shape of the head. The flat top is also short, but hair on the top of the head is trimmed flat rather that graduated.

17. The ducktail was nicknamed the "DA," which stood for "duck's ass."

Chapter 7

1. So pervasive was the sense of competition with the Russians that a musical comedy about rock 'n' roll—*Bye, Bye Birdie*—included the line "How'll we beat the Russians?" if kids spent their time and money worshipfully chasing after rock stars. Conway Birdie, the subject of the show, was a thinly disguised Elvis Presley.

2. The formal name was European Economic Community (EEC), the forerunner of today's European Union. From six member states, the EU has swelled to 25.

3. By this was meant that women felt as free as men did to engage in recreational sex.

4. Lois Gordon and Alan Gordon, *American Chronicle: Year by Year Through the Twentieth Century* (New Haven: Yale University Press, 1999), 594.

5. *Time,* September 9, 1966, 66.

6. The preferred terms were "black" and "Afro-American" during this period.

7. Joel Lobenthal, *Radical Rags: Fashions of the Sixties* (New York: Abbeville Press, Inc., 1990), 186.

8. This is an electronic device that could imitate the sounds of various musical instruments. First used on a rock recording in 1964.

9. Marimekko prints in housewares are still sold in the United States, e.g. via Crate and Barrel catalogues.

10. "Flower power" referred to antiwar sentiments, and was coined in 1965 by activist-poet Allen Ginsberg.

11. A Hindu spiritual teacher and guide.

12. An open air event featuring drugs and music.

13. M. G. Lord, *Forever Barbie: The Unauthorized Biography of a Real Doll* (New York: William Morrow and Co., 1994).

14. Marnie Fogg credits John Bates, another boutique designer, with introducing the miniskirt. *Boutiques: A '60s Cultural Phenomenon* (London: Mitchell Beazley, 2003), 38.

15. "Fashion," *Time* (September 1966), 67.

16. Vogue Book of Fashion Photography: 1919–1979 (New York: Simon & Schuster, 1979): 140–141.

17. A muumuu is the long, variably loose or semifitted print dress of Hawai'i.

18. A 1960s term of approval.

19. "Bra burning" was a misnomer, coined by a journalist to describe the tossing of bras into a trash can at a feminist rally.

20. A phrase used in advertising.

21. Several of these youth and ethnic typologies draw on the descriptions in Jane Stern and Michael Stern, *Sixties People* (New York: Alfred A. Knopf, 1990).

22. Martha Weinman, "3-year-olds in $200 Dresses," *New York Times Magazine*, January 31, 1960, 35, 37, 40.

Chapter 8

1. The "Me Decade" was coined by author Tom Wolfe. See Bruce J. Schulman, *The Seventies: The Great Shift in American Culture, Society, and Politics* (New York: The Free Press, 2001).

2. Hubert H. Humphrey was the democratic candidate who ran against Nixon.

3. "Stagflation" was a term coined in the 1970s to describe a simultaneous occurring of high rates of inflation and high rates of unemployment. It was a combination of the terms "stagnation" and "inflation."

4. Kissinger served as secretary of state from 1973 to 1977 under both Presidents Nixon and Ford.

5. Ford was the first president who was not elected as either president or vice president. When Vice President Spiro Agnew resigned in 1973, Nixon appointed Ford after confirmation by Congress. When Nixon resigned Ford assumed the presidency.

6. Postmodernism is difficult to define but can be seen as the rejection of boundaries between high and low forms of art and an appropriation of many styles blended together.

7. "Ralph Nader Reports", *The Ladies' Home Journal, November 11*, 1973, p. 52.

8. Beth Bailey and David Farber (eds.) *America in the Seventies* (Lawrence, KS: University of Kansas Press, 2004), 218.

9. The day before the Munich Olympics were to begin, Palestinian terrorists took 11 Israeli team members hostage. In a failed rescue attempt, all the hostages were killed, as well as five of the terrorists. The controversial decision was made to allow the Games to continue.

10. Schulman, *The Seventies*, 148.

11. Much of the specific detail in this section comes from Mary D. Troxell and Beatrice Judelle, *Fashion Merchandising* (New York: Gregg/McGraw-Hill, 1971) or Mary D. Troxell, *Fashion Merchandising*, 2nd ed. (New York: Gregg/McGraw-Hill, 1976).

12. Observant retailers predicted a rise in mail-order sales because of gasoline shortages. "Gas Drought May Cause a Flood in Mail Order," *Women's Wear Daily*, January 30, 1974, 1, 30.

13. Anne-Marie Schiro, "Discount Chic," *Women's Wear Daily*, November 7 1976, 70–72.

14. Michele Wesen Bryant, *WWD Illustrated: 1960s–1990s* (New York: Fairchild, 2004), 81.

15. Kennedy Fraser, *The Fashionable Mind: Reflections on Fashion, 1970–1981* (New York: Alfred A. Knopf, 1981), 132.

16. "Franco-American Follies," *Time*, December 10, 1973, 70–73.

17. Jerry Bowles, "Will Halston Take Over the World?" *Esquire*, August 1975, 69–73.

18. Linda Bird Francke, "Princess of Fashion," *Newsweek*, March 22, 1976, 52–58.

19. Valerie Steele, *Women of Fashion: Twentieth-Century Designers* (New York: Rizzoli).

20. "What to Wear at Night—Depending," *Vogue*, November 1976, 212.

21. Bryant, *WWD Illustrated.* 70.

Chapter 9

1. John Ehrman, *America in the Age of Reagan* (New Haven: Yale University Press, 2005), 185.

2. Designer Perry Ellis and illustrator Antonio Lopez were two who died of AIDs.

3. Ehrman, *America in the Age of Reagan*, 216.

4. Beverly Russell, *Architecture and Design 1970–1990: New Ideas in America* (New York: Harry N. Abrams, Inc., 1989), 32.

5. The "brat pack" was a play on a label from the 1960s used to identify a group of actors and singers who socialized together. The "rat pack" included Frank Sinatra, Dean Martin, Joey Bishop, Peter Lawford, and Sammy Davis, Jr.

6. Elaine Stone and Jean A. Samples, *Fashion Merchandising* (New York: Gregg/McGraw Hill, 1985), 160.

7. Ehrman, 216.

8. Between 1980 and 1990, 80 percent of department stores were involved in mergers or buyouts. Ellen Israel Rosen, *Making Sweatshops: The Globalization of the U.S. Apparel Industry* (Berkeley: University of California Press, 2002), 189.

9. Exhibits included Man and Horse in 1984 and Vanity Fair in 1977.

10. *Details* became a men's fashion publication in 1991.

11. See Valerie Steele, *Fifty Years of Fashion: New Look to Now* (New Haven: Yale University Press, 1997).

12. The term "avant-garde" is used to define fashion that is in opposition to established conventions of design or construction.

13. The prevalence of historic inspiration for designers was so remarkable that the museum at The Fashion Institute of Technology presented an exhibit called The Historical Mode, showing the many borrowings from the past. See Richard Martin and Harold Koda, *The Historical Mode: Fashion and Art in the 1980s* (New York: Rizzoli, 1989).

Chapter 10

1. Haynes Johnson, *The Best of Times: America in the Clinton Years* (New York: Harcourt Inc., 2001), 20.

2. Ellen Israel Rosen, *Making Sweatshops: The Globalization of the U.S. Apparel Industry* (Berkeley: University of California Press, 2002).

3. Mark Oxoby, *The 1990s* (Westport, CT: Greenwood Press, 2003), 3.

4. Oxoby, *The 1990s*, 19.

5. In-line skating is often referred to as Roller Blading, a term that is derived from the trademark name of the earliest brand of skates—Rollerblades.

6. While the editing of photographs to change the content is not new to the digital age, digital cameras and computer editing software made the process much simpler. For example, in July 1992 the photo on the cover of *Texas Monthly* showed then Texas Governor Ann Richards on a motorcycle. The picture was created by splicing Richard's head onto the body of a model.

7. Teri Agins, *The End of Fashion: The Mass Marketing of the Clothing Business* (New York: William Morrow and Company, 1999), 187.

8. Agins, *The End of Fashion*, 188.

9. Buying from predetermined large suppliers within each category of merchandise. Only vendors on a retailer's matrix list may show their lines to buyers. Grace I. Kunz, *Merchandising: Theory, Principles, and Practice* (New York: Fairchild, 1998), 226.

10. Frederick H. Abernathy, John T. Dunlop, Janice H. Hammond, and David Weil, *A Stitch in Time* (New York: Oxford University Press, 1999), 4.

11. Edna Bonacich, Lucie Cheng, Norma Chinchilla, Nora Hamilton, and Paul Ong, eds. *Global Production: The Apparel Industry in the Pacific Rim* (Philadelphia: Temple University Press, 1994), 3.

12. Marian H. Jernigan and Cynthia R. Easterling, *Fashion Merchandising and Marketing* (New York: Macmillan, 1990), 108.

13. Ruth E. Glock and Grace I. Kunz, *Apparel Manufacturing: Sewn Product Analysis* (New York: Macmillan, 1990), 39, 522.

14. Kunz, *Merchandising*, 35.

15. As quoted in Valerie Steele, *Fashion, Italian Style* (New Haven: Yale University Press, 2003), 107.

16. Deconstruction in fashion can be described as a rejection of the traditional conventions with regard to arrangement of components of a garment, use of fabric, or placement of body proportions. It also often reveals the inner construction of a garment or the construction process.

17. Combs went by the nicknames "Puffy" and "Puff Daddy" in the 1990s, changing his name to P. Diddy in 2001, and then to just Diddy in 2005.

18. Holography is a method of producing a three-dimensional image of an object.

19. For an overview of technology and textiles, see Sarah E. Braddock and Marie O'Mahony, *Techno Textiles: Revolutionary Fabrics for Fashion Design* (New York: Thames and Hudson, 1998).

20. Gershenfeld, Neil. "Digital Dressing, or Software to Wear." *The New York Times Magazine: Men's Fashion of the Times*, March 24, 1996, 14..

21. Valli Herman, "Nip & Tuck," *The Des Moines Register*, March 16, 1995, 1T–2T.

Chapter 11

1. The flag-patterned dresses by Catherine Malandrino belonged to an earlier collection but gained prominence among wearers of designer apparel after the terrorist attacks.

2. Al-Qaeda is an Islamic fundamentalist group committed to waging *jihad* or "holy war" against non-Muslims.

3. The following details came from Bridget Foley, "Fashion Regroups," *W*, November 2001, 200, 202, 204, 206, 212, 214.

4. This refers to 2000–2004. Previously there had been substantial outsourcing to Mexico and South and Central America.

5. Material in this section is taken from "A Nation Apart: A Survey of America," *The Economist*, November 8, 2003, special section.

6. [TC]² communication, March 14, 2006. Research summaries were also to be shared via the popular press and scholarly communications.

7. Eleena de Lisser and Ann Zimmerman, "Behind the Dressing-Room Door," *The Wall Street Journal*, May 29, 2003, D-1, D-2. Another type of vanity sizing entails increasing dimensions of a garment while holding the labeled size constant.

8. Valerie Seckler, "Fashion Missing Sizeable Segment," *Women's Wear Daily*, October 8, 2003, 16.

9. "Beyond Botox," *The Economist*, November 22, 2003, 61–62.

10. "A Body of Work," *USA Today*, July 29, 2004, 8D.

11. This according to Malcolm Carfrae, Calvin Klein's head publicist. Conor Dougherty and Kate Kelly, "The Fashion Oscars," *The Wall Street Journal*, March 3, 2006, W-1, W-12.

12. Stephanie King, "How a Small Boutique Gets $25 Moccasins on Celebrities' Feet," *The Wall Street Journal*, November 9, 2004, A1, A10.

13. *The Economist*, October 16, 2004, 58.

14. "In Bow to Retailers' New Clout, Levi Strauss Makes Alterations," *The Wall Street Journal*, June 17, 2004, A1, A15.

15. Ann Zimmerman and Sally Beatty, "Wal-Mart's Fashion Fade," *The Wall Street Journal*, July 2, 2004, B-1, B-2.

16. *The Economist*, October 16, 2004, 58.

17. Dominic De Sole, a legal and financial expert in sympathy with Tom Ford, departed at the same time.

18. Cecile Rohwedder and Teri Agins, "Clothing Makers Sew New Labels," *The Wall Street Journal*, November 5, 2005, B1, B3.

19. Gabriel Kahn, "Making Labels for Less," *The Wall Street Journal*, August 13, 2004, B1, B3.

20. Sally Beatty, "Clothes Firms Hail Quotas' End," *The Wall Street Journal*, December 3, 2004, C1, C3.

21. Apparel styles worn by minority young people in city areas.

22. Information above from Matthew Rose and Shelly Branch, "Consumer-Friendly Shopping Magazines Rewrite the Rules," *The Wall Street Journal,* February 10, 2004, B1, B9; and Virginia Postrel, "Where Snobbery is Out of Style," *The Wall Street Journal,* November 26, 2004, W11.

23. Teri Agins, "A Hot Designer Can Generate Buzz but not Profits," *The Wall Street Journal,* September 16, 2005, A1, A6.

24. Teri Agins, "New Kors Line Stars Luxury Look-Alikes 'Carpool Couture,'" *The Wall Street Journal,* August 20, 2004, B1, B3.

25. A hip yoke is a contoured upper section of a skirt or pant that does the fitting normally performed by darts, gathers, or pleats.

26. Sue Shellenbarger, "Undercover Mom: How Working Women Swap Wardrobes, Roles Through the Day," *The Wall Street Journal,* January 22, 2004), D1. The following week, Ms. Shellenbarger published a piece on Undercover Dads, who also made quick changes from business to fathering and coaching attire. *The Wall Street Journal,* January 29, 2004: D1.

27. Naomi Aoki, "Once Again Preppy Rules," *Boston Globe* (online, September 3, 2004).

28. Teri Agins, "Nuevo Casual," *The Wall Street Journal,* May 21, 2004, B1, B4.

29. Karen Monget, "Lingerie's Brave New World," *Women's Wear Daily,* October 25, 2004), 12–13.

30. Ellen Byron, "How Coach Won a Rich Purse by Inventing New Uses for Bags," *The Wall Street Journal,* November 17, 2004, A-1.

31. Cartoon, B. Smaller, *Barron's* (March 12, 2001).

32. Elizabeth Lazarowitz, "More Men Suit Up as Jackets, Ties Make a Comeback," *USA Today,* September 1, 2004, 1.